THE CAMBRIDGE
WOMEN'S WRITING IN

Women writers played a central role in eighteenth-century Britain. Featuring essays on female writers and genres by leading scholars in the field, this *Companion* introduces readers to the range, significance, and complexity of women's writing across multiple genres in Britain between 1660 and 1789. Divided into two parts, the *Companion* first discusses women's participation in print culture, featuring essays on topics such as women and popular culture, women as professional writers, women as readers and writers, and place and publication. Additionally, Part I explores the ways that women writers crossed generic boundaries. The second part contains chapters on many of the key genres in which women wrote, including poetry, drama, fiction (early and later), history, the ballad, periodicals, and travel writing. The *Companion* also provides an introduction surveying the state of the field, an integrated chronology, and a guide to further reading.

CATHERINE INGRASSIA is Professor of English at Virginia Commonwealth University in Richmond, Virginia. She is the author of *Authorship, Commerce, and Gender in Eighteenth-Century England: A Culture of Paper Credit* (Cambridge, 1998); editor of a critical edition of Eliza Haywood's *Anti-Pamela* and Henry Fielding's *Shamela* (2004); and co-editor of *A Companion to the Eighteenth-Century Novel and Culture* (2005) and the anthology *British Women Poets of the Long Eighteenth Century* (2009).

A complete list of books in the series is at the back of the book.

THE CAMBRIDGE
COMPANION TO

WOMEN'S WRITING IN BRITAIN, 1660–1789

EDITED BY
CATHERINE INGRASSIA

CAMBRIDGE
UNIVERSITY PRESS

CAMBRIDGE
UNIVERSITY PRESS

University Printing House, Cambridge CB2 8BS, United Kingdom

Cambridge University Press is part of the University of Cambridge.

It furthers the University's mission by disseminating knowledge in the pursuit of education, learning and research at the highest international levels of excellence.

www.cambridge.org
Information on this title: www.cambridge.org/9781107600980

© Cambridge University Press 2015

This publication is in copyright. Subject to statutory exception and to the provisions of relevant collective licensing agreements, no reproduction of any part may take place without the written permission of Cambridge University Press.

First published 2015

Printed in the United Kingdom by Clays St Ives, plc

A catalogue record for this publication is available from the British Library

Library of Congress Cataloguing in Publication data
The Cambridge companion to women's writing in Britain, 1660–1789 / edited by Catherine Ingrassia.
    pages   cm. – (Cambridge companions to literature)
Includes bibliographical references and index.
ISBN 978-1-107-60098-0 (paperback)
1. English literature – Women authors – History and criticism.   2. English literature – 18th century – History and criticism.   3. English literature – Early modern, 1500 – 1700 – History and criticism.   I. Ingrassia, Catherine, editor.
PR448.W65C36   2015
820.9′928709033 – dc23
2015008278

ISBN 978-1-107-01316-2 Hardback
ISBN 978-1-107-60098-0 Paperback

Cambridge University Press has no responsibility for the persistence or accuracy of URLs for external or third-party internet websites referred to in this publication, and does not guarantee that any content on such websites is, or will remain, accurate or appropriate.

CONTENTS

Notes on contributors   vii
Chronology   xi

Introduction   1
CATHERINE INGRASSIA

PART I   WOMEN IN PRINT CULTURE

1   Women as readers and writers   21
MARK TOWSEY

2   The professional female writer   37
BETTY A. SCHELLENBERG

3   Place and publication   55
SARAH PRESCOTT

4   Women and popular culture   70
PAULA R. BACKSCHEIDER

5   Genre crossings   86
KATHRYN R. KING

PART II   GENRES, MODES, AND FORMS

6   Poetry   103
DAVID E. SHUTTLETON

7   Drama   118
FELICITY NUSSBAUM

CONTENTS

8	History RIVKA SWENSON	135
9	Satire MELINDA RABB	147
10	Early fiction NICOLA PARSONS	164
11	Later fiction KATHERINE BINHAMMER	180
12	Travel writing HARRIET GUEST	196
13	Ballads RUTH PERRY	210
14	Periodical writing MARY WATERS	226
	Guide to further reading	242
	Index	254

NOTES ON CONTRIBUTORS

PAULA R. BACKSCHEIDER, Philpott-Stevens Eminent Scholar at Auburn University, is a former president of the American Society for Eighteenth-Century Studies and the author of several books, including *Daniel Defoe: His Life*, winner of the British Council Prize; *Spectacular Politics*; and *Eighteenth-Century Women Poets and Their Poetry*, winner of the MLA James Russell Lowell Prize. She has published articles in *PMLA, Theatre Journal, ELH*, and many other journals. Her most recent book is *Elizabeth Singer Rowe and the Development of the English Novel*.

KATHERINE BINHAMMER is a Professor in the Department of English and Film Studies at the University of Alberta, Canada. She has published *The Seduction Narrative in Britain, 1747–1800* (Cambridge, 2009), edited *Women and Literary History* (2003), and written numerous articles on gender and sexuality in the eighteenth century. Recently, her research has explored the economics of loss in the late eighteenth-century novel; articles from this work appear in *Studies in the Novel* and *Eighteenth-Century Fiction*.

HARRIET GUEST is Professor Emerita from the Centre for Eighteenth Century Studies and Professor in the Department of English and Related Literature at the University of York, UK. Her books include *Small Change: Women, Learning, Patriotism, 1750–1810* (2000) and *Empire, Barbarism, and Civilization: Captain Cook, William Hodges, and the Return to the Pacific* (Cambridge, 2007).

KATHRYN R. KING is Professor Emerita of Literature at the University of Montevallo at the University of Montevallo. She is author of *Jane Barker, Exile: A Literary Career* (2000) and *A Political Biography of Eliza Haywood* (2012), and coeditor (with Alexander Pettit) of Haywood's *The Female Spectator* (2002). She has published numerous articles on English women writers and continues to pursue Haywood biographical leads for a project that will focus on mortality, late careers, and literary legacies.

NOTES ON CONTRIBUTORS

FELICITY NUSSBAUM is Professor of English at the University of California, Los Angeles. She is author of *Rival Queens: Actresses, Performance, and the Eighteenth-Century British Theater* (2010); *The Limits of the Human: Fictions of Anomaly, Race, and Gender in the Long Eighteenth Century* (Cambridge, 2003); *Torrid Zones: Maternity, Sexuality and Empire in Eighteenth-Century English Narrative* (1995); and *The Autobiographical Subject: Gender and Ideology in Eighteenth-Century England* (1989). She has been awarded numerous academic honors, including a Guggenheim Fellowship, an Andrew Mellon Fellowship at the Huntington Library, and an NEH Fellowship. She has also held a Marta Sutton Weeks Fellowship at the Stanford Humanities Center and has been a Rockefeller Humanist-in-Residence Fellow at the Institute for Research on Women, Rutgers University.

NICOLA PARSONS is a Senior Lecturer in Eighteenth-Century Literature at the University of Sydney. Her first book, *Reading Gossip in Early Eighteenth-Century England* (2009), centers on the development of the novel in the early century and, focusing on texts by Delarivier Manley, Daniel Defoe, Richard Steele, and Jane Barker, argues that gossip modeled an interpretative strategy that shaped readers' participation in both literary culture and public debates. She has published essays on Manley, Barker, Defoe, and Queen Anne's correspondence and also coedited *Reading Historical Fiction: The Revenant and Remembered Past* (2013) with Kate Mitchell. Her new project, funded by the Australian Research Council, centers on connections between poetry and the novel in early eighteenth-century novels by women.

RUTH PERRY was past President of the American Society for Eighteenth-Century Studies and founding Director of the Women's Studies program at MIT, where she is currently the Ann Fetter Friedlaender Professor of Humanities. She is the author of many books on literary subjects, including *Women, Letters, and the Novel* (1980); an edition of *George Ballard's 1752 Several Ladies of Great Britain* (1984); *The Celebrated Mary Astell* (1986); and *Novel Relations: The Transformation of Kinship in English Culture and Literature 1748–1818* (2004). She guest-edited a special issue of *The Eighteenth Century: Theory and Interpretation* on "Ballads and Songs in the Eighteenth Century" in 2006. Her current project is a biography of Anna Gordon Brown, an eighteenth-century Scotswoman who preserved some of her country's finest ballads. Perry is herself a folksinger and teaches courses on folk music.

SARAH PRESCOTT is Professor of English Literature at the University of Aberystwyth, Wales, where she is also Director of the Centre for Women's Writing and Literary Culture. She is the author of *Women, Authorship, and Literary Culture, 1690–1740* (2003); *Eighteenth-Century Writing from Wales: Bards and Britons* (2008); and editor, with Stewart Mottram, of *Writing Wales from the Renaissance to Romanticism* (2012) and, with David Shuttleton, *Women and Poetry, 1660–1750* (2003). Prescott has received external funding from the Arts and Humanities Research Council; the British Academy; and most recently the Leverhulme Trust, which awarded her a three-year, £248,395 Research Project Grant on "Women's Poetry 1400–1800 in English, Irish, Scots, Scots Gaelic, and Welsh."

MELINDA RABB is Professor of English at Brown University. She is the author of *Satire and Secrecy in English Literature 1650–1750* (2007). She has published widely on Swift, Manley, Pope, Richardson, Fielding, Sterne, Godwin, and Defoe. She has edited *Lucius: The First Christian King of England* for *The Broadview Anthology of Restoration and Early Eighteenth-Century Drama*, edited by Douglas Canfield (2000) and a special issue of *Modern Language Studies* titled "Making and Rethinking the Canon: The Eighteenth Century," XCIII: 1 (1988).

BETTY A. SCHELLENBERG is Professor of English and Department Chair at Simon Fraser University. Her most recent book publications are *Reconsidering the Bluestockings* (2003, coedited with Nicole Pohl), *The Professionalization of Women Writers in Eighteenth-Century Britain* (Cambridge, 2005), and the forthcoming Volume 11 of *The Cambridge Edition of the Correspondence of Samuel Richardson*. She is writing a book on the interface of manuscript practices and print in the mid-eighteenth century, and her work on media collaboration and contention in domestic travel writing, Bluestocking networks, and other literary circles of the 1750s has appeared in *Eighteenth-Century Studies, The History of British Women's Writing, 1750–1830*, and *Bookish Histories*.

DAVID E. SHUTTLETON is Reader in Literature and Medical Culture in the School of Critical Studies (English Literature) at the University of Glasgow where he is codirector of the Medical Humanities Research Centre. He has published widely on Restoration and eighteenth-century literature, including essays on the poetic careers of Anne Killigrew and Mary Chandler. He also addresses women's poetry in his monograph *Smallpox and the Literary Imagination, 1660–1820* (Cambridge, 2007). With Sarah Prescott, he coedited the groundbreaking essay volume *Women and Poetry, 1660–1750* (2003) and, with John Dussinger, he recently edited Volume 2 of *The Cambridge Edition of the Correspondence of Samuel Richardson: Correspondence with George Cheyne and Thomas Edwards* (Cambridge, 2014).

RIVKA SWENSON is Assistant Professor of English at Virginia Commonwealth University. Her book *Essential Scots and the Idea of Unionism in Anglo-Scottish Literature* is forthcoming. Other new work is forthcoming in the *Oxford Handbook of British Poetry, 1660–1800* and *The Cambridge Companion to "Robinson Crusoe."* She recently coedited with Manushag N. Powell a special issue of *The Eighteenth Century: Theory and Interpretation* ("Sensational

Subjects"), and she is coediting with John Richetti Daniel Defoe's *The Farther Adventures of Robinson Crusoe*. Currently, she serves on the executive committees of the Defoe Society and the MLA Scottish Literature Discussion Group, and as the delegate for the executive committee of the MLA Restoration and Early Eighteenth-Century Division.

MARK TOWSEY is a Lecturer in History at the University of Liverpool, having previously held visiting fellowships at the Universities of London, Harvard, and Yale, as well as the Huntington Library. He is a Fellow of the Royal Historical Society and has published extensively on the history of reading and the cultural history of libraries, including *Reading the Scottish Enlightenment: Books and Their Readers in Provincial Scotland 1750–1820* (2010).

MARY A. WATERS, Associate Professor of English at Wichita State University, is the author of *British Women Writers and the Profession of Literary Criticism, 1789–1832* (2004). She is also the editor of *British Women Writers of the Romantic Period: An Anthology of Their Literary Criticism* (2009). Her work has appeared in *Eighteenth-Century Studies, Women Writers*, and *Nineteenth-Century Prose*. She is currently working on a digital archive of literary criticism by Romantic-era British women writers.

CHRONOLOGY

This chronology is a representative list of relevant events, publications, and birth and death dates between 1660 and 1800. Dates are given new style. Here, and throughout the volume, dates of birth (or in some cases baptism) and death correspond with those in the *Oxford Dictionary of National Biography* and use the same dating format. To that end, if a birth date is uncertain, a question mark appears; if a birth date cannot be dated to a single year, "/" marks alternative years; "x" indicates a range of years; c. (circa or about) signifies a date that is approximate; fl. (*floruit* or flourished) represents the dates a person was active when neither date of birth or death is known. The listing of works published is not, of course, exhaustive and not every text published by the authors in the volume is included here; rather, the chronology primarily marks texts discussed within or relevant to the essays of this *Companion*.

Authors, Events, and Texts

1658	Mary of Modena (1658–1718) born
1660	Restoration of the monarchy with the return of Charles II
	Anne Killigrew (1660–85) born
	Daniel Defoe (1660?–1731) born
1661	Anne Finch, Countess of Winchilsea (1661–1720) born
1663	Katherine Philips, *Pompey* produced in Dublin
1664	Katherine Philips (b. 1632) dies
1665	Mary Evelyn (1665–85) born
	Queen Anne (1665–1714) born
	Great Plague of London begins
1666	Mary Astell (1666–1731) born
	Mary Pix (c. 1666–1709) born
	John Dryden (1631–1700) made Poet Laureate
	Great Fire of London (September 2)

CHRONOLOGY

1667	Jonathan Swift (1667–1745) born
1669	Susanna Centlivre (1669?–1723) born
	France Boothby (fl. 1669–70), *Marcelia*
1670	Delarivier Manley (c. 1670–1724) born
	Sarah Fyge Egerton (1670–1723) born
	Aphra Behn, *The Forced Marriage*
1671	Sarah Dixon (1671/72–1765) born
	Anne Bracegirdle (1671–1748) born
	Aphra Behn, *The Amorous Prince*
1672	Joseph Addison (1672–1719) born
1673	Aphra Behn, *The Dutch Lover*
	Margaret Cavendish, the Duchess of Newcastle (1623?–73) dies
1674	Mary Davys (1674–1732) born
	Elizabeth Singer Rowe (1674–1737) born
	Catharine Trotter Cockburn (1674?–1749) born
	John Milton (b. 1608) dies
1675	Elizabeth Thomas (1675–1731) born
1676	Aphra Behn, *Abdelazer* and *The Town-Fopp*
1677	Aphra Behn, *The Rover*
	Mary (Molesworth) Monck (1677?–1715) born
	Mary Stuart marries William of Orange
1678	Aphra Behn, *Sir Patient Fancy*
1679	Penelope Aubin (1679?–1738) born
	Aphra Behn, *The Feign'd Curtizans*
1681	Aphra Behn, *The Second Part of The Rover*
1682	Aphra Behn, *The City Heiress*
1683	Anne Oldfield (1683–1730) born
1684	Aphra Behn, *Love-Letters between a Nobleman and His Sister; Poems Upon Several Occasions*
1685	Death of Charles II and accession of James II
	Monmouth's Rebellion
	Jane Brereton (1685–1740) born
	Mary Barber (c. 1685–1755) born
	John Gay (1685–1732) born
1687	Mary Chandler (1687–1745) born
	Nell Gwyn (b. 1651?) dies
	Aphra Behn, *Emperor of the Moon*
1688	"Glorious Revolution": the deposing of James II and the accession of William II and Mary

	Thomas Shadwell (c. 1640–92) replaces John Dryden as Poet Laureate
	Alexander Pope (1688–1744) born
	Mary Collier (1688?–1762) born
	Jane Barker, *Poetical Recreations*
	Aphra Behn, *Oroonoko*
1689	Aphra Behn (b. 1640?) dies
	Martha Fowke Sansom (1689–1736) born
	Lady Mary Wortley Montagu (1689–1762) born
	Samuel Richardson (1689–1761) born
	Susanna Highmore (1689/90–1750) born
1690	Mary Evelyn, *Mundus Muliebris*
1691	Edward Cave (1691–1754) born
1693	Eliza Haywood (1693?–1756) born
1694	Mary Astell, *A Serious Proposal to the Ladies*
	Bank of England established
1696	Anne Ingram (c. 1696–1764) born
	Catharine Trotter, *Agnes de Castro*
	Delarivier Manley, *The Royal Mischief* and *The Lost Lover*
	Elizabeth Singer Rowe, *Poems on Several Occasions*
1697	Richard Savage (1696/97–1743) born
	Mehetabel Wesley Wright (1697–1750) born
1698	Catherine Trotter, *Fatal Friendship*
1699	Frances Seymour (née Thynne), Countess of Hertford (1699–1754) born
1700	John Dryden (b. 1631) dies
	Elizabeth Mure (1700–90) born
	James Thomson (1700–48) born
	Margaret Davies/Marged Dafydd (c. 1700–1785?) born
	Mary Astell, *Reflections on Marriage*
1701	Act of Settlement establishing Hanoverian succession
	Anne Finch, *The Spleen*
	Lady Mary Chudleigh, *The Ladies Defence*
	Jane Wiseman Holt, *Antiochus the Great*
1702	Death of William II and accession of Queen Anne (1665–1714)
	Judith Madan (1702–81) born
1703	Sarah Egerton, *The Emulation*
1704	Robert Dodsley (1704–64) born
	Jean Adam (1704–65) born

	John Locke (b. 1632) dies
	Constantia Grierson (1704/5–32) born
1705	Delarivier Manley, *The Secret History of Queen Zarah*
	Susanna Centlivre, *The Gamester*, *The Basset Table*
1706	Anna Williams (1706–83) born
1707	Act of Union unifying Scotland and England into "Great Britain"
	Henry Fielding (1707–54) born
	Mary Jones (1707–78) born
	Delarivier Manley, *Almyna; or, The Arabian Vow*
1709	First Copyright Act, the Statute of Anne
	Susanna Centlivre, *The Busie Body*
	Delarivier Manley, *New Atalantis*
	Samuel Johnson (1709–84) born
	Teresia Constantia Phillips (1709–65) born
	Laetitia Pilkington (c.1709–50) born
	Mary Pix (b. 1666) dies
	Abigail Baldwin publishes *Female Tatler* (1709–10)
1710	Lady Mary Chudleigh (b. 1656) dies
	Sarah Fielding (1710–68) born
1711	David Hume (1711–76) born
1712	Laetitia Pilkington (1712–50) born
1713	Treaty of Utrecht
	Elizabeth Barry (b. 1656x58) dies
	Jane Barker, *Love Intrigues: Or, the History of the Amours of Bosvil and Galesia* (unauthorized)
	Anne Finch, *Miscellany Poems*
	Charlotte Charke (1713–60) born
1714	Death of Queen Anne, accession of George I (1660–1727)
	William Shenstone (1714–63) born
	Delarivier Manley, *The Adventures of Rivella*
	Susanna Centlivre, *The Wonder: A Woman Keeps a Secret*
	Alexander Pope, *The Rape of the Lock*
1715	Jacobite Rebellion
	Elizabeth Vesey (1715–91) born
	Jane Collier (1715–55) born
	Alexander Pope publishes translation of *Iliad* (1715–20)
	Jane Barker, *Exilus; or, The Banish'd Roman*
1716	Mary Monck, *Marinda*
	Thomas Gray (1716–71) born
	Esther Lewis Clark (1716–94) born

CHRONOLOGY

	Mary Davys, *The Northern Heiress: or the Humours of York*
	Sarah Butler, *Irish Tales: or, Instructive Histories for the Happy Conduct of Life*
1717	Elizabeth Carter (1717–1806) born
	David Garrick (1717–79) born
	Jane Holt (*fl.* c. 1682–1717) dies
1718	Elizabeth Montagu (1718–1800) born
	Alexander Pope, *Eloisa to Abelard*
	Susanna Centlivre, *A Bold Stroke for a Wife*
1719	Eliza Haywood, *Love in Excess* (two volumes, 1719–20)
	Jane Barker, *Love Intrigues* (second edition with Barker's approval)
	Daniel Defoe, *Robinson Crusoe*
	Frances Boscawen (1719–1805) born
1720	South Sea Bubble
	Sarah Scott (1720–95) born
1721	Penelope Aubin, *The Strange Adventures of the Count de Vinevil and His Family*
	Catherine Talbot (1721–70) born
	Robert Walpole (1676–1745) becomes prime minister
1722	Mary Leapor (1722–46) born
	Eliza Haywood, *The British Recluse*
1723	Susannah Centlivre (b. 1669?) dies
	Eliza Haywood, *Lasselia: Or the Self-Abandon'd*
	Jane Barker, *A Patchwork Screen for the Ladies*
1724	Mary Davys, *The Reform'd Coquet*
	Eliza Haywood, *The Arragonian Queen* and *The Tea Table*
	Frances Brooke (1724–89) born
	Frances Sheridan (1724–66) born
	Delarivier Manley (b. 1670) dies
1725	Eliza Haywood, *Mary Stuart, Queen of Scots; Secret Histories, Novels, and Poems*
	Mary Davys, *The Works of Mrs. Davys* (two volumes)
1726	Jane Barker, *The Lining of the Patchwork Screen*
	Eliza Haywood, *City Jilt* and *The Perplexed Duchess*
	Jonathan Swift, *Gulliver's Travels*
1727	Death of George I; succeeded by George II (1683–1760)
	Hester Mulso Chapone (1727–1801) born
	Elizabeth Griffin (1727–93) born
	Eliza Haywood *The Perplex'd Duchess*
1728	Mary Ann Yates (1728–87) born

	Oliver Goldsmith (1728?–74) born
	Alexander Pope, *The Dunciad* (1728, 1729, 1742, 1743)
	Elizabeth Singer Rowe, *Friendship in Death*
1729	Anne Hughes Penny (1729–80/84) born
	Clara Reeve (1729–1807) born
	Jonathan Swift, *A Modest Proposal*
	Elizabeth Singer Rowe, *Letters Moral and Entertaining* (1729–32)
	Eliza Haywood, *Frederick Duke of Brunswick-Lunenburgh*
1730	Anne Oldfield (b. 1683) dies
	Stephen Duck (1705?–56), *The Thresher's Labour*
	Henry Fielding, *The Author's Farce*
1731	Edward Cave begins publishing *The Gentleman's Magazine*
	Charlotte Lennox (1730/31–1804) born
	Catharine Macaulay (1731–91) born
	Mary Astell (b. 1666) dies
	Daniel Defoe (b. 1660?) dies
	Elizabeth Thomas (b. 1675) dies; Edmund Curll publishes *Pylades and Corinna* (vol. 1)
1732	Jane Barker (b. 1652) dies
	Mary Davys (b. 1674) dies
	Elizabeth Thomas, *Pylades and Corinna* (vol. 2), published posthumously
	Jonathan Swift, *The Lady's Dressing Room*
1733	Mary Chandler, *Description of Bath*
	Excise Crisis
1734	Lady Mary Wortley Montagu, *The Reasons that induced Dr. S. to write a Poem called "The Lady's Dressing Room"*
	Alexander Pope, *Epistle to Cobham*
	Jonathan Swift, *A Beautiful Young Nymph Going to Bed*
	Mary Barber, *Poems on Several Occasions*
	Jean Adam, *Miscellany Poems*
1735	Alexander Pope, *An Epistle to a Lady, Of the Characters of Women; Epistle to Arbuthnot*
1736	Anne Ingram, *Epistle to Mr. Pope*
	Elizabeth Singer Rowe, *The History of Joseph*
	Eliza Haywood, *Eovaai*
	Frances Seymour, *The Story of Inkle and Yarico*
1737	Stage Licensing Act
	Elizabeth Moody (1737–1814) born
	Elizabeth Singer Rowe, *Devout Exercises of the Heart*

CHRONOLOGY

1738	Mary Whateley Darwall (1738–1825) born
	Elizabeth Carter, *Poems upon Particular Occasions*
1739	Elizabeth Carter, *Sir Isaac Newton's Philosophy Explain'd for the Use of the Ladies* (trans. of Francesco Algarotti)
	Mary Collier, *The Woman's Labour*
1740	Samuel Richardson, *Pamela*
	James Boswell (1740–95) born
	Jane Brereton (b. 1685) dies
1741	Eliza Haywood, *Anti-Pamela*
	Henry Fielding, *Shamela*
	Hester Thrale Piozzi (1741–1821) born
	Mary Alcock (1741?–98) born
	Lady Anna Miller (1741–81) born
1742	Prime Minister Robert Walpole resigns (February 11)
	Henry Fielding, *Joseph Andrews*
	Anna Seward (1742–1809) born
1743	Anna Letitia (Aikin) Barbauld (1743–1825) born
	Hannah Cowley (1743–1809) born
1744	Death of Alexander Pope (b. 1688)
	Eliza Haywood begins publishing *The Female Spectator* (1744–46)
	Sarah Fielding, *David Simple*
	Jane Brereton, *Poems on Several Occasions*, published posthumously
1745	Jacobite Rebellion
	Hannah More (1745–1833) born
	Jonathan Swift (b. 1667) dies
1746	Elizabeth Hands (1746–1815) born
	Mary Leapor (b. 1722) dies
	Battle of Culloden (April 16)
	Eliza Haywood, *The Parrot*
1747	Anna Gordon Brown (1747–1810) born
	Charlotte Lennox, *Poems on Several Occasions*
	Susanna Blamire (1747–94) born
	Samuel Richardson, *Clarissa* (1747/48)
1748	Mary Leapor's *Poems upon Several Occasions* published posthumously
1749	Charlotte Smith (1749–1806) born
1750	Laetitia Pilkington (b. c.1709) dies
	Sophia Lee (1750–1824) born

	Mary Jones, *Miscellanies in Prose and Verse*
	Sarah Scott, *The History of Cornelia*
1751	Eliza Haywood, *The History of Miss Betsy Thoughtless*
	Mary Leapor, *Poems upon Several Occasions. The Second and Last Volume* published posthumously
	Mary Scott (1751/2–93) born
1752	Frances Burney (1752–1840) born
	Charlotte Lennox, *The Female Quixote*
	George Ballard, *Memoirs of Several Ladies of Great Britain*
1753	Elizabeth Inchbald (1753–1821) born
	Ann Yearsley (1753–1806)
	Jane Collier, *An Essay on the Art of Ingeniously Tormenting*
	Charlotte Lennox, *Shakespeare Illustrated* (1753–54)
	Robert Shiel, *Lives of the Poets of Great Britain and Ireland*
	Samuel Richardson, *Sir Charles Grandison*
1754	Sarah Fielding and Jane Collier, *The Cry*
	John Duncombe, *The Feminiad* (second edition in 1757 published as *The Feminead*)
	Jane Cave Winscom (1754/5–1813) born
1755	George Colman and Bonnell Thornton, *Poems by Eminent Ladies*
	Frances Brooke begins publishing the *Old Maid* (November 15, 1755–July 24, 1756)
	Samuel Johnson, *Dictionary of the English Language*
	Sarah Siddons (1755–1831) born
	Jane Collier (b. 1715) dies
1756	Beginning of Seven Years' War
	Frances Brooke, *Virginia, a Tragedy*
	Elizabeth Hamilton (1756?–1816) born
	Mary Robinson (1756/58?–1800) born
1757	Georgiana, Duchess of Devonshire (1757–1806) born
	Harriet Lee (1757/58–1851) born
1758	Elizabeth Carter, *All the Works of Epictetus*
	Charlotte Lennox, *Henrietta*
	Anna Larpent (1758–1832) born
1759	Mary Wollstonecraft (1759–97) born
	Mary Hays (1759–1843) born
	Robert Burns (1759–96) born
	Janet Little (1759–1813) born
	Sarah Fielding, *The History of the Countess of Dellwyn*

CHRONOLOGY

1760	Death of George II; succession of George III (1738–1820)
	Charlotte Lennox serializes *The History of Harriot and Sophia* (1760–61)
	Charlotte Lennox, *The Lady's Museum* (1760-61)
	Frances Brooke, *Letters from Juliet Lady Catesby* (translation)
1761	Frances Sheridan, *Memoirs of Miss Sidney Bidulph*
1762	Joanna Baillie (1762–1851) born
	Mary (Becky) Wells (1762–1829) born
	Charlotte Lennox, *Harriot Stuart*
	Sarah Scott, *Millenium Hall*
1763	Catharine Macaulay, *History of England*
	Frances Sheridan, *The Discovery*
	Frances Brooke, *The History of Lady Julia Mandeville*
1764	Julia Ann Hatton (1764–1838) born
	Mary Whateley Darwall, *Original Poems on Several Occasions*
1765	Sarah Dixon (b. 1671/72) dies
	Jean Adam (b. 1704) dies
	Thomas Percy, *Reliques of Ancient English Poetry*
1768	Maria Edgeworth (1768–1849) born
	Captain James Cook's first expedition
1769	Elizabeth Montagu, *Essay on Shakespeare*
	Frances Brooke, *The History of Emily Montague*
	Elizabeth Griffith, *The Delicate Distress*
1770	William Wordsworth (1770–1850) born
1771	Elizabeth Griffin, *The History of Lady Barton*
	Sir Walter Scott (1771–1832) born
	Anne Hughes Penny, *Poems, with a Dramatic Entertainment*
	Sophia Briscoe, *Miss Melmoth; Or, The New Clarissa*
1772	Samuel Taylor Coleridge (1772–1834) born
1773	Hester Chapone, *Letters on the Improvement of the Mind*
	Georgiana, Duchess of Devonshire, *Emma; or, the Unfortunate Attachment*
	Anna Letitia Barbauld, *Poems*
1775	Beginning of the American War
	Jane Austen (1775–1817) born
	Matthew "Monk" Lewis (1775–1818) born
	Samuel Johnson, *Journey to the Western Islands of Scotland*
1777	Frances Brooke, *The Excursion*

xix

1778	Frances Burney, *Evelina*
	Hannah More, *Percy*
	Anne Hughes Penny, *Invocation to the Genius of Great Britain*
	Frances Burney, *The Witlings* (written but not produced or published)
1780	Hannah Cowley, *The Belle's Stratagem*
	The Gordon Riots
1781	Frances Brooke, *The Siege of Sinope*
1782	Frances Burney, *Cecilia*
	Frances Brooke, *Rosina*
	Hannah More, *Sacred Dramas*
1784	Anna Seward, *Louisa, A Poetical Novel*
	Charlotte Smith, *Elegiac Sonnets* (first edition)
1786	Hannah More, *The Bas Bleu, or, Conversation*
1788	Charlotte Smith, *Emmeline, the Orphan of the Castle*
	Elizabeth Inchbald, *Such Things Are*
	Hannah More, *Slavery, a Poem*
	Ann Yearsley, *A Poem on the Inhumanity of the Slave-Trade*
1789	Start of the French Revolution
	Elizabeth Hands, *The Death of Amnon*
1790	Mary Robinson, *Ainsi va le Monde*
1791	Elizabeth Inchbald, *A Simple Story*
	Mary Robinson, *Impartial Reflections*
	Anna Letitia Barbauld, *Epistle to William Wilberforce*
1792	Mary Wollstonecraft, *A Vindication of the Rights of Woman*
1793	Charlotte Smith, *The Old Manor House*, *The Immigrants*
	Mary Robinson, *Modern Manners*
	Elizabeth Inchbald, *Every One Has His Fault*
1794	Mary Robinson, *The Widow*
1796	Elizabeth Inchbald, *Mogul Tale*
	Elizabeth Inchbald, *Nature and Art*
1797	Elizabeth Inchbald, *Wives as They Were, and Maids as They Are*

CATHERINE INGRASSIA

Introduction

Virginia Woolf observed that the fact non-aristocratic women "took to" writing and publishing in the seventeenth century "matters far more than I can prove in an hour's discourse."[1] Her words – that women's writing *matters* – remain as relevant today as they did nearly a century ago. Narratives of literary history change as each successive generation of scholars and students refines, revises, and perhaps transforms the understanding of a literary period. Nowhere is that transformative process more evident than in the literary history of women's writing in England.

In the early twentieth century, some scholars championed individual woman writers through, in part, the recovery of primary texts: Myra Reynolds's 1903 publication of the poems of Anne Finch (1661–1720), Montague Summers's 1915 edition of the works of Aphra Behn (1640?–89), or William McBurney's 1963 collection of novels from the 1720s that included texts by Eliza Haywood (1693?-1756) and Mary Davys (1674–1732). Woolf herself briefly mentions women writers discussed within these pages – from Behn, Finch, and Haywood to Laetitia Pilkington (1709–50), Elizabeth Carter (1717–1806), and Frances Burney (1752–1840) – giving a tantalizing glimpse of the wealth of primary materials available. These isolated efforts did not constitute a sustained, systematic, or, frankly, accepted critical tradition on women writers. Indeed, early twentieth-century criticism is the legacy of what Clifford Siskin has termed "The Great Forgetting" – the gendering of the discipline of literary studies in ways that excluded writing by women.[2]

In the past three decades, however, a recovery project of women writers has occurred – the process of identifying forgotten or ignored writers, making their primary texts available, and incorporating a consideration of their work into scholarship and classrooms. Scholars have been able to use sophisticated theoretical, bibliographic, and biographical tools to write women into literary history across the full range of genres. These developments coupled with the profound influence of feminist criticism on eighteenth-century studies specifically and literary studies generally and the increasing presence of women in the academy have produced foundational work on women writers of this period and reshaped the field.

Consequently, a current generation of students expects anthologies and syllabi that include women writers, often unaware of the conditions necessary for that integration to occur. No longer can (or should) scholars teach or write about the period known as the "long eighteenth century" without meticulous attention to women and their texts. Women wrote extensively across multiple genres – fiction, drama, memoirs, translations, periodicals, histories, poetry – and had a significant presence in print culture. Their writing constituted a significant portion of the literary marketplace throughout this period. Similarly, for many literate women, the practice of reading and writing comprised an important part of their daily lives.

This *Companion* is designed to provide a general introduction to women's writing in Britain between 1660 and 1789 by offering recent scholarship, discussions of both canonical and lesser-known women writers, and an understanding of the scope of women's writing during this period. It highlights the differences in class, geography, or employment that define women writers and presents a representative range of genres to illustrate their variety and versatility. It also illustrates how women writers operated as professional, published authors during the long eighteenth century, how they engaged in central issues of the public sphere, and how they created a literary space through their work. As a point of entry for the fourteen essays that follow, this introduction provides a context for thinking about women's writing in the Restoration and eighteenth century; briefly highlights the work that has been done on eighteenth-century women writers heretofore, work on which these essays build; and proposes where scholars and students of women's writing in Britain between 1660 and 1789 might go from here. While scholars and students can no longer imagine writing literary history or engaging in a critical practice that excludes women writers, so integral were they to the period, they must recognize the past work these women's presence represents and the future work it still demands.

Women's writing in Britain 1660–1789

The eighteenth century began its own process of writing a kind of women's literary history. Publications such as George Ballard's biographical offering *Memoirs of Several Ladies of Great Britain* (1752) or George Colman and Bonnell Thornton's *Poems by Eminent Ladies* (1755), the first substantial printed collection of women's verse, intertwined biography, morality, and aesthetics, privileging writers who exhibited propriety, modesty, and decorum. Colman and Thornton celebrated a very specific type of woman writer – refined, domestic, and adhering to the heteronormative expectations of a patriarchal culture. The anthologies effaced impulses inconsistent with the vision of women writers as a virtuous group advancing moral and aesthetic claims of the period; consequently, these texts, and others like them, constituted a kind of ad hoc literary history.

Similarly, John Duncombe's 1754 *The Feminiad* celebrated the efforts of British women writers, highlighting, as critics did throughout the century, the ways British national identity was enhanced by such illustrious women. In Britain, asserts Duncombe, women do not live within a "seraglio's gloomy walls" where "Nor sense, nor souls for women are assign'd." Rather "our British nymphs with happie omens rove / at Freedom's call, thro' wisdom's sacred grove."[3] Duncombe creates a tradition that begins with poet Katherine Philips (1632–64) "the chaste ORINDA" (110) and continues to Anne Finch "a lady of great wit, and genius" (130) and Catharine Trotter Cockburn (1674?–1749), "Philosopher, Divine, and Poet join'd!" (138). Similarly, Elizabeth Singer Rowe (1674–1737) and Frances Seymour, Countess of Hertford (1699–1754) receive Duncombe's praise. By contrast, Delarivier Manley (c. 1670–1724), Susannah Centlivre (1669?–1723), Behn, and Pilkington, although "harmony thro' all their numbers flow'd" (145), fall victim to what Duncombe terms "the dangerous sallies of a wanton Muse" (148).

Duncombe's celebration, a selective history, exalts predominantly poets (the most elevated and socially acceptable genre) of the gentry or aristocracy who published anonymously (Finch and Rowe initially) or with apparently noncommercial motives. Duncombe embraces writers who appear to value female modesty and morality above literary ambition. Duncombe singles out for criticism writers such as Manley, Centlivre, Behn, and Pilkington, who all circulated actively and with varied success in the emergent London literary marketplace and the world of print culture, a site of commercial activity. For example, Behn, regarded by many as the first professional female author, wrote variously and copiously across poetry, drama, and prose fiction, producing at least eighteen plays; five short fictions; two collections of poetry; translations; and a variety of other poems, prologues, and epilogues. Although she actually lived in an economically precarious position for most of her professional life, she sought both reliable financial compensation and an enhanced literary reputation. She defied the cultural expectations for appropriately "feminine" behavior with her prolificity, political engagement, frank representation of sexuality, and clearly stated literary ambition. Consequently, she ran afoul of the prescribed expectations for gentility and feminine modesty.

Duncombe's mid-century text, with its critique of "immoral" female writers and celebration of those whose virtuous, edifying discourse enhances national pride, aligns with dominant cultural norms. For example, Anne Finch in "The Circuit of Appollo," her tribute to female poets, notes that Behn wrote "a little too loosly [sic]."[4] Similarly, poet and memoirist Laetitia Pilkington, herself a figure of scandal, criticizes the "wicked Art of painting up Vice in attractive Colours, as too many of our Female Writers have done to the Destruction of Thousands, amongst whom Mrs. *Manley*, and Mrs. *Haywood* deserve the foremost Rank."[5] (Pilkington's somewhat gratuitous comment seems a strategic move to deflect criticism from her own personal history, revived with the publication of her memoirs.) This moralistic attitude, feigned or legitimate, persisted through the end of the century and beyond. In *The Complete History of the English Stage* (1800), Charles Dibdin characterizes playwright Centlivre as immoral, stating that "when women lose that female delicacy which is their worthiest designation and become Saphos [sic] in writing they may be as well Saphos in every other respect."[6] Allegations of immorality, often borne of professional anxiety, plagued women writers consistently in the eighteenth century.

Women writers confronted obstacles other than the allegations of immorality, however. Cultural anxiety existed about women's intellectual activity beyond regulated boundaries. Poet Elizabeth Thomas (1675–1731) describes women as confined by pervasive social mores or "custom": "By Customs *Tyranny* confin'd / To foolish *Needle-work*, and *Chat*,"[7] relegated to "domestick Tools" (7); "if we enquire for a *Book*, / Beyond a *Novel*, or a *Play*, / ... how soon th' Alarms took" (50–53). Although Thomas describes a world where women's writing is severely circumscribed to a "novel or a play," pleasure reading itself was often suspect. As detailed in "Instructions to Youth of Both Sexes in Proper Choice of Books" (1778), "reading ought not to be confined to mere amusement: that is its lowest form." The "impious buffoonery, false wit, and indelicacy [of] a Haywood, a Behn, a Pilkington [are] the delight of the gay, the volatile, and the inconsiderate." As a result, they should be avoided like "the worst poison" for they have been "injurious to thousands" and their "consequences" are often discovered "too late to be easily remedied."[8]

Women who wrote and published faced criticism about their position as, in the ironic words of Finch, "an intruder on the rights of men"; " Such a presumptuous Creature, is esteem'd / The fault, can by no virtue be redeem'd."[9] In the Dedication to *The Platonick Lady* (1707), Centlivre observes that readers, booksellers, and audience members, upon discovering a play they like has been written by a woman, "alter their judgment, by the Esteem they have for the Author, tho' the Play is still the same." "Why this

Wrath against the Women's works?" she continues. "Perhaps you'll answer because they meddle with things out of their Sphere."[10] This attitude extended to the belief that women's capacity and appropriateness for literary pursuits were limited purely on account of their gender. In his infamous tract *The Unsex'd Females* (1798), Richard Polwhele vociferously condemns "A female band despising NATURE's law" – writers he identifies as Elizabeth Carter, Frances Burney, and Anna Seward (1742–1809) – who "court prurient Fancy" in their literary pursuits.[11] Women certainly questioned these cultural assumptions about the intellectual disparity between the genders – "Why in the Age has Heaven allow'd you more / And Women less of Wit than heretofore?" asks Behn in the Epilogue to *Sir Patient Fancy* (1678). Yet, this cultural belief sometimes compelled women to adopt a strategic rhetorical position that displayed affected modesty in the appraisal of their own skills. In the dedication to the play *The Busie Body* (1709), Centlivre claims to be "conscious of the inequality of a Female Pen." Throughout *Oroonoko*, Behn regrets "only a female pen" could celebrate the title character.

Although a twenty-first-century reader might assume that the dominant resistance to women writing came primarily from men, eighteenth-century women writers prove otherwise. In the Dedication to *The Platonick Lady*, which she directs "To all the Generous Encouragers of Female Ingenuity," Centlivre laments that "even my own Sex, which shou'd assert our Prerogative against such Detractors, are often backward to encourage a Female Pen."[12] Similarly, Mary Barber ventriloquizes her female contemporaries who denounce her pursuit of poetry. Fulvia affirms that "Verses are only writ by Men / I know a Woman cannot write."[13] To label a woman "a wit," a desirable appellation in a man, "means self-conceit, ill nature, pride" in a woman as poet, writes Esther Lewis Clark (1716–94).[14] Women writers also regularly faced accusations of plagiarism; confronted barriers to education; and, later in the century with the rise of the critic and professional reviews, experienced biased critiques that highlighted gender.

While literacy rates for women climbed steadily during the eighteenth century, women's access to education was uneven, contingent on class, resources, and family attitudes. Certainly, some women were well educated. Elizabeth Carter or Constantia Grierson (1704/5–32) acquired the formidable language skills necessary to publish highly regarded translations of Epictetus and Tacitus, respectively. Servants such as Mary Leapor (1722–46) and Mary Collier (1688?–1762), "the washerwoman poet," used access to their employers' libraries to educate themselves. Collier describes reading as "my Recreation," devoting "what leisure time I had to Books."[15] At the opposite end of the social spectrum, Lady Mary Wortley

Montagu's well-known letter of January 28, 1753, to her daughter, Lady Bute, famously endorses the value of reading as part of a female education: "No Entertainment is so cheap as reading, nor any pleasure so lasting." She similarly encourages women to learn "the Languages" because, unlike a man, a girl's "time is not so precious. She cannot advance herself in any profession, and has therefore more hours to spare."[16] (Although, as Elizabeth Thomas notes in "On Sir J – S –, saying in a Sarcastick Manner, My books would make me Mad. An Ode" when women marry, they "in their House a full Employment find, / And little Time command to cultivate the Mind."[17])

As Montagu's letter confirms, while women might find opportunities for education, meaningful employment was largely nonexistent (women cannot "advance ... in any profession"). Eliza Haywood's *Anti-Pamela* (1741), a satiric response to Richardson's *Pamela* (1740), offers a trenchant appraisal of the dearth of employment options for women: Syrena Tricksey moves from an apprenticeship in a milliner's shop to domestic service (ranging from a lady's maid to housekeeper) and ultimately, and necessarily, pursues various forms of sexual labor. As Mary Hays illustrates very differently in *A Victim of Prejudice* (1799) at the end of the century, even well-educated women found it difficult to earn a living, find meaningful employment, or escape the limiting conditions of the sexual economy. Unable to own property and becoming their husband's property upon marriage, women, unless widowed, faced limited financial options.

Writing, however, potentially presented a means for women to earn a living. Mary Robinson's Mrs. Morely in *The Natural Daughter* (1799) turns to writing (after a short-lived career as an actress) because she has calculated it as a means "for the attainment of fame and profit."[18] The literary marketplace and the opportunities provided by print culture presented women working as professional authors the chance to publish in multiple genres and to earn some sort of income, ranging from a living wage to possibly a sustainable sum. Laboring-class poets such as Ann Yearsley (1753–1806) and Mary Chandler (1687–1745), like their middling-class counterparts, recognized the opportunity to exploit the ways subscription publication could operate as a form of charity to their potential advantage. As Mary Collier recounts in the preface to *The Woman's Labour* (1739), "the Author, whose Life is toilsome, and her Wages inconsiderable" confesses honestly "that the View of putting a small Sum of Money in her Pocket ... had its Share of Influence upon this Publication," which was done by subscription.[19] Poignantly, Collier recounts in a subsequent collection of poems (1762) that she actually profited little from the poem that initially brought her fame; having printed her poem "at my own charge," she writes, "I lost nothing, neither did I gain much, others run away with the profit."[20]

For some writers, however, publication (especially by subscription) offered a chance to earn a sum that would potentially allow them to move into another, more reliable form of employment and to escape what Elizabeth Boyd (fl. 1727–1745) terms "the exigencies of fortune." Boyd, also known as "Louisa," provides an interesting example of a woman writer navigating the cultural and commercial dynamics of the literary marketplace to achieve a specific financial, rather than purely literary, end. In 1732, Boyd issued a proposal for "printing a novel entitled 'The Happy Unfortunate: or, the Female Page'" by subscription. The price to subscribers was "Five Shillings; Half a Crown to be paid down, and Half a Crown on the Delivery of the Book," which would "be printed in Octavo, on good Paper, and a fair Letter"; the specific elements about the quality of the book bespeak a relatively knowledgeable consumer who recognizes the importance of the size of the book (octavo) and quality of typeface ("fair letter").[21]

In the March 2, 1732, advertisement to the published novel itself, Boyd claims she "was never ambitious of the Name of an Author" (despite having previously published two poems and publishing again after *The Happy-Unfortunate*), "nor ever designed to indulge my Inclinations in writing any Thing of this Nature, more then for my own private amusement." Rather, she claims to publish "this Manuscript (which otherwise I never had done) with a View of settling my self in a Way of Trade; that may enable me to master those Exigencies of Fortune." Now, she hopes her "honourable Subscribers (who are not already engag'd) [might] be so very good as to be [her] Customers" at her stationery shop: "I shall directly sell Paper, Pens, Ink, Wax, Wafers, Black Lead Pencils, Pocket Books, Almanacks, Plays, Pamphlets, and all Manner of Stationary Goods,"[22] a listing of wares that also reveals much about the material culture of reading and writing.

While this publication allegedly marks Boyd's removal from the literary marketplace, the prefatory materials actually position her within it as a potential rival to Eliza Haywood, revealing Haywood's commercial stature and literary reputation. The poem "On *Louisa*'s NOVEL, call'd *The Happy-Unfortunate*," situated between the list of subscribers' names and the novel itself, begins "Yield Heywood [sic] yield, yield all whose tender Strains, / Inspire the Dreams of Maids and lovesick Swains; / .... / A new Eliza writes –." Boyd, potentially "a new Eliza," illustrates the permeable nature of the commercial marketplace as an author could transition into a bookseller and then back into an author – or something else altogether. Boyd

7

was not alone in this professional shifting. Novelist and playwright Mary Davys earned enough money from her writing to open a coffeehouse in Cambridge in 1718. In the 1740s, Haywood operated a book shop while still writing, illustrating the integrated activities of writing, publishing, and printing, a fluidity that informs the careers of a number of women writers, especially those located primarily in London.

Print culture provided women writers with previously unimagined opportunities – to earn money; to achieve self-actualization; to secure some modicum of independence; to express their political, religious, or social views; and to experiment with literary form. They had a consistent and active engagement with the discursive world and the public sphere. One career path does not accommodate the movement of all women writers – indeed, to suggest that all these writers had the level of control or intentionality associated with the term "career" is a bit of a misnomer. Some, like Boyd or Haywood, carefully navigated the literary marketplace, seeking to position themselves advantageously for opportunities in writing or publishing that might arise. Others, like Carter or Seward, worked to preserve their high cultural capital and published strategically. Still others, like Jane Barker (1652–1732) or Finch, for example, operated in a hybrid culture, circulating within literary coteries in which they shared work and ideas before they ultimately published. These varied paths – and certainly many more exist – reveal the impossibility of using generalities to describe "women writers" during this period. To do so flattens the differences in age, place, class, education, political orientation, and cultural perspective that informs their texts and their professional choices (to the degree they had control of those choices). Such categories also predispose scholars and students to read the narratives of these women's lives through a preexisting lens. As becomes abundantly apparent, it is imperative to shed preconceptions about "women writers" in order to come close to understanding the complexity of the commercial and cultural world in which they operated. While a volume such as this one cannot exhaustively represent every perspective – nor could any – it should enable the reader to recognize the diversity and significance of women's writing during this period.

Previous work on women's writing in Britain, 1660–1789

The feminist recovery of women writers has been well documented and the foundational work in multiple disciplines (some represented in the "Guide to further reading") has demonstrated the unquestionable centrality of women writers, examined the gender hierarchies and sociocultural limitations confining them, and succeeded in writing them more accurately into literary history. The field has moved far from early feminist work that often focused on biography, constructed narratives of feminist triumph, and concentrated primarily on prose fiction. At times, the early efforts of recovery placed greater importance on identifying the presence of women writers and the quantity of their work than on the quality of those texts. Eager to construct a tradition of "women writers," scholars sometimes did so at the cost of the finer delineations and subtle differences necessarily effaced with that general term.

In the past two decades, however, with increasing sophistication scholars have brought a more refined and nuanced approach to women's work in multiple genres. Scholars such as Paula McDowell, Cheryl Turner, and Catherine Gallagher, among others, situated women within the commercial world of print culture. Ros Ballaster and Jane Spencer enriched our understanding of the kind of prose narratives women produced and their connection with contemporaneous discourses. Within specific genres, Paula Backscheider's work on women poets introduced a completely new way of considering that genre; Felicity Nussbaum, Misty Anderson, and Laura Rosenthal brought fresh perspectives to drama, Devoney Looser and Ruth Mack to women's writing of history. Similarly, work on individual authors, both major and minor, has advanced significantly: Claudia T. Kairoff on Anna Seward, Norbert Schürer on Charlotte Lennox, and Kathryn King on Jane Barker and more recently Eliza Haywood. The list of foundational work is extensive (and included in the "Guide to further reading").

These efforts of recovery and recuperation bring the current generation of scholars and students to the point where they can use the rigorous skills of biography, textual studies, and emergent theoretical approaches to complicate existing and formulate new, more precise narratives that further advance the understanding of women writers. Such gains have already occurred for a number of important writers. For example, the history of the scholarship on Eliza Haywood, acknowledged as one of the period's most prolific and significant writers, provides a revealing perspective on the changes within the treatment of female writers over the past decades. As with many women writers, scholarship on Haywood was shaped by the work of her earliest critics, who often read with the limitations of their own cultural moment. Haywood's first modern biographer George Frisbie Whicher, in *The Life and Romances of Eliza Haywood* (1915), at times grasped Haywood's "significance," noting her contributions "cannot safely be ignored;"[23] however, he too often blurred the discursive and the biographical, allowing his attitude toward the "lady novelist" to color his (mis)readings of the sparse biographical information then available.

The biographical inaccuracies he introduced, borne of his culturally bound assumptions, remained unrefuted until newly rigorous biographical work emerged in the early 1990s and culminated, most recently, with Kathryn King's *Political Biography of Eliza Haywood* (2012). Painstaking archival work – work habitually done on many male writers – provided a completely new understanding of Haywood.

Similar advances occurred with the interpretation of Haywood's prose fiction (the genre most frequently treated). In the 1960s, scholars such as William McBurney expressed hope his edition of Haywood's *Philidore and Placentia* (1727) would "send students" to the author, recognizing her importance.[24] Similarly, John Richetti helped bring Haywood to the fore by discussing her as a precursor to the more developed novel of the 1740s. However, they, like many of their contemporaries, read with a model of the novel informed by Ian Watt's privileging of realistic fiction and an artificially stable definition of genre.[25] Consequently, early scholars regarded Haywood as a writer who did not meet the formal or aesthetic expectations for a "novel." Subsequently, serious and sustained attention incorporated Haywood's work into the history of the novel, identified her work's philosophical and political dimensions, and revealed her high degree of narrative experimentation. Such scholarship helped explode what Paula Backscheider terms "the Story" of Eliza Haywood – the too-familiar, ultimately erroneous narrative of her life and works.[26] Many other women writers similarly bear the burden of that kind of critical shorthand, a "story" that helps characterize their contribution – stories scholars must continue to revise.

Within the past decades, scholars have benefited from a multivolume collection of Haywood's works (2000–2001), an invaluable bibliography by Patrick Spedding (2004), and the previously mentioned biography by Kathryn King. Together these fundamental tools of scholarship, which themselves confirm Haywood's significance as an author, have enabled entirely new, highly refined, often revisionary, insights. For example, using Spedding's bibliographic work as a foundation, Al Coppola recently showed that characterizations of Haywood as purely a "scandalous" writer are, in fact, erroneous.[27] Haywood's publishers carefully advertised various texts to different market segments (in something that resembled niche marketing), commodifying her as both a writer of elevation and refined sensibilities and a writer of amatory fiction; they then determined which model offered greater saleablility. This insight, impossible without the tools for careful textual history, helps explode "the story." Haywood serves as just one example of the rich possibilities next steps in the recovery project offer.

Introduction

Essays in this volume

This *Companion* has two sections. The first, "Women in print culture," provides information on how women writers operated within the emergent literary marketplace. Women wrote from diverse cultural positions in terms of class, geography, education, and their fluid relationship with the print trade. Careful examination reveals women were not necessarily marginalized, ignored writers laboring under the shadow of their male counterparts, nor were they always barred from the opportunities necessary for textual production. Rather, they were vital contributors to a vibrant literary culture. Mark Towsey proves how reading and writing were seamlessly integrated and mutually reinforcing in the daily lives of women from various classes and geographic locations. Both women who considered themselves professional authors and those who, by contrast, wrote for pleasure or publication, operated in what Towsey describes as "mutually supportive reading circles." He rightly urges scholars to consider the centrality of reading and writing for women, and the ways literary activities provide the basis for thinking about women writers at that time. Similarly, Sarah Prescott adds another lens for reading, introducing place – and a reflective awareness of the same – as a central consideration. Using an archipelagic approach, Prescott provides, in her words from this essay, "new templates for understanding how writers can interact with and be shaped by multiple geopolitical contexts," a theoretical move that substantially broadens the implications of women's sense of identity and place. Her essay offers keen insight into how place, too often elided, informed women writers' identities, publication strategies, and literary reputations.

While women wrote from the four constitutive parts of Great Britain (Wales, Ireland, Scotland, and England), London and the urban literary marketplace remained important for many, as Betty Schellenberg observes. Whether negotiating with individual publishers, selling books by subscription, or seeking the support of a patron, women navigated myriad opportunities to see their work in print. Schellenberg's discussion of writers such as Behn, Haywood, Charlotte Lennox (1730/31–1804), and Anna Letitia Barbauld (1743–1825) illustrates women's different career trajectories. Women operated as professional authors within the trade, evinced tremendous savvy about the marketplace, and secured significant respect and popularity. The material conditions of production; the forms of publication; the marketing, selling, and circulation of texts; and the exploitation of the dynamics of popular culture are all important elements of their careers. Indeed, as Paula Backscheider's essay illustrates, women were keenly aware of the power of popular culture. A feared characteristic of popular culture is its potential as an ideological vehicle, and women, less suspected of making it so, were actually alert, shrewd, and expert at exploiting such potential. Authors such as Elizabeth Inchbald (1753–1821) harnessed the power of their celebrity and the vehicle of the dramatic stage, which consistently garnered public fascination, to integrate their (often radical) political messages into ostensibly mainstream dramatic texts. The layering of meaning and message and the intersection of gender, politics, and literary discourse reveal the complexity of their texts and the degree to which, in Backscheider's words, "they helped devise the practices that created mass culture."

Complexity also emerges in the strategic use of multiple genres, variously deployed, the subject of Kathryn King's essay. While curricula and scholarship often focus on one genre at a time, women, like their male counterparts, frequently wrote in multiple genres and experimented with hybrid combinations to a degree previously unrecognized. Behn wrote fiction, poetry, and drama and edited a periodical. Haywood produced those four genres, as well as translations and conduct books. Mary Davys was poet, playwright, and novelist. Frances Brooke (1724–89) was a novelist, poet, translator, and playwright. The list could continue. Certainly, the versatility stemmed in part from economic necessity, but hybridization and experimentation centrally characterize many women writers of this period. While some women imitated existing models, striving to emulate their male contemporaries and predecessors, an equal number sought to revise those models, modifying them for distinctly different rhetorical purposes.

The second part, "Genres, modes, and forms," offers a discussion of the range and diversity of women's writing in multiple genres, modes, and forms over the course of the eighteenth century. While the essays in Part II, by definition, focus on women writing within specific genres, they do so in a way that complicates an understanding both of the genre as a genre and of women's engagement with that genre and contemporaneous authors, male and female. For example, Melinda Rabb's essay on satire reveals the significant intersection between male and female satire, as well as the gendering of the genre. She forcefully explodes the idea present in the eighteenth century – and to some degree now – that women did not write satire. Rabb skillfully demonstrates how, at its furthest reach, satire actually touches on the moments of the sentimental. The gendering of satire she describes complicates the genre as written by both men and women.

In poetry, women simultaneously wrote in competition, collaboration, and imitation of their male and female counterparts, as David Shuttleton's essay describes. The most elevated genre, poetry was written by women across all social levels and, in Shuttleton's words, "addressed a broad range of poetic themes, domestic, romantic, and polemical." The sheer volume of

Introduction

women's poetry during the period (according to Judith Phillips Stanton, between 1660 and 1800, women published 243 books of poetry[28]) makes it an important genre for consideration, and one that often yields as many observations about material cultural and social mores as contemporaneous fiction. The study of women's poetry has undergone what Shuttleton describes as a "seismic shift" in the last ten years and, with the increasing availability of primary texts, the field only promises to grow further.

In an essay that has rich cross-currents with Backscheider's discussion of women and popular culture, Felicity Nussbaum looks at continuities among female dramatists in their navigation of the theatrical marketplace and examines how women experimented with form, competed with their male counterparts, and strategically exploited the dissonance between the play's message and its paratexts. Similar experimentation marked Eliza Haywood's engagement with the genre of history, the subject of Rivka Swenson's essay. Exploring the expectations associated with writing history, Swenson asserts that Haywood's treatment of Mary Queen of Scots constitutes a kind of "recessive" history.

The difference between early and later fiction, discussed by Nicola Parsons and Katherine Binhammer, respectively, marks the shifts in the genre, readers, and cultural interests and preoccupations. Changes in reader expectations, the increasing ascendancy of the bourgeoisie, and a culture with more stringently enforced gender norms accounts, in part, for the movement from amatory fictions and secret histories of the 1720s to the more sentimental fiction of the latter part of the century. In her essay, Parsons explores generic hybrids, highlighting what she characterizes as the connection between poetic and novelistic form. This essay, implicitly in dialogue with King's, complicates the expectations for genre. Similarly, Binhammer, writing of the sentimental novel, asserts in her essay that "far from a single plot line following feminine self-sacrifice and acquiescence," as has often been characterized, late-century novels instead present "an array of intelligent, physically aggressive, and witty heroines confronting the major social questions of their day." Together these essays represent the development of the genre.

Women also played a crucial role in genres transmitted in less formal ways. Ruth Perry vibrantly discusses women's role as preservers of the ballad, a form seamlessly integrated with life, as lived, as remembered, as recorded. Perry's treatment of Anna Gordon Brown (1747–1810) and the Scottish ballads she shared, ballads that in many cases drew on her own family's history, reveals the significance of that genre for women of all classes and for a constructed sense of national identity. The ideas about place and publication that Prescott advances share an orientation with Harriet Guest's essay on travel writing. Examining Hester Thrale Piozzi's (1741–1821) and Mary Robinson's (1756/58?–1800) narratives about their travels to Wales, Guest reveals the importance of place and the degree to which women used travel narratives to "shape and advance their identities as authors in a period in which the cultural and literary authority of women was markedly increasing." Mary Waters provides a clear examination of women's participation in the periodical as readers, writers, and narrative personae. Emerging at a crucial time, "periodicals allowed women access to the professionalism of print culture, eventually affording sustained career opportunities that supported increasing numbers of professional woman writers." This volume obviously cannot cover all modes in which women wrote. Some forms such as religious writing, political tracts, or journalistic accounts, for example, are absent not because they are unimportant; such coverage would exceed the scope and size of a *Companion*. Together, these essays, like the volume as a whole, offer a diversity of written perspectives to provide an introduction to women's writing in Britain.

Considerations for subsequent work

Scholars of a certain generation likely remember the publication of Dale Spender's *Mothers of the Novel* in 1986. An important text early in the recovery project, it served for many as a clarion call for the kind of work that was increasingly possible – work nearly inconceivable at the time that now, thirty years later, is integral to and expected of the field. On the heels of *Mothers of the Novel*, Felicity Nussbaum and Laura Brown's *The New Eighteenth Century* (1987), although not focused exclusively on women or feminist approaches, completely broke open eighteenth-century studies, revising critical practices and introducing sophisticated theoretical approaches that have now become commonplace. These books, like the early special issues of *Eighteenth-Century Studies* devoted to "The Politics of Difference" (1990) or "Questions of Gender" (1997), emerged from the recognition that the then-current theoretical and methodological approaches could not accommodate or accurately represent the complex dynamic of print culture. Scholars engaged in the recovery of women writers reconceptualized received literary history. This *Companion* (which itself might have been nearly unthinkable in the not-too-distant past) establishes how much work has been done on women writers, and the degree to which scholars recognize women's significant contribution to and participation in print culture in every form.

Yet, such work is far from complete. Indeed, the moment scholars and students become comfortable with present understandings and the state of the field is the moment they risk losing an awareness of the rich interpretative possibilities still before them. While recovery as it was originally conceived may be nearing completion, scholars must still ask what remains to be done and how can we continue to move forward?

It is imperative that scholars continue to recover women writers' texts and ensure their dissemination in affordable, accessible forms. Great strides have been made in this direction. The production and increasing availability of primary texts by women in anthologies of poetry, fiction, and drama confer materiality and credibility to these writers. Sometimes, the reality of the publishing industry dictates that often "teaching" editions (e.g., those published by Broadview or Oxford Classics) serve as de facto scholarly editions. However, that is not the case for all authors. Cambridge's publication of the works of Anne Finch or Pickering and Chatto's publication of the selected works of Eliza Haywood are just two examples of excellent, authoritative editions.

Further, the extensive number of digitized texts on both proprietary databases such as Early English Books Online (EEBO) or Eighteenth-Century Editions Online (ECCO) and open-source resources such as HathiTrust or Google Books means students and scholars can increasingly find materials previously available only in archives and research libraries. Other databases and the search capacity they afford have also fundamentally changed the nature of scholarship. British newspapers found in the *Burney Collection of Seventeenth- and Eighteenth-Century Newspapers*, court proceedings in *The Proceedings of the Old Bailey, 1674–1913*, or poems and other content in the searchable *Gentleman's Magazine* database that enables the identification of often anonymous female contributors, all allow scholars and students to gather data at a level of detail previously unimaginable. Women, often rendered invisible by earlier methodologies and cataloging systems, become newly visible and populate these eighteenth-century cultural texts. No longer discursive ghosts, their presence waits to be revealed as they are more fully situated within the cultural, literary, and historical context.

All these resources facilitate the kind of high-level bibliographic work, discussed earlier in relation to Haywood, that more precisely and carefully locates women writers within print culture – work essential for scholarship to continue to move forward. Such focused scrutiny, common with generations of male writers, reveals particular modifications in women's commercial interactions, their narrative experimentation, and fine gradations of self-presentation within print culture. Similarly, biographical work, done only with careful research in record offices and archives, can provide a more refined understanding of a writer's career. The revision and extension of entries in the *Oxford Dictionary of National Biography* begun in 2004, and the rich biographical information and search capacity provided by the invaluable *Orlando Project: Women's Writing in the British Isles from the Beginnings to the Present*, dramatically improve scholars' ability to gather the fine points on which revelatory insights depend.

The availability of primary texts through digital and print resources should also compel scholars and students to move beyond those authors and texts already widely familiar (although, to be sure, work on the canon of women writers is hardly exhausted). The pages of this *Companion* are filled with the names of writers across all genres whose work and authorial path warrant more attention both in their own right and in connection with their contemporaries. Scholars and students of women writers must not be content with the gains gotten heretofore – rather, they must push beyond the "canonized." It is also crucial to mine literary periods previously dismissed as unimportant to see what insights they yield. For example, recent work on previously "ignored" or "forgotten" decades such as the 1730s and 1750s indicates how periods that literary history has suggested are somehow unimportant might in fact prove to be central.[29] (It was that same critical dismissal that rendered women writers invisible for so long.) Finally, we have to consider how these efforts translate into the classroom. If new generations of scholars and students do not have access to the recovered work and subsequent scholarship on women writers, it is as though the work never happened. The Modern Language Association recently published *Teaching British Women Playwrights of the Restoration and Eighteenth Century* (a collection cited by a number of contributors within these pages) that validates both the depths of women's contributions to dramatic form (something Felicity Nussbaum's essay highlights) and how seamlessly teaching and scholarship – particularly, perhaps, for women writers – are mutually reinforcing and informing activities.

Efforts to move beyond the "discovered" and canonized will be bolstered by concomitant reflection upon critical and theoretical practices. Scholars and students must interrogate the methodological assumptions and inherent biases that shape the discipline – whether cultural narratives about women, a heteronormative perspective, or an unexamined aesthetic orientation. To that end, scholars and students – particularly with the wealth of materials increasingly available – must continue shifting from the more accessible genre of prose fiction and forge ahead into poetry, drama, periodicals or hybrid forms. Narratives about the history of women's writing in the Restoration and eighteenth century do not – and cannot – focus solely on women, on the domestic, or on fiction. The consistent and appropriate move to situate them within the wider scope of cultural, literary, political, and economic activity more fully and richly presents their lives and

Introduction

their work. Curricula and publishing often still compel scholars to think of genre discretely, when in fact genres impinge upon one another as writers borrow from, imitate, refine, and strategically deploy multiple forms simultaneously.

The essays within this *Companion*, serving as a point of entry to the current state of the field, also harbor opportunities for further exploration of genre, writers, and theoretical approaches. Many of the poets mentioned in David Shuttleton's article lack sustained significant bibliographic, biographical, and interpretative work. Sarah Prescott's rich essay urges scholars to consider the implications of an archipelagic approach, and the resonance that would have with women writers residing in all parts of Great Britain. The generic mixing and the strategic deployment of multiple genres discussed by Kathryn King uncovers opportunities for more refined and sophisticated thinking about genre, form, and reader expectation. The lively discussion about women's writing in Britain between 1660 and 1789 will continue with the fresh perspectives of a new generation of students and scholars.

NOTES

1. The full quotation reads "it matters far more than I can prove in a hour's discourse that women generally, and not merely the lonely aristocrat shut up in her country house among her folios and her flatterers, took to writing." Virginia Woolf, *A Room of One's Own* (London, 1929; rpt. Harcourt, 1981), p. 65.
2. Clifford Siskin, *The Work of Writing: Literature and Social Change in Britain, 1700–1830* (Baltimore: The Johns Hopkins University Press, 1999), Part Four, "Gender: The Great Forgetting," pp. 193–210.
3. John Duncombe, *The Feminiad* (London, 1754), p. 8, lines 49–50.
4. Anne Finch, "The Circuit of Appollo," *British Women Poets of the Long Eighteenth Century*, ed. Paula R. Backscheider and Catherine E. Ingrassia (Baltimore: The Johns Hopkins University Press, 2009), p. 716, line 14.
5. Laetitia Pilkington, *The Memoirs of Mrs. Laetitia Pilkington*, Vol. 2 (Dublin, 1748), p. 239.
6. Charles Dibdin, *A Complete History of the English Stage* (London, 1800), p. 311.
7. Elizabeth Thomas, "On Sir J – S – saying in a sarcastick Manner, My Books would make me Mad," *Miscellany Poems on Several Subjects* (London, 1722), pp. 181–82, line 3.
8. "Instructions to Youth of Both Sexes in the Proper Choice of Books for Miscellaneous Reading," *The Weekly Entertainer and West of England Miscellany*, December 28, 1778, p. 297.
9. Anne Finch, "The Introduction," *British Women Poets of the Long Eighteenth Century*, p. 800, lines 10–12.
10. Susanna Centlivre, *The Platonick Lady* (London, 1707), A2.
11. Richard Polwhele, *The Unsex'd females; a poem* (London, 1798), p. 7.

12. Centlivre, *The Platonick Lady*, A2.
13. Mary Barber, "To a Lady, who commanded me to send her an Account in Verse, how I succeeded in my Subscription," *Poems on Several Occasions* (London, 1734), p. 276, lines 53–54.
14. Esther Lewis Clark, "Slander Delineated Address'd to a Friend," *British Women Poets of the Long Eighteenth Century*, p. 828, lines 13–15.
15. *Poems, on Several Occasions, by Mary Collier, Author of the Washerwoman's Labour, with some remarks on Her Life* (Winchester, 1762), p. iii.
16. *The Complete Letters of Lady Mary Wortley Montagu, Vol. III: 1752–1762*, ed. Robert Halsband (Oxford at the Clarendon Press, 1967), p. 21.
17. Elizabeth Thomas, *Miscellany Poems on Several Subjects* (London, 1722) p. 182, lines 22–23.
18. Mary Robinson, *A Letter to the Women of England and The Natural Daughter*, ed. Sharon M. Setzer (Peterborough, ON: Broadview Press, 2003), p. 207.
19. Mary Collier, *The Woman's Labour: An Epistle to Mr. Stephen Duck* (London, 1739), A2.
20. Mary Collier, *Poems on Several Occasions* (Winchester, 1762).
21. Elizabeth Boyd, *Proposals for printing by subscription a novel. Entitled, The happy-unfortunate; or, the female page. In three parts.* (London, 1732).
22. Boyd, *The Happy-Unfortunate*.
23. George Frisbie Whicher, *The Life and Romances of Mrs. Eliza Haywood* (New York: Columbia University Press, 1915), p. vii.
24. William McBurney, *Four Before Richardson: Selected English Novels, 1720–1727* (Lincoln: University of Nebraska Press, 1963), p. viii.
25. John Richetti, *Popular Fiction Before Richardson: Narrative Patterns 1700–1739* (1969, Oxford: Clarendon Press, 1992); Ian Watt, *The Rise of the Novel: Studies in Defoe, Richardson and Fielding* (London: Chatto and Windus, 1957).
26. Paula R. Backscheider, "The Story of Eliza Haywood's Novels: Caveats and Questions," in *The Passionate Fictions of Eliza Haywood: Essays on Her Life and Work*, ed. Kirsten T. Saxton and Rebecca P. Bocchicchio (Lexington: University Press of Kentucky, 2000) pp. 19–47.
27. Al Coppola, "The Secret History of Eliza Haywood's Works: The Early Novel and the Book Trade," in *1650–1850: Ideas, Aesthetics, and Inquiries in the Early Modern Era*, Vol. 19 (2012), pp. 133–61.
28. Judith Phillips Stanton, "Statistical Profile of Women Writing in English from 1660–1800," in *Eighteenth-Century Women and the Arts*, ed. Frederick M. Keener and Susan E. Lorsch (New York: Greenwook Press, 1988), pp. 247–53.
29. Susan Carlile, ed., *Masters of the Marketplace: British Women Novelists of the 1750s* (Bethlehem, PA: Lehigh University Press, 2011); Lacy Marschalk, Mallory Anne Porch, and Paula R Backscheider, "The Empty Decade? English Fiction in the 1730s," *Eighteenth-Century Fiction*, 26.3 (2014), 375–426.

PART I

Women in print culture

I

MARK TOWSEY

Women as readers and writers

> It is a happy revolution in the history of the fair sex, that they are now in general readers – and what is better, thinkers too, which adds charms to their conversation that outlive those of mere beauty ... Not above two centuries and a half ago, they were few to be found who could read or write. It is now difficult to find any, unless among the very lowest classes, who cannot read and write.
> "Hints on Reading," *The Lady's Magazine*, 20 (1789), 79

The notion that women readers had become an important force in the literary marketplace was one that struck many of the most astute cultural commentators of the eighteenth century. Edward Gibbon thought that "women in general read much more than men," while Samuel Johnson observed that "all our women read now."[1] If these assertions emerged from the very epicenter of contemporary print culture, readers on its margins often echoed them. For example, Elizabeth Mure (1700–90) was convinced that women's literary opportunities in provincial Scotland had changed dramatically in the course of her long life, recalling that in the first decades of the century,

> the weman's knowlege was gain'd only by conversing with the men not by reading themselves, and not picked up at their own hand, as they had few books to read that they could understand. Whoever had read Pope, Addison and Swift, with some ill wrot history, was then thought a lairnd Lady, which character was by no means agreeable.[2]

As part of the feminist recovery of women's writing in the long eighteenth century, scholars have become increasingly impressed by the importance of reading in the lives of Georgian women. For Jacqueline Pearson, the female reader is "one of the most striking phenomena of the eighteenth century," while Amanda Vickery asserts that women "enjoyed unprecedented access to the public world of print."[3] Such arguments are endorsed by the extravagant growth in female literacy documented in this period – 10 percent of women could sign their names in 1640, rising to 25 percent in 1714, and 40 percent in 1750. Virtually all women from aristocratic, gentry, and professional families were able to engage to some degree with print by 1780, although functional literacy was likely to be much more limited in the lower ranks of society. This great influx of new women readers into print culture had important implications commercially and culturally at a time when the marketplace was itself undergoing fundamental transformation. Female readers became "thinkers," capable of engaging in the public realm of information and politics to a far greater extent than before. The act of reading, and especially the tendency to read collectively, sociably, and in mutually supportive reading circles, encouraged women to become writers – whether as amateur producers of manuscript poetry for private consumption or as professional writers in their own right. Female readers also helped shape the sort of books women wrote; women writers spoke through their works to the expanding audience of female readers, guiding their entry into the unfamiliar realm of reading.

If women readers thereby inhabited an important new space at the junction between production and consumption in the literary marketplace, their cultural meaning was deeply contested. Pearson argues that the troubled figure of the female reader was a "key icon for this period," infusing "debates, about authority, gender and sexuality, the economics and morality of consumption, national identity and stability, class and revolution."[4] In some quarters, the rise of the female reader was thought to signify eighteenth-century Britain's unrivaled place at the apex of social history. David Hume, Joseph Addison, and other leading commentators of the Enlightenment regarded well-read women as a "touchstone of civilization" and the "cornerstone" of politeness. Female education, usually derived from the books women read in the absence of more formal pedagogical opportunities, was thought to guarantee the moral security of the family. Mary Wollstonecraft (1759–97) argued that by improving their minds through reading, women could approach more closely the contemporary ideal of virtuous domesticity, preparing them "to fulfil the important duties of a wife and mother."[5] But women had to maintain a careful balance – reading could enhance virtue, domesticity, and reason, but reading the wrong kind of books or the right books in the wrong way was thought to breed idleness, vanity, and sexual indiscretion. Troubled moralists complained that women's desultory reading tended to subvert their duty of care to the household, with one correspondent to the *Edinburgh Evening Courant* protesting "Johnson's Lives have nearly starved my youngest daughter at breast."[6]

While reading books of any kind might thus distract wives and mothers from their fundamental responsibilities, particular concern was expressed for the deleterious impact of novels, which could weaken young women's minds, making them susceptible to vice. The author of *New and Elegant*

Amusements for the Ladies of Great Britain (1772) warned against the "swarms of insipid Novels, destitute of sentiment, language or morals," while the popular conduct writer James Fordyce considered

> the general run of Novels utterly unfit for you. Instruction they convey none. They paint scenes of pleasure and passion altogether improper for you to behold, even with the mind's eye. Their descriptions are often loose and luscious in a high degree; their representations of love between the sexes are almost universally overstrained ... In short, the majority of their loves are either mere lunatics or mock-heroes.[7]

These fears converged particularly on the circulating library, where young girls could apparently indulge their obsession for romantic fiction unsupervised, and with no thought of the consequences. Thus, Richard Sheridan's Sir Anthony Absolute famously decried the circulating library as "an evergreen tree of diabolical knowledge! It blossoms through the year! – and depend on it, Mrs Malaprop, that they who are so fond of handling the leaves, will long for the fruit at last."[8] Alongside such moral hysteria, however, women readers also faced more deeply entrenched cultural hostility to female learning. Convention dictated that women should read within their intellectual limitations, keeping their learned pretensions to the private sphere so as not to compete with men in public. The York dissenter Catherine Cappe (1744–1821) recalled that her aunts "had a great horror of what they called learned ladies, and ... were continually warning me against spending my time in reading."[9] Such was the social stigma attached to women's reading that Elizabeth Hamilton (1756?–1816) once felt compelled to hide a copy of Lord Kames's eminently orthodox *Elements of Criticism* (1762) beneath her cushion "lest she be detected in a study which prejudice and ignorance might pronounce unfeminine."[10]

Such hostility toward women's reading was a natural function of the newly expanded market for print. As Jan Fergus suggests, because "suddenly male writers could not control women's reading or writing, and perhaps for this reason imagined threatening scenarios."[11] The stereotype of the female novel reader, deluded by reading fantastical accounts of love and romance, was what William Warner describes as a "discursive formation" designed to disseminate information and advice on good reading practices as part of a "cultural struggle" to control the new reading public.[12] Many women writers fully expected the storm of disapproval and suspicion to pass, with Sarah Maese (1744–1811) advising readers of *The School* (1766) to "wait till this change is effected, before you indulge yourselves in the most moderate display of your reading; for more than the most moderate, even custom could not sanctify" (Vol. 3.142). Nevertheless, the contemporary struggle to come to terms with the cultural significance of female reading has had important repercussions for the way modern scholars have viewed the rise of women's reading and writing. This essay explores some of the ways in which historians and critics have sought to uncover the historical experience of women readers, asking how far the stereotypical image of women's reading was rooted in reality and, crucially, highlighting the relationship between women's reading and women's writing in the long eighteenth century.

Women's access to books

A natural place to start is to consider the means by which women could come into contact with books in the first place. Family wealth was the primary determinant of female reading, although women could possess large libraries of their own in exceptional circumstances. Elizabeth Rose (1747–1813), the widowed lady laird of Kilravock in Nairnshire, owned nearly 2,000 books, including many legal tomes inherited from her father and grandfather. Many of the more recent books in the collection (including Fordyce's *Sermons*) were explicitly listed as being kept in "Mrs Rose's Closet," while she continued to add books to the collection, including *The British Poets* (1773–76) and Johnson's *Journey to the Western Isles of Scotland* (1775). Celebrated women such as Mary Wortley Montagu (1689–1762), Hester Thrale (1741–1821), and Elizabeth Vesey (1715–91) left library catalogs as basic indices of their reading lives, but most women from professional, clerical, and landed backgrounds had to rely on books belonging to their male relatives, making it impossible to identify books that appealed particularly to women in family libraries.

Booksellers' records are much more suggestive, linking specific titles with the individuals known to have bought them. In her exhaustive studies of the Clay family of booksellers in the Midlands, Jan Fergus finds that their business accounts reveal a more complicated story of women's reading practices than the conventional stereotype would allow and disprove the notion of the middle-class female's addiction to fiction. The impoverished spinsters Mary and Frances Westley ordered one novel for themselves (Richardson's ubiquitous *Clarissa* [1748]) but generally preferred devotional material, including Gastrell's *Christian Institutes* (1707) and the *New Week's Preparation for a Worthy Receiving of the Lord's Supper* (1737). As Fergus details in her work on women readers, Jane Williamson, a landed widow, preferred plays to novels, while Catherine Huddesford, the wife of a parish rector, bought ten novels alongside thirty-four other books, including plays, poetry, history, biography, voyages, and divinity. On the rare occasions when they can be found ordering books, female servants also eschewed novels in favor of different kinds of texts – especially practical texts aimed at improving specific skills, such as Susannah Carter's *The Frugal Housewife, or Complete Woman Cook* (1772) and Anne Barker's *The Complete Servant Maid; or, Young Woman's Best Companion* (c. 1770). In fact, the only two servants to show any interest in the Clays' stock of novels were both men, while subscriptions were evenly divided between men and women when *The Lady's Magazine* was first released in 1770.

Although suggestive, booksellers' records only allow us to glimpse the reading lives of a small minority of Georgian readers, the vast majority of whom could not afford to buy new books. James Raven estimates that the book-buying population was limited mainly to families with a minimum annual income of £50, or to just 150,000 households altogether. Richard Altick pointed out that the market could absorb only 9,000 copies "of even the most talked-of novel in a single year," while an unbound, three-volume novel would have cost a London tradeswoman the proceeds of an entire week's work.[13] Working-class readers still relied on less expensive, more traditional forms of print culture such as ballads, chapbooks, pamphlets, and news sheets, although little is known about their circulation and reception, especially among women. But female readers were not restricted in their reading choices by the books they (or their families) could actually buy, since it became increasingly easy to borrow books.

Sharing books became something of a social obligation in the eighteenth century, with anecdotal evidence of informal lending and borrowing rife among contemporary letters and diaries. Jane Patteshall and Elizabeth Shackleton allowed their books to circulate widely among their extensive social networks in Herefordshire and the northwest respectively, while Elizabeth Rose borrowed books from neighbors, clergymen, and female confidantes, including Richard Hurd's *Introduction to the Study of the Prophecies* (1772), Claude-Étienne Savary's *Letters on Egypt* (1786), and Charlotte Turner Smith's (1749–1806) newly released *Emmeline, the Orphan of the Castle* (1788). Such practices filtered easily down the social scale, so that the housekeeper Philippa Haye borrowed books from her employer's library at Charlecote, as did the working-class poet Elizabeth Hands (1746–1815).[14] The kitchen maid Mary Leapor (1722–46), another working-class poet, made extensive use of her employer's library at Weston Hall in Northamptonshire, reading Shakespeare, Locke, Chaucer, Gay, Swift, and Pope. Indeed, the benevolent reach of privately owned books became something of a cultural cliche; Pearson recounts how *The Lady's Magazine* regularly featured stories in which deprived young girls visited country houses to profit morally from their books.

Many relatively impoverished women also borrowed books from more formal lending libraries, including parish libraries, cathedral libraries, school libraries, and charitable town libraries, all of which often loaned books without charge to the broader community. At the charitably endowed Gray Library in Haddington, female borrowers were more likely than men to borrow fiction and poetry, but they still rated the complete works of Samuel Johnson, Robert Henry's *History of Great Britain* (1771), William Robertson's *History of America* (1777), and Charles Rollin's *Ancient History* (1730–38) among their favorite titles, alongside the imaginative works of Henry Fielding, Alexander Pope, Robert Burns, and Ossian. Stackhouse's *History of the Bible* (1733) was borrowed from the Gray Library by the daughters of a local butcher and a local millwright, while the octogenarian widow Martha Lockhart, Lady Castlehill (1668–1752), borrowed George Buchanan's classic *History of Scotland* in 1750. History was also popular at the Maidstone Parish Library in Kent, where twenty-six of thirty-one lay borrowers were women, at least ten of whom borrowed volumes of Thomas Salmon's *Modern History* (1724–38).[15]

Similarly eclectic reading tastes are evident in the surviving borrowing records of the more exclusive subscription libraries, which were usually perfectly happy to welcome female members as long as they could afford the subscription fee. The Lancaster Amicable Society voted to admit women in 1775 and had thirty-two female members by 1812, while the Suffolk Subscription Library had sixteen female members in 1791 (out of 116 members in total), and the Norwich Library had eighty-three women out of a total membership of 456 in 1792.[16] Where borrowing records survive, they show women to have been every bit as bookish as their male peers. At Wigtown, women borrowers accounted for 151 loans out of 898 overall in the early 1790s, with the widows McCulloch and Milroy ranking among the top five most active borrowers of all with more than fifty separate loans apiece. Milroy borrowed novels such as Johnstone's *Chrysal* (1760) and *The Fashionable Tell-Tale* (1778) alongside histories by Hume and Gibbon, Captain Cook's *Voyages* (1784), and the occasional issues of the *Monthly Review* and *Annual Register*. McCulloch borrowed Brooke's *Fool of Quality* (1765–70), the collected works of Henry Fielding, and Bell's collection of *British Theatre* (1776–78) but also returned time and again to work through all eight volumes of the library's copy of Hume's *History of England* (1754–62).

While closely related to the subscription libraries in cultural function and self-improving mission, the smaller and less formal book clubs proved of particular benefit to women readers eager to join together to buy books collectively that they could not afford individually. At the Oswestry Book Society, twenty-two of the thirty-four members were women, while all-female book clubs could be found in Bishop Wearmouth, Saffron Waldon, and Shrewsbury, with the latter thought to have been founded in the early 1750s. The Penzance Ladies' Book Club was founded in 1770 on the basis that "no gentleman be admitted as subscriber," and the membership went about collecting books that they considered most useful for their own purposes, including history, biography, travel writing, works of popular morality, and a carefully selected range of imaginative works such as Shenstone's poems, Smollett's novels, and Anstey's satirical *The New Bath Guide* (1766).[17]

Although women could thereby borrow books from libraries in both the private and the public spheres, they were especially associated with the commercial circulating libraries that sprang up in towns across the country from the 1740s. As we have seen, these exercised a persuasive hold on the popular imagination, with almost every contemporary writer who mentioned them alleging that they supplied the most objectionable kind of novels to a mainly young, impressionable female readership. Such allegations are simply not borne out by the historical record, with Jan Fergus suggesting that historians "may overestimate the libraries' importance in the market outside London."[18] Surviving membership lists indicate that they catered equally to male and female readers, with many of the longer-established circulating libraries offering impressive catalogs to rival even the most serious-minded subscription libraries in respectable genres such as history, natural philosophy, devotional literature, and self-help guides. Although such sources suggest that circulating library stock was more morally wholesome than contemporary commentators would have us believe, David Allan concedes that they must have served large numbers of women by virtue of being "more reasonably priced" than other forms of collective reading, "generally more widely available, and also rather less questioning as to the status and motives of readers who were, of course, simply paying customers."[19]

The experience of reading

While scholars have thus worked hard to sketch out the physical landscape of women's reading, they remain aware of the limitations of library records. The problem of identifying concealed readers is particularly acute, since married women, spinsters, and young girls tended to be dependent on male relatives in monetary transactions throughout our period. More broadly, to show that women had the opportunity to read a specific book is not to prove that they ever actually read it. Nor is it to demonstrate why they read it, whether they understood it, or how they responded to its ideas. For these reasons, scholars have increasingly turned to material that illuminates the reading experience itself, including diaries, commonplace books, correspondence, marginalia, and reading notes of other kinds. Of course, these more personal accounts of reading present their own problems, not least because so much of the psychological and intellectual work involved in reading takes place in the mind. Such sources can reveal only partial and incomplete impressions of the reader's interaction with a text, already discursively constructed by the reader herself. Countless acts of reading that have taken place in the past were never recorded for posterity, and reading notes (where they do survive) inevitably downplay the significance of reading for pleasure and entertainment. Even so, anecdotal sources occasionally allow us to glimpse some of the supposedly detrimental effects of novel reading on the female mind. Some thought that novels really did raise unrealistic expectations, such as the Scottish gentlewoman Alison Cockburn (born in 1713), who called for *Sir Charles Grandison* (1753) to be burned "by the hands of the hangman. The girls are all set agog seeking an ideal man, and will have none of God's corrupted creatures."[20] Lady Bradshaigh (1705–85) was famously overwrought by the emotional appeal of *Clarissa*: "Would you have me weep incessantly? ... in Agonies would I lay down the Book, take it up again, walk about the Room, let fall a Flood of Tears, wipe my Eyes, read again ... throw away the Book crying out ... I cannot go on."[21] The spinster Gertrude Savile (1697–1758) regretted her unhealthy attachment to risqué texts such as Eliza Haywood's *Perplex'd Dutchess* (1727) and *The Arragonian Queen* (1724), confessing that "such books I read as people take Drams, to support for an hour sinking Spirits,"[22] while Laetitia Pilkington (1709–50) serves what Pearson describes as the "perfect negative role-model" (127), reading transgressively to challenge parental authority, flout the conventions of virtuous domesticity, and prostitute herself in the world of print.

Nevertheless, the documentary record tends to confirm that women's reading experiences were much broader in scope than the conventional stereotype would allow. In the first place, many women clearly thought novels could be read with moral purpose and discipline, "a means of overcoming rather than encouraging female frivolity." Anna Larpent (1758–1832) "refused to accept" that the contemporary stereotype "applied to her own case," filleting at least forty-six novels for moral exemplars and advice on good conduct, including those of female writers such as Elizabeth Griffith (1727–93) and Charlotte Lennox (1730/31–1804).[23] Esther Edwards Burr (1732–58), the daughter of the evangelical theologian Jonathan Edwards, treated *Pamela* as a moral handbook, using it to learn how to behave in polite society, while Sally Chapone approached "any unusual situation by asking what Clarissa would do."[24] Elizabeth Rose used Frances Burney's (1752–1840) *Cecilia* (1782) to endorse her own lifelong bookishness, and she collected an extensive compendium of female conduct models from a wide range of recently published novels. No wonder, then, that in her retrospective account of the rise of the novel, Anna Letitia Barbauld (1743–1825) could insist that novels "had a very strong effect in infusing principles and moral feelings," whatever the weight of contemporary criticism.[25]

Importantly, the same themes emerge in women's encounters with other types of books, reinforcing Leonore Davidoff and Catherine Hall's influential argument that reading played a crucial role in disseminating and solidifying conventional notions of virtuous domesticity among women. Gertrude Savile mined poetry, plays, and periodicals for moral maxims that could be removed from their original context and stored away for later use, including extracts from James Thomson's *Sophonisba* (1730) on "love," "content, ease or relief," and "pain or grief." Jane Pateshall's prolonged engagement with Pope's *Iliad* (1715–20) reflected especially on "parts of the epic narrative that probed individuals' responses to significant moral or emotional stress," while a teenage farmer's daughter in Essex entered verses from William Cowper into her commonplace book on such conventional themes as humility, comfort, and peace.[26] As Lady Mary Chudleigh (1656–1710) advised, history could be read with moral "advantage" too, revealing the "wonderful turns of Fortune, surprizing Occurences, and an amazing variety of Accidents" that shaped people's lives.[27] Martha Fletcher fastidiously collected "the salutary characters of public figures from whom she could hope to learn" in the 1740s, as did her fellow Scotswoman Elizabeth Rose, who focused especially on the moral lives of historical women – including Margaret of Anjou's ultimately fruitless struggle to secure a prosperous future for her son, which Elizabeth read as an allegory for her own life as a single mother.[28] Even classical literature could provide such moral guidance for women readers, in spite of its peculiarly close association with masculine learning. Mary Chorley admired the civic virtue of Plutarch's Rome in the mid-1770s, while a teenage Quaker girl found Stoic inspiration in reading the *Life of Caius Marius*. Jane Johnson (1706–59), a vicar's wife from Olney in Buckinghamshire, ultimately found spiritual consolation in moral sententiae taken from heathen philosophy, while Elizabeth Rose fashioned a strongly devotional interpretation of Scottish Enlightenment philosophy in her extensive commonplace books of the 1770s and 1780s.[29]

If books of all kinds could bolster conventional notions of female morality, newspapers allowed women to engage to an unprecedented degree with political debate. Barbara Johnson (1738–1825; Jane's equally bookish daughter) was well known as a font of opinion on national and international affairs, reporting in February 1776 that she had read "no less than NINE different magazines last month and two reviews."[30] Elizabeth Shackleton subscribed to four London newspapers in the 1760s, as well as provincial periodicals published in Leeds, Manchester, and Preston. As Amanda Vickery contends, "the reader who wept over the fate of Clarissa Harlowe was equally capable of fuming about the progress of the American war, or applauding the release of John Wilkes."[31]

The public sphere impinged on women's reading in other ways. Jane Pateshall's breathless notes from George Anson's *Voyage round the World* (1748) reflect "something of the giddy excitement" with which she followed "the perils braved by the British squadron that had recently circumnavigated the globe."[32] Jane read into Shakespeare's *Measure for Measure* the contemporary politics of the Jacobite rebellion of 1745–46, while Elizabeth Freke (1641–1714) used George Story's *True and Impartial History* (1691) to "place her own life in context" – as well as taking extracts from John Gerard's *The Herball* (1597) and Nicholas Culpepper's *School of Physick* (1659) for more obvious practical purposes.[33] Anna Larpent occasionally read with particular purposes in mind, as when she studied the aesthetic works of Reynolds, Ramsay, Akenside, and Shaftesbury before attending art exhibitions in the 1780s, while Christian Ramsay, Countess of Dalhousie (1786–1839), read Robertson's *History of America* and Kames's *Sketches of the History of Mankind* (1774) as she made landfall in Halifax as consort to the new governor of British North America.

While women thereby fashioned autobiographical and political meanings from the wide range of texts they read, their reading had broader social functions. Naomi Tadmor challenges the "image of the impressionable and idle female reader" by reconstructing reading practices in the household of village shopkeepers Thomas and Peggy Turner, where reading, like work and religious discipline, took place routinely. Peggy read to her husband while he worked, just as Humphrey Repton's wife read to him while he drew.[34] Shared reading helped consolidate bonds of affection between husband and wife, with the Dalhousies sharing intimate re-readings of Blair's *Sermons* (1777–1801) both before and after their marriage; books also played a central role in Frances Burney's marital home. Far from distracting them from domestic duties, women's reading could be fully integrated into their daily lives, with girls taking turns reading while their sisters worked. Most importantly, women took seriously the conventional expectation that they would supervise domestic education, guiding dependents through their earliest experiences as readers – and often maintaining tight control over their children's reading long into adulthood. Reading aloud was a favorite family occupation, not least because a young woman's reading could be more carefully monitored in the shared sociability of the domestic reading circle, where she could be handily corrected.

The particular delights of shared reading encouraged women to look far beyond their homes in search of "kindred spirits," a term used by Elizabeth Rose to describe her preferred reading companions.[35] Women's letters throughout the period included recommendations for and commentaries on reading material, allowing readers not only to refine their own literary sensibilities but also creating a supportive community of female readers. Jane Johnson's letters discussed the moral dilemmas encountered in everyday life by reference to the books she had read, and her daughter Barbara became "a sought after literary critic" among epistolary friends.[36] Esther Burr addressed her reflections on *Pamela* in diarized form to her childhood friend Sally Prince, the two young women self-consciously working out the moral lessons of the book between them, while Betty Fletcher (1731–58) and Margaret Hepburn (1734–59) wrote literary letters to each other to cultivate "the sense of being absorbed together in a common activity."[37] The cultural currency of shared reading stretched back at least to the late seventeenth century, recalling the Utopian vision sketched out in Mary Astell's (1666–1731) *Serious Proposal to the Ladies* (1694), "where women could spend their time in study and contemplation, reading 'judicious authors' and enacting good works, enjoying the friendship and ingenious conversation of one another."[38] Shared reading was also a noteworthy feature of the published (and much talked about) letters of the Bluestockings Elizabeth Carter (1717–1806), Catherine Talbot (1721–70), Elizabeth Montagu (1718–1800), and Elizabeth Vesey (1715–91), which confirmed on nearly every page the centrality of collective reading to the way these literary celebrities experienced the world of print. The Bluestockings demonstrated that shared reading and rational conversation could enhance polite sociability and virtuous domesticity. Informal reading circles that built up around libraries and book clubs can in part be read as an attempt to emulate such cultural practices, providing opportunities for conversation between likeminded women and men, based on the shared discussion of books.

Reading and writing

If collective reading helped shape the way women performed polite sociability, it ultimately provided a crucial link between reading and writing. Georgian men and women "wrote for their own pleasure and edification and that of their relatives and friends," so that all readers whose notes survive can in one sense be considered writers – deliberately fashioning meaning from the books they read, whether for external display or internal self-improvement.[39] Sustained engagement with fiction could inspire readers' own experiments in amateur storytelling. Thus, Jane Johnson sent a short "History of Miss Clarissa of Buckinghamshire" to one of her epistolary friends, relocating Richardson's fable to Johnson's local environment and addressing the moral dilemmas she faced as a clergyman's wife in a poverty-stricken parish: "She distinguished it from scandalous romance, identified with its heroine, and used it to examine her own moral values."[40] Lady Frances Montagu, a Cambridgeshire viscountess (d. 1788), entered her friends' unpublished poems in her commonplace book, while both Margaret Hepburn and Elizabeth Rose composed verses for private consumption within their reading circles. The great success of *The Lady's Magazine* was that it provided an outlet for such amateur writing, fostering the sense of a broader female reading community "by, eliding the roles of writer and reader, encouraging readers contribute ... so that a hierarchical distinction between readers and writers is replaced by ... a less hierarchical community of literary women" (Pearson, 97).

Women readers played their part elsewhere in what Robert Darnton influentially terms the "communications circuit" of eighteenth-century print, often called upon to read drafts of published works for male friends and relatives.[41] Richardson famously encouraged his female readers to become actively engaged in the process of writing, soliciting their opinions on the realism of his fictional narratives and relying on them to calibrate his representation of elite manners. An eighteen-year-old Hannah More (1745–1833) corrected the unpublished works of the mechanic James Ferguson, while novelist Henry Mackenzie, playwright John Home, and historians Robertson and Hume all called on women for advice on early drafts of their works. Margaret Hepburn was so deeply involved in drafting Robertson's *History of Scotland* (1759) that his Mary Queen of Scots had "grown up to her present form under your eyes, you have seen her in many different shapes; and you have now a right to her." Mackenzie's letters to his cousin Elizabeth Rose are packed with comments on her broader reading experiences, and he trusted her to provide detailed feedback on drafts of his novels as they emerged: "I expect your sincere opinion, not only of the Parts you approve, but also of those which admit of Censure ... You see you are not only Mistress of my Thoughts but have them even in Embryo."[42]

Shared reading practices had a particularly important role in shaping female authorship, providing a sense of a collaborative literary community that informed women writers' conception of themselves and underpinned many of the major landmarks of women's writing in this period. Mary Astell was encouraged into print by the circle of well-read learned friends that gravitated around her and in turn encouraged Mary Wortley Montagu to publish her Turkish Letters, writing a preface for them in 1724 before

Montagu's reticence won the day. Catherine Talbot sought out Elizabeth Carter as a famous literary correspondent with the hope one day of following her into the Republic of Letters; her works circulated in manuscript among the Bluestockings, to be collected and published posthumously by Carter in 1772. Carter's own poetry was read in manuscript by the group before she was persuaded to publish it, while Elizabeth Montagu's *Essay on Shakespeare* (1769) emerged from a particularly intense period of shared reading and discussion. Female reading circles also opened up more material opportunities. Elizabeth Montagu paid annuities to Anna Williams (1706–83) and Elizabeth Carter to support their writing, while the practice of shared reading, coupled with the mechanics of the eighteenth-century print trade, allowed ladies of more modest means to engage in literary patronage. Having received Ann Yearsley's (1753–1806) poems in manuscript from her own cook, Hannah More circulated them to other readers in her circle to secure their support in publishing the poems by subscription. She then set about improving Yearsley's self-awareness as a reader, exposing her to landmark works by Ossian and John Dryden.

At the same time, their commitment to a shared sense of reading community ultimately helped frame the type of books women often chose to write. The proliferation of didactic books written by and for women that sought to validate the much criticized figure of the female reader was an external expression of the mutual encouragement given to women writers by their immersion in shared reading practices. Charlotte Lennox's *The Female Quixote* (1752) was one of the earliest novels to dwell explicitly on the thorny issue of women's reading, with the protagonist Arabella reading in exactly the way she is meant to read, taking moral lessons from her reading and applying them to the way she behaves – although as many critics note, Arabella *mis*reads and applies the lessons to the wrong texts. The Bluestockings were famously committed to the education of young girls, and many of them wrote with the emerging role of middle-class women in domestic education very firmly in mind. Talbot asked Carter to write an "edifying essay" for girls who hoped to release themselves from society's conventional suspicion of learned ladies. Elizabeth Montagu encouraged Hester Chapone (1727–1801) to publish the informal letters she had written to her niece in the 1760s, later correcting the manuscript of Chapone's *Letters on the Improvement of the Mind* (1773). Such texts legitimized female literacy by showing how reading could enrich the lives of women both intellectually and emotionally.

In her influential book *The Woman Reader, 1837–1914* (1993), Kate Flint warns about the danger of blurring together the reading experiences of "the fifteen-year-old or the grandmother, the woman on a Yorkshire farm or the society hostess," each of whom Pearson agrees had "different needs, attitudes, and horizons."[43] Scholars seeking to document and understand the reading practices of women in the eighteenth century face formidable challenges. Women are frequently concealed in libraries' and booksellers' records, while more personal accounts of reading experiences tend to come from the aristocracy, the gentry, and published writers of the professional class. Nevertheless, enough evidence does survive to cast considerable doubt on the conventional stereotype of the morally delinquent female novel reader. This familiar figure was largely fictitious, but she remains important for revealing the significance of women's reading – both for contemporaries and for scholars seeking to understand the role of women in eighteenth-century politics, culture, and society. It was through reading that women could negotiate their place in the world, making sense of their responsibilities and relationships, and opening up new spaces in which they could participate in rational conversation, intellectual exchange, and even political debate. In this sense, every woman whose reading notes survive was also a writer – a cultural agent busy framing a sense of self amid her extracts, annotations, commonplace books, and literary correspondence. But women's reading is central to the development of women's writing in this period in a much broader sense. Encouraged by the mutually reinforcing activities of reading and writing, women started to enter the print marketplace in increasing numbers. They did so by subscribing to the works of impoverished writers with whom they were familiar and by advising celebrated authors, thereby contributing to some of the great intellectual and literary landmarks of the age. Most dramatically, they did so by taking up the pen themselves, addressing the needs and desires of the reading community to which they belonged.

NOTES

1. Edward Gibbon, *The Autobiography and Correspondence of Edward Gibbon* (London, 1869 reprint of original editon), p. 154. James Boswell, *The Life of Samuel Johnson* (London, 1792) Vol. 3, p. 62.
2. Elizabeth Mure, "Some Remarks on the Change of Manners in my Own Time, 1700–1790," in *Selections from the Family Papers Preserved at Caldwell*, ed. William Mure, Maitland Club, 71 (Glasgow, 1854), vol. 1, p. 269.
3. Jacqueline Pearson, *Women's Reading in Britain, 1750–1835: A Dangerous Recreation* (Cambridge University Press, 1999), p. 22; Amanda Vickery, *The Gentleman's Daughter: Women's Lives in Georgian England* (New Haven: Yale University Press, 1998), p. 287.
4. Pearson, *Women's Reading*, pp. 219–20, 1.
5. Quoted by Katie Halsey, *Jane Austen and Her Readers, 1786–1945* (London: Anthem, 2012), p. 30.

6. Quoted by Michèle Cohen, "'To think, to compare, to combine, to methodise': Girls' Education in Enlightenment Britain," in *Women, Gender and Enlightenment*, ed. Sarah Knott and Barbara Taylor (Basingstoke: Palgrave, 2005), p. 224.
7. James Fordyce, *Sermons to Young Women*, 2 vols. (London, 1766), vol. 1, p. 149.
8. Richard Sheridan, *The Rivals*, ed. Elizabeth Duthie (London: Black, 1979), p. 26.
9. *Memoirs of the life of the late Mrs Catharine Cappe, written by herself*, ed. Mary Cappe (London, 1822), p. 47.
10. *Memoirs of the Late Mrs. Elizabeth Hamilton*, ed. Elizabeth Benger, 2 vols. (London, 1818), Vol. 1, pp. 49–50.
11. Jan Fergus, *Provincial Readers in Eighteenth-Century England* (Oxford: Oxford University Press, 2007), p. 72.
12. William B. Warner, *Licensing Entertainment: The Elevation of Novel Reading in Britain, 1684–1750* (Berkeley: University of California Press, 1998), p. 141.
13. Richard D. Altick, *The English Common Reader: A Social History of the Mass Reading Public, 1800–1900* (University of Chicago Press, 1957), pp. 50, 52.
14. David Allan, *A Nation of Readers: The Lending Library in Georgian England* (London: British Library, 2008), p. 213; Vickery, *Gentleman's Daughter*, pp. 258, 343; Jan Fergus, "Provincial Servants' Reading in the Late Eighteenth Century," in *The Practice and Representation of Reading in England*, ed. James Raven, Helen Small, and Naomi Tadmor (Cambridge University Press, 1996), p. 213.
15. Drawn from Vivienne S. Dunstan, "Glimpses into a town's reading habits in Enlightenment Scotland: Analyzing the borrowings of Gray Library, Haddington," *Journal of Scottish Historical Studies*, 26.1 (2006), 50, 47. Graham Best, "Libraries in the Parish," in *The Cambridge History of Libraries in Britain and Ireland, Volume II: 1640–1850*, ed. Giles Mandelbrote and Keith A. Manley (Cambridge University Press, 2006), pp. 339–40; Pearson, *Women's Reading*, p. 161.
16. David Allan, *Making British Culture: English Readers and the Scottish Enlightenment, 1740–1830* (New York: Routledge, 2008), p. 66; Allan, *Nation of Readers*, pp. 78–82.
17. William St. Clair, *The Reading Nation in the Romantic Period* (Cambridge University Press, 2004), pp. 249–51; Allan, *Nation of Readers*, pp. 39–40, 51–52.
18. Jan Fergus, *Provincial Readers in Eighteenth-Century England* (Oxford: Oxford University Press, 2007), p. 54.
19. Allan, *Nation of Readers*, p. 154.
20. Quoted by Katherine Glover, *Elite Women and Polite Society in Eighteenth-Century Scotland*. (Woodbridge, UK: The Boydell Press, 2011), p. 64.
21. Quoted by Pearson, *Women's Reading*, p. 28.
22. Quoted by Stephen Colclough, *Consuming Texts: Readers and Reading Communities, 1695–1870* (Basingstoke: Palgrave, 2007), p. 61.
23. John Brewer, "Reconstructing the Reader: Prescriptions, Texts, and Strategies in Anna Larpent's Reading," in *The Practice and Representation*, ed. Raven, Small, and Tadmor, pp. 235, 233.
24. Ned C. Landsman, *From Colonials to Provincials: American Thought and Culture, 1680–1760* (Ithaca: Cornell University Press, 1997), p. 48; Thomas

C. Duncan Eaves and Ben D. Kimpel, *Samuel Richardson: A Biography* (Oxford: Clarendon, 1971), p. 352.
25. Quoted by William McCarthy, *Anna Letitia Barbauld: Voice of the Enlightenment* (Baltimore: The Johns Hopkins University Press, 2008), p. 38.
26. David Allan, *Commonplace Books and Reading in Georgian England* (Cambridge University Press, 2010), p. 197; Leonore Davidoff and Catherine Hall, *Family Fortunes: Men and Women of the English Middle Class, 1780–1850* (University of Chicago Press, 1987), p. 157.
27. Quoted by Devoney Looser, *British Women Writers and the Writing of History, 1670–1820* (Baltimore: The Johns Hopkins University Press, 2000), pp. 17–18.
28. Glover, *Elite Women*, p. 59; Mark Towsey, *Reading the Scottish Enlightenment: Books and Their Readers in Provincial Scotland, 1750–1820* (Leiden: Brill, 2010), pp. 204–5.
29. Vickery, *Gentleman's Daughter*, pp. 7, 259; Susan E. Whyman, *The Pen and the People: English Letter Writers, 1660–1800* (Oxford University Press, 2009), pp. 173–74; Towsey, *Reading the Scottish Enlightenment*, pp. 204–6, 212–15, 223–25, 285–86.
30. Quoted by Whyman, *The Pen and the People*, p. 202 (emphasis is original).
31. Vickery, *Gentleman's Daughter*, p. 260.
32. Allan, *Commonplace Books*, pp. 238–39.
33. Allan, *Commonplace Books*, p. 194; Colclough, *Consuming Texts*, p. 46.
34. Naomi Tadmor, "'In the even my wife read to me': Women, Reading and Household Life in the Eighteenth Century," in *The Practice and Representation*, ed. Raven, Small, and Tadmor, p. 165; Pearson, *Women's Reading*, p. 172.
35. National Records of Scotland, GD125 Box 35; letter from Elizabeth Rose to Euphemia Russell dated 15 March 1809.
36. Whyman, *The Pen and the People*, pp. 177, 204.
37. Landsman, *From Colonials to Provincials*, pp. 50–51; Glover, *Elite Women*, p. 58.
38. Ruth Perry, "Mary Astell and Enlightenment," in *Women, Gender and Enlightenment*, ed. Knott and Taylor, p. 360.
39. Davidoff and Hall, *Family Fortunes*, p. 162.
40. Whyman, *The Pen and the People*, p. 183.
41. Robert Darnton, "What Is the History of Books?" *Daedalus*, 111.3 (1982), 65–83.
42. Glover, *Elite Women*, pp. 100, 73; *Henry Mackenzie: Letters to Elizabeth Rose of Kilravock on Literature, Events and People, 1768–1815* (Edinburgh: Oliver and Boyd, 1967), pp. 25, 57.
43. Kate Flint, *The Woman Reader, 1837–1914* (Oxford: Clarendon, 1993), p. 42; Pearson, *Women's Reading*, p. 14.

2

BETTY A. SCHELLENBERG

The professional female writer

While her successful 1678 London stage play *The Luckey Chance* lay "all printed off and the Press waiting," the playwright Aphra Behn (1640?–89) dashed off a preface in which she defiantly stood her ground against critics who condemned her work for its allegedly scandalous wit and immoral action. Insisting that these critics were biased against her as a woman, she issued a ringing assertion of her right to inhabit the literary marketplace: "All I ask, is the Priviledge for my Masculine Part the Poet in me (if any such you will allow me) to tread in those successful Paths my Predecessors have so long thriv'd in." Behn makes it clear that these "successful Paths" are not only monetary, but reputational: "I am not content to write for a Third day only. I value Fame as much as if I had been born a *Hero*." Although she is not above, in the same passage, appealing for indulgence as "a defenceless Woman," Behn's ambition and her sense of a legitimate claim are unmistakeable.[1] Significantly, the combined right to both remuneration and recognition was becoming in 1678 an increasing possibility for writers of both sexes, and yet it was not a universally accepted ideal. In other words, the writer as respectable professional, rather than as either cultivated amateur or disreputable hack, was a model in the making over the course of the long eighteenth century.

Virginia Woolf's much-cited observation in *A Room of One's Own* that "[t]he extreme activity of mind which showed itself in the later eighteenth century among women – the talking, and the meeting, the writing of essays on Shakespeare, the translating of the classics – was founded on the solid fact that women could make money by writing"[2] – oversimplifies a sequence of cause and effect that included improved literacy levels among women, changing ideas of women's intellectual capacity and even expertise in certain forms of knowledge and writing, and Britons' nationalistic pride in their increasingly refined intellectual and artistic cultures as demonstrated by the achievements of British women. Her argument has also been critiqued and qualified in important ways – to point out, for example, the degrees to which

37

women of the higher ranks were influential as writers prior to the eighteenth century, to which women before Behn were paid for their writing, or to which women writers at this time relied on manuscript-based "publication" rather than on print. Nevertheless, Woolf's striking conclusion that "towards the end of the eighteenth century a change came about which, if I were rewriting history, I should describe more fully and think of greater importance than the Crusades or the Wars of the Roses. The middle-class woman began to write"[3] remains sound in its fundamental insight into the link between the growth of the print marketplace after the Restoration of 1660 and the expansion of female authorship.

In focusing on the professional woman writer, this chapter traces that relationship, beginning with an overview of the conditions that newly enabled both men and women of letters to develop and adopt the role of professional author. Following a brief elaboration of the modern notion of a profession, itself an eighteenth-century development, and its application to an emerging model of the author, the remainder of the chapter is structured around the careers of five representative female professional authors of the period. All these women achieved a significant degree of remuneration and recognition as writers, whether measured by contemporary references to them, by the publication of editions of their works, or by critical reception in their lifetimes and from succeeding generations. All produced work in a range of the genres that were central to the republic of letters at the time, and that came to be included in the category of "literature" as it was defined by the end of the period: drama, poetry, translations, periodical essays, prose fiction, criticism, writing for children, and editing.

Aside from women's improved literacy and education levels through the course of the seventeenth century, as detailed by J. Paul Hunter, the preconditions for the emergence of professional women writers were not very different from those of professional writers in general. Brean Hammond has argued that the theater "was temporally prior to the publishing industry in affording a living to imaginative writers" through its "direct and often brutally frank" contact between playwrights and audiences. At the same time, Hammond observes that the Restoration dramatist's income consisted in part from the sale of playtexts to booksellers (publishers) and the additional rewards of dedications to patrons.[4] It should be noted further that right to the end of the period considered in this chapter, professional writers' incomes tended to include a combination of patronage income (connected to dedications, or in the form of modest pensions allowed by a benefactor) and the income from subscription publication. Subscription publications could be marketed either through booksellers and advertisements or through social connections. In this hybrid form of distributed patronage, a broad social range of sponsors paid half of the subscription price in advance of a work's production, thereby subsidizing its costs in exchange for having their names printed in the front matter of the published work; they then paid the remainder on receipt of the book after its publication.

Whether or not an author benefited from patronage in its more traditional or subscription form, the necessary precondition of viable professional authorship was the existence of a print-based literary marketplace, with enough readers to create demand and make the printing business attractive to entrepreneurs, and with the freedom of the press that became permanent when the 1709 passage of the Statute of Anne replaced state censorship with a system placing legal responsibility on authors or booksellers (publishers) as the holders of copyrights. Once such a marketplace was relatively stabilized and growing, there was an increasing need for writers who could reliably provide "copy" to the booksellers. Because of the unique nature of the commodity supplied by writers – requiring some degree of education, knowledge, and skill, whether acquired formally or informally – they could resist being categorized simply as hacks, as laborers for hire. By means of a series of legal innovations and much public discourse about the claims and cultural responsibilities of authors throughout the century, the work of the professional author as a servant of the public good, worthy of remuneration, became an accepted notion. Aiding the cause were the marketing strategies developed by an expanding and competitive print industry, which found the organization of publications around known authors (often identified as "the author of … " rather than by name) to be an effective tool. The poet Alexander Pope's successful self-representation as a well-connected gentleman who nevertheless earned a comfortable fortune by pleasing a reading public provided a model for subsequent writers, including a number of women.

The emerging discourse of original genius from the mid-eighteenth century onward fuelled the push for recognition of the author as having a unique gift and therefore a unique cultural role. Such theories accorded well with the move toward professionalization of certain services in eighteenth-century society – particularly those of the law, the military, medicine, and the Church – which tended to be provided by men of the middling and gentry orders. Emphasizing vocation, specialized training, and an internally regulated system of ranking and accreditation in exchange for social prestige and substantial remuneration, the model of the profession was somewhat at odds with that of natural genius, but together they served to undergird claims for the primacy of the author in the system of literary production. At the same time, this consolidated model tended, as the eighteenth century drew to a close, to marginalize women writers, since the established professions were all by definition masculine, and late-century debates about the appropriateness and limits of female engagement in the public sphere were inconclusive at best. Nevertheless, the idea of authorship as a profession, whether pursued by a male or a female author, came in the course of the eighteenth century to entail more than simply writing for money; it offered the kind of social respectability that the young novelist Frances Burney (1752–1840) could recognize in the late 1770s as having been attained by her musician-father Charles Burney and by her new friend Samuel Johnson, both of whom had achieved substantial increases in income and status through their authorial labors, as well as honorary doctorates from Cambridge and in Johnson's case a royal pension. The working definition of "professional" for the purposes of this chapter, then, entails not only earning much of one's living from writing but also a general degree of recognition and respect for having produced an accomplished body of work.

While no women (and very few men) in this period achieved comparable professional status to that of Pope and Johnson, the five female writers considered in this chapter fulfilled these criteria in a manner that was acknowledged by their contemporaries, while living from their writing over a sustained period of decades. They are Aphra Behn, who flourished as playwright, poet, and prose fiction writer during the reigns of the Restoration Stuart monarchs Charles II and his brother James II; Eliza Haywood (1693?–1756), whose career as author of amatory fictions, scandal memoirs, plays, theater history, periodicals, advice books, and realist novels spanned almost forty years; Elizabeth Carter (1717–1806), who won renown as a poet and translator furnishing copy for the *Gentleman's Magazine* and booksellers in the 1730s and then published a major Greek translation and a volume of poems several decades later; Charlotte Lennox (1730/31–1804), who began with a precocious volume of poems in 1747; produced an outpouring of novels, translations, plays, periodical writing, and criticism in a very energetic two decades at mid-century; and then tapered off to the slow death of her reputation in the last two decades of the century; and finally, Anna Letitia Aikin (later Barbauld, 1743–1825), who also gained early renown as a poet with an acclaimed volume published in 1772, then expanded to educational and political writings and major editorial projects as well as politically engaged pamphlets and poetry at the turn of the century.

In reviewing each career, this chapter traces the shifting models of authorship represented by these writers, as well as changes in the forms of writing they produced in response to contemporary readerships and market conditions. While space constraints prevent discussion of the numerous women whose achievements could fall within the purview of this chapter, passing mention is made of other female professional writers who successfully negotiated the period's shifting sociopolitical and literary climate, which extends from the late Stuart monarchy to an increasingly Whiggish and commercial culture; a mid-century literary field of genteel urbanity; a new reign (of George III) whose literary culture was dominated by sentimentalists, nationalists, and would-be reformers; and finally the consolidation of literary niches such as fiction and educational writings in which women were dominant.

While the women in this group came from different political, educational, and social contexts, they shared some common biographical characteristics. Chief of these were a background in the lower gentry or the upper middling classes and a good but informal education, often under the tutelage of a father or brother. These commonalities are no accident – for members of the higher social orders in the period, publishing for money continued to carry a stigma that was even more strongly marked for women, as the uneasy relationship between print and such talented poets as Anne Finch (Countess of Winchilsea) (1661–1720) and Lady Mary Wortley Montagu (1689–1762) demonstrates. For those of the middling sort and the lower gentry, on the other hand, the emerging professional model described earlier created an opportunity for which they, even more than high-born women, might be qualified by a social milieu that valued study and self-improvement. Generally not in line for a substantial inheritance, and therefore not expected to make a financially advantageous marriage, these women's precarious situations provided an incentive (though not necessarily the sole incentive) to incur the risks of engaging the literary marketplace. They also built careers centered on London, the only major publishing center of the period – even Carter, who spent much of her life in the country town of Deal, launched her career in London and in later years benefited from the assistance of London friends in furthering the business of her publications.

A final caveat: the women discussed here may have been among the most prominent women writers of the period, but they do not represent the majority of women writing, or even the majority of those appearing in print. A vigorous culture of letter writing and manuscript exchange in which women held a prominent place continued well into the century, often resulting in considerable fame for leading female practitioners, including Finch, Elizabeth Singer Rowe (1674–1737) for a part of her writing life, and the Bluestocking hostess and patron Elizabeth Montagu (1718–1800). Conversely, many of those women who did use print appeared in only a few periodical publications or published one volume of poetry and achieved only ephemeral recognition at best – or, more unusually, like Margaret Cavendish, the Duchess of Newcastle (1623?–73), used print as a form of vanity publication rather than as a source of income. Thus, although the works of such writers as the talented laboring-class poet Mary Leapor (b. 1722), whose untimely death in 1746 at the age of twenty-four cut short a promising trajectory, have gained importance in the canon of poetry in recent years, she is not considered in this chapter because her contemporary reputation was based only on two posthumously published volumes.

To return to Woolf's pronouncement, then, the period from 1660 to 1780 saw a significant shift toward the normalcy of women being known as literary writers, publishing their writing, and earning income, even a potentially comfortable living, from their writing. Indeed, it can be argued that the period from 1750 to the late 1780s, before the twin impediments of the conservative backlash to the French Revolution and the increasing institutionalization of high literary forms as largely masculine preserves, was a high point in the cultural positioning of women writers. Although historians of eighteenth-century women's writing have sometimes emphasized the emergence of a domestic ideal of womanhood in the mid-eighteenth century as a deterrant to the active engagement of women in the literary marketplace, such arguments should be viewed with healthy skepticism. As the century progressed, many women writers did indeed present themselves to the public with modesty tropes emphasizing financial need and the support of family as their motivations. However, this pose can be seen as a strategic mode of self-promotion that helped win over the increasingly influential reviewers, just as Behn's appeal to be treated gently as a woman writer might have been calculated to disarm her readers.

Similarly, their prominent participation in "domestic" literary genres such as the courtship novel and educational writing reflects both a general shift in the publishing landscape and the exploitation of a niche opened up to female expertise. If, on the one hand, James Raven's statistical studies of prose fiction published between 1750 and 1799 indicate that women authored a steadily increasing proportion of novels up to the decade of the 1780s, when novels by identified female authors overtook those by men (although almost 45 percent of novels' authors remain unidentified), on the other hand, some very public voices assigned them a much broader cultural significance. Witness eighteenth-century celebrations of female accomplishment such as John Duncombe's 1754 poem *The Feminiad*; George Colman the Elder and Bonnell Thornton's 1755 *Poems by Eminent Ladies*; Mary Scott's 1774 *The Female Advocate*; and Richard Samuel's 1779 group portrait of *The Nine Living Muses of Great Britain*, which included the professional writers Carter, Lennox, Barbauld, Elizabeth Griffith (1727–93), and Hannah More (1745–1833). As Harriet Guest has shown in detail, learned, publicly visible women such as Carter and Barbauld signifed both "a triumph of civilized national progress" and a classical ideal of female virtue that could combine private and public responsibilities.[5]

Aphra Behn: The playwright as professional writer

Aphra Behn's remarkable accomplishments as a successful playwright, poet, and pioneering writer of fictions are matched by her explicit and unapologetic representation of herself as a professional writer motivated by a desire to win both applause and money. Although her exact origins are uncertain, she appears to have come from a middle-class background, possibly with gentry connections, and certainly with Royalist, libertine, Tory, and Roman Catholic leanings that, together with a wide general education and enterprising nature, suited her for involvement in the cultural life centered around the Restoration court, initially as a spy and later as a member of literary and theatrical circles. With the Restoration of Charles II in 1660, a monopoly system of two patent theater companies operated in London with relative stability through to the end of the eighteenth century, although other venues of theatrical and operatic performance did arise at various times. For authors of plays, this situation meant that a first source of income was the sale of new plays to one of the theater companies; at times, an author might even be retained as a house writer for a profit share or a stipend. Added to this potential source of income were the third-night profits (generally repeated every third night thereafter, if the play's initial run continued) and a strong spin-off market in the sale of play copyrights to printers. Because the theater existed at the crossroads of court patronage and a more socially diverse paying audience, the professional playwright's income was supplemented by support from patrons and dedicatees. Behn, along with John Dryden and Thomas Shadwell, was one of the first of these professionals, seeing staged in 1670 the first of more than fifteen performed plays, including *The Rover*, which became a regular part of the theatrical repertoire and now holds a firm place in the canon of Restoration comedies.

A number of Behn's plays were adapted from earlier English and French works, and like many of the period's professional writers, she also produced several translations of French prose. Although some of the short novellas (or "novels," as they were then called) that she produced in the last few years of her life were adaptations, her well-known and influential story of an enslaved African prince, *Oroonoko* (1688), and her three-part epistolary fiction *Love-Letters between a Nobleman and His Sister* (1684) based on a contemporary court scandal were original works. In addition to publishing two collections of her poetry, Behn also edited at least two volumes and contributed to numerous others. Her poetry, often libertine or commendatory, is described by the database *Orlando: Women's Writing in the British Isles from the Beginnings to the Present* as "mostly opportunistic in some way, seizing the chances offered her, either by projects of literary colleagues or by royal or other grand occasions, to make some money." Thus, Behn stands out among women writers as the first professional literary writer because of the generic range and the market success of her writing. *Orlando* estimates that her income during the most active playwriting period might have been between £50 and £100 per year;[6] although she experienced severe financial constraints both before the 1670s and in the last years of her life, such an income on a regular basis could have provided an adequate, even respectable living for a single person in Restoration London. In her lifetime, she was at once admired and criticized; these criticisms could attack gender as well as status and were often politically motivated. Behn certainly did not view these criticisms as convincing arguments against her professional work, as her preface to *The Luckey Chance* (1686) indicates. Despite eighteenth-century impediments to even imagining a line of influence for a woman writer, as noted by Jane Spencer in *Aphra Behn's Afterlife*, Behn's body of work remained prominent in its own right throughout the period and can be shown to have influenced her contemporaries and successors. In a broad sense of the term, then, Behn was a professional, a pioneering one as the very groundwork of the profession was laid.

Eliza Haywood: From stage to print professional

When Eliza Haywood published her first work of prose fiction, *Love in Excess* (1719–20), almost fifty years after Behn's first staged play, a number of professional women playwrights – Catharine Trotter Cockburn (1674?–1749), Mary Pix (c. 1666–1709), Delarivier Manley (c. 1670–1724), and especially Susanna Centlivre (1669?–1723) – had found substantial success, if not to rival Behn's, through the opportunities offered by the stage. Centlivre produced fourteen staged comedies between 1700 and 1722. Haywood's largely print-based career, then, is representative of a shift in the media balance as entrepreneurial booksellers took advantage of a lively, factional, and increasingly broad-based London literary scene to feed their presses with materials that carried either the cachet of court connections or the appeal of novelty. As detailed by Haywood's biographer Kathryn King, Haywood in the first twenty years of her professional life, from about 1714 to the passage of the Stage Licensing Act in 1737, had an ongoing connection with the stage as actress and playwright. Her primary energies in the 1720s, however, were devoted to prose fiction in every guise – original narratives such as the three-part 1719–20 *Love in Excess*, novellas, scandal fiction (featuring figures of public interest in thin disguise), and translations/adaptations – of which, altogether, she had produced dozens by 1729. Like contemporary political alignments, book-trade and theatrical cliques of the time erupted into print, and Haywood's series of conjunctions and fallings-out with figures such as Richard Savage, Martha Fowke Sansom (1689–1736), and Alexander Pope is reflected in both her scandal writing and contemporary responses to her. While *Love in Excess* won her praise as the "great Arbitress of Passion" for elegant, refined analysis of heterosexual desire, by the end of the 1720s she was also satirized in print and on the stage as Pope's "Eliza ... With cow-like udders and with ox-like eyes," and lampooned as Fielding's "Mrs. Novel."[7] Clearly, she had established a high-profile reputation and a very saleable one at that.

Like many details of Haywood's life, her authorial earnings are impossible to determine, but given her apparent entire dependence on income she generated herself, it is likely that she earned only a modest and precarious living; the very careful calculations of her bibliographer Patrick Spedding arrive at an estimated average of about thirty-two guineas per year. Whereas she was paid between £16 and £20 per volume of a 1734 two-volume theater history and its reprint thirteen years later,[8] novella copyrights were among the lowest paid; even with up to ten publications per year in the 1720s, Haywood might just have made ends meet to support herself (and two young children, it seems). After the passage of the 1737 act, which severely inhibited the production of new stage plays, Haywood devoted her energies entirely to the medium of print. In addition to briefly operating as a pamphlet-shop proprietor and minor publisher at the Sign of Fame in Covent Garden, as King details, she produced advice literature for servants, husbands, and wives; fiction that at once responded to and imitated Samuel Richardson and Henry Fielding (notably *The History of Miss Betsy Thoughtless*, 1751); translations; and materials responding to or exploiting political or scandalous events. Even if some current Haywood attributions ultimately prove uncertain,[9] there can be no question that in terms of generic range, significant output, and popularity, Haywood was a professional writer to be reckoned with in her own time, and remains so in literary histories of the period. Recent criticism of the mid-century novelist Richardson, as William Warner, for example, has asserted, makes her influence on the eighteenth-century novel abundantly clear. Haywood's personal reputation in the later years of her life seems to have been dubious, however. Its flavor is reflected in Thomas Birch's 1750 observations from London to a correspondent in the country that Haywood is "a much more harmless Writer" than recent female producers of scandalous memoirs, "notwithstanding her Novels & Romances of no very edifying a Tendency"; according to Birch, himself a well-connected author and antiquarian, the now almost sixty-year-old Haywood "is still living here, in spite of Brandy and viler Liquours, & instructing us weekly in her Tatler and Xtian Philosopher."[10] Thus, although James Raven has found her to be the most popular female novelist by number of editions printed between 1750 and 1769, thirteen years after her death, the London circles of increasingly respectable professional writers, both male and female, appear to have been closed to her.[11]

Elizabeth Carter: Citizen of the republic of letters

In the middle decades of the century, the print trade saw the emergence of an increasingly numerous and prosperous class of businessmen-entrepreneurs, including Robert Dodsley, the footman-turned-bookseller and author who had been patronized by Pope; Edward Cave, editor of *The Gentleman's Magazine* and member of the Prince of Wales's circle; Samuel Richardson, the printer-novelist; and Andrew Millar, an important publisher of literary writing, including fiction. As promoters and often commissioners of projects such as the canon-creating *Collection of Poems by Several Hands* (1748), Johnson's *Dictionary* (1755), or the posthumous edition of Leapor's poems, these middle-class printers and booksellers were described by Johnson as the new patrons of literature, referring specifically to Dodsley, as the new patrons of literature. James Boswell, in *Life of Johnson*, reports the assertion of Johnson that "Doddy, you know, is my patron."[12] The writers they welcomed into their circles and introduced to one another, the subscription projects they promoted, and the copyrights they owned helped establish the market for learned and refined, yet broadly appealing and accessible writing. Elizabeth Carter was one of the early beneficiaries of this networking system when, as an extremely well-educated twenty-year-old from the country village of Deal, she came to London to work as a contributor to Cave's *Gentleman's Magazine* in 1738. Carter quickly won fame for her accomplished Latin verses and went on to publish several translations of scientific and religious works, including the Italian Francesco Algarotti's *Sir Isaac Newton's Philosophy Explain'd for the Use of the Ladies* (1739). Yet this fame seems also to have created discomfiting situations that led Carter to return to her home in Deal, where she cultivated an alternative identity as a retired woman of letters, perhaps in imitation of her admired predecessor Elizabeth Singer Rowe (1674–1737). King has analyzed in detail how Rowe "mov[ed] between and exploit[ed] the resources of" traditional scribal cultures and "the new forms of cultural authority offered by print," beginning with success in the periodical press of the early 1690s, followed by a return to the country, where she cultivated connections with the elite Thynne family coterie and reemerged in print, beginning in 1728, as a writer of visionary poetry and prose focused on death and the afterlife, gaining enormous fame and influence (161). Like Rowe, Carter effectively combined print and coterie literary practices to build her career, establishing a reputation in London's print-based circles which led to friendships with London literary women such as Catherine Talbot (1721–70) and Susanna Highmore (1689/90–1750), and through them, with Richardson; Johnson was an even earlier, and always loyal, admirer.

The friendship with Talbot and her guardian Thomas Secker (then Bishop of Oxford and later Archbishop of Canterbury) was particularly productive. First, it led Carter to a major publishing project, the first English translation from the Greek of *All the Works of Epictetus* (1758), with a "who's who" subscription list of intellectual and social leaders that enabled her to purchase a house in Deal for herself and her father (her original teacher in languages). The further fame of this edition brought Carter into contact with the coalescing social circle of Elizabeth Montagu, thereby making her one of the founding members of the group of elite and learned women and men that came to be known as the Bluestockings. With their encouragement, she published a further volume of poems in 1762; like Rowe, she was urged to do so as a means of "communicating the pious, virtuous sentiments that breathe[d] in all [her] verses."[13] Although she printed no further works in her lifetime, her correspondence, along with a memoir, was published after her death in 1806. Despite the relatively few works Carter saw printed, her career demonstrates not only the potential range of women's publishing activity in the period but also the kind of living and influence a woman writer could achieve in the middle decades of the century. She edited (with Montagu) the work of writers they patronized, such as the Scottish poet James Beattie, and her longevity meant that she served as an admired mentor to younger writers such as Hester Chapone (1727–1801), Barbauld, and Burney. As Duncombe described her, Carter transcended her nationality as a true citizen of the republic of letters: "Joy sparkles in the sage's [i.e., Plato's] looks, to find / His genius glowing in a female mind; / Newton admiring sees [her] searching eye / Dart thro' his mystic rage, and range the sky; / By [her] his colours to [her] sex are shown, / And Algarotti's name to Britain known."[14] In demonstrating what a learned Englishwoman could achieve, Carter became a symbol of the advancement of British civilization itself.

Charlotte Lennox: A bookseller's author

Launched almost a decade after Carter's, in 1747, Charlotte Lennox's career was much more prolific than that of her forerunner; it is also a career that demonstrates, in its combination of significant accomplishment and constant insecurity, the vicissitudes of professional authorship in the period. Although commercialization of her writing enabled Carter to earn a living and establish an authorial reputation, she succeeded in appearing as though she did not depend on the marketplace, emphasizing her limited needs and desire for a simple country lifestyle. Lennox, on the other hand, practiced a more openly professionalized model of the writer, making no secret of the fact that she had to make a living from her writing, and aggressively working her collegial networks to obtain both opportunities with booksellers and patronage from social leaders. Carter's correspondence, indeed, contains a number of critical references to Lennox, seemingly stemming from the moral ambiguity of the speaker's position in Lennox's 1747 poem "The Art of Coquetry"; for a period of time, Carter seems to have defined herself against Lennox's brand of authorship. In the end, this stance may have negatively influenced Lennox's reputation in the eyes of other socially influential Bluestocking women through to Frances Burney in the late 1770s.

Nevertheless, Lennox's early career experience is not so different from Carter's. She attracted attention and admiration as a young woman in London through her 1747 volume of *Poems on Several Occasions*, published when she was only eighteen and promoted in the *Gentleman's Magazine*, and like Carter, she gained the active friendship of Richardson and Johnson, which was especially significant in getting her breakthrough novel *The Female Quixote* (1752) accepted for publication by Andrew Millar. Within the next ten years, Lennox published at least five translations of French works, a three-volume translation of Shakespeare's sources accompanied by critical commentary entitled *Shakespeare Illustrated* (1753), a periodical magazine, three other novels (two serialized in her magazine, *The Lady's Museum*), and a play. Further fiction, translations, and plays followed, although at a slower pace. Lennox's published output likely rivals or exceeds Haywood's in sheer page length and covers a wider generic spread. Many of these works were well received and repeatedly reprinted into the nineteenth century. Certainly, as Susan Carlile has determined, the fact that Millar paid Lennox £86 17s 6d. for her 1757 translation of the *Memoirs of Madame de Maintenon* indicates that Lennox's work was a good investment.[15]

Lennox's career after the early 1760s illustrates some of the ways in which an author under duress might seek to build on established literary capital. Perhaps as a result of a period of very intense work under challenging household circumstances (a financially dependent husband and an infant child), her health collapsed at least temporarily, and she left London for a period of time around 1759–60. Upon her return to the city, Lennox's output was characterized by a certain amount of recycling, adapting, and re-issuing of previously published work.[16] Lennox continued to work patronage connections, particularly with the Duke and Duchess of Newcastle, through whom her husband obtained a Custom House post in the early 1760s, and to seek the assistance of contacts in the trade such as Johnson. Lennox's extant correspondence provides insight into the degree to which a mid-century professional author had to actively manage her own career, from borrowing books for research, to seeking colleagues' support in convincing booksellers to take on a project, to requesting permission to dedicate to a patron, thereby enhancing the earnings of a publication both through an outright gift and the enhanced sales an endorsement might produce. The underlying theme of these exchanges is the income insecurity, and, therefore, the continual need to work connections and generate new projects experienced by a professional writer who could not, or chose not to, retire to a frugal country life funded by investment income as Carter had done.

Although Johnson continued a loyal friend, and members of his circle aided Lennox even after his death in 1784, she ended her long life as an impoverished beneficiary of one of the earliest institutions of the authorial profession, the Royal Literary Fund. Thus, although Lennox conducted her career effectively within the relatively narrow confines of her urban business connections and a traditional court-based system of patronage, she failed to combine reputational, financial, and social success into a foundation for middle-class professional respectability. Some of the correspondence suggests that Lennox might have been, as her biographer Susan Carlile puts it, "politically clueless"; while successful professional authorship still depended on social connections, these were now less importantly with political elites than with cultural leaders such as salon hostesses.[17] As a young Frances Burney, just entering the professional world herself, discovered in the Streatham literary circle presided over by Hester Thrale and Samuel Johnson, "[Lennox's] *Female Quixote* is very justly admired here; indeed, I think *all* her Novels far the best of any *Living* Author, – but Mrs. Thrale says that though her *Books* are generally approved, Nobody likes *her*."[18] Without the endorsement of this larger social network, Lennox's arguably more significant record of achievement could not, in the long run, enable her to benefit as fully as did Carter from professional authorship.

Anna Letitia Barbauld: The professional author as public intellectual

As a member of the Dissenting community at Warrington Academy in Lancashire, where her father was a tutor throughout her formative years, Anna Letitia Aikin had educational opportunities arguably exceeding those of Carter, adding to the earlier emphasis on learned languages an exposure to the new sciences and political economy. Dissenting culture's encouragement of frank and spirited debate, moreover, is reflected in Barbauld's style and her willingness to speak publicly about controversial political issues; as her biographer William McCarthy has put it, with her "enquiring mind, temperamentally sceptical towards received views, distrustful of established power and devoted to the rights of conscience," Barbauld was a true Dissenter.[19] Although her 1768 poem *To Dr. Aikin on His Complaining that She Neglected Him* reveals her pain at being left behind when her younger brother John, until then her fellow student, moved on to pursue medical studies, she can be seen as pursuing the less formal career alternative of writer and educator, which was much more open to her as a woman. Already famous for her 1772 volume of *Poems* and other publications, Aikin, after her marriage to Rochemount Barbauld in 1774, co-founded with him a school for boys. This endeavor led to her production of a series of curricular materials for very young children such as *Lessons for Children* (1778–79) that saw multiple editions through the century; the later multivolume *Evenings at Home* (1792–96), intended for family reading and coauthored with her brother, was similarly successful. At the same time, Barbauld continued to engage on the liberal side of events and issues of public debate such as long-standing legislation against Dissenters, the slave trade, the uprising of the French populace, the state of the British poor, the rights of women, and the health of the British polity in pamphlets and in poetry appearing in magazines throughout the period of the French Revolution and the subsequent Napoleonic wars. In the final decades of her lengthy publishing career, she carried out several substantial and pathbreaking editorial projects, including the first (and until now, only) edition of the *Correspondence of Samuel Richardson* (1804); a fifty-volume collection entitled *The British Novelists* (1810); and an elocutionary anthology, *The Female Speaker*. Her final major publication, the 1812 poem *Eighteen Hundred and Eleven*, is a bleak, antiwar assessment of the state of the nation; it remains controversial to this day.

Although Barbauld's authorial career, apparently ending with two New Year's poems published in late 1822, extends forty years beyond the time period covered by this volume, it is relevant here in that it represents, more fully than the earlier careers discussed previously, the new possibilities offered by professional authorship for eighteenth-century women, and the prominent cultural and political role that such women could play. The wide range of Barbauld's authorial activity – poetry and other creative literature, educational writing, political writing, journalism, and literary history and criticism – has already been noted. On the basis of her initial publications in the early 1770s, she was greeted with enthusiasm in the press as one of a handful of British women worthy of an "MA" (Mistress of Arts) degree[20] and as one of the "Nine Living Muses of Great Britain" (along with Carter and Lennox in both cases), and she was the subject of a cameo and medallion in the Roman style by Josiah Wedgewood. Although it is impossible to calculate Barbauld's lifetime or annual earnings from publishing work, McCarthy demonstrates not only Barbauld's long-term saleability but also the improved rates of pay for professional writers when he calculates that her first book of poems sold 1,000 copies at six shillings each, and that she was paid between £240 and £300 for five months' intensive work on the Richardson edition, with its 200-page biographical preface, as well as £100 for the single poem *Eighteenth Hundred and Eleven*. Her literary friendships over her lifetime cast her in the roles of admirer, peer, and mentor and included Montagu, Carter, Burney, Hannah More, Maria Edgeworth (1768–1849), William Roscoe, Samuel Coleridge, Joanna Baillie (1762–1851), and Sir Walter Scott. At the same time, she was one of the casualties of a changing literary, social, and political climate from the 1790s onward. Coleridge went from walking forty miles to meet her in 1797 to publicly attacking her a decade later; his attacks are representative of a rising generation of young male writers whose repudiation of the socially engaged and accessible writing represented by Barbauld took an explicitly gendered form. Such tactics may have been influenced by the social debates of the 1790s, which tended to group Barbauld with women such as Mary Wollstonecraft (1759–97), whose politics may have been similarly radical but whose views of gender roles were considerably more unorthodox than Barbauld's. Certainly Barbauld's uncompromising support for oppressed groups such as the Dissenting community and the poor, in opposition to reactionary and Tory politics, drew attacks in the post-revolutionary period, culminating in the backlash against her with the publication of her sweepingly critical *Eighteen Hundred and Eleven*. While these circumstances are specific to Barbauld, they may suggest a broader backlash against the woman writer taking on the role of public intellectual, and thus a curtailment of possibilities for the professional female author.

Conclusion

When Frances Burney (1752–1840) burst onto the literary scene in 1778 with the publication of her novel *Evelina*, her professional models, as indicated by her journals and letters, included not only women writers such as Carter, Brooke, and Lennox but also the male professionals who socialized with her father and were lionized in the circles of salon hostesses such as Hester Thrale (1741–1821). Many of these men were authors as well as practitioners of other arts (Sir Joshua Reynolds, David Garrick, Richard Brinsley Sheridan), but a few were authors by primary trade (John Hawkesworth, the playwright Arthur Murphy, and particularly Samuel Johnson). Johnson explicitly encouraged Burney to be ambitious, to aim not only to topple the salon hostess Montagu from her position of cultural prestige but also to rival Richardson and Fielding as the generally accepted fathers of the modern novel.[21] Burney did indeed succeed, not only in establishing herself as the foremost of respectable contemporary novelists, but also in maintaining herself, and ultimately her French emigré husband and their son, in a middle-class lifestyle. While subscription sales by leading Bluestocking women and even endorsement by the royal family were still an important element in such professional recognition, the appointment as lady-in-waiting to the queen that Charles Burney carefully arranged for his daughter served not to further, but rather to hinder, Frances's career. Although with the publication of her final novel *The Wanderer* in 1814 and her memoir of her father in 1832 Burney suffered a critical repudiation somewhat like that experienced by Barbauld, her early reception, particularly with her second novel *Cecilia* (1782), matched the professional aspirations she had been encouraged to entertain.

Other women working in the literary genres – Charlotte Smith (1749–1806), for example, who published her first collection of sonnets in 1784 and went on to write ten novels as well as translations and shorter fiction, or Hannah More, who was endorsed by Garrick and the Bluestocking circle, had her first London play staged in 1775, and over decades wielded significant influence as a social critic and educational and religious writer – also experienced the financial benefits and prestige of successful professional authorship. Although Smith continued to lament the need to write to support her family, Jennie Batchelor has shown that such rhetoric functioned to foreground her work ethic and authorial achievements as a source of identity and pride, as much as to distance herself from her publications.[22] In the area of writing for the stage, Frances Brooke (1724–89) in her late career and Hannah Cowley (1743–1809), as well as More, demonstrated the possibility that the stage could offer remuneration and acclaim, if not security, as it had in the days of Aphra Behn. One price of the gradual solidification of a model of the professional female writer, however, was the fact that earlier women whose literary talents were proven in the marketplace, but whose personal lives did not adhere to the social respectability expected of the new professional, particularly the professional woman, were marginalized both in the present and in literary history: Behn (posthumously), Haywood, and Lennox all experienced this marginalizing effect. More broadly, with the turn of the century the increasingly hierarchical and institutionalized structures of the literary field resulted in a sense on the part of some commentators that women were not qualified to produce the highest, most public forms of poetry and political writing. This view, arguably exemplified by the late-career attacks on Barbauld and Burney, not only hurt these authors personally but would have surprised and disheartened many of their female colleagues of the previous century. Having convincingly demonstrated their claim to the "Masculine Part" of "the Poet" in themselves, the daughters of Aphra Behn found themselves with a new battle to fight.

NOTES

1. Aphra Behn, "Preface" to *The Luckey Chance, or an Alderman's Bargain*, in *The Works of Aphra Behn*, 7 vols., ed. Janet Todd (Columbus: Ohio State University Press, 1996), Vol. 7, p. 217. The "third day" was traditionally the playwright's day to receive the profits of a play's performance.
2. Virginia Woolf, *A Room of One's Own*, ed. Morag Shiach (Oxford University Press, 1998), p. 84.
3. Woolf, *A Room of One's Own*, p. 84.
4. Brean Hammond, *Professional Imaginative Writing in England, 1670–1740: "Hackney for Bread"* (Oxford University Press, 1997), pp. 48–49, 55–69. J. Paul Hunter, *Before Novels: The Cultural Contexts of Eighteenth-Century English Fiction* (New York: Norton, 1990), pp. 65–75. The discussion of copyright is informed by Mark Rose, *Authors and Owners: The Invention of Copyright* (Harvard, 1993) and Martha Woodmansee, "Genius and the Copyright," *The Author, Art, and the Market: Rereading the History of Aesthetics* (New York, 1996), pp. 35–55.
5. Harriet Guest, *Small Change: Women, Learning, Patriotism, 1750–1810* (University of Chicago Press, 2000), pp. 132, 236–51. For a discussion of the culture of letter-writing and manuscript exchange, see especially Margaret J.M. Ezell, *Writing Women's Literary History* (Baltimore, 1993), pp. 30–38; *Women's Writing and the Circulation of Ideas: Manuscript Publication in England, 1550–1800*, ed. George L. Justice and Nathan Tinker (Cambridge, 2002) and within that, Kathryn R. King, "Elizabeth Singer Rowe's Tactical Use of Print and Manuscript," pp. 158–181. For an overview of the women's participation in the literary marketplace, see Judith Stanton, "Statistical Profile of Women Writing in English from 1660 to 1800," in *Eighteenth-Century Women and the Arts*, Frederick M. Keener and Susan E. Lorsch, ed. (New York, 1988), pp. 247–54; Cheryl Turner, *Living by the Pen: Women Writers in the Eighteenth Century* (New York, 1994); and James Raven, "The Novel Comes of Age," in James Raven and Antonia Forster, with the assistance of Stephen Bending, *The English Novel 1770–1829: A Bibliographical Survey of Prose Fiction Published in the British Isles, Vol. I: 1770–1799* (Oxford, 2000), pp. 46–49.
6. "Aphra Behn," in *Orlando: Women's Writing in the British Isles from the Beginnings to the Present*, ed. Susan Brown, Patricia Clements, and Isobel Grundy (Cambridge University Press, 2006), orlando.cambridge.org.
7. James Sperling, "To Mrs. Eliza Haywood on Her Writings" (1732), in *Love in Excess*, 2nd ed., ed. David Oakleaf (Peterborough, ON: Broadview Literary Texts, 2000), p. 278; Alexander Pope, "The Dunciad," in *Pope's Poetical*

Works, ed. Herbert Davis (Oxford University Press, 1966), Vol. 2, pp. 157–64; Henry Fielding, *The Author's Farce*, in *Henry Fielding: Plays Volume I: 1728–1731 (Wesleyan Edition of the Works of Henry Fielding)*, ed. Thomas Lockwood (Oxford: Clarendon Press, 2004), pp. 221–93.

8. Patrick Spedding, "Appendix H," in *A Bibliography of Eliza Haywood* (London: Pickering and Chatto, 2004), *Eliza Haywood*, pp. 763–64. Kathryn R. King, *A Political Biography of Eliza Haywood* (London, 2012); see especially 'The Theatrical Thirties,' pp. 55–72.

9. Leah Orr, "The Basis for Attribution in the Canon of Eliza Haywood," *The Library*, 7th series, 12.4 (2011), 335–75. For influence of Richardson on eighteenth-century novel, see William B. Warner, *Licensing Entertainment: The Elevation of Novel-Reading in Britain, 1684–1750* (Berkeley and Los Angeles, 1998), pp. 196–230.

10. Hardwicke Papers, British Library Add. Ms. 35397, f. 291.

11. James Raven, *British Fiction 1750–1770: A Chronological Check-List of Prose Fiction Printed in Britain and Ireland* (Newark: University of Delaware Press, 1987), p. 14, Table 2; this list excludes editions of translated fiction, of which Haywood published two works in this period.

12. James Boswell, *Life of Johnson*, ed. Robert W. Chapman (Oxford University Press, 1980), p. 231.

13. Montagu to Carter, in *The Letters of Mrs. E. Montagu, with Some Letters of her Correspondence*, 4 vols. (London, 1809–13), Vol. 4, p. 350.

14. John Duncombe, *The Feminiad; or, Female Genius, A Poem* (London, 1754), lines 252–57.

15. Private communication from Susan Carlile, August 17, 2012.

16. See, for example, the relationship between the novel *Henrietta* and its stage adaptation *The Sister*, discussed by Susan Carlile in "*Henrietta* on Page and Stage," in *Masters of the Marketplace: British Women Novelists of the 1750s*, ed. S. Carlile. (Bethlehem, PA: Lehigh University Press, 2011), pp. 128–41.

17. Private communication from Susan Carlile, September 13, 2012.

18. Frances Burney, *Early Journals and Letters: Volume III, The Streatham Years: Part I, 1778–1779*, ed. Lars E. Troide and Stewart J. Cooke (Oxford University Press, 1994), p. 105. Italics in original.

19. Private communication from Michelle Levy, August 5, 2012; William McCarthy, "How Dissent Made Anna Letitia Barbauld, and What She Made of Dissent," *Religious Dissent and the Aikin-Barbauld Circle, 1740–1860*, ed. Felicity James and Ian Inkster (Cambridge University Press, 2012), pp. 52–69 (p. 56 quoted).

20. *The Westminster Magazine*, July 1773.

21. Burney, *Early Journals and Letters: Volume III*, p. 151; pp. 114–15.

22. Jennie Batchelor, *Women's Work: Labour, Gender, Authorship, 1750–1830* (Manchester, 2010), pp. 67–107.

3

SARAH PRESCOTT

Place and publication

The years from 1660 to 1780 witnessed profound changes in the circumstances of women's literary production as a cultural world primarily dominated by manuscript circulation slowly gave way to a marketplace for literature dominated by print. Accounts of women's writing in the light of these broader phenomena tend to emphasize shifts in gender roles, the increasing acceptance of the figure of the woman writer in public life, and women's expanding access to print alongside the rise of the novel form as the dominant literary genre. What is less fully documented is the way in which women's writing develops in response to the changes happening throughout Britain in relation to the geographical development of the English provinces and the interactive and sometime oppositional relationship of the constituent parts of the British archipelago – England, Ireland, Scotland, Wales – to one another. This chapter takes the geographical location of women writers as its main object of enquiry to ask the following questions: how does geographical location directly shape what women were publishing, their perception of themselves as writers, and their reception in literary culture? In what ways might a provincial location have enabled women's literary production? And finally, who were the women writing from Ireland, Scotland, and Wales in this period and how did national affiliation shape them as writers and inform their texts?

Focusing on non-metropolitan, provincial, and rural locations as enabling sites of literary production opens up new ways of constructing women's literary history that move away from conventional binaries of center/margin, core/periphery, and indeed manuscript/print culture. Furthermore, archipelagic perspectives that take into account all four nations of Britain not only allow for a study of writers from non-English locations but also provide new templates for understanding how writers can interact with and be shaped by multiple geopolitical contexts. The conventional view of a stark division between life in London and that in the English provinces, as well as between England and its Celtic neighbors, is starting to be challenged by early modern and eighteenth-century scholarship on women's engagement in provincial literary networks, coteries, and different national traditions. Similarly, as Margaret Ezell's work on seventeenth-century women's writing has admirably demonstrated, manuscript and print publication often overlapped and existed simultaneously, often within the career of one writer. Scholars are also increasingly recognizing the persistence, well into the eighteenth century, of models of coterie and literary practices usually associated with the seventeenth century and earlier. Across the period represented here, however, it appears that poets, rather than novelists or dramatists, were more likely to write from non-metropolitan sites and benefit from regional networks of support. In turn, these localized support systems often led to subscription as a route to publication for provincial women poets in particular.

Epistolary networks were of key importance for disseminating texts and connecting to the world outside an immediate circle of readers. By the 1660s, Katherine Philips's (1632–64) extensive network centering on her famous Society of Friendship had widened to include the Anglo-Irish elite in Dublin as well as the connections to court and Royalist circles forged in the 1650s. The presence of these epistolary networks and other connections that transcended geographical place suggest that we need to think beyond the binaries of core and periphery that underpin the association of provinciality (and non-metropolitan nationality) with marginality. For example, it is not enough to say that Katherine Philips achieved her wider reputation despite spending most of her writing life in Cardigan in West Wales. Instead, we need to consider also the poems she wrote that arose specifically from that location as well as those aspects of her work produced in Ireland in addition to the print world of London. In this sense, the networked provincial writer (and in Philips's case the Welsh writer) can be said to act as the "interface" between her specific locality and a world beyond (which, as in Philips's case, may also be archipelagic in scope).

Provincial women writers also benefited from what we might term the "hub" or "node" of the aristocratic country house. These crucial epistolary connections, friendships, or religious networks often emerged and developed across and beyond geographical boundaries. Therefore, in addition to rethinking the structural framework of core and periphery, it is also necessary to reassess the ways in which the direction of cultural traffic and literary influence is perceived. As the geographer Doreen Massey has noted, it is still the case, even in the context of twenty-first-century globalization debates, that the global "is imagined as an external force that arrives to affect the local place. The direction of relationality, in other words, is conceptualized as being one way, from the outside in." However, as Massey goes on to argue, this imagining of the relation between the local and global is erroneous, as "those relations with the wider world are two way. Globalization is not always an external force, arriving from somewhere else ... As there is the global production of the local, there is also the local production of the global."[1] In a similar way, the seventeenth- and eighteenth-century non-metropolitan literary systems inhabited by women interrelated with metropolitan culture through a process of reciprocity, not dominance. It was not the case that London literary culture simply directed its values and practices onto rural, provincial, and Celtic locations as passive recipients of "an external force."

Poetry from the English provinces

Lady Mary Chudleigh (1656–1710), Anne Finch (1661–1720), and Elizabeth Singer Rowe (1674–1737) are all key women poets of the late seventeenth and early eighteenth centuries who were associated with provincial locations yet who also interacted extensively with the London world of print culture as their writing moved from being targeted at a small coterie group to being oriented toward a commercial reading public. For all three writers, their provincial circumstances were not a barrier to broader literary success in the marketplace but rather actively enabling. In his work on the "coterie provincial network," Michael Gavin notes that the dual development in the late seventeenth and early eighteenth centuries of the postal service and "the improvements of country roads meant that communication and travel between towns and estates, and between London and the provinces were easier than ever before, enabling the proliferation of what Gary Schneider has called 'epistolary communities.'"[2] All these developments were crucial for the careers of provincial women writers. Chudleigh was born Mary Lee in Clyst St. George in Devon and after her marriage (to Sir George Chudleigh in 1674) spent the majority of her life at her husband's family seat Place Barton in Ashton, also in Devon. Nevertheless, Chudleigh's family (the Sydenhams) and her husband's family, as Margaret Ezell notes in her introduction to Chudleigh's works, were part of wider intellectual circles that included Richard Boyle and John Locke as well as members of the royal family to whom she dedicated some of her verse. At the start of the eighteenth century, Chudleigh began to publish her work starting with *The Ladies Defence* in 1701; Bernard Lintott, her publisher, was "a prominent and influential figure, who published Pope, Gay, Steele and Nicholas Rowe." Chudleigh's early work was thus written for a close geographically proximate circle, but after "the publication of *The Ladies Defence*, she moved into a new mode of authorship. She became a public figure, a poet whom strangers read; they sought her friendship and they sent their own verses to her for comment."[3]

As Rebecca Mills describes, Chudleigh embodied the "turn-of-the eighteenth-century learned lady" who participated in the worlds of manuscript and print culture. The surviving material evidence suggests Chudleigh was involved in several epistolary networks that worked in her provincial context but also smoothed her entry into print.[4] As Chudleigh mentions in one of her letters to the poet Elizabeth Thomas (1675–1731), there was an excellent library at Ashton and it is clear that her family background encouraged her literary pursuits. Access to libraries in provincial country estates was central to the literary development of women of rank. For example, the family library also enabled the Irish poet and translator Mary (Molesworth) Monck (1677?–1715) whose father, in the dedication to *Marinda* (1716), mentions his daughter's literary and linguistic accomplishments being developed "in a Remote Country Retirement, without any Assistance but that of a good Library."[5] Non-elite women also benefited from the use of a family library as in the case of the servant-class dramatist and poet Jane Holt (d. 1717) and the Scottish laboring-class poet Jean Adam, discussed later.

Like Chudleigh, Anne Finch's career spans the seventeenth and eighteenth centuries, and her shifting modes of authorship equally reflect these different contexts from a provincial angle. The perception that geographical distance from London inhibited women's literary production is overturned again in the case of Finch. Like Katherine Philips in Wales, Finch's provincial context at Eastwell in Kent in many ways actively enabled her writing career. Although her political exile as a Jacobite after the Glorious Revolution of 1688 might seem to signal cultural disempowerment, as Michael Gavin notes, while disenfranchisement and exile were disastrous in many other respects, Anne Finch often portrays these circumstances as "serendipitous to her writing career." In fact, not only did Eastwell provide the material ease and reflection to write, the readership contained in these locations provided a community of readers who encouraged her poetry: Finch's particular connections were with Longleat House and the Thynne family, who were also patrons of Elizabeth Singer Rowe and encouraged the latter's juvenilia. Gavin thus reads Finch's poetry in terms of her preoccupation with geographical position rather than her anxiety about print culture as dangerously public: "Finch's poetry is deeply concerned with what she thought it was like to be a woman poet outside London." In a reversal of the expectation of the urban as textually productive and networked, however, "For Finch, patriarchal estates like her country homes or the Thynne's manor at Longleat bring men and women together under the banner of shared poetic tradition."[6]

In Finch's poetry, it is provincial readers and audiences who are favorably positioned as offering a supportive context for poetic production, in contrast to their urban counterparts.

As the eighteenth century progressed, a provincial subscription system based on supportive and sometimes charitable middling-rank social circles could be said to replace the role of the country house and library with its base in an older model of aristocratic literary production and patronal encouragement. Many laboring and middling-class provincial women poets benefited from subscriptions arising from networks of encouragement and support often involving local clergy. Sarah Dixon (1671/72–1765) (Kent), Elizabeth Hands (1746–1815) (Coventry), Mary Jones (1707–78)(Oxford), Mary Leapor (1722–46) (Brackley), Mary Masters (fl. 1733–1755) (Norwich), and Mary Whateley Darwall (1738–1825) (Walsall in the West Midlands), for example, all benefited from local networks of support that enabled publication by subscription. As Paula Backscheider and Catherine Ingrassia note, "through the assiduous efforts of two local clergymen, Henry Homer, the vicar of Birdingbury, and his son, the Reverend Philip Bracebridge Homer, and a 'network of rural social contacts,'" the servant-class Elizabeth Hands had 1,200 names on her subscription list for *The Death of Amnon: A Poem* (1789). Whateley Darwall similarly benefited from "a provincial social network mobilized by clergy" who created support for the subscription list for her *Original Poems on Several Occasions* (1764).[7]

Elizabeth Singer Rowe's career, which started in the 1690s and peaked in the early eighteenth century, is especially interesting as it intersects with most of the main drivers connecting provincial women writers to the metropolitan publishing world: the periodical press; epistolary networks; the country house; aristocratic connections made by middling-class writers; and in Rowe's case, the networks established by her dissenting connections, particularly Isaac Watts who edited some of her later religious work.[8] However, Rowe is a slightly newer model of provincial literary authorship as her geographical location becomes bound up with her authorial persona in ways that, while ostensibly eschewing a commercial impetus for authorship associated with the print world of London, actually enabled her as a writer through the association of provincial location with virtuous retirement. She is an early example of the way in which writers became closely linked with their place of birth and/or geographical location. Like Anna Seward (1742–1809), the "Swan of Lichfield," and Susanna Blamire (1747–94), "The Muse of Cumberland" active later in the eighteenth century, Rowe was known as the "Poetess of Frome," a town in Somerset where she was born, lived, and wrote her poetry and fiction. The association of writers with a specific location was, as we shall see in the case of Jean Adam (1704–65), increasingly common for lower-class women and linked to their occupations – for example, Mary Collier (1688?–1762), the "washerwoman" of Petersfield in Hampshire, whose *The Woman's Labour* (1739) was published in response to Stephen Duck's *The Thresher's Labour* (1730), and Ann Yearsley (1753–1806) or "Lactilla the milk-maid poet" of Bristol.

Rowe entered print at an early stage in her career when, in the 1690s, she sent a number of poems under the name the Pindarick or Pindarical Lady to the *Athenian Mercury*, a Whig-inflected periodical edited by the entrepreneurial John Dunton. Rowe was able to contact the *Mercury* by post and thus her involvement demonstrates the key role played by the periodical press in connecting province and city; the postal system and the periodical press linked the metropolis and the province together in ways that overcame geographical distance and the need for writers to live in London. Rowe's epistolary connections with Dunton's periodical led to him publishing her first volume of poems in London in 1696 entitled *Poems on Several Occasions. Written by Philomela*. A similar process can be seen later in the eighteenth century when Mary Whateley Darwall's previous publications in the *Gentleman's Magazine* and the *Royal Female Magazine* generated the interest in her work that led to the publication of the collection of poems mentioned earlier. Rowe's connections beyond Frome were also enabled by what Rosemary Sweet has termed "supra-local allegiances between members of the same denomination" which transcended geographical location.[9] As a nonconformist, Rowe's dissenting cultural networks led to further publication in London and she was also connected through her marriage to Thomas Rowe to the intellectual circles around the dissenting academy at Newington Green. Although from an oppositional denomination, Rowe's circles are comparable to the seventeenth-century Anglican Royalist coterie within which Katherine Philips operated. Both of these supra-local networks were not confined by place and provide further evidence of the two-way exchange between London and the provinces.

Poetry to fiction: Jane Barker

Jane Barker (1652–1732) is a fascinating and complex example of the interrelation of geographical location, political allegiance, print culture, and social authorship. Her position is further complicated by what Kathryn King has identified as her "exiled" position both in political and religious terms as a Jacobite and a Catholic and in relation to her geographical location, first in St. Germain (a literal exile) and then in Wiltsthorp in Lincolnshire where she lived after her return to England in 1704. However, her first collection of poetry, which formed the first part of *Poetical Recreations* (1688), shows a very different vision of Barker than the Galesia figure she created in her later work, the self-image King has interpreted as "the mythology of the female poet as Virtuous Outsider." By contrast, verse printed in *Poetical Recreations*, "written in the 1670s and 1680s when Barker was still a young woman, tells a striking different story. Composed for a small but sympathetic circle (or circles) of fellow amateur poets, this is pre-eminently sociable verse ... It also offers scholars today a considerable glimpse into the world of the provincial literary coterie" (King, 29). Nevertheless, Barker's example complicates the sense that provinciality enabled creativity for women writers. Indeed, when Barker returned from France to Wilsthorp (where she had passed her early years) in 1704 and where, as a result of taxes, she was struggling to manage the farm she inherited: "One gets the impression that she lived in the village of her girlhood virtually as an alien. Such documents as have come to light give glimpses of a woman estranged from her rural Protestant community and at odds with such family members as she could claim in England."[10]

Although she may have left Wilsthorp by 1717, she is nevertheless marketed as a provincial writer in her 1723 publication *A Patchwork Screen for the Ladies*. The text is advertised as "By Mrs. JANE BARKER, of *Wilsthorp*, near *Stamford*, in *Lincolnshire*." The introduction is also bound up with place the way in which it impinges on Galesia's life history. Galesia/Barker has come from St. Germain to England and is traveling in a stagecoach to the North from London when the coach crashes and Galesia falls off the bridge into a river. After the accident, she meets a lady and joins her making a patchwork screen out of various texts including her own poetry. Recalling Finch, *A Patch-Work Screen* can be read not as expressing anxiety about commercialism per se, but as a nostalgic glance back to a residual patronage system based on a provincial coterie of readers and symbolized by the lady she meets in the garden. As King argues, the "nostalgic scene" is set up in relation to an "older, aristocratically oriented, and more sheltered literary system [and] seeks refuge at a country house, one of the main traditional sites of literary production, where she will tell her lifestory to a noble Lady."[11]

Writing provincial life

As the eighteenth century progressed, however, more women poets took provincial and local life as the subject of their writing. As Susan Staves notes, "The increasing wealth and cultural activity of provincial towns meant that provincial women writers of the middling classes now appear to record provincial life."[12] Mary Chandler's (1687–1745) poetry provides another model of provincial authorship for women that can expand further our sense of the opportunities for non-metropolitan women writers. Chandler was born at Malmesbury, Wiltshire, but moved to Bath and ran a shop as a milliner. Her most famous poem is the loco-descriptive *A Description of Bath*, which was published in 1733 and then in 1734 when it was inscribed to Princess Amelia, the second daughter of George II, and printed for the Bath bookseller (and brother-in-law of Samuel Richardson) James Leake and J. Gray, a bookseller in the Poultry, London. Chandler lived and worked in a trading environment and knew the town as someone who was engaged economically as well as culturally in provincial life. As David Shuttleton has argued, Chandler's *Description* "actively constructs an ethically prescriptive topography of sociability, portraying Bath as a model landscape for the enactment of an emerging Enlightenment ideal of civilized, consumerist pleasure." The poem is also a mix of traditional pastoral and a proto-commercial celebration of local patriotism in its attempt at civic mapping or what Staves calls "local boosterism": "Chandler's *Description*," asserts Shuttleton,

> celebrates this burgeoning city by painting an idealised portrait of the resort as a utopia reminiscent of ancient Athens where 'in comely Order, Rows of Buildings stand' and 'Squares, and Hospitals, and Temples rise.' This is a therapeutic urban pastoral space where palaces and fountains 'o'erspread the verdant Ground' and where clean water and fresh produce are in abundance.[13]

Chandler's celebration of civic pride is consistent with what Peter Borsay has influentially identified as the "urban renaissance" in England between 1660 and 1770. Similarly, Joyce M. Ellis has described as emergent a "new awareness and appreciation of urban forms."

> The year 1680 marked the beginning of a golden age for the prospect as increasing public demand transformed a trade previously dominated by foreign artists and by views of London. Native artists and provincial now played a far greater part in the business; the most successful and prolific publishers of printed prospects, Samuel and Nathaniel Buck, succeeded in depicting nearly 80 different towns in the years between 1721 and 1753.[14]

Other writers representing non-metropolitan cities and urban and university towns include the Irish writer Mary Davys (1674–1732). Davys lived briefly in the northern English town of York, which resulted in a comedy called *The Northern Heiress; or the Humours of York* (1716). The play provides a precursor of Mary Chandler's *Description of Bath* in its focus on the trade, commerce, and leisure context of York life. As Staves outlines, the play "captures the tensions between the prosperous tradesmen in the northern country seat and the leisure class who gather there to spend money and enjoy amusements including biweekly Assembly entertainments and horse races."[15] After the death of her husband, Davys ran a coffee house in Cambridge whose university clientele subscribed to her 1724 novel *The Reform'd Coquet* as well as the two-volume collection of her *Works* in 1725. The university town of Oxford was also the location for another provincial dramatist, Jane Holt (née Wiseman) (fl. c. 1682–1717) who, as a servant for William Wright, Recorder of Oxford, had access to her employer's library. The result was a play called *Antiochus the Great: Or, The Fatal Relapse. A Tragedy*, which she completed after a move to London and which, as Roger Lonsdale records in the biographical note on Davys in his *Eighteenth-Century Women Poets: An Anthology*, was performed in 1701 at the New Theatre, Lincoln's Inn Fields and published in 1702. She did not pursue a career as a dramatist but, writes Lonsdale, "married a young vintner named Holt and, with the profits of *Antiochus*, opened a tavern in Westminster." Holt is an interesting and rare example of a provincial female servant achieving success (albeit limited) on the London stage and using this success to build a future life as a tradeswoman in the metropolis.

Celtic women writers: Ireland, Scotland, and Wales

Moving up the spatial scale from local and provincial to national concerns, a range of women writers also wrote primarily outside of an English context. This is not to say, however, that women were tied to a national context or that they were not mobile across national boundaries. Indeed, many of the women discussed in this concluding section did travel on a number of occasions and wrote from multiple locations. England, Ireland, Scotland, and Wales developed at different rates in this period. As Staves notes, Dublin's literary culture was well advanced: "the Irish capital being earlier supplied with its own printers and other cultural institutions like theatres before English provincial towns were."[16] One example of an early eighteenth-century Irish woman writer is Mary Monck, who was the daughter of Viscount Molesworth and whose husband George Monck was a MP in the Irish Parliament. Monck's poems and translations, according to Lonsdale, were published by her father for Jacob Tonson in 1716 after her death at Bath in 1715. Mary Barber (c. 1685–1755), another poet, also moved between Ireland and England, but her status as the widow of an unsuccessful linen draper produced a different set of verses from the accomplished productions of Monck. Barber moved from Dublin to Bath in 1730 and was supported by Jonathan Swift, who was influential in arranging the publication of her *Poems on Several Occasions* (1734) by subscription.

The poems are variously set in the English spas of Bath and Tunbridge, and other verses such as "An Invitation to *Edward Walpole*, Esq; upon hearing he was landed in *Dublin*" have a distinct Irish inflection. The subscribers are a varied mix and include prominent Irish people (Lord Lieutenants of Ireland past and present; Earls of Orrery), who Staves suggest sought to demonstrate support for Irish cultural achievement.

Irish history and national politics have a much more prominent role in Sarah Butler's fascinating prose fiction *Irish Tales: or, Instructive Histories for the Happy Conduct of Life*, which was published in London by Edmund Curll in 1716. Comparable with Jane Barker's 1715 *Exilus; or, The Banish'd Roman* (also published by Curll), *Irish Tales* is a fascinating mix of romance and nationalist allegory.[17] Drawn from a range of sources in Irish history as outlined in the preface, Butler's prose fiction, like much eighteenth-century writing on Welsh history concerning resistance to Saxon invasion, frames the historical romance of the lovers Murchoe and Dooneflaith in terms of Irish resistance to the "the *Danish* Yoak" (p. 72): when Dooneflaith prevents Murchoe from being killed by his rival Turgesius, the lover declares: "how inglorious you have made my Name! that, had you given me leave, might have resounded through the World, and born the Title of its Countrys Saver! *Ireland* should then have had its native Liberty again, and I perhaps been chose their King, proud only in that Glory, to lay my Crown beneath your feet" (p. 56). While weaving a narrative of doomed love and the conflict between patriotic duty and romantic passion, the text ends not with the marriage of the noble lovers but with a celebration of Irish resistance to invasion. It is uncertain that Sarah Butler ever existed and any information about her is restricted to the claim in the dedication by Charles Gildon that "The Fair Authress of the following Sheets" is dead (p. 35). Nevertheless, as her editors note, "it is striking that Butler's version of Irish history, her emphasis on Ireland as 'insula sanctorum et doctorum', predated all of those works that modern historians have indicated as important" in the Gaelic revival in the early eighteenth century (p. 30). Furthermore, "What makes *Irish Tales* still more noteworthy, of course, is that Sarah Butler combines her positive revaluation of Irish Gaelic culture with Roman Catholic and Jacobite polemics in a London-published novel" (p. 30).

Women writers from Wales in this period are decidedly less oppositional; nevertheless, we do see national distinctiveness even in a poet such as Jane Brereton (1685–1740), who was a pro-Hanoverian Whig. All the writers of Welsh origin who published from 1660 to 1775 write in English and mostly publish in London. The earliest example and seemingly the only Anglophone woman writer in Wales in the entire seventeenth century was Katherine

Philips, who spent the majority of her writing life in Cardigan, West Wales. Philips, of course, also spent a significant point of her career in Ireland, where she saw the production of her heroic drama *Pompey* (1663) performed in Dublin and enjoyed the patronage and support of a number of the Anglo-Irish aristocracy.

Women were also writing in Welsh in this period, as shown by the circle surrounding Margaret Davies/Marged Dafydd (c.1700–1785?) in North Wales in the eighteenth century. Davies was a collector of manuscripts and a poet herself. She corresponded with male figures associated with the London Celticism movement, but the core of her activity was local poetic/bardic circles in the Snowdonia area of North Wales. None of her poems were published.[18] By contrast, the Anglophone poet Jane Brereton, born in Mold in Flintshire in 1685, moved between Wales and London on a number of occasions and published her work in London; her posthumous collection of *Poems on Several Occasions by Mrs. Jane Brereton* was published by Edward Cave in 1744 (she died in 1740). Cave was the editor of the *Gentleman's Magazine* in which Brereton had published an exchange of poems in the 1730s. She is also interesting as a Welsh poet who in her later years (after she separated from her husband) lived in the provincial town of Wrexham in North-East Wales, close to the border with England. Jane Cave Winscom (1754/55–1813) is a slightly later example of an eighteenth-century Welsh woman poet who also lived and published in the provincial town of Winchester. The cultural value of the country house, in this case nearby Erddig, and local literary circles, here a group of Welsh antiquarians surrounding Mary Myddleton at Croesnewydd, thus continue to be important for maintaining a woman's literary career outside of London.

Jane Brereton's connections with antiquarian scholars fed directly into some of her poetry on Welsh historical themes, and she self-identified as a Welsh writer or a "Cambrian Muse." Public self-identification as a Welsh writer is, however, comparatively rare, and it is not until the end of the eighteenth century that we see a writer (who was actually English born) being described in terms of a Welsh location – Julia Ann Hatton (1764–1838) was known as "Ann of Swansea," because of her loco-descriptive poem "Swansea Bay" (1811). Another Welsh-born writer was Anne Hughes Penny (1729–80/84) from Bangor in North Wales. Penny subsequently lived in London and was, like Brereton, sometimes drawn to Welsh antiquarian themes. Her *Poems, with a Dramatic Entertainment* (1771) was published by subscription and includes Samuel Johnson in the list. Although based in London, Penny's collection shows a marked interest in topics of a Welsh inflection. Although mostly known for her patriotically British *Invocation to the Genius of Great Britain* (1778), as a Welshwoman,

Penny was also drawn to eighteenth-century Celticism as shown by her interest in Thomas Gray and her versification of two poems from Evan Evans's *Some Specimens of the Poetry of the Antient Welsh Bards* (1764): "Taliesin's Poem to Prince Elphin" and "An Elegy on Neest." As Jane Aaron details, it is not until the end of the eighteenth century and into the nineteenth century that Welsh women writers published in any great numbers.

Unlike Wales, Scotland could boast the cultural and print capital of Edinburgh. Joyce M. Ellis has shown that "Welsh towns did not experience the sustained growth commonplace in both English and Scottish centers after 1700 until quite late in the century." In contrast, "research which is currently transforming our knowledge of Scottish towns suggests that their cultural and economic development increasingly converged with that of England."[19] However, my final example, Jean Adam, did not emerge from the Edinburgh context but was born in Cartsdyke, near Greenock, Renfrewshire, in the west of Scotland, as is made clear on the title page of her *Miscellany Poems by Mrs Jane Adams in Crawfordsdyke*, which was published in Glasgow in 1734.[20]

The preface "To the Reader" by Archibald Crauford refers directly to the locality of her authorship and her social position: "her Father was a Shipmaster in that Place: her Breeding was as is ordinary for Girls of her Station, and Circumstances." Adam later ran a school and tried to earn a living by needlework and domestic service but "died in Glasgow's Town's Hospital (a workhouse) on 3 April 1765."[21] Like many other women poets of a lower social station, Adam benefited from access to the library of a family above her socially. The preface states: "having several Years ago lost her Father, Providence ordered her Lot for some Years in the Family of a Reverend Minister in the Neighbourhood, where she had Access to peruse such of that Minister's Books, as her Fancy led her to read." The prefatory material, the dedication, and the first poem in the collection, aptly titled "The Gratefull Muse," all construct Adam as an object of charitable sympathy. Religion is the hallmark of her poems and readers looking to find any Scottish national sentiment will be disappointed in her work. Indeed, as Crauford insists in his preface, Adam's work appears strenuously to emulate English style: "the Phrases, Allusions and Figures, will not be found disagreeable to the best *English* Poets, that have written within Seventy Years last past," and he emphasizes her use of English meter and Miltonic blank verse. Thus, it is somewhat surprising that Jean Adam is best known as the author of the much admired Scots poem "There's nae luck aboot the hoose," which was published in R. H. Cromek's *Select Scotish songs, ancient and modern* in 1810. Much controversy exists over whether the poem is actually by Adam or by the male poet William Julius Mickle; as Bill Overton notes, however, many critics suggest that the following lines about an absent lover are clearly from a female perspective:

> And will I see his face again?
> And will I hear him speak?
> I'm downricht dizzy wi' the thocht,
> In troth I'm like to greet [weep].

Paying attention to culturally and geographically specific linguistic traditions of women's writing can lead to further revisionary interpretations of women's engagement in the literary culture of their day. In the case of Adam, the key role played by the oral Scottish ballad tradition for women writers complicates the sense of her as a working-class poet who is directly comparable to those in England. The argument over the attribution to Adam of a poem in Scots is thus interesting on a number of levels. Her example not only demonstrates the key significance of place and location for a broader understanding of British women's writing but also raises what Overton characterizes as further questions "about the relations between evidence originally from oral and from written and printed sources, and between dialect and standard English." Jean Adam thus exemplifies how an attention to place, location, and nation can fundamentally unsettle the narratives of women's writing we have inherited and often still employ.

In a broader context, therefore, the impact of an archipelagic critical approach that attends to all the constituent nations of Britain has the capacity to transform current understanding of women's literary history. However, revisionist histories of women's writing are not simply a matter of inserting token representatives from the English provinces, Ireland, Scotland, and Wales into the picture to offset a London-centered metropolitan framework for women's literary culture. Indeed, just as Jean Adam cannot easily be compared to her English counterparts who were writing from the same marginal class context, it would also be an equally complex task to read her work in relation to women's writing in Scottish Gaelic, for example. Archipelagic criticism, as John Kerrigan explores it, is an inclusive model of both reciprocity and difference that focuses on the dynamic interactions as well as the tensions between local and national literary and linguistic cultures.[22] In this sense, archipelagic women's literary history provides an important transferable model for thinking more broadly about women's engagement with the literary culture of their day most clearly, perhaps, in relation to the growing area of "transatlantic feminism." By moving away from singular national and linguistic contexts, scholars of both British literary culture and women's writing of the Atlantic world will be able to see more clearly the ways in which geographical location is precisely not a limiting marker of marginality but a site of multiple cultural, linguistic, and literary affiliations.

NOTES

1. Doreen Massey, "A Counterhegemonic Relationality of Place," in *Mobile Urbanism: Cities and Policymaking in the Global Age*, ed. Eugene McCann and Kevin Ward (Minneapolis & London: University of Minnesota Press, 2011), pp. 1–14.
2. Michael Gavin, "Critics and Criticism in the Poetry of Anne Finch," *English Literary History*, 78.3 (2011), 635.
3. *The Poems and Prose of Mary, Lady Chudleigh*, ed. Margaret J. M. Ezell (Oxford University Press, 1993), p. xix.
4. Rebecca Mills, "Mary, Lady Chudleigh (1656–1710): Poet, Protofeminist and Patron," in *Women and Poetry, 1660–1750*, ed. Sarah Prescott and David Shuttleton (Basingstoke and New York: Palgrave Macmillan, 2003), p. 51.
5. *Marinda: Poems and Translations upon Several Occasions* (1716), sigs b7v–b8v. I am grateful to Gillian Wright for sharing her work on Monck for her book *Producing Women's Poetry, 1600–1730: Text and Paratext, Manuscript and Print* (Cambridge University Press, 2013).
6. Gavin, "Critics and Criticism," pp. 636, 643.
7. Paula R. Backscheider and Catherine E. Ingrassia, eds., *British Women Poets of the Long Eighteenth Century: An Anthology* (Baltimore: The Johns Hopkins University Press, 2009), pp. 703–4, 705–6.
8. Elizabeth S. Rowe, *Devout Exercises of the Heart, In Meditation and Soliloquy, Prayer and Praise* (London, 1739).
9. Rosemary Sweet, *The English Town, 1680–1840: Government, Society and Culture* (New York: Pearson Education Limited, 1999), p. 189. Discussed further in Sarah Prescott, *Women, Authorship, and Literary Culture, 1690–1740* (Houndsmill: Palgrave McMillan, 2003), chapter 6.
10. Kathryn R. King, *Jane Barker, Exile: A Literary Career 1675–1725* (Oxford: Clarendon Press, 2000), pp. 29, 13.
11. King, *Jane Barker*, p. 212.
12. Susan Staves, *A Literary History of Women's Writing in Britain, 1660–1789* (Cambridge University Press, 2006), pp. 197–98.
13. David Shuttleton, "Mary Chandler's *Description of Bath* (1733): The Poetic Topographies of an Augustan Tradeswoman," *Women's Writing*, 7.3 (2000): 447–67.
14. Peter Borsay, *The English Urban Renaissance: Culture and Society in the Provincial Town, 1660–1770* (Oxford: Clarendon Press, 1989); and Joyce M. Ellis, *The Georgian Town, 1680–1840* (Basingstoke and New York: Palgrave, 2001), p. 20.
15. Staves, *A Literary History of Women's Writing*, p. 204.
16. Staves, *A Literary History of Women's Writing*, p. 199.

17. *Irish Tales by Sarah Butler*, ed. Ian Campbell Ross, Aileen Douglas, and Anne Markey (Dublin: Four Courts Press, 2010). All further references are to this edition and cited parenthetically in the text.
18. For a groundbreaking anthology of Welsh women's poetry, see *Beirdd Ceridwen: Blodeugerdd Barddas o Ganu Menywod hyd tua 1800*, ed. Cathryn Charnell-White (Llandybïe: Cyhoeddiadau Barddas, 2005). For a discussion of later Welsh women writers see Jane Aaron, *Nineteenth-Century Women's Writing in Wales: Nation, Gender and Identity* (Cardiff: University of Wales Press, 2007).
19. Ellis, *The Georgian Town*, p. 4.
20. Jean Adam is the Scots singular spelling of the Anglicized plural Jane Adams. See Bill Overton, "The Poems of Jean Adam, 1704-65," *Women's Writing*, 10.3 (2003), p. 427.
21. Karina Williamson, "Adam, [Adams] Jean (1704–1765), *poet*," in the *Oxford Dictionary of National Biography* (Oxford University Press, 2004–12).
22. John Kerrigan, *Archipelagic English: Literature, History and Politics 1603–1707* (Oxford University Press, 2008).

4
PAULA R. BACKSCHEIDER
Women and popular culture

Mary Robinson's heroine Mrs. Morley, after experiencing the incredible difficulties, damaging misunderstandings, and setbacks of the typical late eighteenth-century heroine of the woman's novel, finds herself confined to a private mental institution and put in a straitjacket.[1] (Not to say that many authors and booksellers did not conceive of their books as appealing to both sexes.) On becoming calmer and released from the straps, she asks for a novel and is given one in the sixth edition. She shrieks, throws the book, and yells repeatedly, "Six editions for ten pounds." She is declared "in the most decided state of raving insanity." Her head is shaved; she is "bled, blistered, and tortured"; and "her limbs bruised even to the privation of the powers of motion." She is the author of the novel. Nearly destitute and in need of an occupation, she decided "on making the *modern* experiment, both for the attainment of fame and profit, by writing a Novel" (emphasis mine). She invested six weeks of "incessant labour" in completing a two-volume novel; after peddling it on Paternoster Row, then Pall Mall and Bond Street, "a dashing publisher," Mr. Index, gave her £10 for her six weeks' work.[2] Robinson (1756/58?–1800) had succeeded Robert Southey as poetry editor for the *Morning Post* the same year that she published this novel, *The Natural Daughter* (1799), and the next year she was arrested for debt.

Robinson and her novel illustrate a number of important facts about women and popular culture. A former actress, a perennial presence in gossip periodicals because of her affairs with the Prince of Wales and with Sir Banastre ("Bloody") Tarleton, and then a retired woman with a disability forced to live by her pen, Robinson had been exploited in theatrical and print culture and then tried to use that knowledge to exploit the opportunities for economic sustainability if not security. After the first attack of rheumatism and the forced sale of her personal belongings for debt in 1784, she attempted to profit from her knowledge of France with publications such as *Ainsi va le Monde* (1790) and *Impartial Reflections on the Present Situation of the Queen of France* (1791). She published her first of seven novels in

1792, and for the rest of her life that she followed trends and tried to profit from them is clear, as monodies, translations, sonnet sequences, and memoirs indicate. For example, she began her memoirs the year that William Godwin published *Memoirs of the Author of A Vindication of the Rights of Woman* (1798), and her *Letter to the Women of England, on the Injustice of Mental Subordination* came out in 1799.

Robinson has Mrs. Morley assess the state of novel genres before she begins her novel. Like Robinson, Mrs. Morley is trying to predict the likelihood of publication and profit. Among other things, she notes, "the sentimental would no longer suit the languid nerves of those who were devoted to dissipation" (p. 207). Writing in the wake of the social revolution that plays and places such as Carlisle House and the Pantheon had made familiar, she can simply refer to the fashionable life led by many rich enough to purchase novels. Mr. Index tells Mrs. Morley to write a satiric novel based on a private event conducive to juicy gossip, such as "an highly-fashionable elopement, ... an ungrateful runaway daughter, or a son ruined by sharpers" (p. 209). These were popular plot lines for plays and novels, and allusions that allowed audiences to speculate on the people who inspired the text did indeed add to sales, especially to what Morley called "the whole phalanx of fashionable readers," readers whom Robinson knew well. Robinson was aware that society had changed; the word "modern" reverberates in her work, as with Morley's "modern experiment." Among her titles are *Modern Manners* (1793), a verse satire, and *The Widow, or A Picture of Modern Times* (1794), a novel. The titles that Mr. Index suggests consistently use the word "modern," including one that may gesture toward one of Elizabeth Inchbald's most popular plays.

Popular culture is by definition time sensitive and "modern," forward looking and trendy; to identify a new direction or fad is to appeal to women and also to "the whole phalanx of fashionable" consumers. Women and popular culture are always to some extent defined by their relationship to the dominant culture, which they make into an arena of consent and resistance, a space of perpetual tension and critique.[3] Both also make obvious the complex relationships between high and low culture and between performer and spectator. Dominic Strinati argues that "a set of generally available artefacts" is a satisfactory working definition, given the disagreements, ideologies, and theories surrounding the term.[4] I am not interested in the "life" of "ordinary people" and the "authentic art" they allegedly produced, but with available, widely familiar texts and performances calculated to succeed because composed with high awareness of audience-pleasing elements (therefore, to some extent self-consciously "manufactured"). The importance of profit and potential commodification is taken for granted. Men have always been adept at recognizing the ways they can employ women to increase the appeal of their work, and the heartbeat of modern popular culture is women. In this brief discussion, I will begin with Elizabeth Barry (1656/58–1713) and Aphra Behn (1640?–1689) who made sure women will always be driving forces, then move to Frances Brooke (1724–89) and Mary Ann Yates (1728–87), representatives from mid-century, and then to Elizabeth Inchbald (1753–1821), an example from the end of the century. Their careers illustrate some typical, even archetypal practices, and they helped devise the practices that created mass culture.

Barry, Behn, and the rise of commercial theater

The introduction of actresses on the Restoration stage is a familiar example of a radical innovation, and theater managers went from one creative way to exploit the women to another. Exotic, revealing costumes, breeches parts, prologues and epilogues spoken by actresses written as though personal rather than in character, proviso scenes, cat fights between rival queens, and she-tragedies were just some of the fads that fascinated and then faded. Men wrote almost all of the prologues and epilogues, but, as Elizabeth Howe notes, between 1660 and 1720 more than 100 were written for a specific actress. And the women exploited them. They were quick to learn that they were commodities and could commodify themselves. Nell Gwyn (1651?–87) with her saucy comic genius and unforgettable prologues and epilogues offered models for later women. As prologues and epilogues became more explicit in their references to women's bodies and reputations, there is some evidence that actresses and others reacted to the power imbalance and pushed back. Certainly, they increasingly entered sites of immediate interest and debate. An example is when Anne Oldfield (1683–1730) refused to speak an epilogue Alexander Pope wrote for her for *The Tragedy of Jane Shore* and Anne Finch (1661–1720) wrote a counter epilogue highlighting the "triumphs of her blooming age."

More often than noticed, women were implicated in creating something new. Plays were written to feature Elizabeth Barry, the "main 'draw'" of the Duke's Company, and they introduced innovations.[5] After Barry's success as Monimia in Thomas Otway's *The Orphan* (1680), Nahum Tate rewrote *King Lear* for her as a love story between Cordelia and Edgar with highly emotional scenes between her and Lear; a year later in 1682, Otway's *Venice Preserv'd* and John Banks's *Vertue Betray'd: or, Anna Bullen* solidified her preeminence and the popularity of the she-tragedy form. A poem by Otway captures her mesmerizing force:

> I am the Famous She, Whose moving Arts
> Give Life to Poetry, to Poets Fame:
> I Charm Spectators Eyes, and chain their Hearts.[6]

"Arts" cannot be read without the moving *parts* of actresses coming to mind, and, as in subsequent lines in the poem, the woman's body and craftsmanship are called to mind simultaneously. Barry provides an example of how rapidly women came to understand the workings of popular culture and themselves as able to operate within its commercial possibilities. She was the first player, male or female, to receive a benefit night and the only one until 1695. She negotiated ever higher wages, and with Thomas Betterton and Anne Bracegirdle (1671–1748) went before King Charles II and was granted the license for a second theatrical company.

Barry was central to Otway's plays, and she became friends with Aphra Behn, the first woman since Katherine Philips (1632–64) to have a play performed at a royal theater. One of Barry's first roles was Leonora in Behn's *Abdelazer* (1676), and she created the important role of the canny ingénue Hellena in *The Rover* (1677). Behn and Barry became friends, and, more than other playwrights, Behn created roles for her that brought out a variety of talents and changed with her age. Barry played, for instance, Lady Galliard, a rich City widow, in *The City Heiress* (1682). It opened with a prologue written for her by Otway, whose *Venice Preserved* had been sensationally successful earlier in the season. Recent drama specialists have made much of the advantages Elizabeth Inchbald had because she was friendly with actress Becky Wells (1762–1829), among others, and could discuss and refine performances with them in the way that Emily H. Anderson describes as the "channeling" of "the opinions of the playwright through the medium of the actress."[7] Behn had the same advantage with Barry and, because of her long association with Betterton and his company, with others.

The prologues and epilogues to Behn's plays underscore an agency similar to Barry's in establishing women's place in popular culture. In the small world of London theater in 1670, a time when it was still correct to speak of the "court set," she could advance herself with canny self-reflexive references when *The Forced Marriage*, her first play, was staged. A returned spy for the government, she was well known among this set for her appeals for payment to Thomas Killigrew, Groom of the Bedchamber and patent holder of the King's Company. The important playwrights Robert Howard, Roger Boyle, Thomas D'Urfey, and John Dryden wrote for his theater, and Behn found a home at the more needy Duke's Company, where Thomas Betterton, who was always interested in developing new playwrights, was now co-manager and star. He took the role of Alcippus in her play, his wife Mary Saunderson Betterton that of the leading lady Erminia, and for one night Thomas Otway himself played the king.[8] The prologue declared firmly that a woman was the author:

> They'le joyn the force of Wit to Beauty now,
> And so maintain the right they have in you;
> ....
> The Poetess too, they say, has spyes abroad,
> Which have dispos'd themselves in every road,
> I'th'upper box, Pit, Gallery.[9]

The prologue to *The Amorous Prince* (1671), her second play, was saucy and unapologetic, and the printed play proclaimed, "Written by Mrs A. Behn."

Her third play, *The Dutch Lover* (1673), again had her name on the title page and carried her famous defense of women's ability and right to write plays. Avoiding any pretense to prestige principles of composition, she stated, "I think a Play the best divertissement that wise men have . . . I studied only to make this as entertaining as I could." She then proceeded to attack those who would damn a play simply because it was by a woman by creating a composite of many of the frequent targets of popular culture ridicule and condemnation:

> [T]here comes me into the Pit, a long, lither, phlegmatick, . . . wretched Fop, an officer in Masquerade newly transported with a Scarfe & Feather out of France . . . but no more of such a Smelt. (5:162)

"Lither" meant a person whose actions and disposition were "bad, base, wicked, rascally unjust," and phlegmatic people were cold, dull, and sluggish. Behn piles on insults at his intelligence. "Smelt" was common slang for "simpleton," and at that time "fop" meant "fool," and throughout her plays Behn uses it that way. It was a common insult on the stage and was beginning to take on the French association that Etherege solidified. Disloyal, un-English, naïve enough to imitate the French, this target of Behn's is also "an officer in masquerade" ornamented with scarf and feather, pretending to be things he is too stupid to realize decrease rather than increase others' regard. By using the familiar theatrical diction attached to ridiculous characters who would be humiliated and perhaps even assaulted in farcical scenes, Behn indicated that she and those she addresses are not smelts and enlists these theater-wise connoisseurs against those who would damn a play simply because it was by a woman.

This kind of sophisticated exploitation of the culture of popular rhetoric and entertainment is characteristic of Behn. Before Eliza Haywood (1693?–1756) began the practice of commodifying herself by signing her texts "By the author of ..." Behn was claiming the kind of dual personal and artistic notoriety and distinctive identity that actresses came to have by affixing her name to publications and representing a created self. Following the failure of *Dutch Lover* (1673) and demonstrating her adaptability to fads, Behn produced *Abdelazer, Or the Moor's Revenge* (1676), a blood and guts tragedy with spectacular scene changes that included luxurious rooms, dismal dungeons, and elaborate multicultural costumes. (Nathaniel Lee's *Nero* (1674) and especially John Dryden's *Conquest of Granada* (pt. 1, 1670; pt. 2, 1671) belong to this lurid fad. Dryden's play was also set in Spain; emphasizes Christian-Muslim rivalry and hate; and, like the plays of this type, explores consuming sexual passion and its intersection with power.) "Little Miss Ariell," probably young Anne Bracegirdle who lived with the Bettertons, spoke a feminine and conciliatory epilogue. Similarly charming and noncontroversial, the prologue to *The Town-Fopp: Or Sir Timothy Tawdrey* (1676), her next play, characterizes the play as "a plain Story, that will give a taste / Of what your Grandsires lov'd i' th' Age that's past" (5:323). Strikingly both this play and George Etherege's *The Man of Mode; or Sir Fopling Flutter*, which appeared in the same year, are complex depictions of the fop and important guides to this transition stage of the character type. Both draw out the congruence of rake and fop. The entire first act of Etherege's play centers on Dorimont getting dressed and discussing his wardrobe, and he and Sir Fopling Flutter strut through the rest of the play, while Behn's protagonist, Sir Timothy Tawdrey, combines the characteristics of both types.

After omitting her name from title pages for a year, *Sir Patient Fancy* (1678) came out triumphantly as "Written by Mrs. A. BEHN, the Author of the ROVER." This style of identifying the writer with a work that achieved the status of popular culture would be followed by Daniel Defoe with *The True-Born Englishman* (1701) and, more comparably, by Eliza Haywood with *Love in Excess* (1719). As Elizabeth Taylor came to say, Behn with three, perhaps four, successful plays in twenty months, could say, "I am my own industry. I am my own commodity."[10] Plays that followed showed her astute capitalizing on success, as did *The Feign'd Curtizans* (1679), with a repeat of wandering cavaliers and flirtatious, marriageable women, and *The Second Part of the Rover* (1681), both with courtesan parts for Barry.[11]

Behn had clearly embraced the commercial philosophy inherent in prologues like that for *Sir Patient Fancy*. Betterton in the character of Wittmore said,

> We write not Now as th' Ancient Poets writ,
> For your Applause of Nature, Sense and Wit;
> But, like good Tradesmen, what's in fashion vent.   (6:7)

In the epilogue, she continued to identify herself with the new and crowd pleasing:

> Your way of writing's out of Fashion grown.
> Method, and Rule – you only understand,
> Pursue that way of Fooling, and be Damn'd.
> Your Learned Cant of Action, Time, and Place,
> Must all give way to the unlabour'd farce.   (6:79)

Here and elsewhere, she mentions the vicious exchanges over the rules and unities, arguments developed in Dryden's *Of Dramatick Poesy* (1668), and makes clear her position.

Plays to novels and back

Frances Brooke (1724–89) with the actress Mary Ann Yates (1728–87) followed Barry and Bracegirdle seventy-eight years later in managing a theater, King's in the Haymarket. David Garrick (1717–79) had been able to block the Brooke-Yates group (Richard and Mary Ann Yates, Brooke's brother-in-law James) from performing anything but music and ballets. Brooke wrote and succeeded in many genres including drama, translation, and the novel, and adapting her writing to popular culture is especially visible in her career. She knew poverty. By the time she was twenty-four, she had had four homes, "taken in" by a succession of relatives after her father's death. She came to know the literary marketplace, too, and in 1770 a reviewer for the *Critical Review* wrote that she was so well known that "it would be superfluous ... to say anything of her literary abilities."[12] Her literary career began with the essay periodical *The Old Maid*; in a very competitive market, it survived for thirty-seven issues beginning with the November 15, 1755, number. Styling it governed by the goddess of Great Britain, Caprice, she frequently wrote on politics, current events, marriage, and plays.

Her periodical had the polished register of Addison, Steele, and Johnson, and she was offering to David Garrick a blank verse tragedy *Virginia* (1756), based on Livy's story of the tyrant Appius's desire for Virginia. Two other plays on the same subject appeared on the stage, and Brooke accused Garrick of holding her play until after he produced Henry Crisp's *Virginia*.[13] She published it in an ambitious volume intended to win her a place in the Republic of Letters, *Virginia. A Tragedy with Odes, Pastorals, and*

Translations, noting that she had given up all hopes of seeing it produced. Next, she translated Marie Jeanne Riccoboni's novel *Letters from Juliet, Lady Catesby* (1760), a decisive move into popular success and one that gave her lasting fame. *Letters* was the third of Riccoboni's wildly popular novels, and by 1800 there were twenty editions as well as almost immediate translations into Dutch, German, Swedish, Russian, and other languages. Brooke is credited with introducing Riccoboni to English readers, and her translation required a second edition in the year of its publication.[14] Translations from the French, considered to be a more elegant, polished, and literary than English novels, were popular; women were often engaged to do them, and they were important to Behn's and Inchbald's careers as well as hers.

From this point on, Brooke purposefully and successfully moved between publishing texts that protected her reputation as an elegant, literary writer and others that maintained her identity as an *au courant* exploiter of the popular. Her first novel, *The History of Lady Julia Mandeville* (1763), which required four editions in two years, was identified as "By the Translator of Lady Catesby's Letters," and *The History of Emily Montague* (1769), an ambitious epistolary novel marked by her periodical experience, advertised, "By the Author of Lady Julia Mandeville."

Just as Riccoboni's novel had been news, Guiseppe Sarti's opera, *Mitridate a Sinope* (1779), was notable for the English public. He had produced many operas, Brooke and Yates had included several of them at King's, and this one was recent. Her *The Siege of Sinope* (1781), another blank verse tragedy, was published shortly after the reasonably successful ten-day run, with "By Mrs. Brooke, Author of Julia Mandeville, &c." Drawing upon her experience with opera, the talent of Yates, and her sense of her contemporaries' continued taste for heroic tragedy, a form she admitted was ridiculed but she found "noble and affecting," Brooke gave unstinting praise to the actors and to Thomas Harris, the owner-manager of Covent-Garden and, not coincidentally, one of the purchasers of the King's Theatre.[15] Aphra Behn had had Betterton's help and obviously learned techniques on the job, and Brooke specifically mentions Harris's revisions and the "advantage of decoration" that he added.

Taking advantage of an even closer relationship to an actress than Behn had had with Barry, Brooke expanded the part of Thamyris and gave Yates the opportunity to run the scales of strong, differing emotions that she-tragedy stars had enjoyed. Yates provides a good example of the way public women were forced to experience themselves as sex objects and then control and, if possible, use that reality. She had a stormier career than most of the great tragedians, and a major reason was her continual battle for higher pay, which led to numerous changes in venue, but in the 1779–80 season she moved to Covent Garden and remained there until her retirement in 1785.

Popular culture is always a site for the dramatization of sexual tensions and the commodification of its most important creators, and the performance of *Sinope* provided that for Yates. On stage and in life, she had a reputation for haughtiness, and she excelled in parts requiring a commanding, noble woman who experienced grief, despair, and strong passion. She was a magnificent Jane Shore, rivaled Sarah Siddons as Constance in *King John*, and had been a sensation as Louisa in Robert Jephson's *Braganza* (Brooke gives an eye-witness description in her fashion novel, *The Excursion* [1777], pp. 56–57). Even the *Biographical Dictionary of ... Stage Personnel in London*[16] mentions Yates's reception in the part of Constance in *King John*: "They clapped, shouted, hussaed, cried bravo, and thundered out applause," Walpole reported (16:329). Thamyris had been promised by her father Athridates to Pharnaces, but he reneges. Pharnaces kidnaps and marries her. Athridates besieges Sinope to recover her and, on the day in which the play is set, a peace treaty is to be signed. Brooke holds Yates's appearance back until scene 2 of Act 2. Thamyris, "Bright as Aurora" and surrounded by priests and "Virgins in white," is standing by the altar in the center of an elaborate temple setting. Only two speeches into the scene, there is thunder, the temple shakes, the flames on the altar die, and the stage goes dark. "Avert these omens, heaven!" Orontes, the High Priest, exclaims (14).

The great tragic dilemma for women in fiction and plays was the choice between father and husband epitomized by Sarah Siddons's riveting line spoken to her husband in *Venice Preserved*: "Kill my father?" With the heightened emphasis on the domestic and material in the 1780s, writers like Brooke heightened the tragic dilemma with the triad of husband-father-son, a ghosting of many classical plays. "Ghosting" is Marvin Carson's conceptual term for the experience of audiences when presented with "the identical thing they have encountered before, although now in a somewhat different context" and becomes part of the reception process.[17] In fact, a great deal of the conflict in *Sinope* comes from Athridates's threats to kill the child or take him to Rome and parade him through the city as a captured slave. Brooke's part for Yates included "the indignant queen, the tender wife, the steady heroine," and the noble, fearless confrontation of death that she had praised in the *Braganza* role. Displayed in poses, tableaux, and dramatic speeches that made her the center of attention, Yates's body is frequently described by other characters, and the prologue gestured toward it, even using the word "gaze": "on perfection's height we gaze intent" (vi).

The epilogue continues the duality of the exploitation of Yates's sexuality. Written by Brooke's friend the popular playwright Arthur Murphy, Yates begins, "In all this bustle, rage, and tragic roar" and "Have I not wept, and rav'd, and tore my hair?" (73). These formulaic elements of what had become the signature components of she-tragedy led into a shift in the type of prologue meant to remove the actress from her character to speak in her "own" voice, offering intimacy to the audience. She diagnoses,

> Behind the curtain you must have a peep.
> Tho' bright the tragic character appear,
> Our private foibles you delight to hear.
> ....
> But 'tis the secret anecdote we like.

In the final lines, the epilogue gestures toward Brooke as "Mother, Daughter, and the faithful Wife" who has "copied" Thamyris "true to her [Brooke's] sex."

The Excursion (1777), Brooke's only truly popular culture novel, had as its theme the positioning of woman as sexual object, the scrutiny and "reading" of bodies, and the part speculation about private hours plays. Rather than Pharnaces's and Atridates's struggle to identify Thamyris exclusively with *one* status-locating category, "wife" or "daughter," and her consciousness of the demands of two equally determining categories, "queen" and "mother," Maria Villiers, the protagonist in the novel, is drawn with considerable status ambiguity and, as one character summarizes, everyone in contact with her must decide "to support Miss Villiers as a person of family and character ...; or to give her up as a little adventurer" (68). Although most of the status ambiguity comes from her unprotected situation in London lodgings, her undefined family and fortune, and indiscretions that the most naïve reader would recognize, her body contributes. Several times as characters are ready to slot her as "a little adventurer," they will be drawn up and puzzled by her "elegantly formed" body and charming conversation, which speaks of family and breeding and, on occasion, her ability to awe a detractor with her regal reaction. Brooke, then, who had written a blank verse tragedy and several novels and translations judged to be elegant and appropriate for high culture could use an apparently slight fashion novel to continue her depiction of the fact that women are forced to compete with society for control of their interpretation as sex objects. She followed *Sinope* with her great popular culture, theatrical triumph, *Rosina* (1782), a comic opera performed more than 200 times before 1800. Loaded with many of the most crowd-pleasing tricks in commercial drama, the play also depicts a woman's status ambiguity and the positioning of her as sexual object.

The epilogue for *Sinope* ends with the description of a statesman who is inseparable from an actor.[18] In private life, however, he reveals himself, as he hurries away "to shake the box, and be undone at dice" (74). Making the gestures, Yates calls attention repeatedly to bodies:

> ... in attitude he stands,
> Sprawling his feet, and stretching forth his hands;
> "In this petition, Sir – the nation begs;
> And Mr. Speaker – while I'm upon my legs"

She makes a parallel between the audience's reaction to her performance (some weep and some "stare") and to the politician's ("All gaze; all wonder"), and, as about her, the spectators ask, "But how does he employ his private hours?" Here we have an example of women writers' awareness of the inseparability of the private and public and their ability to exploit the dynamic tension between popular and dominant cultures to release the potential for political commentary, something women tirelessly sought. As Stuart Hall details, this tension is sometimes perpetuating, sometimes antagonistic, but always a site of potential critique. A feared characteristic of popular culture is its potential as an ideological vehicle, and women, less suspected of making it so, were actually alert, shrewd, and expert at exploiting this potential.[19]

In the long eighteenth century, many aspects of governance were under pressure and changing. Behn wrote that plays and public "Divertisements" "are secret instructions to the People, in things that 'tis impossible to insinuate into them any other Way" (dedication of *The Luckey Chance*, 7:213). "Insinuate" is an inspired word choice, for in writing politically, women wrote, in Emily Dickinson's word, "slant" and subversively. By no means were women's subversive purposes limited to "women's issues" such as courtship, marriage, and the economics of widowhood, although they wrote a lot about these topics. Long a place where women could express dissatisfactions, expose abuses, and even encourage resistance to comfortable masculine abuses, popular culture became increasingly an important participant in the new emphasis and pressing need for reconstructing the middle term of the still potent configuration of father of a family; earthly ruler of subject peoples; and, typologically, a figure for God. Elizabeth Inchbald (1753–1821), author of two novels, was one of the most successful dramatists in the century. She had nineteen plays produced on the London stages between 1784 and 1805; fourteen of them ran ten or more nights in their first seasons, and six ran twenty or more. Inchbald made empire and the kind of ruler it encouraged a driving subject in many of her plays. Like Brooke, she wrote popular novels as well as plays and like Behn and Brooke adapted many continental texts for the stage. Unlike Brooke, however, Inchbald's domain was the popular, and although her plays grew in ambition and skill, she, like Behn, dedicated herself to her life as a dramatic "tradesman" as Behn had styled herself.

Inchbald was "fascinated by the stern, nearly tyrannical, father figure,"[20] and Lord Elmwood in *A Simple Story* (1791) is one of the most famous in the eighteenth-century novel. She had an exceptionally clear understanding of some of the implications of the fact that the figure of the father was now being styled the father of a growing number of colonies. That he is the father of the thoroughly submissive Matilda, an owner of a West Indian estate, and a former priest draws together all of the components of the patriarchal concept. The novel went through five London and four Paris editions by 1810, and today it is better known than any of her plays. "Rigor," strict justice, and governance are major terms for fathers (few as extreme as Elmwood) in Inchbald's plays as well as in her novels. Lord Norland in *Every One Has His Fault* (1793) epitomizes the character who believes in them above all other virtues. His judgments, including the exile of his daughter, are not to be questioned. Sir William in *Wives as They Were, and Maids as They Are* (1797) tells his kneeling, begging daughter that he must do his duty and turns her over to the bailiff who is taking her to prison for debt. He says to him, "I give myself joy in being the instrument of your executing justice" (2:66). However, his feelings are quite different; after she is dragged away, he says, "this is justice – this is doing my duty – this is strength of mind – this is fortitude – fortitude – fortitude" (2:68). He has been warned by a friend that his conduct could "degenerate into rigour" (2:3), a pattern that Inchbald builds into Lord Elmwood, whom she describes as becoming "a hard-hearted tyrant ... an example of implacable rigour and injustice."[21] Popular comic drama demanded sentimentality, while Inchbald could develop a thrilling depiction of a tyrant with a virtuous daughter-victim. Both, however, as most popular culture does, dichotomize characters and ideologies.

Inchbald's father-rulers mimic the action of the British colonial governor, whose care comes from obligation, what will become "the white man's burden." His style is designed to accomplish three things: discipline the subject, put it in a highly controlled situation, and set up the conditions in which the governor can expect no further trouble of any kind from it. Elmwood, for instance, pronounces "in a stern and exalted voice 'let me *never* hear again on this subject – You have full power to act in regard to the persons you have mentioned'" (208). As many scholars have pointed out, the parallels between Georgian marriage and colonial governance are strikingly strong. Inchbald often compares English women to subjects of imperial rule. Even so light a play as *Mogul Tale* (1796) opens with the harem women discussing the benefits of being the Mogul's favorite, and one of them refers to "our wretched sex" (1:4). *Such Things Are* (1788) is filled with comic characters whose reasons for being in Sumatra are not funny at all. There are fortune hunters, position seekers, and women unwillingly sent to find husbands; every example of government is self-seeking, corrupt, or dishonest. Lord Flint, for instance, will do or say anything to keep his place with the Sultan, and a prison is the central setting. Inchbald's play takes advantage of the interest in John Howard, the prison reformer who visited prisons in England and then in Europe, whom she depicts as Haswell.

Aphra Behn saw this coming. *Emperor of the Moon* (1687), her most popular play after *The Rover*, is a stunning combining of commedia dell'arte (especially as it had evolved on the French stage), English farce, opera, and court masque, and the kinds of songs and dances common in comedy; it held the stage for seventy-five years and is far more influential than anyone has noted. The play features a father obsessed with the Emperor. He spends his time aiming his twenty-foot telescope at the Emperor in his closet hoping to see scheming, private meetings. Crazed and mad with ambition, he thinks he is marrying his wards to nobility from the moon. In *Wives as They Were*, in spite of hiding the fact that he is Miss Dorrillon's father, Sir William will thunder commands. It is possible to link his autocratic paternity to his Eastern career when he silences his daughter as she begins to assert her own determination of her future and forces her to marry Sir George. Thus, the difficulty of the middle term, to be justly sovereign as God is and in command without crossing into tyranny, becomes a new topic of exploration with the multiplication of kinds of subject people and the rising self-consciousness of women and the lower classes. Popular culture often slips in coded ideas to be picked up or go unnoticed, and, similarly, Inchbald finds ways to define and critique nationhood. Sir William explicitly compares his governance to Sir George's and says that Maria is choosing "to become the subject of a milder government" – a less imperial one (2:94).

The consistency of Inchbald's thematic drives comes out in a dialogue between Norland and the child Edward. Tangling Norland in his own words, Edward asks, "It is not *just* to be unmerciful, is it?" Norland says, "Certainly not." Then Edward says, "Then it must be *just* to have mercy." This brings from Norland the pronouncement that "Great as is the virtue of *mercy, justice* is greater still," and he leaves to prosecute his daughter's husband who, out of dire necessity, has robbed him (2:77). Ghosting the words describing British colonial governors, Harmony describes Norland as "amidst all your authority, your state, your grandeur" (2:78). Edward's questioning is highly similar to several exchanges between the child Henry, who has been reared on an island in Africa, and William, a dean in the Church who has adopted him, in Inchbald's novel *Nature and Art* (1796). A typical one comes about as Henry tries to learn the difference between "massacre" and "war." The provoked dean finally explains, "Consider, young savage, that in battle, neither the infant, the aged, the sick, nor infirm are involved, but only those in the full prime of health and vigour."[22] This offhand way of identifying the different categories of dead in massacres is a flirtation with ridiculing a pompous man while stating horrible facts. It is a major tactic of popular culture but often judged inappropriate in high art, which is more bound by decorum, mode, and genre purities.

Although the mastery of ways to appropriate and prosper by exploiting popular culture strategies and commodifying themselves demonstrated by the women featured in this chapter was unusually fast, they are not either unusual or rare examples of women's ability to adapt and profit. In fact, it would be worthwhile to explore whether the majority if not all of the long eighteenth-century women writers we appreciate most were not exceptionally tactical in their moves between genres identified with prestige literature and those "manufactured" from popular content and rhetorical strategies. Certainly, we are only beginning to recognize encoded commodifying tactics. For instance, never abandoning the kind of references to herself and her plays in prologues and epilogues that Behn employed, Inchbald added another kind of "can-you-recognize-it" game that collapses the distance between text and past successes. On a single page in *Wives as They Were*, Oliver says, "I can tell you what" and "I have faults of my own," both references to titles of her earlier plays and said at moments that recall central plot elements in each (2:35). "I'll tell you what" referred to a risqué question usually about sex, one that exposed what should be unspoken, and *Every One Has His Faults* is interpreted by Misty Anderson and Katherine S. Green as Inchbald's very political response to William Godwin's insistence on absolute truth telling and "the aristocracy as the root of injustice."[23] Thus, these references are sophisticated examples of two of the most frequent uses of popular culture, evidence of women's ability to exploit its potential in the moral and political spheres.

NOTES

1. By the last quarter of the eighteenth century, women were seen as a market segment, and novels, often in pastoral, sentimental, or even gothic modes, centered on their lives, experiences, and interests and became a significant publishing phenomenon.

2. Mary Robinson, *The Natural Daughter*, in *A Letter to the Women of England and The Natural Daughter*, ed. Sharon M. Setzer (Peterborough, ON: Broadview, 2003), pp. 207–10, 221, 242–43.
3. I have adapted Stuart Hall's identification of what he describes as "essential" to the definition of popular culture to include women; see "Notes on Deconstructing 'The Popular'" in *People's History and Socialist Theory*, ed. Raphael Samuel (London: Routledge, 1981), pp. 234–39. See also, s.v. "Popular" in *New Keywords: A Revised Vocabulary of Culture and Society*, ed. Tony Bennett, Lawrence Grosberg, and Meaghan Morris (Oxford: Blackwell, 2005), pp. 262–64.
4. Dominic Strinati, *An Introduction to Theories of Popular Culture* (London: Routledge, 2004), pp. xvi, 241–45.
5. On Barry, see my *Oxford Dictionary of National Biography* entry, and Elizabeth Howe, *The First English Actresses: Woman and Drama, 1660–1700* (Cambridge University Press, 1992), pp. 27–28, 108–28.
6. Thomas Otway, "Under Mrs. B[arry]'s Picture," quoted in Felicity Nussbaum, *Rival Queens* (Philadelphia: University of Pennsylvania Press, 2010), p. 31.
7. Emily H. Anderson, *Eighteenth-Century Authorship and the Play of Fiction* (London: Routledge, 2009), pp. 77–78. Wells is Mary Davies Wells, later Sumbel.
8. The prompter John Downes describes Otway being overcome by stage fright, quoted in *Works of Aphra Behn*, 7 vols., ed. Janet Todd (Columbus: Ohio State University Press, 1992–96), Vol. 5, p. 3. All references to her plays are to this edition.
9. Aphra Behn, *The Forc'd Marriage*, 5:7–8.
10. Elizabeth Taylor, quoted from her lawsuit to stop the showing of an unauthorized account of her life; Greil Marcus, *Lipstick Traces: A Secret History of the Twentieth Century* (Cambridge, MA: Harvard University Press, 1989), p. 106.
11. On the date of composition for *The Young King* and the authorship of *The Revenge*, which has sometimes been attributed to Thomas Betterton, see Todd, *Works of Aphra Behn*, respectively 7:80–81 and 6:163.
12. *Critical Review* 30 (December 1770), 420.
13. Frances Brooke, *Virginia. A Tragedy with Odes, Pastorals, and Translations* (London, 1756), p. viii. Crisp's play was produced at Drury Lane on February 25, 1754, and John Moncrieff's *Appius* at Covent Garden on March 6, 1755 (*London Stage*).
14. Emily A. Crosby, *Une romancière oubliée Madame Riccoboni* (Geneva: Slatkine Reprints, 1970), p. 141. And on Garrick persuading Riccoboni not to make Brooke her official translator, see Backscheider, "Introduction," *The Excursion*, ed. Paula Backscheider and Hope D. Cotton (Lexington: University Press of Kentucky, 1997), pp. xvii–xviii.
15. Frances Brooke, Preface to *The Siege of Sinope. A Tragedy* (London, 1781), p. iii.
16. Philip H. Highfill, ed., *Biographical Dictionary of Actors, Actresses, Musicians, Dancers, Managers & Other Stage Personnel in London, 1660–1800* (Carbondale: Southern Illinois University Press, 1973–93), 16 volumes.
17. Marvin Carlson, *The Haunted Stage: The Theatre as Memory Machine* (Ann Arbor: University of Michigan Press, 2003). For an example with Betterton, which could be applied to Barry, see pp. 58–63.
18. Epilogue to *The Siege of Sinope*, pp. 73–74; the epilogue raised accusations that Charles James Fox was intended and reviewers accused Yates of "taking him

off"; see Lorraine McMullen, *An Odd Attempt in a Woman: The Literary Life of Frances Brooke* (Vancouver: University of British Columbia Press, 1983), pp. 193–94.

19. An example is Inchbald's ability to include the line "Provisions are so scarce" in *Every One Has His Fault* (1793) during a tumultuous time marked by food riots; for an analysis of how she got away with it, see my "Retrieving Elizabeth Inchbald" in *Oxford Handbook of the Georgian Theatre 1737–1832*, ed. Julia Swindells and David F. Taylor (Oxford University Press, 2014), p. 609.

20. Paula Backscheider, "Introduction," *The Plays of Elizabeth Inchbald*, 2 vols. (New York: Garland, 1980), Vol. 1, p. xxxii. Quotations from her plays are from this edition.

21. Elizabeth Inchbald, *A Simple Story*, ed. Joyce M. S. Tompkins (Oxford University Press, 1988), p. 195. Quotations are from this edition.

22. Elizabeth Inchbald, *Nature and Art*, ed. Shawn L. Maurer (London: Pickering and Chatto, 1997), pp. 28–29.

23. Misty Anderson, *Female Playwrights and Eighteenth-Century Comedy: Negotiating Marriage on the London Stage* (Houndmills: Palgrave, 2002), 177–78; Katherine S. Green, "Mr Harmony and the Events of January 1793: Elizabeth Inchbald's *Every One Has His Fault*" *Theatre Journal*, 56 (2004), 50–51, quotation at 50 (numerous critics agree with Green). The fact that there are lengthy discussions by modern critics makes my point about Inchbald's sophistication.

5

KATHRYN R. KING

Genre crossings

Discussions of the interplay of gender and genre in our period often begin and end in the novel. A generic latecomer, open to transgressive possibilities and not entirely respectable, a product of the distinctively modern culture of print, the novel as a form seems supremely suited to bear women's upstart ambitions. But prose fiction made up a small fraction of women's total literary output in the eighteenth century. They wrote poetry and drama, to name the major literary genres they inherited, and they experimented with so wide a variety of established kinds and emerging subgenres that it has become almost obligatory in essays such as this one to celebrate the generic diversity of their achievements: elegies, retirement poems, female friendship poems, scandal chronicles, scandalous memoirs, amatory romance, Gothic romance, satiric anti-romance, and so on – the list of genres, modes, and forms women made their own over the course of the long eighteenth century has come to seem virtually endless.

This chapter surveys trends in gender/genre study since the 1980s and then turns to a topic that has recently begun to attract attention: the genre crossings that energized some of the liveliest writing by female authors in the first half of the century. Many women wrote across multiple genres. Aphra Behn (1640?–89), Jane Barker (1652–1732), Eliza Haywood (1693?–1756), Mary Davys (1674–1732), Charlotte Lennox (1730/31–1804), and others moved between and among genres over the course of their long and varied writing careers. In addition, they moved strategically between genres within given texts. The discussion takes as its chief exemplary case Haywood's *Love in Excess* (1719–20), a hybrid narrative that falls somewhere between narrative and drama, romance and erotic lyricism. It then looks at generic crossovers within the careers and individual works of two other playwright-novelists, Behn and Davys. By way of comparison, it considers the evocative genre crossings of the poet-novelist Barker, who does not so much mix genres as cut them up into bits and pieces to be collaged in patchwork narratives. The mingling of genres that is one of the most important features of writing by women in this period offered unprecedented opportunities to tell new kinds of stories about female life.

Genre and feminist recovery

In its early days, the feminist recovery project was animated by news from the archival front of the sheer numbers of women writers left out of literary history. Gender/genre study provided weapons (as it seemed back then) for canon expansion by calling attention to distinctively female subgenres that had been ignored or overlooked – the mother's legacy to an unborn child, to take an unusually clear example – and by highlighting female contributions to familiar genres, the novel preeminently. Scholars from various vantage points sought to map the course of twinned rises: the rise of the woman writer as a cultural force and the rise of the novel as a culturally dominant genre. The broad aim was to revise male-centered accounts that, at least from Ian Watt's classic study *The Rise of the Novel* (1957), located the novel's emergence in the paternal exertions of Daniel Defoe, Henry Fielding, Samuel Richardson, and other "masters." Revisionary work by Jane Spencer in *The Rise of the Woman Novelist* (1986) and Janet Todd in *The Sign of Angelica: Women, Writing and Fiction, 1660–1800* (1989) offered pioneering rejoinders to the male literary genealogies constructed by the Watt tradition. Nancy Armstrong's *Desire and Domestic Fiction: A Political History of the Novel* (1987) connected the genre with a distinctively feminine consciousness that shaped the way the middle class came to understand itself and assume cultural power. In another broadly invigorating move, Ros Ballaster in *Seductive Forms* (1992) focused on the amatory fiction of Behn, Delarivier Manley (c.1670–1724), and Haywood in the earlier part of the period, inaugurating an inquiry into the persistence of romance elements in women's writing that remains vigorous to this day.[1] Early gender/genre investigations such as these put the contributions of women novelists front and center and made it hard to ignore the importance and complexity of the representations of female desire and erotic experience that they infused into prose fiction.

The 1980s saw the beginnings of crucial work in poetry and drama as well. The landmark contributions in poetry are two hugely enabling wrest-from-the-archives anthologies that appeared at the decade's close: *Kissing the Rod* (1988), the provocatively entitled anthology of seventeenth-century verse compiled by a team assembled by Germaine Greer, and the equally revelatory *Eighteenth-Century Women Poets* (1989), edited by Roger Lonsdale. The study of women and the drama was slower to take hold. In 1991, the first-ever collection of essays devoted entirely to women's contributions to the stage during this period, *Curtain Calls: British and American Women and the Theater, 1660–1820,* edited by Mary Anne Schofield and Cecilia Macheski, appeared. Despite illuminating studies of individual playwrights and topic-oriented treatments of specific aspects of women's drama, we await a synthetic overview in this area. For the time being, readers can consult a collection of short pieces, *Teaching British Women Playwrights of the Restoration and Eighteenth Century* (2010), edited by Bonnie Nelson and Catherine Burroughs, which includes a section on the "Playwright-Novelist."

Alongside this push to include women's writings within an expanded canon based on traditional formal genres was a growing emphasis on generic diversity within the canon of literature by women. In an important critique, Clare Brant argued that canon expansion had come "at the price of a conservative attitude to genre. Many women writers in eighteenth-century Britain were not novelists, poets, or dramatists."[2] She drew attention to the importance of dialogues, letters, diaries, memoirs, and essays. Scholars such as Margaret Ezell in *Writing Women's Literary History* (1993) and Paula McDowell in *The Women of Grub Street* (1998) had already insisted on the importance of political and religious polemic in women's literary output and helped establish the point that assessment of women's writings would require engagement with unfamiliar forms that fall outside traditional generic boundaries. The new stress on generic multiplicity, even miscellaneity, brought scrutiny to previously marginal and in some cases nearly invisible forms of writing – works possessing what Brant describes as "uncertain status then and certainly liminal status now."[3] Establishment of generic diversity as an organizing principle in histories of women's writing is perhaps best exemplified by the remarkable work of synthesis achieved by Susan Staves in *A Literary History of Women's Writing in Britain, 1660–1789* (2006), a generically embracing account that seeks to reflect period interests in such nonfictional prose forms as the memoir and travel literature. Staves's insistence that "much of women's best writing" is to be found in forms other than the novel is now widely endorsed, although her emphasis on aesthetic or literary merit as a principle of inclusion remains controversial.[4]

In addition to serving historical aims of revision and redress, genre-based analysis lends itself to the investigation of gender difference that is a hallmark of feminist literary criticism. Studies of individual writers and works show that women of all classes, religions, social settings, and geographical locations manipulated existing genre systems to buck the patriarchal system, either by talking back or by creating their own counter-traditions. A recent overview of the interplay of gender and genre at mid-century provides suggestive examples of ways that women used genre – specifically prose fiction – to deconstruct fictions of gender. In the hands of a Sarah Scott (1720–95), Jane Collier (1715–55), or Sarah Fielding (1710–68), the novel pitches artifice against artifice to "reveal how nature had been supplanted by culture speciously passed off as 'truth.'"[5] Analyses of drama and poetry yield similar conclusions. Women's relationships to established poetic forms, for example, were inevitably fraught: "Women were, after all, working within genres and poetic conventions created and shaped by men," and like men they appropriated conventions "for their own ends, and to juxtapose masculine and feminine in revelatory ways."[6] Poetic kinds that flourished during the Restoration and well into the eighteenth century, retirement poems and female friendship poems, for example, provided what amounted to oppositional spaces in which poets such as Katherine Philips (1632–64), Barker, Anne Finch (1661–1720), and Elizabeth Singer Rowe (1674–1737) could slip out of the subject/object relations dictated by conventional love lyrics and explore instead feelings of mutuality, sometimes with a homoerotic tinge. Gender/genre analysis is often fascinated with transgression of boundaries and is nearly always sharply attuned to the potential for resistance to gender ideologies offered by generic manipulations.

Another vein of genre-based analysis considers issues of authorial legitimacy, including negotiated positions vis-à-vis literary tradition, discursive authority, and literary identity and the crafting of signature and voice as well as the formal choices that enable women to express, however obliquely, the truth of their experience as opposed to the fictions and clichés of gender lodged within existing generic forms. Genre-based analysis also exposes the limitations of the difference paradigm which, as Brant has observed, tends to make "women writers inescapably *women* writers" by bringing into play the vast and endlessly workable world of allusions, conventions, frames, traditions and possibilities that constitute the common stock of meaning into which any writer can dip at any given moment.[7] Genre analysis can be used, that is to say, to magnify the *writerly* side of women's authorial identities. Lady Mary Wortley Montagu (1689–1762) uses imitation, parody, and allusion to deliver the withering contempt of a response poem such as *The Reasons that induced Dr. S. to write a Poem called "The Lady's Dressing Room"* (1734), but related techniques also make possible the respectful but searching meditation on Pope conducted by the working-class poet Mary Leapor in her *An Essay on Woman* (1748). By revealing the particularities of women's engagement with literary tradition, genre-based analysis affords a means of assessing their artistry and craftsmanship, as well as their sense of difference. In sum, gender/genre analysis has served the feminist recovery project in a host of ways: it calls attention to the limitations of inherited genre systems; renders visible previously obscured work by women; opens to view female counter-traditions within the established genres of poetry, drama, and prose fiction; and, in the most conceptually ambitious studies, invites rethinking entire literary fields from the perspective of the generic experiments pursued by female practitioners.

Genres mixed and remixed

The inventiveness and even exuberance of women's experimentation with hybrid forms is often celebrated these days, but it would be a mistake to think of hybridized texts as distinctively female. The first half of the eighteenth century was the great age of mixed forms. Neoclassical theory assumed a hierarchy of fixed literary types descending from epic and tragedy to pastoral and short lyric, but in practice men and women of varying backgrounds and interests combined "high" and "low" genres to a degree unmatched until our own moment of "creative remix." This is not to deny the existence of gender-marked differences. University-educated men enjoyed a comfortable familiarity with Greek and Latin literature seldom shared by their home-educated sisters and were thus better equipped, psychologically and technically, to pursue the mock-epic strategies that resulted in some of the most memorable work of the period by the likes of Pope, Swift, Gay, and Fielding. Haywood's wry comment on women's educational disadvantages in the dedication to *Fatal Secret* (1725) should be recalled: she is "a Woman, and consequently depriv'd of those Advantages of Education which the other Sex enjoy" and therefore dare not "imagine it in my power to soar to any Subject higher than that which Nature is not negligent to teach us," that is, "LOVE." Haywood's ironies notwithstanding, women did not lack literary resources and many approached authorship with a well-honed critical intelligence – or as Haywood put it, "a tolerable share of Discernment."[8] Writers from Behn and Barker to Lennox were well schooled in vernacular traditions, especially the stage, and drew freely on French works in the original and in translation, including the seventeenth-century heroic romances that stand behind prose fictions ranging from Behn's *Oroonoko* (1688) and Barker's *Exilius* (1715, but mostly written earlier) to Lennox's satiric mid-century novel *The Female Quixote* (1752), where a latter-day Quixote, her mind bent by uncritical reading of heroic romances, exposes the disjunction between real and unreal often explored in novels.

Hybridizing characterizes some of women's most important work in the period. Behn is known to be our first professional woman playwright but is arguably the first English novelist, as well. *Oroonoko* – part heroic romance, part exotic travel narrative, and part memoir of a hero who is paradoxically a "royal slave" – mixes heroic, courtly, and romance discourses with a gritty here-and-now realism associated with the emerging novelistic discourse. An "innovator in the search for the novel who changed the course of literary history," Behn is a playwright-novelist who turned narrative inward and beyond the constraints of dramatic form.[9] Her pioneering efforts at mapping complex psychosexual worlds opened up new territories for amatory writers such as Manley and Haywood, but the amatory elements that she popularized shaped a range of work by genre-hopping women in the first half of the century. The poet and prose fiction writer Elizabeth Singer Rowe, immensely popular in her own time but known nowadays for an intense piety that modern readers may find daunting, drew unabashedly on the appeal and conventions of amatory fiction in religious works such as the prose fiction *Friendship in Death* (1728) and the narrative poem *The History of Joseph* (1736). The poet-novelist Penelope Aubin (1679?–1738) did likewise in Crusoe-esque travel fictions such as *The Strange Adventures of the Count de Vinevil and His Family* (1721). Haywood, who reigned supreme in the amatory field in the 1720s, went on to recycle her own amatory themes and devices in her later fictions. *Eovaai* (1736), a famously savage attack on Walpole's England, is a satiric travel narrative-cum-seduction tale partly modeled on that most mixed of proto-novels *Gulliver's Travels* (1726) that includes episodes that deliberately recall Swift's shocking use of cross-species sex. It also recasts from a female point of view the "mirror for princes" tradition, framing it within a set of expectations established by Haywood's own seduction fictions interwoven with threads of early modern pornography and Oriental political fable. Further study will doubtless deepen appreciation of the complex workings of generic hybridizing in women's narratives and within their careers.

Bakhtin has influentially encouraged students of the novel to understand the genre not as a bounded or fixed form but rather as a range of possibilities perpetually in a process of becoming that is ceaselessly shaping and reshaping the genres in which it comes into contact, a process that he calls "novelization." A genre always "in-the-making," the novel exhibits an "indeterminacy, a certain semantic open-endedness, a living contact with unfinished, still-evolving contemporary reality."[10] A suggestive recent application of the idea of contiguous genres mutually shaping each other is advanced by Gabrielle Starr in *Lyric Generations* (2004), a study of the interrelations among the novel and lyric poetry. Theories of the novel seldom notice, much less seek to account for, "the presence of poetry in 'prose' romance"; although it is true that the lyric declined as a poetic kind during the Restoration and for much of the eighteenth century, the lyric impulse remained vigorous. It resurfaced in novels by Behn, Haywood, and Samuel Richardson, among others, sometimes in stand-apart verse and sometimes in lyrically inflected prose, and it served many strategic purposes. Starr's subtle analysis of the interplay of novel with the language, forms, and affect of lyric poetry brings her to the conclusion that the "generic boundaries" during this period are "as open to imaginative crossing as the boundaries of personal experience."[11]

The imaginative crossings of three writers from the 1720s are the subject of the remainder of this chapter. The writing careers of Barker, Davys, and Haywood overlap from the 1680s through 1756, and taken together their lifetimes span more than a century. They represent three writing generations, in other words, but it is fascinating to find that the genre-crossing narratives to be discussed now appeared within five years of one another, between 1719 and 1724, at the precise midpoint of the period under study in this volume. These writers are usually classified as early novelists, and their work is accordingly read backward through a progressive narrative of the intertwined rises of the novel and the woman writer. But when their narratives from the early 1720s are read together, synchronically, and in relation to the genre fluidity of their cultural moment, they reveal some of the ways stories of women's lives were told at this time within a Bahktinian contact zone in which prose fiction, poetry, and drama formed a dynamic continuum of expressive possibilities.

Gender fluidity in the twenties: The case of *Love in Excess*

Haywood's disregard for generic boundaries is well known: she was "omnivorous in her consumption and use of various popular genres and forms – they were all grist for her mill."[12] But apart from scattered attention to theatrical elements in her narratives – in the plots, characters, and settings of *Fantomina* (1725), *Anti-Pamela* (1741), and *The History of Miss Betsy Thoughtless* (1751) to take the usual instances – and a few discussions of genre blending in the "wildly" hybridized Orientalized political satire *Eovaai*, the phenomenon of genre crossing within individual texts is little broached. Although seldom analyzed from a genre-studies point of view, Haywood's first novel, *Love in Excess* (1719–20), strikingly illustrates the way narrative at this time occupied a zone of contact with other genres, most importantly stage tragedy and comedy, to be discussed shortly, and lyric poetry. Starr argues convincingly that the "absorbed lyricism" of this novel – its incorporation of the language and feeling of Renaissance and seventeenth-century courtly lyric, with some rapturous Donne and even a little Milton thrown in – serves to create affective bonding or "emotional consensus" among reader, author, and characters. The passion-infused prose aligns "speaker and reader with ideals of love so that the language intimates the structure of delight" and invites "consensuality."[13]

Focus on the lyricism of the language and its fostering of shared sensibility brings into view aspects of *Love in Excess* easily overlooked when attention is trained instead on the characters and their bodily experiences. We notice the Romeo-and-Juliet–like exchange of couplets between a pair of lovers at the base of a statue of Diana; the translation into exalted prose of Donne's "Extasie"; and, most interestingly, because it seems largely to have escaped critical attention, the tendency of the prose to fall into iambs at moments of high passion. Perhaps Richard Savage had this in mind when he praised the metrical patterning and musicality of her prose, which *"in sweeter harmony refines, / Than numbers flowing thro' the Muses's lines."*[14] Recognition of the artful lyricism of Haywood's prose offers an attractive alternative to approaches that regard the amatory fictions as fantasy-delivery systems for panting chambermaids. Framing the "sexy bits" as potential sites for communities of shared affect may help us understand the popular appeal of her short novels of passion from 1719 to 1726 when they dominated the market for fiction.

If *Love in Excess* incorporates and rearranges lyrical elements within its narrative structure, it also exists in a "mutually informing relationship" with drama.[15] This relationship remains little explored; indeed, it is an often "overlooked fact" that a number of women novelists at this time were also playwrights. They include professionals such as Behn, Manley, Davys, and Lennox, the latter of whom seems to have been the first to rework one of her own novels for performance on stage, as well as amateur poets such as Anne Finch and, earlier, Katherine Philips.[16] Haywood, the consummate professional, began her career as an actress and when her stage aspirations failed, she took up writing prose fictions (mostly) and plays. Her imagination was steeped in the techniques of stagecraft, and from the start her narratives were strongly shaped by her theatrical background. *Love in Excess* shows the influence of Renaissance and Restoration drama, from Shakespearean tragedy to romantic comedy, and it is filled with echoes of and allusions to *Hamlet, Lear, Twelfth Night,* and *Midsummer's Night Dream*. Her stagier characters speak in monologues and soliloquies, and the narration is indistinguishable at times from stage directions. She seems often to be transcribing for the page scenes first conceived visually as if occurring on stage, as when characters "fling" themselves outside a room and then, in effect, disappear.

In addition, *Love in Excess* declares its affiliation with the theater by way of several paratextual signals. The dedication is addressed to Anne Oldfield, the most renowned actress of this period, and signed by the bookseller William Chetwood, who had worked with Haywood during her actress days at the Smock Alley Theatre in Dublin and who would have been associated by her first readers with Drury Lane Theatre where he was prompter. The word "novel" appears nowhere in the dedication; it refers instead, twice, to "the following lines" as if in reference to a play or poem. The 1722 edition features a stagey frontispiece by Elisha Kirkall that could easily be taken for the frontispiece of a printed tragedy. It illustrates the double death-by-sword that closes Part II, showing two bodies downstage and behind them a group of five figures all gesturing with "speaking hands" in the manner of stage performers at this time; the intensely dramatic grouping set within a wainscoted room is reminiscent of London theatrical interiors since the Restoration. All that is missing is the proscenium arch.

The entire novel is imbued with theatrical elements, but they are nowhere more evident or purposeful than in the construction of the rivalry between a pair of women, Alovisa, the jealous wife, and Melliora, the orphaned ingénue who is her rival for Delmont's love. Alovisa, an actress by instinct and practice, inhabits tragic theatrical space from the start to her death in Part II. She speaks in monologues and dialogues; her language, rendered in the "dost thou" and "can'st thou" idiom of the playhouse, often swells into the heightened feeling of the tragic heroine: "Oh the villain! ... What misfortunes are these thou talk'st of?" (95). Her stormy feelings are conveyed by way of stereotyped stage actions: "She tore down the Count's picture which hung in the room, and stamped on it, then the letter, her own cloths, and hair" (133). Emotionally inflexible, driven by jealousy and rage, she is unable to find her way into the new world of the novel where the recognizably modern forms of love, feeling, and community promoted by Haywood's consensus-seeking narrator are beginning to inform the narrative. She dies by the sword a stage heroine. Melliora, on the other hand, embodies dimensions of female life figured by the emerging novel – a life that combines agency and complicated interiority. She carries within her "a world of troubled meditations" (102). It is the delicate tangle of her feelings that interests Haywood, an interior world not easily expressed via older generic forms. Its expression requires a sympathetic narrator able to articulate the inchoate feelings of this new kind of heroine and enlist the support of the reader through a direct address that is a distinguishing feature of Haywood's methods in the 1720s: the narrator of *Love in Excess* reaches out to readers who "have delicacy enough to feel what I imperfectly attempt to speak" and seeks to elicit their "pity" for Melliora's "distress" (122). In such moments, we catch a glimpse of the stage performer turned popular fiction writer using the resources of prose narrative to engender empathy, sympathy, and other new affective bonds and to forge relationships with audiences learning to seek their pleasures on the page as well as in the playhouse.

Paula Backscheider has pointed out that in Haywood fictions such as *British Recluse* (1722) and *City Jilt* (1726), Haywood uses a technique of narrative doubling by which a story is told first within the conventions of a romance and then retold in updated, novelistic terms, sometimes in the "straightforward prose of the novel-to-be." In *The City Jilt* (1726), for example, "the old, familiar story" of seduction and abandonment is balanced by the story of Glicera learning to act "in a very modern world."[17] In *Love in Excess*, the story of Melliora's happy marriage to Delmont replicates, in romance-comedy register that includes several generic twists, the tragic story of Alovisa's death at Delmont's hands. Alovisa, the doomed tumultuous wife, is stuck in her overly familiar, stage-worn passions; her evolving double Melliora is able to grow out of her passive helplessness (the name means "better"). Over the course of an increasingly novelistic storyline that anticipates the bildungsroman and novel of courtship and marriage that would flourish later in the century, she learns to shape her own life story – figured, interestingly, when she plays a self-created part allowing her to bestow herself in marriage in a comedic plot of her own devising. She is the first and ultimately the most successful in a long line of Haywood's actress-heroines – Fantomina and Syrena Tricksy are others – who survive and even thrive, at least temporarily, by dint of their virtuoso acting performances. Haywood's career is sometimes framed as a movement from playwriting to novel writing, but she is better regarded as a genre-crossing author who, from the start, crafts updated stories of female life within Bahktin's zone of contact with an unfinished and still evolving contemporary reality. Armstrong observes that "the internal composition of a given text [records] the history of its struggle with contrary forms of representation."[18] *Love in Excess* uses contrary forms of representation, the conventions of stage tragedy as against those of the emerging female-centered novel, to depict female existence in the modern world.

The case of Mary Davys and Jane Barker

Mary Davys's indebtedness to the conventions of the stage is often remarked. She came to prose fiction in the 1720s after having enjoyed some success in the theater. *The Northern Heiress: or the Humours of York*, performed and published in London in 1716, earned her enough to open a coffeehouse in Cambridge. She wrote at least one other play, an unacted comedy *The Self-Rival*. During her coffeehouse days, with the encouragement of her customers, she wrote and published *The Reform'd Coquet* (1724), a lively story of female education strongly influenced by comedic stage conventions. The preface to the *Works* (1725) invokes the rule of dramatic unity in relation to her novels:

they are constructed around *"one entire Scheme or Plot"* according to the *"great Rule prescribed by Criticks, not only in Tragedy, and other Heroick Poems, but in Comedy too."* (On this business of "rules," Haywood was typically sarcastic: "I know myself beneath the Censure of the Gyant-Critics of this Age," she writes in the preface to *Frederick Duke of Brunswick-Lunenburgh* (1729), "yet have I taken all imaginable Care not to offend the Rules"). Paratextual elements link the narrative with the stage. Although the title page of *The Reform'd Coquet* uses oversized uppercase letters to proclaim the narrative's identity as "A NOVEL," the Dedication to the Ladies associates the novel with the "Masquerades, Operas, New Plays, Conjurers, Monsters, and feigned Devils [of] the Town," conflating theatrical entertainments and other fashionable spectacles with those delivered by prose fictions. Many of the characters are lifted from Restoration comedy of manners and bear stage-comedy names – Froth, Lord Lofty – and the narrative proceeds by way of sprightly dialogue and soliloquy. The witty repartee, professed (in passing) cynicism about marriage, besieged heiress plot, sexual intrigue, and allusions point toward and continuously activate the generic affiliation with the stage.

At the same time, *Reform'd Coquet* recycles elements from the French heroic romances so popular in the seventeenth century, including the gallant rescue of an endangered heroine, and in this way anticipates the more openly satiric exposure of the absurdities of seventeenth-century heroic romance in Lennox's *The Female Quixote* at mid-century. It also looks forward to the didacticism of the later novel. The emphasis on the education and reform of an overly self-regarding coquette places Davys at the head of "a long line of women writers who create coquettish heroines and lover-mentors to reform them."[19] *Reform'd Coquet* deftly mingles the language and themes of Restoration comedy with elements of French romance and those of the educative novel "in-the-making." For insight into the significance of this generic fluidity, we can turn to Rosamund Colie, who was first to develop the perception that at any given moment genres and kinds provide frames or sets of interpretation available for recombination and rearrangement by writers no longer satisfied with existing modes of expression. She does not examine women's generic crossovers in the 1720s, but she might have. Genre mixing in both *Love in Excess* and *The Reform'd Coquet* illustrates with clarity and force her observation: "Experience can be seen as searching for its own form, after all: the kinds may act as myth or metaphor for a man's" –we can now add "woman's" – "new vision of literary truth."[20] Colie arrived at this insight in 1973, just as the feminist recovery project was getting under way. Were she to return to her thinking today with the benefit of the feminist scholarship that has flourished in the intervening years, she would surely be struck by the way genre and kind provided women writers in the first half of the eighteenth century with vehicles for articulating their new visions of the truth of female experience.

Jane Barker, who has always figured as something of a sport in literary history, is unusual among the crossover women of this period in having no known interest in writing for the stage (although her fictional alter ego, Galesia, does decide to imitate the Faithful Shepherdess of the Fletcher play by that name in her "perpetual Chastity"). Barker's first and most sustaining love was poetry. She was involved in coterie exchange with a group of Cambridge students in the 1680s and at the century's turn acted as a kind of unofficial poet laureate to the Jacobite court at St. Germain. Later she would recall being "dropp'd" as a girl into a "Labyrinth of Poetry, which has ever since interlac'd all the Actions of my Life."[21] However, it is her generically mixed "patchwork" narratives – *A Patchwork Screen for the Ladies* (1723) and *The Lining of the Patchwork Screen* (1726) – along with the earlier and more conventionally structured *Love Intrigues* (1719) that compel most readers today. These narratives were once mischaracterized as pious polemics but a new generation of readers has discovered in them the captivating life story of a woman of strong if quirky intelligence who chose poetry over marriage. More recent work still has restored these deliberately miscellaneous narratives to their Jacobite, Roman Catholic, and early Georgian political and economic contexts. They intersperse scraps of verse and prose in a loosely structured narrative repeatedly likened to a patchwork. The first-person narrator, the poet-heroine Galesia, describes these patches as the record of a writing life, "Pieces of *Romances, Poems, Love-Letters*, and the like" (*PWS*, 74), but they are drawn from an almost bewildering variety of generic sources. The prose includes small essays, proverbial stories exchanged by passengers in a coach, realistic contemporary tales (one offers an intriguing glimpse of what appears to be a proto-lesbian relationship), tales of the supernatural, an allegorized and teasingly enigmatic preface "To the Reader" that evokes among other things the bursting of the South Sea Bubble and, in the manner of Margaret Cavendish's self-invoking fictions fifty years earlier, even includes a cameo appearance by "Jane Barker."

No less striking is the variety of poetic kinds that go toward making up the patchwork: odes, pastorals, landscape poems, love lyrics, to take just a few of the established genres, as well as a number of poetic performances that are hybrids in themselves, including a versified recipe for French soup and an account of the circulation of the blood taken from a medical textbook and "reduc'd" to verse – a procedure the poet-narrator attributes to Ovid. Many of these verse fragments are taken from poems written and published by Jane Barker during her earlier amateur coterie days in Lincolnshire, London, and at the Jacobite court at St. Germain. Presumably some or most of the prose fragments were written earlier. They are pieced together to tell the story of a life less ordinary. At one time critics professed themselves baffled by the open-ended generic diversity of the patchwork narratives; some were dismissive. These days, critics are more likely to find narratological complexity where once there was disorder. Essays by Rivka Swenson and Constance Lacroix, to name two of the more suggestive, argue convincingly that the "increasingly polyphonic and intricate" patchwork narratives, assembled out of a diversity of forms and genres, represent a fractured modern subjectivity in a way that enables Barker – a woman, a poet, a Roman Catholic, and a Jacobite – to confront the dissatisfactions of modern life from a position of political resistance.[22]

Conclusions

In 1722, the poet Elizabeth Thomas (1675–1731) exclaimed, "Yet, if we enquire for a book, / Beyond a novel or a play, / Good lord! how soon th' alarm's took."[23] But women read and wrote widely outside the gender-appropriate formal genres of fiction and drama and, despite the cultural "alarm," had few inhibitions about crossing generic lines and mixing forms. Genre theory and criticism have been a vital part of the feminist recovery project. Genre analysis has traced women's interlinked transgressions of gender and genre boundaries, exposed omissions in traditional histories, and contributed to the remaking of literary histories that reflect the full range of genres that constitute women's writing past. Ralph Cohen has observed that "generic theory ... reemerged as a critical force" in the second half of the twentieth century because the study of genre "reveal[s] a historical process that provides a valuable, practical, and theoretical understanding of the changes, gaps, incompletions, and transformations that take place in the writing of literary history and other histories." Awareness of the evolving ins and outs, ups and downs, of genre history makes us aware of "the functions of repression and renewal in our society" and helps us "realize the limits of any monolithic classification."[24] To this, we might add the idea, which emerges from even this brief discussion of genre-crossing women of the 1720s, that mixed forms and genres can stand in for and to some extent convey their authors' new understandings of female existence. The generic gridlines established by traditional literary histories – to say nothing of academic course offerings, syllabi, anthologies, library classification systems – tend to reinforce notions of generic boundaries that bear a misleading relation to women's actual genre-crossing practices and, almost certainly, their conceptions of themselves as writers. Boundaries that may appear fixed or rigid viewed through the lens of inherited generic gridlines can be seen to be porous or even, perhaps, nonexistent viewed through the eyes of creative practitioners such as Behn, Barker, Davys, and Haywood. From the writer's vantage point, generic choices are probably better regarded as a set of interactive and evolving practices that involve engagement with tradition, convention, readers, and fellow writers. At their most interesting, genre crossings point toward possibilities for women's lives and modes of expression that lie outside and possibly beyond the imaginings of established genre.

NOTES

1. For the persistence of the appeal of romance into the present, see Janice Radway, *Reading the Romance: Women, Patriarchy, and Popular Literature* (1984; Chapel Hill: University of North Carolina Press, 1991).
2. Clare Brant, "Varieties of Women's Writing," in *Women and Literature in Britain 1700–1800*, ed. Vivien Jones (Cambridge University Press, 2000), pp. 285–305, at p. 285.
3. Brant, "Varieties of Women's Writing," p. 285.
4. Susan Staves, *A Literary History of Women's Writing in Britain, 1660–1789* (Cambridge University Press, 2006), p. 2.
5. Jennie Batchelor, "'[T]o strike a little out of a road already so much beaten': Gender, Genre, and the Mid-Century Novel," in Jacqueline M. Labbe, *The History of British Women's Writing, 1750–1830* (Houndsmills, Basingstoke, Hampshire: Palgrave Macmillan, 2010), pp. 84–101, 92.
6. Paula R. Backscheider, *Eighteenth-Century Women Poets and Their Poetry: Inventing Agency, Inventing Genre* (Baltimore: The Johns Hopkins University Press, 2005), p. 19.
7. Brant, "Varieties of Women's Writing," p. 286, emphasis in original.
8. Eliza Haywood, Dedication, *The Fatal Secret; or Constancy in Distress* (J. Roberts, 1725), pp. i–ii.
9. Rose Zimbardo, "Aphra Behn: A Dramatist in Search of the Novel," in *Curtain Calls: British and American Women and the Theatre, 1660–1820*, ed. Mary A. Schofield and Cecilia Macheksi (Athens: Ohio University Press, 1991), p. 379.
10. Mikhail M. Bahktin, "Epic and Novel," in *The Dialogic Imagination*, ed. Michael Holquist, trans. Caryl Emerson and Michael Holquist (Austin: University of Texas Press, 1981), p. 6.
11. G. Gabrielle Starr, *Lyric Generations: Poetry and the Novel in the Long Eighteenth Century* (Baltimore and London: The Johns Hopkins University Press, 2004), pp. 47, 46.
12. Juliette Merritt, *Beyond Spectacle: Eliza Haywood's Female Spectators* (Toronto, Buffalo, and London: University of Toronto Press, 2004), p. 8.
13. Starr, *Lyric Generations*, p. 63.
14. Richard Savage, "To Mrs. Eliz. Haywood, on Her Novel Called Love in Excess, &c" reprinted in *Love in Excess; or, The Fatal Enquiry,* 2nd ed., ed. David Oakleaf (Peterborough, ON: Broadview, 2000), p. 82. All subsequent references to *Love in Excess* will be to this edition and will appear parenthetically.

15. Catherine Ingrassia, "'The Stage Not Answering My Expectations': The Case of Eliza Haywood," in *Teaching British Women Playwrights of the Restoration and Eighteenth Century*, ed. Bonnie Nelson and Catherine Burroughs (New York: Modern Language Association of America, 2010), pp. 213–22, 215.
16. Emily H. Anderson, *Eighteenth-Century Authorship and the Play of Fiction: Novels and the Theatre, Haywood to Austen* (New York and London: Routledge, 2009), p. 4.
17. Paula R. Backscheider, Introduction, *Selected Fiction and Drama of Eliza Haywood* (Oxford University Press, 1999), p. xxi.
18. Nancy Armstrong, *Desire and Domestic Fiction: A Political History of the Novel* (Oxford University Press, 1987), p. 23.
19. Jane Spencer, *The Rise of the Woman Novelist: From Aphra Behn to Jane Austen* (Oxford: Basil Blackwell, 1986), p. 146.
20. Rosalie Colie, *The Resources of Kind: Genre-Theory in the Renaissance* (Berkeley: University of California Press, 1973), p. 30.
21. *The Galesia Trilogy and Selected Manuscript Poems of Jane Barker*, ed. Carol S. Wilson (Oxford University Press, 1997), p. 76. Subsequent references to this volume appear as *PWS*.
22. The quotation is from Constance Lacroix, "Wicked Traders, Deserving Peddlers, and Virtuous Smugglers: The Counter-Economy of Jane Barker's Jacobite Novel," *Eighteenth-Century Fiction*, 23.2 (Winter 2010–11), 269–94, 274. See also R. Swenson, "Representing Modernity in Jane Barker's Galesia Trilogy: Jacobite Allegory and the Patch-Work Aesthetic," *Studies in Eighteen-Century Culture* 34 (2005), 55–80.
23. Elizabeth Thomas, "On Sir J– S– saying in a Sarcastic Manner, My Books would make me Mad. An Ode," in *Eighteenth-Century Women Poets: An Oxford Anthology*, ed. Roger Lonsdale (Oxford University Press, 1989), p. 41.
24. Ralph Cohen, "Genre Theory, Literary History, and Historical Change," in *Theoretical Issues in Literary History*, ed. David Perkins (Cambridge, MA, and London: Harvard University Press, 1991), pp. 85–113, 85, 89, 90.

PART II
Genres, modes, and forms

6

DAVID E. SHUTTLETON

Poetry

Critical engagement with eighteenth-century women's poetry has undergone a seismic shift since the last decade of the twentieth century through a project of radical recovery and reassessment largely enacted by feminist literary historians, editors, critics, and biographers. Throughout most of the past century, the canon of eighteenth-century poetry was largely presented as entirely male: patrician, rigidly neoclassical, dominated by satire until the onset of a proto-romantic searching for sublimity. An exception was made for Anne Finch, Countess of Winchilsea (1661–1720), based on admiration for her *Nocturnal Reverie* expressed in William Wordsworth's "Essay Supplementary to the Preface" in his *Poetical Works* (1815). Miscast as a unique anticipation of a truly romantic poetic sensibility, Finch's *Reverie* came to serve as the sole representative of her substantial but otherwise neglected oeuvre; singled out as the exception that proved the rule that when apparently ill-equipped eighteenth-century women presumed to try their hand at poetry, the result was mere *verse*.

Such oversight stemmed from chauvinism but also reflected broader changes in taste; if one steps back to the mid-eighteenth century, one finds women poets being patriotically praised. An emergent female poetic canon evident in George Ballard's *Memoirs of Several Ladies of Great Britain who have been Celebrated for their Writings* (1752) and John Duncombe's versified *The Feminiad* (1754) was consolidated in Robert Shiels's five-volume *Lives of the Poets of Great Britain and Ireland* (1753) and George Colman and Bonnell Thornton's two-volume *Poems by Eminent Ladies* (1755), setting a trend for the editorial "collecting" of women poets that continued into the early-nineteenth century. Finch's flame was kept flickering by Matthew Arnold, Edmund Gosse, and, into the last century, by a passing nod from Virginia Woolf (1882–1941), but when discussed at all, eighteenth-century women were invariably cast with condescension as "minor poets." In sharp contrast, anyone aiming to offer an adequate survey of the field of eighteenth-century women's poetry today is confronted by an embarrassment of riches. Since the appearance of Roger Lonsdale's groundbreaking Oxford anthology in 1989, there have been significant developments in the availability of primary texts and scholarly biographical accounts of individual writers sustaining a sophisticated body of criticism.[1] As now made evident, women worked in virtually all available poetic kinds and genres from pastoral lyrics, ballads, and social satires to verse epistles and dialogues, elegies, verse fables, hymns, and narrative biblical adaptations. Their choice of forms was equally varied, embracing iambic heroic couplets, tetrameters, Pindarics, blank verse, ballad forms, and later the sonnet. The period is now perceived as pivotal in the development of women's poetry.

Despite limited or circumscribed educational opportunities, women of the educated ranks did gain access to literature, and it was not unusual for genteel women to read works in French and Italian. With the encouragement of more liberal-minded scholarly fathers or brothers, a limited number were able to learn Latin and Greek. Constantia Grierson (1704/5–32), an associate of Jonathan Swift, was proficient in Hebrew, Latin, Greek, and French, and she corrected her bookseller husband's editions of Terence and Tacitus for the press. Better known is Elizabeth Carter (1717–1806), who also wrote admired original poetry but was more celebrated for her translation of *Epictetus* (1758). Carter, a close friend of Samuel Johnson, became an influential role model of the "learned lady." For the less privileged, "the Ancients" were increasingly accessible through new English translations, notably by John Dryden, Samuel Garth, and Alexander Pope. Women were also engaging with an emerging canon of British "Moderns," dominated by Shakespeare, Milton, Dryden, and Pope and later James Thomson, William Collins, and Thomas Gray.

Many women were avid consumers and producers of poetry, discussing their reading with friends and circulating their own compositions in manuscript. Such practical interest penetrated virtually all social levels. As a household servant, Samuel Richardson's eponymous heroine Pamela is presented as precocious; nevertheless, such scenes in the novel as that where she recites her own "VERSES on my going away" imply an assumption that poetry plays a social role in ordinary life.[2] Poetry has never been a preserve of courts, but some relaxation of laws controlling the press, the rise of literary journalism, and the widening opportunities for making writing a profession provided by a burgeoning book market encouraged increasing numbers of women to commit their poetry to print. Many, like Carter, found an initial outlet in the periodical press, notably in Edward Cave's *The Gentleman's Magazine*, which from its foundation in 1731 regularly featured poetry by women.[3] Aristocrats such as Lady Mary Wortley Montagu (1689–1762), whose *Six Town Eclogues* appeared without her prior knowledge in 1746, tended to eschew commercial publication, but, as Isobel Grundy details, this was the age of Grub Street "piracy" when many manuscripts conveniently or inconveniently found their way into a bookseller's hands. Women who made their poetic aspirations public were undoubtedly at risk from prevailing social attitudes that tended to stigmatize those who presumed to trespass beyond their allotted domestic sphere – in this context. Phoebe Clinket, the caricature of a "mad poetess" in the Scriblerian drama *Three Hours After Marriage* (1717) is often cited – but the varied means of poetic circulation erode any overly polarized gendered model of public and private literary space. Private did not necessarily mean isolated when original poetry was being committed to commonplace books or personal letters that might then be shown and circulated within and beyond the immediate family circle. Publication in print took different forms: it could be anonymous, pseudonymous, or posthumous and might be achieved through a private transaction with a printer, by public subscription, or after wholesale purchase of the manuscript by a commercial bookseller (publisher). Finch's poetic career, which began in the previous century, exemplifies the porous boundary between a coterie culture of manuscript circulation and the public world of print. Finch's own awareness of the potential pitfalls in making this transition is evident from the opening lines of the versified introduction, *The Introduction*, she placed at the head of an early manuscript volume: "Did I, my lines intend for publick view, / How many censures, wou'd their faults persue."[4] Finch goes on to regret that modern women are not treated with the respect accorded their heroic biblical counterparts; however, by the time of her death in 1720, her poetry had drawn compliments from Pope and Swift, and she had seen her poem "A Song" ("Love, thou art best of human joys") set to music by Henry Purcell in 1694.

Women poets continued to run the risk of abuse from hostile social critics (male and female), the type of crude character assassination exemplified in Pope's offensive allusions to Elizabeth Thomas (1675–1731) as "Curll's Corinna" in *The Dunciad* of 1728 (Book 2, lines 65–66). Angered because Thomas sold some unflattering, youthful letters to notorious Grub Street publisher Edmund Curll, who then published them, Pope represented Thomas in grossly scatological terms. However, such representations, often rooted in a private slight, tended to abate by the 1730s with increasing numbers of genteel women being prepared to put their reputations at risk. The poetic careers of such figures as Jane Brereton (1685–1740), Mary Chandler (1687–1745), Mary Barber (c. 1685–1755), and Mary Jones (1707–78), which signal this growing confidence, tend to follow a similar trajectory from manuscript circulation to periodical submission or singly published poems followed by one or two collected volumes. For such women, poetry rarely amounted to a full-time profession but often formed part of a life devoted to literature that might embrace working in other genres: drama, prose fiction, moral essays, literary reviewing, memoirs, travel narratives, letter writing, conduct literature, children's books, and devotional texts.

A search for literary novelty prompted a fashion for promoting so-called peasant poets. A tradition of women poets born into the laboring poor is often traced back to 1739 with the publication of *The Woman's Labour. An Epistle to Mr. Stephen Duck*, by Mary Collier ('Now a WASHER-WOMAN at *Petersfield*') (1688?–1762), who offers a polite but assured riposte to Duck's blindness to the double burden of women who have to run households as well as work in the fields (Duck having just enjoyed some ultimately fleeting recognition at court as "The Thresher Poet"). Collier's poem went even further than Duck in overturning artificial pastoral conventions to present a self-conscious, socially realistic account of rural life. Collier is remembered for the one poem, but the more substantial corpus of Mary Leapor (1722–46), a gardener's daughter, which includes *Crumble-Hall* (written 1742; published 1751), her re-working of the country-house poem from an ironic, "below-stairs" perspective rewards attention. The mixed poetic fortunes of Hannah More's (1745–1833) gifted, but wayward protégée Ann Yearsley (1753–1806), whose pen name "Lactilla" registered her early life as a milkmaid and her Scottish counterpart, Janet Little (1759–1813), who elicited some practical support from Robert Burns, prompt important critical questions concerning authenticity of voice, literary agency, and the pressures of polite patronage.

Women from all social levels addressed a broad range of poetic themes, domestic, romantic, and polemical. A first wave of editors, responsive to an emergent field of women's literary studies, tended to foreground shorter poems concerned with purportedly "female" subjects – the quotidian, domestic, and local – or poems of complaint addressing inequitable marriage laws, sexual double standards, and educational disadvantages or scoffing at literary aspiration and other evidence of patriarchal oppression. Titles such as Sarah Egerton's (1670–1723) *The Emulation* (written 1703), which rails against the impositions of "tyrant Custom" on women such that "From the first dawn of life unto the grave, / Poor womankind's in every state a slave" were foregrounded for anticipating modern struggles for equality.[5] Poems debating marriage are more prevalent in the first decade of the century when the Revolution settlement of 1688–89 had intensified public debate over the validity of legal contracts, including those pertaining to marriage. As the author of *A Serious Proposal to the Ladies, for the Advancement of their True and Greatest Interest* (1694), the Anglican controversialist Mary Astell

(1666–1731) encouraged a debate over women's roles and education that long predates the first modern rights-based argument for radical reform at the very close of the century presented in Mary Wollstonecraft's (1759–97) *A Vindication of the Rights of Woman* (1792). Astell's essay *Reflections on Marriage* (1700) inspired her adherent Lady Mary Chudleigh (1656–1710) to write her own polemic in verse, *The Ladies Defence* (1701), in response to a recent sermon calling for the subordination of women. In turn, Chudleigh corresponded with the poet Elizabeth Thomas, whose witty satires against male presumptions were overshadowed by a prurient interest in her personal life.

But not all eighteenth-century women poets were proto-feminists, and those who might be so labeled occupied all positions on a contemporary political spectrum that may now seem alien. Anne Finch presents one such conundrum in as much as her proto-feminist statements belong within an otherwise deeply conservative political stance. Born Anne Kingsmill, the daughter of a Hampshire squire, she emerges from obscurity around 1682 when she was appointed a maid-of-honor to Mary of Modena, wife of the Duke of York, who became James II of England and Ireland (and also reigned as James VII of Scotland). As a conventionally pious royal servant, Finch kept her poetic interests largely private, though she shared them with another maid-of-honor, the short-lived Anne Killigrew (1660–85). Their poetic interests were enabled by the coterie culture surrounding Mary of Modena (1658–1718) based on a French tradition of *precieuses* (intellectual female aristocrats). Aspiring to a chaste model of religious devotion drawn from a continental convent tradition, this gynocentric milieu encouraged music, theatrics, and literature. Finch's place at court was consolidated by her marriage to Colonel Heneage Finch in 1684, which, as she celebrated in several poems, proved supportive. But their lives were thrown into disarray in the winter of 1688 when King James II fled into exile. Her husband suffered temporary arrest and Finch followed him into internal exile on the Kent estates of his nephew. Finch's life of rural retirement suited her scholarly temperament, although, as evident in such poems as *Ardelia to Melancholy* it may have exacerbated her constitutional tendency toward depression, a theme more fully explored in what has become her most discussed poem *The Spleen; a Pindaric Poem* (1701), in which the troubled poetic voice struggles to fathom the nature of this fashionable disease of the learned that might be equally associated with affectation, creativity, religious scepticism, and languor.

Finch's repudiations of fashionable London were no doubt sincere, but a pervasive celebration of the pleasures of retirement exemplified in her *Petition for an Absolute Retreat* can also be read as a sustained exercise in pastoral politics made more overt in the fifty-three post-1713 poems her husband carefully copied into what is now known as the Wellesley Manuscript volume. These poems include a number of verses with barely veiled crypto-Jacobite allusions that, more than Finch's gender, explain why the volume was held back from print.[6] Moreover, such self-explanatory titles as *Ardelia's Answer to Ephelia, who had invited her to come to town, reflecting on the coquetterie and detracting humour of the age* betray the fact that Finch's rustication was punctuated by trips to London and fashionable Tunbridge Wells. In 1712, on her husband's succeeding to the Earldom of Winchilsea, Finch relocated back to London, where, again in court favor, she became a maid to Queen Anne (1665–1714). Finch had already accrued considerable literary recognition for poems appearing in fashionable miscellanies. Pope included seven in his *Poems on Several Occasions* (1717), by which date she had published *Miscellany Poems ... Written by a Lady* (1713), the subtitle registering how the booksellers were starting to see a market advantage in advertising poetry as being the work of a woman.

The career of Elizabeth Singer Rowe (1674–1737) belongs more firmly in the eighteenth century, but, despite being one of the most respected poets of her generation, she confounds modern expectations. She is best known for her much reprinted prose work *Friendship in Death. In Twenty Letters from the Dead to the Living* (1728), but, as Sarah Prescott has demonstrated, it was her popular elegy *On the Death of Mr THOMAS ROWE* that sealed her image as the exemplary, pious widow such that her role as the respectable female poet far outstripped the amount of serious critical attention afforded her verse.[7] Rowe spent much of her life at Frome in her native Somerset, although her career does not conveniently conform to an image of the embattled, isolated female for she was supported by a literary network with metropolitan links.

Rowe began publishing poetry in the 1690s as a contributor to John Dunton's *Athenian Mercury*, for which she adopted the pseudonym "The Pindarick Lady"; by the first decade of the new century, her poems were included in prominent London miscellanies. Her "Athenian" poems, drawn together as *Poems on Several Occasions* (1696) under her other pseudonym "Philomela" ("the nightingale," a play on "Singer"), include some blatantly pro-Williamite verses reflecting Rowe's political allegiances as a nonconformist, allegiances that also informed her later eight-book biblical narrative poem *The History of Joseph* (1736). Isaac Watts, Rowe's dissenter associate, published her *Devout Exercises of the Heart* in 1737 and a posthumous edition of her poems, edited with prior consent by her brother-in-law, appeared in 1739. But while commended at the time, the appeal of Rowe's verse, particularly the ecstatic religious poetry composed after the death of her husband, can elude modern readers. Feminist critics initially recoiled at her apparently submissive persona or sought to interpret such passionate religiosity in Freudian terms as evidence of sexual repression. But it has since been observed how such approaches do not afford due attention to an established tradition of eroticized divine lyric verse, including Christian Pindarics, which draws largely on the Psalms (Canticles) within which Rowe's work was originally appreciated, not least by the next generation of women poets.

In elegiac verses *On the Death of Mrs. Elizabeth Rowe*, Carter writes on behalf of all "friends to virtue" to mourn her fellow poet as "our sex's ornament and pride" whose "chaste style" had served to direct female wits away from wanton romance and satire toward the higher themes of "virtue sacred and thy maker's praise."[8] For Carter, an overt contrast was with Pope, who, by the 1730s, had become a focus for admiration, emulation, and contestation. Mary Jones conveys something of his daunting presence when she fears that "Whilst Pope erects his laurelled head, / No lays like mine can live beneath his shade."[9] But somewhat ironically these lines appear at the opening of her *An Epistle to Lady Bower* (1750), in which Jones successfully adapts the breezily exasperated tone of the beleaguered Pope in his *Epistle to Arbuthnot* (1735) to enter into a mock dialogue with her own patroness over the social pitfalls of a woman who aspires to being respected as a poet. Pope shared in a prevalent cultural assumption that women should remain "ornamental," yet his own marginalized social position as a Roman Catholic combined with his compromised masculinity as a physically impaired invalid, his carefully orchestrated stance of distanced political retirement, and his apparent fascination with feminine concerns most evident in *The Rape of the Lock* (1714) and *An Epistle to a Lady, Of the Characters of Women* (1735), all drew attention from aspiring women poets. Lady Mary Wortley Montagu's withering riposte in *Verses Addressed to the Imitator of the First Satire of the Second Book of Horace* (1733), co-written with Lord Hervey, came out of a war of words after a spoiled friendship, whereas Anne Ingram's (1696–1764) *Epistle to Mr. Pope* (1736) is a measured, intellectually astute response to *The Characters of Women* that seeks to flatter and shame Pope into doing something positive toward enabling women to escape from the cultural trap by which they are simply encouraged to believe beauty is their sole source of power: "Bred to deceive even from their earliest youth; / Unused to books, nor virtue taught to prize; / Whose mind, a savage waste, unpeopled lies."[10]

For all his denunciations of Grub Street, Pope's success had been partly commercial and many women followed his example by turning to subscription publishing. Publishing by subscription involved an author's friends, family, patrons, and the general public being asked to pay for a proposed volume in advance either by word of mouth or through advertisements circulated as handbills or placed in newspapers (the list of subscribers would then appear at the front of the book). This method had a number of practical advantages: it avoided the potentially creative constrictions of being overly obliged to one particular patron and held out the potential to at least secure an advance on the costs of printing if not provide any immediate income. Subscriptions were also raised to secure a posthumous reputation. For example, following Leapor's premature death from measles in 1746, with the assistance of the friend and patron Bridget Freemantle (the "Artemisia" of the poems), her *Poems upon Several Occasions* appeared in 1748 bearing a subscription list of more than 600 names and, in accordance with the poet's dying wish, the profits went to support her aged father. Mary Barber's lines *To a Lady, who commanded me to send her an Account in verse, how I succeeded in my Subscription* imply that securing a subscription could be a taxing business, even prompting carping from other women: "Servilla cries 'I hate a wit; / Women should to their fate submit, / Should in the needle take delight; / 'Tis out of character to write.'"[11] Nevertheless, when Barber's *Poems on Several Occasions* appeared in 1734 they carried an impressive list of subscribers including John Arbuthnot, John Gay, and Pope alongside chief minister Sir Robert Walpole and many leading nobles. The printer was future novelist Samuel Richardson, who also subscribed.

Barber, the daughter of an English woolen draper settled in Dublin, was one of several literary women in the immediate circle of Swift, who, valuing her "poeticall Genius," made considerable practical efforts to further her career including writing letters of introduction to potential patrons when she visited England in 1730 and providing a prefatory letter of commendation for her 1734 volume.[12] Given the frequent charges of misogyny leveled against him, Swift may seem like an unlikely poetic role model but, as Louise Barnett details, his forging of a deliberately anti-romantic, self-deprecating poetic persona and his use of unaffected, colloquial, rhymed tetrameters to create a willfully "unpoetic" poetics provided Barber and other women with a useful model for developing an apparently deferential, yet pointed public voice.[13] Barber's subject matter is not confined to matters maternal. Nevertheless her lines *Written for my Son ... at his First Putting on Breeches*, in which she voices her infant's protestations against "tyrant Custom," the rite of passage from babyhood to boyhood requiring that he is imprisoned within the unhealthy constraints of tight-laced clothes, presents a rather unique perspective on the role of mothers in literally "shaping" their sons.[14] This said, it should be noted that Barber also wrote many poems on non-domestic subjects, including reflections on public philanthropy.

The struggle to gain the favor of a wealthy literary patron was a necessary evil, not least for a genteel woman with limited access to college, cloister, and debating chamber. The attendant humilities are imagined by Jones in her *Epistle to Lady Bower*, in which she rehearses the humiliations of seeking a patron when she has no friends at court:

> Well, but the joy to see my works in print!
> Myself too pictured in a mezzotint!
> The preface done, the dedication framed,
> With lies enough to make a lord ashamed!
> Thus I step forth, an Auth'ress in some sort;
> My patron's name? 'O choose some lord at court.
> One that has money which he does not use,
> One you may flatter much, that is, abuse.
> For if you're nice, and cannot change your note,
> Regardless of the trimmed, or untrimmed coat,
> Believe me, friend, you'll ne'er be worth a groat.'[15]

Jones's witty, ironic dialogue conveys a genuine sense of frustration but only represents one stage in her literary struggles. As the well-educated sister of an Oxford clergyman, she came to enjoy the friendship of a number of noblewomen, and, with Bower's support, her *Miscellanies in Prose and Verse* appeared in 1750 with a subscription carrying 1,400 names headed by the Princes Royal. We cannot rely on subscription lists as reliable evidence for ascertaining the readership for particular poets – ownership of a book being no guarantee that it was read – but they do at least give some indication of the social circles within which particular poets moved or had some degree of access.

Jones was not unique in finding support from a noblewoman. Rowe enjoyed a lasting supportive literary friendship with Frances Seymour, Countess of Hertford (1699–1754). In turn, Rowe introduced Hertford to Isaac Watts and James Thomson. It was no doubt through Rowe's westcountry dissenter circle that Hertford's attention was also drawn to Mary Chandler (1687–1745), who enjoyed some modest success with her poetic *Description of Bath* (1733), which offered a guide to the historic and social landmarks of the fashionable spa where Chandler ran a milliner's shop. Spa towns, with their bookshops, public assemblies, and local newspapers emerged as significant centers for poetic activity. Bath in particular became a particularly popular seasonal resort where, for the following generation, Lady Anna Miller (1741–81) provided an enabling forum for women poets at nearby Batheaston. If, unsurprisingly, many contributions to her much advertised poetry competitions were mediocre, they did create a favorable milieu for younger poets such as Anna Seward (1742–1809) discussed later. The Bluestockings, the most famous Georgian network of female intellectuals headed by Elizabeth Montagu (1718–1800), Elizabeth Vesey (1715–91), and Frances Boscawen (1719–1805) whose actual activities as patrons were long hidden behind clouds of condescension, are now recognized for their part in encouraging women such as Hannah More (1745–1833), who enjoyed considerable success not just as a poet but as a dramatist, essayist, and educationalist. More's two-part poem *The Bas Bleu, or, Conversation* (1786) highlights the elevated conversation found among the Bluestockings by painting acerbic vignettes of the social pretensions on display at lesser literary assemblies.

Frances Seymour had few ambitions to publish, though she did exchange original poems with Rowe and some inevitably found their way into print. *The Story of Inkle and Yarico* (1736, written earlier), based on "a most moving tale from the Spectator," became popular. It tells a tale of male betrayal: Inkle, a young man compelled to go to seek his fortunes at sea, is left stranded on an exotic island where, as the sole survivor of cannibals, he meets and falls in love with Yarico, a native girl. After being rescued by passing friends and landed at Bermuda, he cruelly sells his lover into slavery: "And now his mind, by sordid interest swayed, / Resolved to sell his faithful Indian maid."[16] As a sentimental critique of mercenary colonial values Hertford's poem – alongside an operatic and other stage adaptations by others – contributed to subsequent antislavery debates in which other women made poetic interventions. More's *Slavery, a Poem* (1788) and Yearsley's *Poem on the Inhumanity of the Slave-Trade* (1788) – the latter implying an identification with the oppression of African slaves on the part of a working-class Englishwoman – were followed by Anna Letitia Barbauld's (1743–1825) *Epistle to William Wilberforce, Esq. on the Rejection of the Bill for Abolishing the Slave Trade* (1791) supporting the leading parliamentary abolitionist.

Already by the 1770s the plight of slaves had joined those of orphans, distressed widows, jilted lovers, lunatics, caged birds, and departed pets as the focus for poems of pathos blatantly aimed at eliciting an immediate emotional response. The sentimental mode of much later eighteenth-century popular poetry proves problematic for modern readers unprepared to engage with the cultural codes that rendered it popular at the time. This challenge particularly applies to its characteristic promotion of a normative model of femininity based on traditionally feminine qualities of sympathy and empathy. The "cult of sensibility" lent cultural capital to "nervous" sensibility by drawing support from fashionable medical theories that posited an innate, physiological disposition toward a more delicate, discriminating taste. In *Sensibility. A Poetical Epistle to the Hon. Mrs Boscawen* (1782), More ponders this elusive, contested attribute that, as she implies, is as much to be known by what it *is not*, as what it is: "Thy subtle essence still eludes the chains / Of Definition, and defeats her pains."[17] As such, More's epistle bears useful comparison with Finch's earlier meditation on the spleen.

Modern cultural commentators remain divided over the extent to which the sentimental movement marked a feminization of the culture at large or merely served to circumscribe female agency by casting women as passive victims of their purportedly weaker constitutions. Certainly titles addressing the iniquities of the slave trade suggest that the poetry of sentiment, for all its often crude exploitation of contrived scenes of pathos, cannot be simply dismissed as solipsistic self-indulgence. Sentimentalism also brought in new attitudes toward animal welfare as evident in Barbauld's much-anthologized *The Mouse's Petition. Found in a trap where he had been confined all night by Dr. Priestley, for the sake of making experiments with different kinds of air* (1773), addressed to the natural philosopher who discovered "phlogiston" (oxygen). These verses, which bear comparison with Robert Burns's *To a Mouse* (1785) as an expression of a libertarian spirit crossing species boundaries, take on new interest in the context of eco-criticism.

Next to More and Barbauld, of the women poets active at the end of the century, Anna Seward (1742–1809) was among the most celebrated. Known nationally as the "Swan of Lichfield," Seward was widely respected as a poet, critical reviewer, salon hostess, musical patron, correspondent, and mentor to a number of younger poets including Walter Scott. In her youth, she received qualified literary encouragement from her father, a canon of Lichfield Cathedral, and from local physician-poet Erasmus Darwin. Seward initially found a readership for her poetry in *The Gentleman's Magazine*, in which, as a letter writer, she subsequently contributed to various literary debates. Her public exchanges with James Boswell over what she considered to be the overblown adulation afforded Johnson, who had been taught by her maternal grandfather, left her vulnerable to mockery by some London literati. Seward has too readily been cast as a parochial figure apparently out of touch with the literary and political mainstream seen as exclusively flowing out of London, ignoring the fact that she first drew widespread public attention for patriotic poems on national themes, including her *Elegy for Captain Cook*, which captured the public mood in 1780.

Seward's most commercially successful work, begun when she was nineteen, was *Louisa, A Poetical Novel in Four Epistles* (1784), which found wide appeal among readers already attuned to the sentimental fiction of Richardson, Laurence Sterne, Oliver Goldsmith, and Henry Mackenzie. This generic hybrid re-works themes from Rousseau's novel *Julie; ou, La nouvelle Heloïse* (1761) and Pope's *Eloisa to Abelard* (1717) through a poetic lens tinted by Milton and Matthew Prior. According to her preface, Seward sought to "unite the impassion'd fondness of POPE's ELOISA, with the chaster tenderness of Prior's EMMA; avoiding the voluptuousness of the first and the too conceding softness of the second."[18] *Louisa* had no obvious imitators but stands as a register of popular taste on the very cusp of Romanticism while illustrating how a poet, whose critical values were essentially conservative, was not afraid to experiment with genre.

Seward's affective life, as reflected in a significant number of her poems, was dominated by an intense attachment to her foster sister Honora Sneyd (1751–80). When Honora left the Seward household to marry in 1773, Anne fell into a disturbed state of emotional loss. *To Honora Sneyd* suggests an intense response to being left behind by her beloved friend: fearfully anticipating a "cruel time" when mere "cold respect" might come to replace the "love-warm looks in which I live," Seward declares how she "could not learn my struggling heart to tear / From thy loved form, that through my memory strays."[19] Such expressions of same-sex love are not uncommon within a tradition of female friendship poetry, which often acknowledges the example set by the seventeenth-century poet Katherine Philips (1632–1664), but the particular intensity of the Sneyd poems has invited "queer" readings. Speculation over Seward's sexuality has also been fed by her verses on *Llangollen Vale* (1796), prompted by a visit to Lady Eleanor Butler (1739–1829) and Sarah Ponsonby (1755–1831), the "Ladies of Llangollen," who famously lived together in a domestic partnership. The first half of *Llangollen Vale*, which gives an historical picture of the landscape around Llangollen as the once bloodstained scene of border warfare between the English and the Cambrians (Welsh) suggests the influence of Thomas Gray's *The Bard* (written 1755–57) and the ensuing fashion for a romantic engagement with British Gothic themes. Set against this violent heroic, masculine backcloth, the home of the virtuous *Ladies of Llangollen* is portrayed as a modern oasis of female domestic harmony and studious virtue.

By the 1790s, Seward's self-consciously high literary language and her pervasive use of personifications were starting to sound dated when set against the more spontaneous voices of the first generation of Romantics. Her contemporary Charlotte Smith (1749–1806) played a more lasting role as a formal innovator. At the start of the eighteenth century, the sonnet form, which had enjoyed such success a century earlier, had fallen out of favor. In his *Dictionary*, Johnson had considered it "not very suitable for the English language," but interest was revived with the first appearance of Smith's *Elegiac Sonnets* in 1784, which, though long overlooked, are now recognized as a crucial prompt for the development of the Romantic ode. Both William Wordsworth and Samuel Taylor Coleridge acknowledged Smith's achievement, with the latter remarking that her "Sonnets appear to me the most exquisite, in which moral Sentiments, Affections, or Feelings, are deduced from, those associated with, the scenery of Nature."[20] Representing a gradual movement away from an aesthetic of sensibility to a fully fledged Romanticism, the melancholic tone of Smith's sonnets was as much an outcome of her troubled personal story as a carefully crafted literary persona. Married off at fifteen to a feckless, abusive, unfaithful man with whom she had a dozen children of whom nine survived infancy, Smith had been forced to turn to publishing when her husband was imprisoned for debt in 1783. She self-consciously presents *The Sonnets* as a plea for sympathy for a woman in distress, but recent readings by scholars such as Jacqueline Labbe emphasize subtle elements of social critique.

Smith's *Elegiac Sonnets* were reprinted (it was in its ninth edition by 1800), but she gained most money as the author of a run of accomplished, popular novels starting with *Emmeline* in 1788 and including *The Old Manor House* (1793). The liberal politics evident in these works of fiction also informs two important longer poems: *The Emigrants* (1793), written in blank verse, in which Smith identifies with the plight of those fleeing the Revolutionary terrors of France, and her posthumously published loco-descriptive poem *Beachy Head* (1807). The latter in particular displays Smith's exquisite, scientifically informed eye for geological, botanical, and other natural phenomena and now occupies its rightful place in the Romantic canon.

More broadly, eighteenth-century poetry by women is starting to be integrated into general period anthologies, and it becomes increasingly possible to access longer poems such as Finch's *The Spleen*, More's *Sensibility*, and Smith's *Beachy Head*, once only represented by extracts, in their entirety. In some respects, such editorial recovery and regrouping take us back to the more heterodox contexts within which this poetry was originally encountered, not only in magazines and miscellanies but even in purportedly single-authored volumes in which poetry often appeared "cheek-by-jowl" with other genres. For example, Finch's *Miscellany Poems on Several Occasions* (1713) is not untypical in also including a play text, her unacted tragedy "Aristomenes." More's *Sensibility* originally formed the conclusion to her *Sacred Dramas: chiefly intended for young persons: the subjects taken from the Bible* (1782). Many of the later poems of Jane Barker (1652–1732) first appeared in the context of *A Patch-Work Screen for the Ladies* (1723), a hybrid volume that employs the conversations of her literary persona Galesia to link together works of prose fiction, moral essays, favorite recipes, and poetry. Barker's work is an extreme case, but the mixing of genres and even contributors was not uncommon; the octavo edition of Barber's *Poems* (1734) includes a poem by her son Constantine, one by her deceased friend Grierson, and another by Rowe. When considered alongside the complex social affiliations linking many of the poets discussed, such bibliographical samplings serve to remind us not only of the engaging wealth of poetry being generated by women in this era but also to alert us to what is lost when we disregard the multiple contexts of its original composition, distribution, and reception.

NOTES

1. *Eighteenth-Century Women Poets*, ed. Roger Lonsdale (Oxford University Press, 1989).
2. Samuel Richardson, *Pamela; or Virtue Rewarded*, ed. Thomas Keymer (Oxford University Press, 2001), pp. 89–91.
3. These poetic contributions are now searchable. See *The Poetry of the 'Gentleman's Magazine', 1731–1800: An Electronic Database of Titles, Authors, and First Lines*, ed. Emily Lorraine de Montluzin, available at gmpoetrydatabase.org.
4. *British Women Poets of the Long Eighteenth Century*, ed. Paula R. Backscheider and Catherine E. Ingrassia (Baltimore: The John Hopkins University Press, 2009), p. 800, lines 1–2.
5. Lonsdale, *Eighteenth-Century Women Poets*, p. 31, lines 3–4.
6. "Petition ..." in *Anne Finch, Countess of Winchilsea, Selected Poems*, ed. Denys Thomson (Manchester: Carcanet, 1987), pp. 53–61. *The Anne Finch Wellesley Manuscript Poems*, ed. Barbara McGovern and Charles H. Hinnant (Athens: University of Georgia Press, 1998).
7. Sarah Prescott, "Elizabeth Singer Rowe (1674–1737): Politics, Passion and Piety," in *Women and Poetry 1660–1750*, ed. Sarah Prescott and David E. Shuttleton (Basingstoke: Palgrave-Macmillan, 2003), pp. 71–78.
8. Lonsdale, *Eighteenth-Century Women Poets*, p. 167, lines 4, 8, 14, 20.
9. Lonsdale, *Eighteenth-Century Women Poets*, p. 157, lines 9–10.
10. Lonsdale, *Eighteenth-Century Women Poets*, p. 151, lines 38–40.
11. Lonsdale, *Eighteenth-Century Women Poets*, p. 127, lines 11–14.
12. *Poems on Several Occasions. By Mrs. Barber. To which is prefix'd, a recommendatory letter from the Revd Dr. Swift, Dean of St. Patrick's, to the Right Honourable the Earl of Orrery* (London and Bath, 1736), p. vi.
13. Louise Barnett, *Jonathan Swift in the Company of Women* (Oxford University Press, 2007).

14. Lonsdale, *Eighteenth-Century Women Poets*, p. 84, line 3.
15. Lonsdale, *Eighteenth-Century Women Poets*, p. 157, lines 29–39.
16. Lonsdale, *Eighteenth-Century Women Poets*, pp. 106–9, lines 83–84.
17. Lonsdale, *Eighteenth-Century Women Poets*, pp. 328–29, lines 5–6.
18. Anna Seward, *Louisa, A Poetical Novel in Four Epistles* (Lichfield: 1784), p. [v].
19. Lonsdale, *Eighteenth-Century Women Poets*, p. 313, lines 1, 5, 4, 11–12.
20. Samuel Taylor Coleridge, *Poetical Works*, ed. Ernest H. Coleridge (London: 1912), Vol. 2, p. 1139.

7

FELICITY NUSSBAUM

Drama

> But you your Sex's Champion are come forth,
> To fight their Quarrel, and assert their Worth.
> Our *Salique* Law of Wit you have destroy'd,
> Establish'd Female claim, and triumph'd o'er our Pride.
> "To the Ingenious Author, on her Tragedy, called *Fatal Friendship*"
> (1698), by an unknown hand

In the "New Commonplace Book," Hester Thrale Piozzi (1741–1821), an avid fan of the theater and herself an aspiring playwright, chats about her admiration for Joanna Baillie's (1762–1851) late eighteenth-century tragedies *Count Basil* and *DeMonfort*, along with the scholarly preface that introduces *Plays on the Passions* (1798). Like many readers, Thrale Piozzi had assumed that the author was a man until Baillie revealed her identity:

> I remember a Knot of Literary characters met at Miss [Harriet] Lee's House in Bath deciding – contrary to *my* Judgment, – that a Learned Man must needs have been the Author, and I – chiefly to put the company in Good humour – maintained that it was a *Woman*. Merely said I because both her Heroines are *Damespassées*: and a *Man* has no Notion of mentioning a Female after she is five & Twenty.
>
> What a Goose Joanna must have been ever to reveal her sex & Name!! Spite and Malice have pursued her ever since, & if she had of a Mind of Gigantic Mold, must have crushed her quite ... I never knew a Writer so ill used ... & *such* a Writer! Why she is a Zebra devour'd by African Ants, – The Termites Bellocosi. If ever I get into the living World again, I will try to be acquainted with her – Though a Soul so *sublime* & at the same Time so *Vulgar* must make a disagreeable Companion – *except on a Shelf* – What lofty Sentiments! ... Pathetic in the Extreme! – Oh brave Joanna!
>
> Never so sure our Passion to create.
> As when She touch'd the Brink of all we hate.[1]

At the turn into the nineteenth century, according to Thrale, a female playwright who dared to tackle difficult psychological issues, and who incorporated every "*grossièreté*, every ludicrous Meanness," required extraordinary courage. Unlike George, Lord Byron, who famously praised the

Scotswoman Baillie for seeming to borrow the "testicles" necessary to be "our only dramatist since [Thomas] Otway & [Thomas] Southerne," Thrale is thrilled to discover the playwright's sex but alarmed at the potential repercussions redounding to her sister author.

The production of Baillie's *De Monfort* at Drury Lane in 1800 had starred Thrale's dear friend Sarah Siddons (1755–1831) as the tragic Jane DeMonfort, and like Thrale, the actress, heroine, and playwright were all *damespassées*, or women well beyond middle age. Thrale expresses mixed sympathies for Baillie: though she believes that her testy personality would not meld easily into her social circle, she marvels at her extraordinary mind. In addition, Thrale's allusion to Alexander Pope's *Epistle to Lady* (1735) recalls not only the subject matter of Baillie's tragedy, the passion of hatred, but also the vulnerability of women playwrights to the sentiments expressed in the classic misogynist satires. Referring to Calypso in Pope's satire on women, Thrale suggests that Joanna Baillie, like Odysseus's temptress, aroused men's powerful emotions only to drive them to their peril. Baillie's brilliance, in other words, inspired men's respect because she did *not* write like a woman, but venturing into such arenas also meant that the playwright braved men's bellicose condemnation.

Women who wrote for the stage from 1660 to 1780, the years under consideration here, earned the extremes of praise and censure. They ranged in reputation from the infamously licentious Aphra Behn (1640?–89) to the very proper Hannah More (1745–1833), from the rebellious transvestite Charlotte Charke (1713–60) to the diffident Frances Burney (1752–1840). According to theater historian Robert Hume, twelve women staged plays in London during the first half of the century, and twenty women successfully mounted plays from 1750 to 1800;[2] but this accounting does not include the many female playwrights who wrote closet dramas or mounted private theatricals or whose plays failed to reach the stage for other reasons. Restoration and eighteenth-century women wrote plays to claim a public profile and to express their ideas, but most wrote primarily for economic reasons. If a play managed to have a successful run, writing for the eighteenth-century stage could prove much more lucrative than publishing in other genres.

As writers, performers, and patrons of dramatic texts, women played a crucial role in the development of the theatrical tradition from the Restoration period and throughout the eighteenth century. Coming to the British stage for the first time in 1660, actresses inspired dramatists to create substantial parts for them. Previously confined to private performances, women players joined the dissenting prophets and petitioning wives who opened public spaces during the Civil War. They also threw open the doors of the theater to women playwrights, although some scholars have argued that demanding actors and managers exerted considerable pressure on these early pioneers to conform to cultural expectations. Establishing literary and publishing networks, women's increasing practice of playwriting extended to London, Dublin, and Edinburgh, as well as the provincial theaters. While women playwrights often shared aesthetic assumptions with their more prolific male colleagues, an evolving female dramatic tradition energized them to imitate popular forms, translate earlier plays, adapt men's interpretations while avoiding charges of plagiarism, and experiment more broadly. In a world that alternately regarded women as both ideal and corrupt, female playwrights shared the experience of being economically and politically marginalized along with women players, patrons, and spectators; these connections, however subtly realized, have not yet been sufficiently emphasized.

As scholars and critics in the twenty-first century, we have, of course, moved beyond employing mere identity politics or relying on the simple binaries of resistance and complicity; we now seek a more thoroughgoing inclusion of women dramatists in the history of the British theater. Jacqueline Labbe's observation that "tracing the history of British *women's* writing open[s] up new avenues for questioning the received wisdom about British *men's* writing" may be extended to include women's playwriting.[3] This chapter draws on the continuities among female dramatists, not because that is the only valid approach, but because doing so allows women writers to be more fully integrated into the full richness of stage and theater history. "Woman" remains a powerful and viable category of analysis, not least because its meaning is never fixed but continues to shift throughout history, and so it depends for its definition on intersections with other social and economic categories. As Dympna Callaghan notes, " 'Woman' is never an already accomplished, cold, hard, self-evident fact or category, but always a malleable cultural idea as well as a lived reality ... *that always already has a history.*"[4]

Tragedy

The Tragedy of Mariam, published in 1613, was the first original tragedy written by an Englishwoman – Elizabeth Tanfield Cary. Although actresses had forged the way a decade earlier, the first woman's play performed in a theater was not until 1669 with the King's Company performance of Frances Boothby's *Marcelia*.[5] By far the most prominent Restoration period female dramatist was Aphra Behn, who wrote at least eighteen plays – including *Sir Patient Fancy* (1678), *Feign'd Courtesans* (1679),

The Widow Ranter (1789), and *The Rover* (1677) – without the benefit of a female dramatic tradition to rely on. Misty Anderson has neatly summarized the contradictory nature of Behn's importance: "She became both the standard of theatrical accomplishment and of moral depravity against which future women playwrights were judged."[6] In her preface "To the Reader" introducing *Sir Patient Fancy*, Behn offers special pleading for her sex and defends her bawdy language in recognition of her uneasy position as the first woman dramatist of note: "The Play had no other Misfortune but that of coming out for a Woman's: had it been owned by a Man, though the most Dull, Unthinking, Rascally Scribbler in Town, it had been a most admirable Play."[7] A woman's sexual reputation was, inevitably, closely aligned with her literary one.

Delarivier Manley (c. 1670–1724) in her preface to *The Lost Lover* (1696) shares the perception that women playwrights bear a special burden: "After all, I think my Treatment much severer than I deserved. The bare Name of being a Woman's Play damn'd it beyond its own want of Merit."[8] Following Aphra Behn's lead, however, women dramatists inspired satirical responses in staging five new plays from 1695 to 1696, including most prominently the anonymous play *Female Wits* (1696) featuring Catharine Trotter (1674?–1749), Mary Pix (c. 1666–1709), and Manley. The activity of women playwrights ebbed and flowed from the flourishing 1670–1717 period, followed by the years 1717–50, dominated by Susanna Centlivre (1669?–1723), leading to a slow accelerating rise when theatricality became fashionable in the late 1770s, and finally tapering off after Baillie's turn-of-the century triumphs. Women writing after 1737, restricted to two patent theaters and subject to the Lord Chamberlain's censoring hand, found means to draw parallels to contemporary political events in their plays; they withstood and sometimes defied the often domineering force of theater managers. Dramatists such as Behn, Manley, Centlivre, and Hannah Cowley (1743–1809) signaled a change in the way that women regarded themselves as writers: they were capable of attracting an audience, and brave enough to express their ideas in a public, scandal-ridden forum.

From their first forays into the theater, women playwrights aroused strong, contradictory reactions among spectators. In an early example, Trotter anticipates not only Joanna Baillie's fascination with her protagonist's hatred in *DeMonfort*, but she, like Baillie, employs the passions as powerful dramatic themes ("anger and love, pity and jealousy").[9] Trotter included frequent soliloquies that set these affective oppositions in motion and explored the interiority of her characters. For example, in *Agnes de Castro* (1696), a tragedy based on Aphra Behn's story of female friendship, Alvaro despises yet desires the eponymous heroine who is more virtuous than her namesake:

> I love, and hate her, both with Violence,
> And both the Passions equally wou'd please,
> T'enjoy her were for Love a happy Fate,
> But 'tis the Rape, wou'd satisfy my Hate.[10]

While some readers have found that Trotter eschews eroticism and unfailingly urges moral reform, her language and characters are often sensual, if not sexy. Further, she prefigures Gothic themes with hints of madness, mayhem, and incest. *Fatal Friendship* (1698), dedicated to Queen Anne, features show-stopping repartée between clever women whose reasoned discourse serves as a spirited antidote to the tyranny of domineering fathers and brothers. Their wit gives them a means to counter the political and domestic disarray that erupts because of men's failure to control their desires. *Fatal Friendship*, her most popular play – performed with an all-star cast of Thomas Betterton, Ned Kynaston, Elizabeth Barry, and Anne Bracegirdle – counters their arbitrary authority with women's life-affirming relationships in Trotter's brilliant vehicle.

In the blank verse tragedy, the central character Bellgard insists on marrying his sister Felicia to Count Roquelaure, whose younger son Gramont, played by Betterton, has already secretly married her and fathered a son. Bellgard's aim is to protect Felicia from poverty, though it becomes clear that she values love far more than fortune. Gramont rationalizes his bigamous marriage to Lamira, a rich widow, thus betraying both his wife and Castalio who loves Lamira himself. Married to the same man, Lamira and Felicia powerfully debate the morality of the choices available to them, while Gramont simply bemoans his unfortunate fate. Ready to kill Gramont, Bellgard asserts, "Honour gives different laws to different sexes, / Mine says this sword alone can do me justice" (Act 5.1). Gramont accidentally kills his dear friend Castalio; regretting his rash actions, he commits suicide: "Oh, what a wretch was I, that could not wait / Heaven's time, the providence that never fails / Those who dare to trust it" (Act 5.1). Danger, Trotter suggests, lurks in failing to recognize human frailty in the face of cosmic forces, but it falls to women to set things right.

In Trotter's memorable rendering, male friendship is fatal in the double sense of being both predestined and deadly. Though Felicia falls in despair on Gramont's dead body, the two blameless women characters survive, bound by a not-so-fatal friendship, and reconciled within the "vicissitude of miseries" (Act 5.1) that surround them. Although Lamira retreats to a convent, and Felicia submits to the protection of the Count, the two women presciently lament the "false pretences of designing men" (Act 1.2 and Act 4.2); in the comic epilogue, Lamira taunts male spectators into behaving differently from the reprehensible men in the play.

Similarly, in Delarivier Manley's *The Royal Mischief* (1696), Bassima (Anne Bracegirdle) protests the ways in which her suffering is the requisite condition for reforming masculine authority gone awry;[11] but the central character, Princess Homais (played by Elizabeth Barry), a "prey to passion" (Act 2.1), is a ruthless enchantress who destroys all in her path in spite of being held captive to her husband. Married to an impotent aged prince who recognizes her exquisite qualities but abhorrent faults, Homais takes up with his nephew, Levan, the Prince of Colchis, after tiring of the libertine Ismael, an Iago-like character. Homais acts as an imperial force in seeking incestuous regions of love. For Homais, the war hero Levan is her "tool to hew ambition" (Act 5.1), and resistance increases her desire to conquer: "How lawless is a woman's love, / The swelling current will admit no bounds" (Act 1.1). If Trotter was cautious about eroticism in her plays, Manley leaps into the fray in steamy Orientalized scenes teeming with raw sexual desire and including mutes, bowstring, veil, and jewels, as well as candle-lit processions, a dumb-show, music, and an exotic "dance of Indians." Homais's eunuch Acmat describes her lust: "How often have I seen this lovely Venus, / Naked, extended in the gaudy bed, / Her snowy breast all panting with desire, / With gazing, melting eyes" (Act 2.1).

Although some have located *The Royal Mischief* in the developing tradition of she-tragedies, the plot does not really fit the pattern of tainted femininity. Bassima, pursued by her captor Osman/Betterton, remains virtuous even until death. In the complicated murderous subplot, Homais and the single-mindedly chaste Bassima contrast as the "two extremes / So foul and yet so fair" (Act 5.1). Featuring spectators within the play who eavesdrop on various intrigues, in *The Royal Mischief* the theater audience too "overhears" plotting that brings about the disastrous ending. Bassima's rejection of the effeminate whiner Osman at first merely confuses him: the rhythms of blank verse desert him as he woos the unwilling Bassima while his wife Selima (sister of the impotent ruler) watches, aghast, from the wings: "So true a love, so innocent a flame, / A heat which, scorned by you, / Disdains its native seat, / Loathes the anxiety it finds within." The consequences of Osman's adulterous passion finally lead to his being shot from a cannon as his gory body splatters into a thousand pieces. Homais, alternately shackled and unshackled by her husband, dies attempting to strangle her lover, and Bassima expires after an appeal to heaven. In Manley's tragedy, women's desire for political and state authority, and the extreme passions that accompany such ambitions, are displaced into the domestic domain: "Survey the globe, choose where our eyes would reign" (Act 1.1). The searing force of a woman's gaze may topple kingdoms, as well as men's hearts.

The Royal Mischief hints at parallels between the lives of playwright and actress, for Manley herself had been seduced into a bigamous marriage and impregnated in her early teenage years. Actresses Barry (whose lover was the rakish Lord Rochester) and Bracegirdle again face off in this play to contrast virtuous and corrupt femininity: both die, but they take the male leads down with them, leaving only a sorry set of male hangers-on – the flaccid Prince of Libardian, the libertine Ismael, and the eunuch Acmat – to lament the horror. The conclusion to *The Royal Mischief* implies that rigidly determinate gender roles only exacerbate women's wish to control their own destinies, while cultural restrictions produce men who become mere caricatures. Enforcing such stereotypes results in a tragic world filled with political and domestic disorder.

Other female playwrights also turned to Oriental themes to explore women's positioning within divine right and patriarchal authority and their imperiling the state during political crises. In Aphra Behn's *Abdelazer* (1676), the passionate Queen Isabella, Queen of Spain, is obsessed with the eponymous Moor, both infidel and invader, who is a sexual, religious, and racial threat to the state and to royal succession. Isabella had earlier coupled with the Cardinal to father the apparent heir to the throne, Ferdinand. Her unconstrained passion, "her black offense," threatens to contaminate Spain.[12] Abdelazer, attempting to reestablish Moorish rule over Spain, kills his rival Ferdinand, and Isabella murders Abdelazer's loyal wife, Florella. After attempting to rape Isabella's daughter Leonora (played by Elizabeth Barry), Abdelazer is stabbed to death, and Spain is freed from the Moorish threat. In spite of the jeopardy to the state that Isabella represents in the play, the sprightly epilogue asserts women's rights, thus highlighting the disparity between the themes of the tragedy and the enthralling actress, Bracegirdle, who speaks the lines to embody women's dual capacity to bewitch and to kill.

Manley's tragedy *Almyna; or, The Arabian Vow* (1707) draws explicitly on *The Arabian Nights*' frame tale and the despotic ruling brothers Schahriar and Schahzenan, who recall recent parallels in the reigns of James Stuart and Charles. The ambitious but chaste Almyna (Barry) seductively convinces Caliph Almanzar, the Moorish conqueror of Spain, that in addition to possessing beautiful bodies (stunningly displayed in the star actresses), women have souls. Almyna is a heroic woman, sharing Scheherazade's characteristic "courage, wit, and penetration infinitely above her sex."[13] She persuades the Caliph that he should not execute his wives as she eventually transforms him from being a misogynist. Her sister Zoradia (Bracegirdle) patriotically frees Abdallah from his Arabian vow to marry her so that the Sultan will stop murdering his brides. At the same time, the language is lushly sexual: "When still aside the King of Tartary / He found the Eastern Empress, all undrest, / Supinely laid, upon a Bed of Flowers, / Her flowing robes, no longer veiled her charms! / But all the bright Adultress, stood Confest! / Enjoying, and enjoy'd by a vile Moorish Slave" (Act 1.1). Still, Zoradia dies a virgin, insisting that she had been terribly wronged. *The Arabian Nights* in its eighteenth-century French and English translations intermixes East with West, and Manley's tragedy similarly blends Eastern exotica with a critique of divine right theory and a demand for better treatment of women. In the concluding epilogue, Almanzor/Betterton reinforces his metamorphosis with appeals to the female spectators to join Almyna in enslaving the despotic sultan. Like her clever heroine, Manley seeks political sway under the guise of sexual manipulation, a common pattern in the period's fiction as Ros Ballaster details.[14]

After the 1737 Licensing Act that mandated the Lord Chamberlain's censorship and limited productions to Drury Lane and Covent Garden, theater managers preferred Shakespeare and adaptations of Voltaire's Oriental tragedies to problematic new plays, although Susanna Centlivre's popular mid-century comedies were an exception. Women wrote few new tragedies from this point until the end of the century, but Frances Brooke (1724–89), drawing on the tradition of woman-centered Oriental tragedy, forwarded *The Siege of Sinope* (1781) as a vehicle for Mary Ann Yates (1728–87), her close friend and a renowned tragedienne who performed more than ninety parts during her remarkable career. In the preface to the play, Brooke praises Yates's "astonishing exertion" in combining manly wisdom with womanly sweetness in the starring role.[15] The pair ranks among the very few female managers, and together with their husbands they oversaw the King's Theatre, Haymarket (1773–78).

In contrast to the earlier tragedies, *The Siege of Sinope* features an ambitious heroine who acts as a potent force in promoting familial, conjugal, and national reconciliation. Unlike the English adaptations of Voltaire's *Zaïre*, *Sémiramis*, and *Les Scythes*, in which the valiant but fallible tragic heroines perish only to be resurrected in the epilogue, in Brooke's play Queen Thamyris/ Yates survives to restore domestic calm and imperial peace. (Similarly hoping that Yates might take a starring role to ensure commercial success, Charlotte Lennox had offered Garrick an adaptation of Racine's *Bajazet* [1672].) The indomitable Thamyris/Yates, like other Oriental queens, sparks discord in marrying an outsider but then negotiates an internecine dispute between the Anatolian regions, Cappadocia and Pontus. She questions whether her private desires should be forfeited to fulfill her public duty to the adopted alien region. Tragically torn by her loyalty to her misogynous father and conjugal family, Thamyris retracts her selfless vow to kill her son to prevent his being made captive of the enemy Cappadocians. But in contrast to other earlier Oriental tragedies, in the sentimental conclusion the father is sacrificed instead of the daughter. Rather than being disinherited or banished, the uncompromising Thamyris takes up a sword to defeat the evil Romans and defend the tomb where she has secreted her child.

Brooke thus asserts the possibility of women's meaningful patriotic action in saving the nation through her heroine's brave interventions in men's political affairs. Brooke's noteworthy preface thanks Covent Garden manager Thomas Harris for surmounting "the shafts of undistinguishing ridicule" directed at the genre of tragedy, and for removing "the dragons which have been supposed to guard the avenues to the theatre" from the female pen. Prominent among the "dragons" was David Garrick, whom Brooke boldly chastised in her novel *The Excursion* (1777) for blocking the path to producing her earlier tragedy *Virginia*. Both prologue and epilogue similarly urge women spectators to emulate the female author and, by implication, to forward her message: "Assert yourselves, ye fair! This chosen right, / And prove your powers to judge as well as write." In the epilogue, the speaker Thamyris/Yates mischievously contrasts the national treasure represented in women dramatists and actresses with the public persona of politician Charles James Fox, who delivered parliamentary orations favoring individual liberty, but in private life was a notorious gambler. In contrast, Brooke, contesting reigning attitudes toward women dramatists, insists on their virtue.

Perhaps the finest later eighteenth-century tragedy written by a woman is Hannah More's very successful tragedy *Percy* (1778), which similarly questions the moral necessity of a daughter's duty to her father. Dedicated to Earl Percy and successfully revived in 1818, the play is bookended by friend David Garrick's prologue and epilogue. Set near the end of the Crusades, it is part of a cluster of medieval tragedies including Robert Jephson's *Count of Narbonne* (1781) and Baillie's *DeMonfort* (1800). The distressed heroine reluctantly agrees to marry her father's choice, Douglas, Earl Raby, after his feud with her beloved Percy. The anguished Elwina explains her decision as dutiful acceptance of the inevitable:

> My barbarous father forc'd me to dissolve
> The tender vows himself had bid me form –
> He dragg'd me trembling, dying, to the altar,
> I sigh'd, I struggled, fainted, and – complied.[16]

Elwina's father coldly questions how she dares to claim purity because "her alien heart doats on another," and she confesses to Percy that loving him is "a fearful deed, / A deed of wild despair, a deed of horror" (Act 3.1). Capturing Percy and discovering that he wears Elwina's scarf, a fatal talisman, Douglas violently accuses her of being a "polluted woman." Refusing to dishonor her father by acknowledging her love for Percy, the crazed Elwina transforms the scarf into a winding sheet and poisons herself. Finally, Douglas murders Percy in a jealous rage before committing suicide.

The focus here has been on tragedies, largely because women's contributions to the genre are so often neglected in favor of their more accessible comedies, but the tragedies too are worthy of consideration because they center on strong, vulnerable women entangled in classic conflicts between love and honor. Like the heroines of eighteenth-century novels, they are caught between personal and public loyalties. Because the tragic denouements predictably bring death to women who question the arbitrary authority of powerful men, one could argue that the suffering women are victims; nevertheless, the tragic conclusions are most often life affirming in commending their heroic struggles. Finally, the comic epilogues appended to the serious plays, most often spoken by the celebrity actresses featured as the play's heroines, create significant tension with the tragedies they follow. The epilogues assert the bonds among women – actresses, playwrights, and spectators – in exercising their right to free themselves from social restraints. Eighteenth-century tragedy is a genre in which the actresses who play these heroines embody the contradictions that most women faced: they represent not only "the brink of all we hate" but also the heroism of the playwrights who create them.

Comedy and romance

Women playwrights frequently liberate and empower their comic female characters through disguise at home in a performative world that resembles the theater itself, the idyllic topsy-turvy world of masquerade. Aphra Behn's *The Rover, or The Banished Cavaliers* (1677), based in part on Thomas Killigrew's *Thomaso* (1654), is still among the most frequently performed Restoration and eighteenth-century plays by women. Positioned somewhere between tragedy and comedy, *The Rover* takes serious subjects – rape, libertinism, prostitution – to an extreme before turning them toward a comic conclusion, and the sequel entertains still darker themes. Behn introduces the madcap spirit of carnival during which the defiant whores Angellica Bianca and Lucetta exert sexual power over the men on whom they prey. The eponymous rover is Willmore, the devil-may-care libertine, but equally Hellena, first disguised as a gypsy who thieves and roams outside the law and later cross-dresses. In a bawdy double entendre, Hellena teases Willmore with her intent to pick his pocket, "which will more vex your English humour, than an Italian fortune will please you." She mocks his plan to part with "things of more value" but ultimately demurs: "Indeed no, that's the business of a witch, and I am but a gipsy yet" (Act 1.2).

Like Willmore and Hellena, Angellica dares to travel a meandering path. Often taken to be a proxy for Behn herself, she knows her own worth and claims to be immune to love; experiencing an "ague of her soul," she proves to be poignantly vulnerable and prefigures the sympathetic prostitute Millwood in George Lillo's mid-century domestic tragedy *The London Merchant* (1731). In the play, disguises, jewels, and literal signage stand in for individuals and threaten to deprive women of their personhood. The sign advertising Angellica is literally the whore's sign, and perhaps that of Behn herself; as various critics have pointed out, Aphra Behn shares Angellica's initials.

Confusion results from mistaken identity: Florinda, mistaking Willmore for her beloved Belvile, is nearly raped, and a second attack darkens the drama. Willmore's bad-boy charm encourages even *female* spectators to have an ambivalent response to him. Desired by both virgin and whore, Hellena and Angellica, he mischievously attracts women but also rails at them:

> A virtuous mistress! Death, what a thing thou hast found out for me! Why, what the devil should I do with a virtuous woman? – a sort of ill-natured creatures, that take pride to torment a lover. Virtue is but an infirmity in woman; a disease that renders even the handsome ungrateful; whilst the ill-favoured, for want of solicitations and address, only fancy themselves so. – I have lain with a woman of quality, who has all the while been railing at whores. (4.1).

Willmore narrowly escapes a tragic ending when Angellica holds a pistol to his breast, and her stormy exit forecasts the gloom of Behn's sequel: "Why must we be either guilty of fornication or murder if we converse with you men – and is there no difference between leave to love me, and leave to lie with me?" (Act 1. 2).

Elizabeth Inchbald (1753–1821) judged Whig Susanna Centlivre to be second only to Tory Aphra Behn, although she criticized her for imitating "the licentious example" of other playwrights.[17] Among the most prolific of women dramatists, the brilliant comedienne and sometime actress Centlivre triumphed with her comedies *The Gamester* (1705), *The Bassett*

Table (1705), *The Busy Body* (1709), *The Wonder: A Woman Keeps A Secret* (1714), and *A Bold Stroke for a Wife* (1718). Although Inchbald found *Bold Stroke* to be too farcical, its popularity continued well into the nineteenth century. More sentimental than *The Rover*, the play revolves around Colonel Fainwell's trickery of "an odd *ragoût* of guardians" (foppish Sir Philip Modelove, the broker Tradelove, the Quaker hosier Prim, and the virtuoso Periwinkle) and a middling woman's attempt to please all of them in choosing her mate.[18] Seeking genuine affection in a world of hypocrisy, the savvy, spirited Anne Lovely hopes to extract her considerable fortune from the guardians in order to marry Fainwell. His disguises become the means to set her free from their tyranny, but like the actress who takes the role, she "must vary shapes as often as a player" (Act 2.2), dressing as a Quaker, if a voluptuous one, both literally and metaphorically to please Prim.

The various masquerades the Protean Fainwell adopts (a Francophile "beau," Dutch merchant, Pennsylvania Dissenter, and Egyptian traveler) define the play's modern British values in contrast to exotic others. Repeating a theme we have frequently encountered, the prologue introduces the xenophobic attitude of individual rights. Lovely, seeking "our country's good" (Act 5.1), reflects her creator's Whig sympathies: "I will rid myself of your [Tradelove's] tyranny, if there be either law or justice to be had; I'll force you to give me up my liberty" (Act 5.1). She asserts that she will "wear what I please, go when and where I please, and keep what company I think fit and not what you shall direct" (Act 5.1), to escape her commodification as a "gewgaw" (Act 3.1) or curio. The atmosphere of unstable commercial markets and financial speculation, most prominent in the scenes taking place in the Exchange, mimics the uncertainty Lovely experiences in ascertaining truth. In the end, the witty couple exemplify British domesticity: Lovely embodies English womanhood, and Fainwell boasts of serving his country's cause as a soldier. Together, the happy couple outwits the guardians in establishing a contract on their own terms. Although Lovely's "liberty of choice" (Act 5.1) merely transfers her property from one set of men to another, from guardians to husband, her naughty epilogue asserts her agency in demanding sexual satisfaction from her new husband who promises to be "a man of war in bed."

More sentimental than Centlivre's comedies, Frances Sheridan's (1724–66) comedy *The Discovery* (1763) flirts with tragic topics such as adultery, incest, libertinism, illegitimate birth, heavy gambling, and insolvency; yet the quarrelsome marriage between newlyweds Sir Harry and Lady Flutter in the farcical subplot turns marital incivility to comic ends. The prologue, derived from a draft by James Boswell, asserts that it is "high treason" for a female playwright to trespass into men's territory.[19] After Sheridan vigorously defended her "child" against David Garrick's critique, he ultimately came to admire it and even to star as the pompous Sir Anthony Branville, along with Frances's actor-manager husband as the bankrupt gambler Lord Medway, a not-so-subtle reference to Thomas Sheridan's considerable debt. The rakish Medway unites the various subplots: he plans to save himself from financial ruin by sacrificing his children George and Louisa to wealthy, objectionable spouses. Lord Medway extracts a promise from his son, a virtuous man of feeling, to marry the widow Knightly instead of his beloved Clara Richly, but the disastrous marriage is narrowly averted. Louisa maneuvers the elder Sir Anthony Branville into postponing their betrothal since she prefers his nephew. The new generation proves sentimentally instructive to the older one when the reformed father reverses patriarchal authority and bows before the son: "I'd give [them] all, nay, the whole world, were I master of it, to be possessed of such a virtuous self-acquitted heart as yours" (Act 5.1).

The witty Lady Medway/Hannah Pritchard, perhaps a stand-in for playwright Frances, outsmarts her husband, who flirts with Lady Flutter (played by Kitty Clive's protégée Jane Pope). The uproarious scenes between the two actresses spotlight their comic talents as Lady Medway coaches the naïve newlywed how to affect being an obedient wife. While Lady Medway has been criticized for her inconsistent transformation from clever termagant into a suddenly satisfied wife who accepts her husband's early philandering, her emphasis on the performative aspects of femininity make her character more credible. The play good-naturedly debates the sovereignty of the sexes so that love (and conveniently, money) ultimately unites the couples. Lady Medway's steadfast nature gives her the authority to reform her husband, yet the epilogue she recites asserts that real women, such as those in the audience, need not be as passive as her character. The actress's person and her role blend together with the female spectators to celebrate women's potential power in spite of cultural limitations.

Like Sheridan, Hannah Cowley (1743–1809) draws attention to the advantages of honoring the potential alliances among women playwrights, actresses, and Englishwomen more generally. Encouraged by David Garrick, who did not always look kindly on female playwrights, Cowley produced twelve plays. Among the most popular was *The Belle's Stratagem* (1780), a woman's counterpart to George Farquhar's *The Beaux Stratagem* (1707), set in the gossipy London social world of assembly halls, masquerades, operas, and auctions. Cowley's purpose, she writes in her dedication to Queen Charlotte, a devoted fan of the play, was "to draw a FEMALE CHARACTER, which, with the most lively sensibility, fine understanding, and elegant accomplishments, should unite that beautiful reserve and delicacy which, whilst they veil those charms, render them still more interesting."[20]

A nationalist play produced more than one hundred times in the 1770s and 1780s, *The Belle's Stratagem* set English liberty against the historical backdrop of the war with America and the threat of turmoil in France. How, it asks, may a principled national character be reconciled to protean theatrical and performative identities? In Cowley's comedy, the fashionable hero Doricourt is betrothed to Laetitia Hardy, who resists the arrangement. Her father, a second son, planned the marriage to consolidate his estate holdings, but each seeks a more romantic connection. Doricourt returns from the Grand Tour a worldly xenophobe: "I have never yet found any man whom I could cordially take to my heart, and call friend, who was not born beneath a British sky, and whose heart and manners were not truly English" (Act 1.3). British *womanhood*, however, is a different matter. Arguing that English beauties are insipid, Doricourt hopes his ideal love match will possess an element of "the restless charmers of Italy and France" (Act 1.2) and combine "domestic joys" with the worldly excitement. Appearing first as an ingénue and later at the masquerade as a mysterious "incognita," in a familiar convention, the idealized Laetitia masks herself to reveal her true character: to be recognized as herself, she impersonates another. Laetitia will indeed be an *English* wife but her very modesty nearly results in a failed courtship, while the freedoms available to English women grant her the ability to choose her own husband: "The timidity of the English character threw a veil over me you could not penetrate" (Act 5.5).

Since dissembling is assumed to be endemic to femininity, and identity appears to be as malleable as donning a costume, how can disguise be disentangled from a woman's essentially debased nature? Sir George Touchwood, introducing his country wife Lady Frances to the town, finds his masculinity threatened by fashionable life: "I should never have had the courage to have married a well-bred Fine Lady" (Act 2.1). He blames the chaos of modern life on the loss of distinction among the ranks, which results in "one universal masquerade, all disguised in the same habits and manners" (Act 2.1). In the topsy-turvy world of the masked ball, for example, strumpet Kitty Willis could be mistaken for the virtuous Lady Frances. But the epilogue, again critical to resolving the comic contradictions, praises the subtler arts of deception and, in a deft turn, redeems the theater as respectable in claiming that the English stage is, unlike other venues, free of deception because its make-believe proves to be transparent.

Toward the end of the century, respectable women found playwriting a path to fortune and fame, although not without barriers along the way. Urging Frances Burney to write for the stage, Hester Thrale tells her,

"A *play* will be something *worth* your Time, it is the Road both to Honour & Profit, –& *why* should you have it in your power to gain [these rewards] & not do it. If you would but *try*, I am *sure* you would succeed, and give us such a Play as would be an Honour to all your Family."[21] Perhaps the most lasting of Burney's plays, her satirical comedy *The Witlings*, was written in 1779 but, ironically, not produced or printed in her lifetime. The play links Lady Smatter, a thinly disguised reference to Bluestocking hostess Elizabeth Montagu (1718–1800), with the other learned women in her social circle:

> A Club she supported of Witlings and fools,
> Who, but for her dinners, had scoff'd at her rules;
> The reason, if any she had, these did shatter
> Of poor empty-Headed, and little Soul'd Smatter.[22]

Describing the author as "a sister of the Order," Burney viciously mocks the Bluestockings' vanity but thus includes herself in the satire against writing women. The ladies' intellectual pretensions, she suggests, are driven by commercial ambitions in a scandal-ridden world where lampoons, poetry, and books are treated as commodities rather than art. Lady Smatter falls into mercantile language: "Where can be the pleasure of reading Books, and studying authors, if one is not to have the credit of talking of them?" The modest Cecilia sees through her affectations: "Your Ladyship's desire of celebrity is too well known for your motives to be doubted" (Act 2.1). The *Witlings*'s subplot centers on the romance between Beaufort, Lady Smatter's dependent nephew, and the impoverished Cecilia. The couple finds heroic freedom in daring to be poor, but Cecilia voices every thinking woman's need, from Aphra Behn to Joanna Baillie, in pleading for an independent income and a room that is hers alone: "Have you, madam, any Room which for a few Hours you can allow me to call my own? – where, unmolested and alone, I may endeavor to calm my mind, and settle some plan for my future conduct?" (Act 3.1).

In sum, women playwrights touched the brink of all we hate, in Alexander Pope's memorable phrase: disdain and fear are bound up with envy and admiration. The Restoration and eighteenth-century theater provided a means for women playwrights to negotiate and resist these demeaning assumptions. Adhering to the conventions available to them, but at other times experimenting with form and content, they collaborated with managers, sponsors, and actors of both sexes even when the gap between the actresses, largely unbound by the conventions of passive femininity, and their roles surfaced in the dissonance between the play's message and its paratexts. Like the actresses for whom they wrote, and the patrons who supported their efforts, women dramatists helped shape a national femininity defined by its liberties in contrast to Continental, American, and Oriental women. Hester Thrale's comments on Joanna Baillie made clear the ongoing concerns about regulating women's talents in spite of, and perhaps because of, the new, profitable opportunities in the marketplace for publication and production they witnessed in the period. We have, then, traced here a part of the emerging story of women dramatists, some of whom aspired to be Judith Shakespeares, and all of whom deserve to be more fully integrated into theater history.

NOTES

1. Hester Thrale Piozzi, "New Commonplace Book" in Houghton Gen MS Hyde 35 No. 18 [p. 23], Harvard University, Cambridge, MA. In a later version of her notes, Thrale remarks, "Well! The Moment a Female Pen owned the Book, – down dropts its Value: – out sprung the faults, and Joan's *Name* ruined all. But English People love to destroy their own Pleasure in every thing. If a concert is good, they find how hot the Room is." O. G. Knapp, ed., *The Intimate Letters of Hester Piozzi and Penelope Pennington 1788–1822* (London: John Lane, The Bodley Head, 1914), p. 173, inexactly cites and abbreviates the passage, and the inaccuracies have been perpetuated in subsequent criticism. The gathering to which Thrale refers occurred in the home of playwright and novelist Harriet Lee (1757/58–1851). *Termites bellicosi* are large African insects, sometimes called "white ants."
2. Robert Hume, "Drama and Theatre in the Mid and Later Eighteenth Century," in *The Cambridge History of English Literature, 1660–1780*, ed. John Richetti (Cambridge University Press, 2005), p. 338. Hume does not discuss plays by women playwrights.
3. Jacqueline M. Labbe, "Introduction: Defining 'Women's Writing'; or, Writing 'The History,'" in *The History of Women's Writing, 1750–1830*, Vol. 5, ed. Jacqueline M. Labbe (Basingstoke, Hampshire: Palgrave Macmillan, 2010), p. 15, emphasis in original.
4. Dympna Callaghan, *A Feminist Companion to Shakespeare* (Oxford: Wiley-Blackwell, 2001), p. xii. See also Ellen Pollak, "The Future of Feminist Theory and Eighteenth-Century Studies," *The Eighteenth Century* 50.1 (Spring 2009), 18, emphasis in original.
5. Derek Hughes, "Aphra Behn and the Restoration Theatre," *The Cambridge Companion to Aphra Behn*, ed. Derek Hughes and Janet Todd (Cambridge University Press, 2004), p. 29.
6. Misty G. Anderson, *Female Playwrights and Eighteenth-Century Comedy: Negotiating Marriage on the London Stage* (Basingstoke, Hampshire: Palgrave Macmillan, 2002), p. 107.
7. Preface to *Sir Patient Fancy* in *The Plays, 1677–1682, The Works of Aphra Behn*, Vol. 6, ed. Janet Todd (Columbus: Ohio State University Press, 1996). All subsequent quotations from the plays discussed will be cited in parentheses by act and scene number.
8. Delarivier Manley, Preface to *The Lost Lover; or, The Jealous Husband* (1696) in *Eighteenth-Century Women Playwrights*, Vol. 1, ed. Margarete Rubik and

Eva Mueller-Zettelmann, gen. ed. Derek Hughes (London: Pickering and Chatto, 2001).
9. Catherine Trotter, *Fatal Friendship, A Tragedy* (1698), Act 4.2.
10. Catherine Trotter, *Agnes de Castro, A Tragedy* (1696), Act 2.1.
11. Delarivier Manley, *The Royal Mischief* (London, 1696).
12. Aphra Behn, *Abdelazar; Or, The Moor's Revenge* in *The Plays, 1671–1677, The Works of Aphra Behn*, Vol. 5, ed. Janet Todd (Columbus: Ohio State University Press, 1996).
13. *Arabian Nights' Entertainments*, ed. Robert L. Mack (Oxford University Press, 1995), p. 10.
14. Ros Ballaster, *Seductive Forms: Women's Amatory Fiction from 1684 to 1740* (Oxford University Press, 1998), pp. 89, 116.
15. Frances Brooke, *The Siege of Sinope, A Tragedy* (London, 1781), p. 12.
16. Hannah More, *Percy, A Tragedy* (London, 1778), Act 1.1.
17. Elizabeth Inchbald, "Remarks" on *A Bold Stroke for a Wife* in *The British Theatre: or, a Collection of Plays ... with Biographical and Critical Remarks*, Vol. 11 (London: Longman, Hurst, Rees, and Orme, 1808), pp. 3–5.
18. Susanna Centlivre, *A Bold Stroke for A Wife*, ed. Nancy Copeland (Peterborough, ON: Broadview, 1995), Act 2.1.
19. Prologue to *The Discovery; A Comedy* in *The Plays of Frances Sheridan*, ed. Robert Hogan and Jerry C. Beasley (Newark: University of Delaware Press, 1984), p. 41.
20. Hannah Cowley, *The Belle's Stratagem*, ed. Melinda C. Finberg (Oxford University Press, 2001), p. 212.
21. Letter from Frances Burney to Susanna Elizabeth Burney, September 3, 1778, *The Early Journals and Letters of Fanny Burney*, Vol. 3, The Streatham Years: Part 1, 1778–1779 (Montreal and Kingston: McGill–Queen's University Press, 1994), p. 133, emphasis in original.
22. Frances Burney, *The Witlings and the Woman-Hater*, ed. Peter Sabor and Geoffrey Sill (Peterborough, ON: Broadview Press, 2002), Act 5.1.

8

RIVKA SWENSON

History

No longer is it a "truth universally acknowledged," as Raymond Williams quipped in *The Country and the City* (1973), that women in earlier centuries did not contribute to the historical project. Scholars have heeded Devoney Looser's call to challenge the "received wisdom" that "history" or historical discourse was "a male enclave devoid of women subjects and practitioners" and followed her recommendation to consider "more broadly."[1] The recommendation is appropriate: generic boundaries were creatively limned during the period; as J. Paul Hunter attests in *Before Novels* (1990), historiography changed significantly. Moreover, Looser urges us to read against the grain of any expected gender-genre nexus, since "women writers," like other writers, "used historical material with widely diverging interests, aims, and results" (2). Thus, we should hesitate to embrace expectations about gender and genre. Demonstrating the benefits of such critical flexibility, I focus on a single fascinating example of "historical discourse": Eliza Haywood's *Mary Stuart, Queen of Scots: BEING THE SECRET HISTORY OF HER LIFE, and the Real CAUSES of all Her Misfortunes. Containing a relation of many particular Transactions in her REIGN; never yet Published in any Collection. Translated from the French, by Mrs. Eliza Haywood* (1725).[2] Haywood's *SECRET HISTORY* counter-intuitively *reduces* material that we might expect to find expanded. As we shall see, Haywood's *SECRET HISTORY* – a translation of Pierre le Pesant de Boisguilbert's *Marie Stuart, Reyne D'Escosse, Nouvelle Historique* (1675) – thus challenges what we think we know not only about the Scottish queen but about genre, gender and genre, and the notoriously seductive *"Mrs. Eliza Haywood"* of 1720s fame.[3] As we illuminate taxonomy's *aporiae*, complexity emerges.

My reading of Haywood's approach to the form of (secret) history in *SECRET HISTORY* is a recessive reading that highlights strangeness within what Ralph Cohen terms the "interrelation of genre."[4] The secret history was an important genre/subgenre, and, like secret histories explored by Rebecca Bullard, Haywood's *SECRET HISTORY* is a "highly self-reflective ... form of historiography," rife with "political and formal complexities."[5] But, Haywood's *SECRET HISTORY*, as both "secret history" and, more broadly, "history," is an unusual example of what it purports to be. As "history," it *omits*. And as "secret history," it is neither a political exposé nor an amatory fiction in disguise; there is no gossip, nor even much attempt (despite the titular promise) at what Noelle Gallagher calls the intimate "rhetoric of disclosure." Haywood's contribution is partly an epistemological critique of historical discourse it deconstructs. Cohen observes, "Genres are open categories" and "each member alters the genre by adding, contradicting, or changing constituents."[6] Indeed, if (as Bullard writes) Haywood's other "overtly historical works that bear the title 'secret history'... have strong generic affiliations with romance-inspired amatory fiction," *SECRET HISTORY* departs even from expected Haywoodian formalism.[7] Moreover, Haywood's *SECRET HISTORY* almost always closely follows her source, scaling back instead of fictionalizing or embellishing. *SECRET HISTORY* is an odd intervention; its silences are radical substitutions for the deeply embodied, extant "reality" of mimetic-dilatory "Marianism" (i.e., the body of writing about Mary, Queen of Scots, and its typical characteristics). Crucially, *SECRET HISTORY* highlights the biographical and historical importance of Mary's decades-long competitive relationship with her cousin Queen Elizabeth, but, instead of bringing to life that drama, *SECRET HISTORY* evacuates and erases, manifesting the fatal absence, the canceling out, at the heart of fraught sorority.

My recessive reading is comparative. "Revising" Boisguilbert mainly by omission, Haywood's feminist text simultaneously revises by omission the extant body of Marian material: the surrounding discourse included songs, memoirs, poems, letters, portraits, and several early-1720s histories and reprintings of histories. These Marian materials included texts such as George Buchanan's (1587) *A Detection of the Actions of Mary, Queen of Scots* (1721), William Camden's (1571) *Annals, or the History of the Actions of Mary, Queen of Scots* (1721), and Samuel Jebb's *The History of the Life and Reign of Mary Queen of Scots, and Dowager of France. Extracted from original records and writers of credit* (1725). These texts were obsessed – like John Banks's popular play *The Albion Queens* (1704) – with the matter of what John Staines has characterized as the pathos of the queen's image.[8] Readers familiar with contemporary Marian depictions – and there would have been many readers who were familiar with Elizabethan history – would expect to see Mary's image displayed copiously in Haywood. As would secret history readers; some twenty-five texts in English from 1700 to 1725 that appeared under the titular generic marker of "secret history" divulged what Peter Burke calls "history from below": "kings, queens, and ministers without their clothes."[9] *SECRET HISTORY* diverges.

Moreover, *SECRET HISTORY* balances strangely against a rival translation/revision: James Freebairn's *LIFE of MARY STEWART, QUEEN of Scotland and France*.[10] Freebairn's intimate *LIFE*, embellishing on Boisguilbert, exemplifies (unlike *SECRET HISTORY)* Marian tradition. Haywood's subtitle signals disingenuously that she, too, will evoke *presence*: "*particular[s] ... never yet Published in any Collection.*" But, compared to Freebairn's "*collected*" (as *his* subtitle says) *LIFE*, Haywood's *SECRET HISTORY OF HER LIFE* is undetailed, unsexy: neither political intrigue nor scandalous romp, it strips down to omit. Indeed, Haywood's Mary lacks a body. Haywood does indicate "*the Real CAUSES of all Her Misfortunes*": Elizabeth's "jealousy" over Mary's royal claim "was indeed the first and principal Motive of that mortal Hatred which Elizabeth ever after bore her, and which at last was the Cause of her Fall" (5) – but this was not news, and Haywood offers no juicy bits.[11] Instead, inside the discursive body, Haywood locates history that does not fill reality's gaps but is the gap.

Haywood thus violates expectations about well-trammeled genre (and its connection to gender), well-trammeled topic (Mary), and Haywood's 1720s author function, which, early, included an arguably sexualized reputation. Haywood resists our desires for an especially intimate portrayal of rival queens, a reach across space and time from (female) author to (female) subject to us. I highlight three areas: Haywood's stripped-down methodology contra Boisguilbert and Freebairn, her oppositional dematerializing of the surrounding Marian corpus, and her challenge to readers' expectations not only of "Haywood" but of genre and gender-and-genre. Giving us what we least expect (of Mary, of secret history, of 1720s Haywood), Haywood leaves us looking toward the essence of the titular "*CAUSE*" of Mary's nineteen-year imprisonment and eventual death sentence: the mutual absences of Mary and her sister-queen/cousin/rival Elizabeth; the meeting that never happened, the face-to-face that never was. Haywood's exhumation reveals the wages of fatally competitive sisterhood. Interpolating readers into its performance of de-intimacy and failed sorority, the *SECRET HISTORY* complicates how we conceive of relationships between women in/and history.

The Marian body: *Nouvelle Historique, LIFE, SECRET HISTORY*

A half century after Boisguilbert's 1675 *Nouvelle Historique*, Freebairn's *LIFE* was published – and followed shortly thereafter by a Mary (Haywood's) that was radically different from extant Marys past or current, positive or negative. A rich tissue of material (everything from Valois courtiers' poems to Elizabeth's counselors' statements about the English queen's jealousy of Mary's legendary beauty) lingered over Mary's seductive matter: her looks, her clothes, even her body's attitudes during her execution and her severed head's appearance. But Haywood's Mary never materializes; SECRET HISTORY omits most of the embodying passages from Boisguilbert that Freebairn amplified.

The first differences between Boisguilbert, Freebairn, and Haywood inhere in their titles. The original, Boisguilbert's, is *Marie Stewart, Reyne D'Escosse, Nouvelle Historique*. Freebairn's title, like his text, expands: *LIFE of MARY STEWART, ... with NOTES Illustrating and confirming the most material passages of this HISTORY*. "Life," "Notes," "Illustrating," "material," "History": these are promises Freebairn keeps. Freebairn's *LIFE is* expansive; supported by even more footnotes than the original, it draws on "fifteen or sixteen authors," Freebairn brags (xvi). Haywood's "secret history" intervenes by offering less – and thus implicitly critiques history *qua* history.

If Freebairn's title is a straightforward advertisement, the head and body of Haywood's text relate more complexly to each other. Haywood's title is difficult grammatically and conceptually (*Mary Stuart, Queen of Scots: BEING THE SECRET HISTORY OF HER LIFE ...*). It is also disingenuous. Despite promising to convey heretofore unrevealed *"particular transactions,"* there is no "particular" access: the text defamiliarizes. Compared to Freebairn's boastingly "swell'd" *LIFE* with its notes, its anecdotes, and its sixty-odd pages of engorged prefatory material, Haywood's SECRET HISTORY OF HER LIFE seems farcically bereft of details (secret, known, sensational, or pedestrian) (vi). Freebairn's Mary is "painted to Life" (xxxii). Twenty-two times, he mentions his "reader's satisfaction," for "I have here taken the Liberty... to in[s]ert (for my reader's Satisfaction) the Papers, at full Length"(173). His text is a "Performance" by "Mary" (vi). Freebairn stokes desire ("my readers, or my own Satisfaction"), and, in the fullness of a pruriently fleshed-out narration, we achieve *"full Satisfaction* in the *Possession"*(v). Freebairn's narrative/Mary is thus a conduit for homosocial desire, specifically male (as denoted by Freebairn's direct address to Sir Thomas Bruce-Hope, dedicatee). Freebairn vows "to open our Eyes" to "a perfect *Model*," fully assembled: "MARY Queen of *Scots*, in a homely Dress, comes to You for *Shelter*, and is sure to find it" (v). Freebairn's Mary is always already embodied. Indeed, his narrative proper begins with a straight translation of Boisguilbert's discomfiting observation about Mary's "qualitez de corps & d'esprit" (7): when "THIS young Princess was just Six Years old, ... the extraordinary Qualities of her Body and Mind began to blossom, which have since been the Wonder of Europe" (4). Haywood, by contrast, writes simply that when "The young Princess was scarce six Years old ... it was easy to discover in this Dawn of Life, what her Meridian would be" (2).

Haywood's relative distance is thus revealed by comparison to forebears' intimacies. For instance, while Freebairn and Haywood both translate closely Boisguilbert's encomium on Mary's beauty (*"Sa veuë sait en un instant le chemin qu'il y a des yeux jusques au coeur"* [8]), Haywood stops there ("The first Sight of her in a Moment found the way from the Eye to the Heart" [2]). But Freebairn, like Boisguilbert, delights to "fill up a Page" with a courtier's ode (28). Haywood merely reports that the ode "describe[d] the Perfections of the too lovely Queen in Colours so lively and natural" (20). If the courtier enjoyed (like readers of Boisguilbert and Freebairn) "feasting his Eyes with those Perfections," Haywood's readers cannot (19).

Indeed, Haywood, unlike Boisguilbert and Freebairn, highlights what we lack. For instance, Freebairn translates closely when he writes that Charles IX saw "his Brother," Mary's first husband, "as the happiest Man upon Earth, however short his Life and Reign were, since he had enjoyed so beautiful a Creature, the Possession of whom no earthly Pleasure could equal" (6).[12] Haywood uses direct address and heightening italics: *"Happy! happy Brother! thou hadst enough of Life and Empire, short as was thy Reign, in the possession of so exquisite a Charmer"* (4). Lucky him, unlucky Haywood, unlucky us.

We "see" Boisguilbert's Mary, and Freebairn's. The former begins with an engraving, *Maria Scotorum Regina*. Assuring us that "The very Pictures of her, which were taken from the Life, made as great Impression on the Eyes and Hearts of the Spectators" as did "the Original," Freebairn displays Mary in the climax/crisis of execution (6). Readying Mary for death, Freebairn includes Robert Wyngfield's infamous eyewitness report to Lord Burghley (reproduced here at length for effect):

> She appear'd . . .; being tall of Body, Corpulent, Round-shoulder'd; her Face fat and broad, Double-chin'd, and Hazle-ey'd; her borrow'd Hair brown. Her attire was; She had on her Head a Dressing of Lawn edg'd with Bonlace, a Pomander Chain, and an *Agnus Dei* about her Neck; a Crucifix in her Hand, and a Pair of Beads at her Girdle, with a golden Cross at the End of them; a Vail of Lawn fasten'd to her Caul, bowed out with Wire, and edg'd round about with Bonlace; her Gown was of Black Sattin printed, with a Train, and long Sleeves to the Ground, set with Accorn Buttons of Jett, trimm'd with Pearl, and short Sleeves of black cut Sattin, with a Pair of Sleeves of Purple Velvet whole; under them her Kirtle, whole of figur'd black Sattin; her Petticoat Upper-Body unlac'd in the Back, of Crimson Sattin, and her Petticoat Skirts of Crimson Velvet; her Shoes of *Spanish* Leather, with the rough Side outwards; a Pair of

green Silk Garters; Her nether Stockings worsted coloured, watch'd and clack'd with Silver, and edg'd on Top with Silver; and next her Legs, a Pair of Jersey Hose white. Thus attir'd, She went chearfully to the Place of Execution.

(318)

At last, the executioner cuts her off mid-prayer: "taking up the Head, he shew'd it openly all full of Blood, and mangled with the Strokes he had given it, yet still carrying those attractive Charms of her Beauty and Majesty"; "her Beauty continu'd for some Time after her Death as brilliant as ever" (318). Freebairn's footnotes describe how her terrier emerged from under-skirts to lay where her head was, lapping blood, and how weepy Elizabeth "order'd [Mary's] Corps[e] to be interr'd after a most sumptuous Manner" (315). Freebairn even includes the tombstone epitaph.

If Freebairn capitalizes on Marian-embodiment tradition, Haywood does not. Preparing for execution, Haywood's Mary distributes her goods to her ladies, "wr[i]te[s] a long Letter to ELIZABETH" (237, letter not given), and

> her Head was taken off at the third Blow, the Earl Marshal crying out at the same time, *Long Live Queen* ELIZABETH, *and thus let all her Enemies perish!*
> THUS have you had an Account of the Life and Death of MARY STUART ... She was buried without any Pomp in a neighbouring Church and her Servants put up an epitaph for her; which was soon taken down, because it spoke so much in her praise, and set forth the Cruelty of those who put her to death. (240)

Haywood stops, gesturing to Elizabeth ("who put her to death") with the omega, circling back to the subtitle's alpha: "*the real CAUSES of all her misfortunes.*" Haywood eschews to include Mary's epitaph, instead ending with uncanny erasure ("soon taken down") – figuratively an erasure of historiography's palimpsest and the exposure of a relationship defined by absences.

Disembodying the rival-queen canon

There is something appropriate about Haywood's decision neither to embody Mary nor bring to life a relationship (the queens') that not only led to Mary's literal disembodiment but was defined, in life, by mutual absences. Could Haywood have offered a fleshier (in any sense) secret history of "the finest she that ever was" (as one Englishman begrudgingly called Mary)?[13] Yes. As indicated by provocative puffs for Haywood's collected *Secret Histories, Novels, and Poems* (1725),[14] her other secret histories resembled their classical forebear: scandalous *Anekdota*, which chronicled the exploits of the lusty empress Theodora.[15] But Haywood's SECRET HISTORY diverges. If, as Ros Ballaster writes, "female desire" is not simply "a ruling metaphor in [Haywood's] fiction, but rather the subject and generating ground of its plot," SECRET HISTORY foregrounds desire frustrated; Haywood, true to life, by implication, in a way that some other historical discourse was not (her introduction reproduces Boisguilbert's promise of "not a *Romance*, but a *True History*"), hardly inscribes Mary's matter within a narrative circle of sustaining female homosocial desire.

Indeed, Haywood goes against grain, omitting Boisguilbert's embodiment passages (amplified by Freebairn) and leaving untouched the larger Marian tissue that could have manufactured presence. Adam Blackwood's *Histoire*, translated by Samuel Jebb in 1725 preceding the SECRET HISTORY, exemplifies the old tradition Freebairn drew on: Blackwood's Mary, facing doom, cannot "contain herself from weeping and from pitiful moan"; she is "stripped down," her wig "pulled" off as the executioner "snatched her rudely by the arms and pulled off her doublet, her straight bodice, which [was] low in the collar, so that her neck, being all naked, appeared to the spectators more white than snow or alabaster" (122).[16] Even "her hardest-hearted enemies – were greatly moved," "weeping" at her "spectacle" (123). Comparatively, Haywood's portrait is unsensational.

But perhaps nothing suggests better what Haywood does *not* do than her treatment of the letter Mary wrote Elizabeth when entering England in 1567. Freebairn writes evocatively, "However Melancholy the Queen's Adventures, ... they may be resembl'd only to the Buds and Blossoms of those Thorns which are to succeed" (160). Haywood is matter of fact: "HOW mournful soever the Adventures of this Queen, ... they may be counted fortunate, when consider'd in competition with those that follow" (126). Later still, Freebairn's Mary, writing to Elizabeth, offers a movingly "full and particular" rendering of "her Sufferings": rebellious subjects *"broke into my Chamber, cruelly Murder'd my Servant before my Face, tho' I was then big with Child"* (162). Comparatively, Haywood's Mary is reserved: her subjects *"have taken up arms against me, and treated me with the utmost Indignities"* (127). Haywood's letter version is key to her methodology of emptying out.

To be sure, Haywood's letter version focuses on Elizabeth in a way that Freebairn's does not, but Mary's invocations of her cousin thus point more fully to lack. Where Freebairn's Mary requests, *"Allow me therefore, my dear Sister, the Honour of seeing you as soon as possible"* (161), Haywood's Mary begs: *"I beseech you therefore, my dear Sister, that I may be conducted to your Presence"* (128). This entreaty for *"Presence"* is striking: readers knew Elizabeth never fulfilled what would become Mary's oft-repeated plea. Moreover, in Freebairn, Mary's pleas are less immediate and desperate. His

Mary triangulates Elizabeth, looking to God for salvation: *"I pray God, that he may crown you with his Favours, and that he may afford me Patience, and those Comforts which I hope to receive from his Holy Grace by your Means"* (162). But Haywood's Mary turns to Elizabeth directly: *"To remind you of the Reasons I have to depend on England, I send back to its Queen this Token of her promis'd Friendship and Assistance"* (128). In Haywood, then, the Mary-Elizabeth relationship is paramount. And, yet, Mary's glancing reference to the *"Token"* highlights all Haywood does not say. Of the token, and the queens' history, Haywood writes only,

> AS soon as [Mary] had left the Borders of Scotland, she dispatched a Gentleman to Queen ELIZABETH, with a Mark of Friendship she had receiv'd from her; it was a Diamond which she sent in exchange of one the Queen of Scots had presented to her, each agreeing to assist the other on all occasions whatsoever, on sight of either of these Tokens. (126–27)

Her translation is close to Freebairn's, but he includes the token's Latin epigram, in dramatic blackletter. In life as in *SECRET HISTORY*, the Token is a cipher: standing for more than itself, it means nothing, yields nothing.

In effect, the Token points to history unrevealed by *SECRET HISTORY*: the fact of the queens' mutual teenage obsession and courtship, all that Haywood might have but did not discuss. In life, as young women, the queens indulged a passionate correspondence of original Italian verse. In life, young Mary viewed a portrait of Elizabeth, asking an advisor, "How like is it unto the queen?" He said she would soon know and "find much more perfection than could be set forth with the art of man," and Mary responded, "That is the thing that I have most desired."[17] Meanwhile, Elizabeth quizzed advisors: who was tallest and "fairest," who "played best" at music, who "danced best"?[18] In January 1562, Mary sent a portrait; when Elizabeth wrote that she was delayed in sending her own in return because the painter was ill, Mary sent a second portrait, in the form of a ring with a miniature behind a heart-shaped diamond. While courtiers wrote odes to Mary's *"visage,"* Mary courted Elizabeth. Elizabeth responded with verses, and Mary wrote back:

> Thus, dear sister, if this verse brings you
> The desire to meet that moves me also,
> I can only be left in pain and sadness
> If the meeting does not soon occur.[19]

Elizabeth finally sent her own token, and the young queens vowed that should either diamond be returned, it would constitute a plea for shelter from the other.

Haywood omits all such intimacies: how they planned to meet, how plans fell through, how Mary swooned with "such a passion as she did keep her bed all that day."[20] Mary's trials in Scotland were underway, and Elizabeth wrote that the breach posed to their sisterhood "gnawed her heart."[21] Mary, soon to seek shelter in England, sent, in French, an anxious poem of "affection" in which she described herself as a ship trying to enter a safe port in a storm; she hoped her woes were not caused by Elizabeth (*Non pas de vous?*), and she asked if it was Elizabeth or *"Fortune"* that tore Mary's sails and ropes, her *"voile et cordage double."*[22] Elizabeth's own poem "Doubt of Future Foes" bespoke similar unease: "mindes" are "cloak[ed]" in "clowdes," buffeted by "changed windes."[23] But none of these details are in *SECRET HISTORY*. Haywood glances over how Mary, imprisoned for nineteen years by Elizabeth, wrote repeatedly to her cousin ("Sister"), begging to meet, sending embroidered petticoats and nightgowns in which Elizabeth's own body might be by Mary inscribed. Elizabeth, responding rarely, never came. Mary begged "to satisfy you in person."[24] Sorrowing, "without seeing or being seen but by you," Mary pleaded for "the favour of your presence."[25] But no; if Elizabeth wished "that we were but as two milkmaids, with pails upon our arms,"[26] she also chided, "Think you that I could love my own winding-sheet?"[27] On February 8, 1587, Mary was executed at Fotheringay after being informed the previous day (not by Elizabeth) that she was to die; Elizabeth was absent; an empty, cloth-draped chair stood in. Haywood's Mary bemoans the wages of unrequited sympathy, asserting that "if she could have spoken to her once, which she had earnestly desired," then "all things might have been friendly made up" (236), but Elizabeth denied Mary's satisfaction and Haywood denies ours. Readers might know from other sources how everything Mary's blood touched was burned to prevent relic hunting. Or how Mary's entrails were buried secretly inside Fotheringay while her embalmed remains sat in a lead coffin for six months before burial in Peterborough – and were later moved, in 1612, to Westminster opposite the sister-queen she never met in life.

Conclusion: Reading recessively

> I rushed through the chamber which divided mine from my sister's ... I gently opened the curtains of her bed – Ah, gracious Heaven, what did I feel when I beheld it empty! – Sophia Lee, *The Recess: Or A Tale of Other Times*

Reading recessively, which is to say reading in a way that unsteadies our sense of naturalized taxonomies, we may find disrupted our understanding of the "interrelation" that Ralph Cohen states is genre. For instance, what happens if we see Sophia Lee's *The Recess: Or, a Tale of Other Times* (1783)[28] – a Gothic novel inspired by the Mary-Elizabeth rivalry – as inheriting not only the unsteadiness of David Hume (1711–76) but the presence *cum* absence of his predecessor, Haywood, whose text Jayne Elizabeth Lewis identifies as the most popular of its kind until Hume's *History of England*. New critical echoes generated by recessive readings may divulge more about the extent and complexity of women's contributions to (and divergences from) generic genetics.

The Recess, along a continuum of historical discourse, may be read as heir to the disembodying SECRET HISTORY. In Lee's fiction, Mary has secret twin daughters, Matilda and Ellinor, fostered underground. The girls know their mother (imprisoned by Elizabeth) only by a picture, and, the one time they see Mary, through a barred window, she does not resemble the picture they have committed to heart of "a lady in the flower of youth"(10). Matilda yearns to "deliver" her mother from bondage, thus to deliver herself by being "received to her arms" (39). Matilda fails. Mary is executed ("That radiant sun of Love seemed to dip into a sea of blood, and sink there forever"); Ellinor dies; a female friend commits suicide (117). If *The Recess* is as Jayne Lewis suggests, a kind of labyrinth, Haywood's SECRET HISTORY is an antecedent. SECRET HISTORY's formalism of loss, as if anticipating Lee, is itself not revelatory but reductive. Matilda is, Lewis avers, "the future female reader" who "becom[es] Mary's reader;"[29] Matilda, "struck on [her] heart at the thought of" Mary's death "with a pang perhaps equal to that which [Mary] bore [Matilda]" (117), poring over documents related to Mary, could be Lee reading Mary through Haywood, with or without Humean mediation.

If Haywood disappoints modern readers' desires and intuitions, she provocatively problematizes our sense of women's contributions to the generic genetics of historical discourse. In fact, women writers of historical discourse negotiated variously the intersections of gender and genre. Jane Barker (1652–1732), in the early 1700s, wrote explicitly contra "the male Patchworkers" and their "Histories at Large." Similarly, Catharine Macaulay (1731–91), in the later 1700s, claimed in the preface to volume 6 of *The History of England* (1781) that her outsider status as a not well-connected "man of genius" (unlike, e.g., William Robertson, Edward Gibbon, Hume) allowed her to pursue "a disinterested principle," an "impartiality."[30] But the diversity of women's contributions to writing history, as this chapter has shown, requires more than a one-size approach. If Haywood's SECRET HISTORY sometimes amplifies emotion, relative to the context of generic Marianism there is very little *there* – in terms of substance – there. Indeed, SECRET HISTORY's recessive gene manifests the formalism of fatally competitive sisterhood, straining the bounds of genre with what it does not do: here is a (secret) history whose ruling affective tale (letters, diamond tokens, poetry, embroidered petticoats, and pleas for presence), sensationalized by other "histories," is never really told. For all its strangeness, indeed because of its strangeness, Haywood's translation *cum* revision, her history *cum* secret history, makes apparent the risks of reading horizontally when it comes to genre and to gender and genre. SECRET HISTORY's disruptive gene, unsettling the history of Mary, 1720s Haywood, gender and genre, and the praxis of historical discourse, suggests the challenges and the benefits of illuminating the *aporiae* within simple taxonomy.

NOTES

1. Raymond Williams, The Country and the City (London: Chatto and Windus, 1973), p. 113. Devoney Looser, *British Women Writers and the Writing of History, 1670–1820* (Baltimore: The Johns Hopkins University Press, 2005), pp. 1, 2. She also warns us that women historians are not "necessarily" either "feminist" or "female-focused" (3).
2. J. Paul Hunter, Before Novels: The Cultural Contexts of Eighteenth-Century English Fiction (New York and London: W.W. Norton & Company, 1990), p. 339. Mary Helen McMurran (The Spread of Novels: Translation and Prose Fiction in the Eighteenth Century [Princeton, 2010]), was first to observe that Haywood has indeed translated. Eliza Haywood, *Mary Stuart, Queen of Scots: BEING THE SECRET HISTORY OF HER LIFE, and the Real CAUSES of all Her Misfortunes. Containing a relation of many particular Transactions in her REIGN; never yet Published in any Collection. Translated from the French, by Mrs. Eliza Haywood* (London, 1725).
3. Pierre le Pesant de Boisguilbert, *Marie Stuart, Reyne D'Escosse, Nouvelle Historique* (Paris, 1675).
4. Ralph Cohen, "History and Genre," *New Literary History* 17.2 (1986), 203–18, 204.
5. Rebecca Bullard, *The Politics of Disclosure, 1674–1725: Secret History Narratives* (London: Pickering and Chatto, 2009), pp. 187, 38.
6. Noelle Gallagher, Historical Literatures: Writing about the Past in England, 1660–1740 (University of Manchester Press, 2012), p. 94. Cohen, "History and Genre," p. 204.
7. Bullard, *Politics of Disclosure*, p. 162.
8. John Staines, *The Tragic Histories of Mary Queen of Scots, 1560–1690* (Farnham and Burlington: Ashgate, 2009), p. 231.
9. Peter Burke, "Publicizing the Rise of the Private: The Rise of Secret History," in *Changing Perceptions of the Public Sphere*, ed. Christian J. Emden and David Midgley (Oxford: Berghan Books, 2012), p. 61.
10. James Freebairn, *The LIFE of MARY STEWART, QUEEN of Scotland and France. Written Originally in French and Now done into ENGLISH. With NOTES illustrating and confirming the most material Passages of this HISTORY, collected from Co[n]temporary, and other Authors of the Greatest Character and Reputation* (Edinburgh, 1725).

11. Haywood translates exactly: "*ce qui sut le premier principe de la haine mortelle qu'Elizabeth conserva depuis contre Marie, & qui la porta enfin à causer sa ruine*" (Boisguilbert, *Marie*, p. 11).
12. Freebairn, *LIFE*, p. 6. Boisguilbert writes, "qu'il estimoit François II. son frère, le plus heureux Prince de la terre, quelque peu qu'eussent duré sa vie & son regne, d'avoir possedé une si belle personne" *(Marie,* p. 9).
13. Thomas Randolph to William Cecil, *Calendar of State Papers Relating to Scotland and Mary Queen of Scots* (Edinburgh, 1880–1969), Vol. 2, p. 229.
14. Eliza Haywood, *Secret Histories, Novels, and Poems* (London, 1725). David Brewer, "'Haywood,' Secret History, and the Politics of Attribution," The Passionate Fictions of Eliza Haywood: Essays on Her Life and Works, ed. Kirsten T. Saxton and Rebecca Bocchicchio (Lexington: University Press of Kentucky, 2000), pp. 217–39.
15. Procopius, *Anekdota: The Secret History of the Court of the Emperor Justinian, faithfully rendered into English* (London, 1674).
16. Ros Ballaster, Seductive Forms: Women's Amatory Fiction from 1684 to 1740 (Oxford University Press, 1992), p. 158. Adam Blackwood, *Histoire de la martyre de la royne d'Escosse* (Paris, 1587), trans. Samuel Jebb, in *The History of the Life and Reign of Mary Queen of Scots, and Dowager of France. Extracted from original records and writers of credit* (1725).
17. Quoted in John Guy, *Queen of Scots: The True Life of Mary Stuart* (New York: Houghton Mifflin, 2004), p. 154.
18. James Melville, *Memoirs* (London, 1683), p. 94.
19. Guy, *Queen,* p. x.
20. Quoted in Guy, *Queen,* p. 154.
21. Quoted in Guy, *Queen,* p. 159.
22. British Library Cotton MS Calig. B.V., fol. 316.
23. Elizabeth Rex, "Doubt of Future Foes," *Poetical Works,* ed. James C. Smith and Ernest de Selincourt (Oxford University Press, 1985), p. 405.
24. A. Labanoff, ed., Lettres, Instructions, et Mémoires de Marie Stuart, Reine d'Écosse, Vol. 2 (London, 1844), p. 384.
25. *Lettres, Instructions, et Mémoires,* p. 83.
26. Quoted in John E. Neale, *Elizabeth I and Her Parliaments* 1584–1601 (New York, 1958), p. 117.
27. Quoted in Guy, *Queen,* p. 151.
28. On Lee and Hume, see Cynthia Wall, "'Chasms in the Story': Sophia Lee's The Recess and David Hume's History of England," in Imagining Selves: Essays in Honor of Patricia Meyer Spacks, ed. Rivka Swenson and Elise Lauterbach (Newark: University of Delaware Press2008), pp. 21–40. SECRET HISTORY was advertised as late as 1743; an edited copy was appended to a 1754 Elizabeth biography (Lewis, Mary, p. 132). Sophia Lee, *The Recess: Or, a Tale of Other Times,* ed. April Alliston (Lexington: University Press of Kentucky, 2000).
29. Jayne Elizabeth Lewis, *Mary Queen of Scots: Romance and Nation* (London: Routledge, 1998), p. 143.
30. Catherine Macaulay, preface, Vol. 6, *The History of England from the Accession of James I. to the Revolution,* 8 vols. (London, 1781), pp. [v]–xiv, [v], xiii.

9

MELINDA RABB

Satire

"[B]ecause they were fond of reading, she fancied them satirical: perhaps without exactly knowing what it was to be satirical; but THAT did not signify. It was censure in common use, and easily given."[1] When Jane Austen (1775–1817) offers this ironic insight into Lady Middleton's unease toward the Dashwood sisters in *Sense and Sensibility*, written in 1795, she casts a backward glance at a century of unease toward the relationship between women and satire. Austen's irony goes further because it identifies three issues fundamental to any critical assessment of this relationship. The first two issues are worrisome: the imputation of satire is a frequent slur against female reputations; such a slur is made ignorantly because most people are confused about the defining characteristics of the genre. The third issue, however, is more hopeful: the satirical is linked to an engagement with language and reading.

The passage from *Sense and Sensibility* reveals that despite improbabilities, the eighteenth century had effectively bequeathed a legacy of female-authored satire to which Austen is self-consciously contributing – that despite obstacles, earlier women writers had cleared a path for her to execute a deft jab at the stupid yet potentially dangerous Lady Middletons of the world. This literary inheritance has been compromised by assumptions about the relationship between gender and genre that deserve to be rethought. We know that the adjective "satirical" applied to a man would not emit the whiff of scandal directed toward Eleanor and Marianne. But we also know that if pleasure in reading, if fondness for language and the pursuit of knowledge, cultivates the "satirical," then the sisters have been crucially endorsed from their author's point of view. The more books one knows (or would like to know), the more likely one is to venture and to be admitted into this exclusive if hazardous realm. Aphra Behn (1640?–1689), arguably the earliest published female satirist in English, voices precisely this yearning to read widely beyond "[t]he fulsome Gingle of the times [that] is all we [women] are allow'd to understand or hear."[2] Excluded from classical education of Greek and Latin, she longed to "tread / The Mighty Paths of Learned Heroes ... Virgil, and great Homer's Verse" that "Like Divine Mysteries are conceal'd from us."[3] While traditions of ancient heroics and learned wit provide one map into the tradition, other routes to the satirical exist.

This chapter argues that satire written by women during the long eighteenth century claims a central position in the period's literary history because satire by women was the locus of the most intense and, therefore, the most revealing literary struggle between cultural constructions of femininity and women's participation in textual production. The intensity of this struggle results from traditional claims that satire is especially masculine. By offering an analysis of the relationship between the cultural history of gender, politics, and what is means to be satirical in literature, this chapter establishes a perspective from which to view a representative group of women authors and publications that preceded Austen. This perspective envisages a more continuous and influential history of female authorship from the apparent scarcity of women satirists in the early eighteenth century to the abundance of "lady-novelists" at the end. The same nexus of gender, politics, and literary representation that informs satire accompanies the shift toward women's production of sentimental or domestic fiction.

Several prevailing attitudes have obscured female-authored texts that castigate public and private abuses of political and social power. (The *Oxford English Dictionary* defines satire as "the employment ... of sarcasm, irony, ridicule, etc. in exposing, denouncing, deriding, or ridiculing vice, folly, indecorum, abuses, or evils of any kind.") Literary history locates the "Golden Age" of satire from approximately the mid-seventeenth to mid-eighteenth-centuries "because many of the most enduring works written during this era were satirical."[4] Scholarly claims are often sweeping: "the literature of the entire century ... is dominated by satire. It would be difficult to find another comparable period of modern literary history whose tone was so firmly established by a single dominant genre."[5] The sturdy pillars of this asserted greatness are men such as John Dryden, Jonathan Swift, Alexander Pope, and John Gay, who wrote poetry, essays, drama, political pamphlets, and narrative fiction – texts that readers perceive as either "a satire" (a form) or as "satirical" (a mode or discourse) because of the impulse to expose, deride, and reform specific evils. After 1750, satire ceases to dominate, although it is absorbed in important ways into the increasingly popular novel (and persists in some drama, verse, and essay). The "satirical" also seems to yield ground to the "sentimental" and the "romantic" by the 1790s.

If women writers were caught up in the rise of the novel and of the sentimental in the later decades of the eighteenth century, might they also have been caught up in the dominating mode of the satirical in the earlier ones? For some critics, the possibility is unthinkable: "the organization of culture has made it difficult for women to write and publish satire ... because women were long permitted little knowledge of the world outside their own domestic domain [and] ... have been trained not to develop or display aggressiveness."[6] The belief, expressed in 1994, that women are unable "to develop and display aggressiveness" differs little from Pope's view in 1728 of "the Sex which ought least to be capable of such malice or impudence." According to another critic, "the moves that satire required a writer to make were entirely inimical to the developing ideologies of femininity and sentimentality. Women were not supposed to laugh at their fellow creatures or to have opinions strong enough to lead them into ridiculing institutions or concepts."[7] Was there no laugh of the Medusa before the postmodern era? Did women do what they were "supposed to"? Is the "central place of women [in] the growing market for reading and writing imaginative literature" predicated only on "the possibilities for exploring sympathetic understanding of other human beings that [the novel] offered"?[8] Perhaps there is a way to connect the cultural work performed by the sentimental/romantic novel at the century's end with the functions of satire before 1750.

Redressing early women satirists

Scholarship on the novel has demonstrated the extent to which female-authored fiction published before 1740 was overwritten without acknowledgment by later writers intent on "legitimizing," "mainstreaming," or "elevating" popular narratives by women. The recovery and reassessment of amatory fiction by Aphra Behn, Delarivier Manley (c. 1670–1724), and Eliza Haywood (1693?–1756), for example, has changed and complicated the story of the novel's rise. "The erasure or forgetting of earlier cultural formations," William Warner notes, "is an obscure process."[9] A similar effort of recovery is required in the case of satire. Evidence suggests that eighteenth-century contemporaries were more aware of the work of women satirists (or the satirical work of women authors) than later generations have acknowledged. Two representative examples are offered here, drawn from the early and the later years of satire's "great age": Mary Evelyn's (1665–85) *Mundus Muliebris* (1690) and Jane Collier's (1715–55) *An Essay on the Art of Ingeniously Tormenting* (1753). They represent the independent accomplishments of early women satirists, as well as the relationship of such work to male traditions of satiric writing, epitomized by writers like Swift and Pope.

Consider these pairs of quotations from poems about the contents of ladies' dressing rooms, a frequent locus for satire. In each, an observer exposes the artificial and sometimes disgusting paraphernalia with which female beauty is achieved. The reader is shown the means of having a youthful round face:

> a) And that the Cheeks may both agree,
> Plumpers to fill the Cavity
> b) Now dexterously her plumpers draws,
> That serve to fill her hollow jaws.

The reader also witnesses the use of a false hairpiece or "tour":

> a) And when this Grace Nature denies,
> An Artificial Tour supplies.
> b) Then seated on a three-legged chair
> Takes off her artificial hair.

Hairs requires combs:

> a) Combs ... the set, and trim the Hair and Face
> Calembuc Combs by dozens fill'd
> b) The various combs for various uses,
> Fill'd up

Each dressing room is permeated with offensive body odors that are mitigated by a deodorizing substance that counteracts the stink of smelly clothing – either from "Scent of Gousset" ("goussset" refers to the fabric of a dress under the armpits where sweat would accumulate) or from a dress's "armpits well besmeared":

> a) Though powder'd Allom be as good,
> Well-strew'd on, and well understood;
> For Vapours that offend the Lass,
> Of Sal Armoniack a Glass:
> b) Here alum flower to stop the steams,
> Exhaled from sour unsavory streams.
> The petticoats and gown perfume
> And waft a stink round every room.

The second or (b) example in each pair of quotations comes from Jonathan Swift's well-known poems *A Beautiful Young Nymph Going to Bed* (1734) and *The Lady's Dressing Room* (1736). The first or (a) of each pair of quotations, however, comes from a satire written more than forty years earlier by a woman: Mary Evelyn's *Mundus Muliebris, or, the Ladies Dressing Room Unlock'd, and her Toilette Spread* (1690).[10] While several dressing room satires occur during the Restoration and eighteenth century, none predates or compares so extensively with Swift's work as Evelyn's.

Additional points of comparison, such as the inventory of objects, emerge. Evelyn's lady has "Pocket Mouchoirs [handkerchiefs] Nose to Drain"; Swift's "lady" Celia has "Handkerchiefs ... all varnish'd o'er with snuff and snot." Evelyn's lady has gloves of animal "skin for night / To keep her Hands plump, soft, and white"; Swift's "nymph" Corinna has "night-gloves made of Tripsy's hide." Evelyn's lady has a pile of eight "petticoats"; Swift's Celia has "petticoats in frowsy heaps." Evelyn's lady keeps "Pomatum ... Washes, Unguents, and Cosmeticks ... in Bottle, Cups / Cover'd or open to wash Chaps"; Swift's Celia keeps "pomatum, paints, and slops / And ointments good for scabby chops." Evelyn's lady uses "Gris" or squirrel's fur, while Swift's Corinna uses "mouse's hide." Evelyn's lady applies to her face "Spanish Paper, Lip and Cheek, / With Spittle ... to belick," while Swift's Corinna can "smooth the furrows of her front / With greasy paper stuck upon't." Evelyn's lady uses "Puppidog Water for the face," and so too does Celia rely on "puppy-water, beauty's help." In both imagined rooms, the poets place mirrors, tokens of the playhouse, and an odorous "chest."

Some shared formal characteristics are notable, such as the use of iambic tetrameter and striking comic end rhymes. Both writers represent the poet as casting up her/his hands in mock despair near the end of the inventory of dressing room things: "But tir'd with numbers I give ore, / Arithmetick can add no more," writes Evelyn; "But how shall I describe her arts / To recollect the scatter'd parts?" writes Swift. One could argue that Swift overwrites Evelyn to make women's things more disturbing: plumpers in Evelyn "fill the cavity," while in Swift they empty it out; the artificial hair goes on in Evelyn and comes off in Swift; "well-strewed on" becomes the harsher "well-besmeared"; squirrel's fur is downgraded to mouse's hide; "spittle" becomes grease. And a quilted storage chest for clothes becomes the container of a stinking chamber pot – although clothes (no dry cleaners, no washing machines) might also offend the nose, for Evelyn's room requires comically vast quantities of perfume: "D-Ange, Orange, Mill-Fleur, Myrtle, / Whole Quarts the Chamber to bespertle."

Did Swift know this poem when writing about women's private chambers and bodies? What other characteristics of the earlier poem would support the assertion that Evelyn's work specifically made an impression on later male satirists and, more generally, that female satirists (willing to castigate their own sex as male satirists castigate their own) may claim a role in the history of the genre? In *The Lady's Dressing Room*, Swift notes that puppy-water was "distilled from Tripsy [the dog's] darling whelp." Evelyn provides a recipe for preparing this concoction in terms worthy of Swift's ironic directions for cooking up a stew of human children in *A Modest Proposal* (1729). In both cases, earnest details are offered for accomplishing a "good" effect (physical beauty and economic prosperity) with apparent obliviousness to the cruelty of mutilating and destroying the young. Here are the directions that Evelyn's delicate nymph, goddess, or belle must follow:

> Take a ... Fat Puppidog, of nine days old and kill it, order it as to Roast, save the Blood, and fling away nothing but the Guts; then take the Blood, and ... the Puppidog, and break the Legs and Head, with all the Liver and the rest of the Inwards, ... put all into the Still if it will hold it, to that, take two Quarts of Old Canary, a pound of unwash'd Butter not salted; a Quart of Snails Shells, and also two Lemmons, only the outside pared away; Still all these together in a Rose Water Still ... Let it drop slowly into a Glass-Bottle.

Such gruesome practical advice ("take a ... Fat Puppidog ... and kill it") pushes Evelyn's work into the kind of satiric excess we have come to associate with Swift.

Swift's dressing room poem includes voyeuristic Strephon as an object of ridicule, and so does Evelyn include the "consummate beau" as an object of derision. Evelyn's preface advises "young Sparks" seeking mistresses and wives that "[t]he Refined Lady expects her ... Admirers should Court her in the Forms and Decencies of making Love in Fashion ... a little Practice will qualifie you for the ... Mystery of the Ruelle." A frustrated idealism underlies Evelyn's poem, which is framed in ways that extend its satiric purview beyond a mere diatribe against women's pursuit of artificial beauty; the modish worship of fashion is a symptom of or metaphor for abuses of wealth and power.

Evelyn imagines the world as a "Great ... Emporium," filled with "cargo" acquired though global trade, in which women's bodies are equated with marketable things. Pope's famous representation of this idea ("the various Off'rings of the World") in Belinda's dressing room in *The Rape of the Lock* (1712, 1714) occurs more than a decade later.[11] Evelyn's poem transmutes belles and beaus into "glittering Store" (Pope's phrase in *The Rape* is "glitt'ring Spoils") from Spain, Turkey, Asia, Flanders, Holland, France, India, Africa, and Rome. Evelyn's lady has inherited a "sapphire Bodkin for the Hair" (in Pope, "a Bodkin grac'd [Belinda's] Mother's Hair ... and now Belinda Wears"), she specifies "Diamond Pendants for the Ears" (Belinda too wears "Drops," defined in the *OED* as diamond earrings), a "Neck lace ... with Diamond Croche for Breast" (on Belinda's "Breast a sparkling Cross she wore").[12] Both women play ombre, and the same metaphor – the vessel – is used to conflate their identities with the merchandise they employ. To "smite" "silly fops," Evelyn's lady styles her hair into "creve-coeurs," which she defines as "heart breakers, the two small curl'd locks at the nape of the neck," exactly Belinda's coiffure.

Here, too, differences are noteworthy. Belinda's things require help from the sylphs; women are praised for labors not their own. Objects are vulnerable to stains, cracks, tears, and scissors. Evelyn's lady knows exactly how many and what kind of goods she wants: four pairs of silk stockings, twenty-four day smocks and twelve for night, two waistcoats, three nightgowns, four cushions cloths, three muffs, and so on. She has a knowing eye for style: every little black dress must be well accessorized: "One black Gown of rich silk. Which odd is / Without one colour'd, embroider'd Bodice." No one snips off the heartbreaker curls dangling at the nape of her neck.

Tita Chico has argued that dressing room metaphors in attacks on women (not work by women) played a crucial role in the development of eighteenth-century satire because they served a double purpose: to expose both the falseness of women and to comment on the art of the (male) satirist by asking "which kind of artifice – women's or satirist's – is ultimately more persuasive."[13] If "[n]early every satire about women reverts in one form or another to a dressing room scene," then the overwriting of the early and arguably paradigmatic *Mundus Muliebris* is even more interesting. Chico finds that Evelyn's "dressing room is a site of failure and delusion" (104) and that the work "jerks awkwardly toward a resolution": "There is no narrative ... [it] labor[s] to name item after item, ... framed by the minimal statements of purpose." To the contrary, Evelyn's satire is not so much a catalogue of existing things as a kind of imaginary shopping spree. It is ironically learned, in that it taps knowledge of women's special area of expertise – the practical and ornamental demands of their bodies – knowledge outside the purview of the beau. He need not envy women this special area of expertise, but he must learn what to provide. He does not ransack an existing scene of excess – although later Strephons would do so. Evelyn's things accumulate by "arithmetic." They do not "scatter" like Corinna's glass eye and false teeth, or suffer rape like Belinda's lock.

Evelyn's complete work consists of a prose preface, a lengthy poem, a mock-dictionary and "recipe," thus satisfying the requirements of Dryden's familiar definition of "Satura ... which signifies Full, and Abundant; and also full of Variety."[14] Her satire ridicules greedy material girls; and also the amoral beaus who willingly objectify them. In many representations of dressing rooms, the woman is missing, although her things remain behind to be inspected and manipulated by a masculine intelligence. So too Evelyn, who wrote precociously and died young, left behind her dressing room – in the form of a verse satire – to provide a satiric venue in her absence.

Further perspective on women satirists may be gained by reversing the sequence of influence and by considering later female-authored texts produced in response to male practitioners, as in the well-studied case of Behn's "The Disappointment" (1680) written in answer to John Wilmot, Earl of Rochester's "Imperfect Enjoyment" (1670–72). Jane Collier's *An Essay on the Art of Ingeniously Tormenting* (1753) shows an awareness of and bears a relationship to Swift's earlier *Directions to Servants* (1745).[15] Swift ironically critiques class and power; Collier ironically critiques class, power, and Swift. *Directions* teaches servants how to get the better of their masters, while *An Essay* teaches masters and mistresses how to dominate their servants and then extends the possibilities of domination over children, lovers, "humble companions," and ultimately "all your acquaintance."

Swift's text offers strategies for avoiding blame: "When you have done a Fault, be always pert and insolent, and behave your self as if you were the injured Person; this will immediately put your Master or Lady off their Mettle" (*DS* 1). Collier's text reverses the power play:

> If, on blaming any servant for a fault, she should be able to excuse herself, in a manner that ought to be perfectly satisfactory to a reasonable person, ... say, "that you will not hear the impertinent disclosure of such a wench ... and that you never knew a servant guilty of a fault, but she had pertness and invention enough to make a good excuse for it." (*IT* 14)

Swift's text recommends taking service in a household full of children and pets to have other creatures on whom to impute culpability: "Lay all Faults on a Lap-dog, a favourite Cat, a Monkey, a Parrot, a Magpye, a Child, or on the Servant who was last turned off" (*DS* 17). Collier recommends a similar household population, but only to trouble and inconvenience the staff:

> If you [Masters and Mistresses] have no children, keep as large a quantity of tame animals as you conveniently can. If you have children, a smaller number will do. Show the most extravagant fondness you possibly can for all these animals: and let them be of the most troublesome and mischievous sort, such as cats, monkeys, parrots, squirrels, and little snarling lap-dogs. (*IT* 16–17)

Swift's cook is counseled on ways to keep the best food for herself and the butler, such as attributing the disappearance of expensive meat and dainties to a hungry pet: "When you roast a Breast of Veal, remember your Sweetheart the Butler loves a Sweet-bread; therefore set it aside till Evening: You can say, the Cat or the Dog has run away with it" (*DS* 24). Collier's cook must watch helplessly while the choicest victuals are fed to the cat and dog:

"feed [pets] with all sorts of rarities, and give them (I mean the cats and dogs) what anyone would be glad of, while you feed your servants with the coarsest and cheapest diet that you can get" (*IT* 17).

Swift's extensive directions to the Housemaid include memorably scatological recommendations for embarrassing the mistress with whom, of all the servants, she has the greatest physical intimacy: "[L]et me advise you, on whom this Office [emptying the chamber pot] lies, to convey away this Utensil, that you will do it openly, down the great Stairs, and in the Presence of the Footmen; and, if any Body knocks, to open the Street-door, while you have the Vessel filled in your Hands" (*DS* 68-69). However, Collier's mistress keeps her distance from, as well as the upper hand over the maid:

> Your housemaid you will have so little intercourse with, that I hardly know how to direct your proceedings with regard to her ... Be kind to her for about a week, that you may raise her expectations of leading an easy, quiet life; for in judicious disappointment lies half the art in every connection whatever ... When Jenny is satisfied, by your kind behavior, that you are very well-disposed towards her ... fly all at once into a violent rage with her, call her saucy, pert, and impudent ... Remember always to tease and soothe her so alternately, that she shall be vastly puzzled. (*IT* 18-19)

Further contrast between the two texts exposes different, although equally compelling satiric goals. The implied dwelling of Swift's *Directions to Servants* is crammed with material objects: earthen drinking vessels, tablecloths, candles, china plates, baskets, snuff boxes, toothpick cases, rice milk, sack-posset, cards, riding jackets, horse shoes, buttermilk, salt cellars, a silver-laced hat, an old bridle and stirrup leather, pin cushions, ribbons, slippers, cold meat, a strange greyhound, fat drippings, cinders, corks, onions, water-gruel, and pistols. The world of things is not only crowded but often is unsavory: sockets full of grease, old snuff, burnt toast, foul smocks and handkerchiefs, greasy spits, singed and flayed larks, raw joints of meat, a lump of soot fallen into the soup, rats, broken mirrors, and water from a pot where cabbage and fish have been boiling then used for tea. Things become the weapons that servants can deploy against their masters:

> [I]f the Poker be out of the Way or broken, stir up the Fire with the Tongs; if the Tongs be not at Hand, use the Muzzle of the Bellows, the wrong End of the Fire Shovel, the Handle of the Fire Brush, the End of a Mop, or your Master's Cane. If you want Paper to singe a Fowl, tear the first Book you see about the House. Wipe your Shoes for want of a Clout, with the Bottom of a Curtain, or a Damask Napkin. Strip your Livery Lace for Garters. If the Butler wants a Jordan, he may use the great Silver Cup. (*DS* 18)

But, curiously enough, the end result of this potentially threatening and disorderly material world is a serene and peaceful state in which masters are happy fools among knaves. Slam the door, Swift counsels, "to put your Master and Lady in Mind that you observe their Directions" to keep entries shut (6). Always blame mishaps on dismissed servants because "[b]y this Rule you will excuse yourself, do no Hurt to any Body else, and save your Master or Lady from the Trouble and Vexation of chiding" (*DS* 17–18). Combine the dregs of various liquors into one mixture and re-serve it to gentlemen because "by this Method you are certain that nothing is lost" (*DS* 4). Do not report broken glasses until all of them are smashed because "this will be but one Vexation ... which is much better than fretting once or twice a Week; and it is the Office of a good Servant to discompose his Master and his Lady as seldom as he can" (*DS* 15).

Collier's departures from Swift create a domestic circumstance in which breakage happens to people, not things. Relatively few material objects command attention. Rather the reader is focused on the damage done to human integrity and well-being by means of "the noble game of Tormenting," a mind game. Both satirists attack abuses of power through the metaphor of domesticity. However, in place of Swift's household of placid dupes and concealed trickery, Collier gives us emotional cruelty inflicted by the powerful on the powerless. She does not restrict her views to "teasing and mortifying a good industrious servant, who has done her very best to please you" but rather expands to include other kinds of dependents – anyone who is vulnerable because of desire (lovers and spouses), economics (poor relations), or age (children). A long chapter addressed to patronesses recommends ways to torment "an Humble Companion" (*IT* 21), that is, "young women who have been well-educated; and who, by the misfortune or death of their friends, have been left destitute":

> There is some difficulty in giving rules for tormenting a dependent, that shall differ from those already laid down for plaguing and teasing your servants, as the two stations differ so very little in themselves. The servant, indeed, differs in this; she receives wages, and the humble companion receives none: the servant is most part of the day out of your sight; the humble companion is always ready at hand to receive every cross word that rises in your mind: the servants can be teased only by yourself, your dogs, your cats, your parrots, and your children; the humble companion (besides being the sport of all these) must, if you manage rightly, bear the insults of all your servants themselves. (*IT* 22–23)

Collier imagines satirical scenes that would reappear in un-ironic form in later sentimental fiction. For example, she proposes to "those who take young women into their houses, as subjects of their power," ingenious ways of abusing "Miss Kitty," "Miss Lucy," "Miss Dolly," and "Miss Fanny": "[Y]ou may, generally insult [an attractive ward] with her beauty, yet be sure, at all times, to say so many mortifying things, as shall make her believe you don't think her in the least handsome ... by right management, every personal perfection may be turned to her reproach" (*IT* 24). Beautiful or plain, shy or vivacious, simple or intellectually gifted, the figures of Collier's satirical portraits easily could become the suffering heroines of later novels.

If Swift is a witty observer of domestic materiality, Collier is an astute analyst of human psychology: "There are several good tricks of mortification, which you may apply properly, by attending to people's characters and dispositions, so as to find out what they most value and pride themselves upon" (*IT* 85). Collier's "ingenious tormenting" takes satire into new territory because aggression is more emotional, more intersubjective than physical. She alters the traditional idea of the satirist as a warrior who stabs, lashes, and pierces the metaphorical body of an enemy. Instead, she targets the vulnerable mind and self-esteem. Eighteenth-century male satirists make frequent use of madness as a metaphor for disorder. Collier's characters are not irrational; they are savvy manipulators of the mental states and feelings of others.

She also re-imagines the ancient idea that satire kills. In *Directions to Servants* (as in *A Modest Proposal*), Swift invokes the death of children as a satiric *coup de grace*. The Nurse is advised: "If you happen to let the Child fall, and lame it, be sure never to confess it; and, if it dies, all is safe" (*DS* 74). But Collier arguably is more vexing in her ironic attack on adult irresponsibility. All is not safe. First, children may be tortured emotionally: "If your children happen to have but weak understandings, upbraid them with every excellence you see abroad; and lament your own hard fate in being plagued with idiots. But, if you see a rising genius in any child ... give that child no assistance nor encouragement" (*IT* 39). The modest proposal of being sold for food during infancy might be preferable to such sustained emotional starvation and torture. In Collier, annihilation is eerily more plausible:

> Suppose your stock of children too large ... To make way with the troublesome and expensive brats [without incurring the laws against whipping and starving] ... [s]uffer them to climb without contradiction, to heights from whence they may break their necks; let them eat everything they like ... to sit up as late as they please at night ... should they chance to die of a surfeit ... your name will be recorded for a kind and indulgent parent. (*IT* 37–38)

The deceptive tranquility – and even triviality – of home and family can camouflage genuine danger. Collier's frontispiece first cites the motto

"Celebrare domestica facta" (Celebrate domestic things) but then quotes ominously from a child's book: "The Cat doth play / And after slay" (*IT* 2). Surely Austen (and others) would have found much in the emotional complexities and interpersonal relationships of the *Essay*'s domestic satire.

Satire and manliness

If we find the case for women participants in the great age of satire to be persuasive, we may wonder why critical interest in them has been long in arriving. There are legitimate reasons for hesitating at the threshold of female-authored satire. What does it mean, as Austen puts it, to be satirical? Despite its status as the dominant form of literature during the Restoration and early eighteenth century, "both the word and the idea of satire were fraught with ambiguity and confusion."[16] Its form, style, etymology, and appropriate character and purpose were matters of long-standing debate. If there was consensus in this debate, it arose from shared belief that satire is "a manly species of invective" expressing "manly indignation"[17] and from frequent use of militaristic and phallic critical terminology to describe its verbal attacks as "thrusts," "stabs," "piercings," and "cuts."

The satiric tradition has a rhetorical arsenal of sharp penetrating implements, like the teeth of Joseph Hall's "byting satyr." For John Milton, satire's weapons "ought to strike high and adventure dangerously" (*Apology for Smectymnuus*, 1642). "[S]trait to the thrusts I go, / And pointed Satyr runs him through and through," writes John Oldham (*Satyrs Upon the Jesuits*, lines 26–27; *Works*, 2: 132). Dryden's ideal satirist commits no "slovenly butchering" but like a Restoration Zorro executes "the fineness of the Stroak that separates the Head from the Body, and leaves it standing in its Place" (71). The *Poetical Register* of 1723 refers to "a very dangerous and unlawful weapon, ... a Sword."[18] Even Swift, who experimented with less traditional metaphors for satire – a bandied ball, a trick mirror, a bowl of cream – skewers his enemies Bentley and Wotton on a spit at the end of *The Battel of the Books*. And Pope embraces the role of embattled hero "arm'd for Virtue" who points his sharpened pen and "pleas'd by manly ways" (*Epistle to Dr. Arbuthnot*, line 347).

Women are specifically excluded from the club of armed warriors: it is "as disagreeable to see a Satyr Cloath'd in soft and effeminate Language, as to see a Woman scold and vent her self in Billingsgate Rhetorick in a gentile and advantageous Garb."[19] Joseph Addison, who insists that "it [is] absolutely necessary to keep up the partition between the two sexes, and to take notice of the smallest encroachments which the one makes upon the other"

(*Spectator* 435, July 19, 1712), associates women satirists with prostitutes: "all the Common Women of the Town are of their Side; for which Reason they ought to preserve a more than ordinary Modesty in their Satyrical Excursions, that their Characters may not be liable to Suspicion" (*Freeholder* 23, March 9, 1716). Twentieth-century literary critics endorse the masculinity of satire. Northrop Frye identifies it with the "blasts" of Saturn; Robert Elliot, with primitive phallic songs and ritual murder; Maynard Mack, with the *vir bonus* and other male personae; Alvin Kernan, with a biological adaptation through which "man has learned to control aggression and manage it to useful ends"; David Worcester, with tragic heroism; Claude Rawson, with the machismo of Norman Mailer; Brean Hammond, with men's "competitive and aggressive" attitudes. Even feminist critiques of satire often assume a male writer challenging or usurping "phallic female power."[20]

Historical context shows, however, that satire's "great age" in England coincides with a so-called crisis of authority when patriarchal authority is challenged in unprecedented ways by the game-changing events of the Civil Wars, Commonwealth, Restoration, and Succession Settlement. The sequence of monarchs from Charles II to George III begins in licentiousness and ends in madness, framing the Restoration and eighteenth century with models of compromised masculinity.

Insistence that the period's dominant form of writing is "manly" also coincides with an effort to define gender roles with greater clarity. *The Universal Spectator* is typical: "[T]he same qualities, which are extremely decent and ornamental to one Sex, are very misbecoming and reproachful in the other, as it is encroaching upon the Boundaries, assign'd to each for a proper Distinction and Discrimination between us" (November 25, 1738). Double standards are operative. Anger may be admirable in a satirist such as Juvenal, but an angry woman is "a scold ... vent[ing] herself in Billingsgate Rhetorick."[21] For women, compulsive behavior betrays weakness, hysteria, or poor self-control. Yet, one of the defining attributes of the satirist is yielding to compulsion: *Difficile est saturum non scribere* ("It is difficult to not write satire") writes Juvenal about the irresistibility of his art. Pope compares his craft to the minister who, seeing ass's ears on King Midas, "was forc'd to speak, or burst" (*Epistle to Dr. Arbuthnot*, 1735, l. 72). A masked woman has salacious connotations; for the satirist the mask is a liberating persona. Unstable or unclear meaning is taken as a sign of women's poor command over language and intellect, yet satiric irony is admired as the crucial destabilizer of language and meaning. Mutability is construed as fickleness when it is a feminine quality, but satire's protean capacity to change forms provides, to adapt Pope's words, creative "elasticity and fire."

Revealing scandalous secrets is demeaned as mere gossip in women, but in satire, exposure of hidden vice is dignified as moral castigation. Female figures who stand apart from society are stereotyped as disappointed spinsters, prudes, or old maids, while the satirist's unapologetic isolation, however bitter, provides a valuable perspective on society.

Finally, the satirist's need to have knowledge of evil to rebuke or reform the world conflicts with the tremendous cultural investment in female innocence and purity. "[T]o be a universal reformer and corrector of abuses," Swift astutely notes of the broom that grows dirty with sweeping, the satirist risks "sharing deeply all the while in the very same pollutions he pretends to sweep away." Cultural constructions of gender begrudge women a single *faux pas*, much less "rak[ing] into every slut's corner of Nature."[22] We should not, then, be surprised at unease toward women who produce satire.

From satire to sentiment: Anger as the antidote to pain

The assertion of satire's manliness and its predication on the relational nature of male and female roles can serve as a means of seeing continuity rather than fundamental change in the emergence of novels and the sentimental in the later part of the eighteenth century when female authorship increases. It allows us to see women writers' abiding practice of the satirical within a shifting literary landscape. Although the sentimental at first seems precisely opposite – humane, generous, inclusive, allied with victims who are taken seriously, not made the butt of jokes – it shares a commitment to fantasies of inflicted pain, of power imbalance, and of excesses that push female practitioners into irony, ridicule, and satire. The circumstances that obscure women satirists and promote women novelists might be said to participate in the same cultural work, despite assertions that "the moves that satire required a writer to make were entirely inimical to the developing ideologies of femininity and sentimentality."[23] The public display of the pains suffered by women in their private spaces, as imagined by male authors, effaces many apparent differences between Swift's satiric representation of a woman's body in *Tale of a Tub* (1704) ("Last week I saw a woman flayed, and you will hardly believe how much it altered her person for the worse") and Burke's sentimental one in *Reflections on the Revolution in France* (1790) (the "persecuted ... almost naked" Marie Antoinette nearly "pierced with a hundred strokes of bayonets and poniards").

Satire and sentiment share a deep political purpose that is inseparable from a need to reify and perpetuate the concept of manliness. Like satire, "sentimentality has a long and exceedingly complex history tied in with the civil war in seventeenth-century England." Like the satirical, the sentimental is "a commanding imaginative response to a world riven with crisis."[24] The political upheavals that frame both ends of the long eighteenth century are testimony that "the calamity of revolution is a crisis of gender."[25] The severed head of one failed patriarch (Charles I) supports the satiric indignation and anger of a writer such as Swift (who gave a sermon every January 30, the anniversary of the king's execution); the head of another (Louis XVI) supports the sentimental tears of a writer such as Burke (whose writing on the French Revolution inspired cartoonist James Gillray to envision Sensibility using the king's skull as a foot rest).[26]

Further affinities between the two modes of discourse are noteworthy. They suggest that some women writers represent strong feelings not because, at last, there was a chance to exude emotion but because they perceive the harsh truth that "woman's presence in a sentimental public sphere is not to be confused with her empowerment there." Both modes of discourse operate at the nexus of affectivity, politics, and gender; each indulges in immoderate extravagant fictions – what Claude Rawson calls "overplus" in satire and Claudia Johnson calls "disfiguring excess" in sentimental novels. The adjectives "strain, incoherence, and excess" Claudia Johnson attributes to fiction of the 1790s might describe as well Swift's great satire of the 1690s, *A Tale of a Tub*. For both, the underlying question is "how the manliness of political subjects is ... constituted."[27] Both encourage fantasies of aggressive domination to test that manliness, whether by skewering an opponent or by dissolving him into tears, by separating the head from his body or disarming him with feeling. Both satire and sentimentalism incur pain; both attribute the ills of society to outrageous egoism. Both rely on fictions of penetration and surfaces, and of making the private public. Both emerge from anxieties within heterosexual culture and often transpose those anxieties onto masculine women and feminine men. The boundary crossings of Pope's Sporus and Behn's Philander, as well as Samuel Richardson's Lovelace and Frances Burney's (1752–1840) Mr. Lovel have the potential to disrupt both gender and the sociopolitical order. Women writers could "be satirical" when they participate in "as well as assail the sentimental tradition at precisely that moment when it is being reasserted in extreme forms as a political imperative."[28]

Woman's private space remains an important metaphor. The dressing room becomes the closet or boudoir, domestic spaces that witness scenes of pain, trespass, and anxiety – of "mangl'd Plight[s]" – from "the Anguish, Toil, and Pain" of Swift's Corinna to the scabbards of *sans culottes* symbolically raping the bed of Burke's French queen. If exposing what women suffer for physical beauty in the dressing room is a means of clarifying the terms of masculinity in satire, then exposing women's physical and emotional suffering in their bedchambers serves a similar purpose in sentimental novels: "Classic texts of sentimentalism by Samuel Richardson, Henry Mackenzie, Hugh Kelly, Henry Brooke, and Oliver Goldsmith recur to the spectacle of suffering womanhood to elicit the melting humanity of male onlookers."[29] These scenes of disgust or dismay bear directly on a revised understanding of women writers and satire by revealing how, over the century, they recognize, expose, and ridicule with varying degrees of self-consciousness abuses framed by gender construction in public and private spheres.

Anyone fond of reading, as the Dashwood sisters knew, might find grounds for being satirical. Eleanor and Marianne had plenty of time to read while they were being genteelly disenfranchised by a culture of patriarchy and primogeniture. The idea, as Wollstonecraft "acidly put it," that "humanity to women is the characteristic of advancing civilization" elicits protest, irony, and anger from women writers throughout the eighteenth century.[30] Austen had a rich inheritance to invest in her own ironic fictions.

NOTES

1. Jane Austen, *Sense and Sensibility*, ed. R. W. Chapman (Oxford University Press, 1988), p. 246.
2. An argument can be made for locating women's satirical writing even earlier, in the work of Mary Wroth (1587?–1651/53). *The Countess of Montgomeries Urania* (1621) and the attached sonnet sequence *Pamphilia to Amphilanthus* are self-consciously parodic of the masculine literary forms of the pastoral romance and the Petrarchan sonnet.
3. Aphra Behn, "To Mr. Creech ... on his Excellent Translation of Lucretius" (1684), lines 33–34, 28–30.
4. Brean Hammond, *Pope Among the Satirists: 1650–1750* (Tavistock: British Council, 2005), p. 1.
5. David Nokes, *Raillery and Rage: A Study of Eighteenth-Century Satire* (New York: St. Martin's Press, 1987), p. 1.
6. Dustin Griffin, *Satire: A Critical Reintroduction* (Lexington: University Press of Kentucky, 1994), pp. 189–90.
7. Hammond, *Pope Among the Satirists*, p. 5.
8. Hammond, *Pope Among the Satirists*, p. 5.
9. William B. Warner, *Licensing Entertainment: The Elevation of Novel Reading in Britain, 1684–1750* (Berkeley: University of California Press, 1998), p. 42.
10. Mary Evelyn, *Mundus Muliebris: or, The Ladies dressing-room unlock'd, and her toilette spread. In burlesque. Together with the Fop Dictionary compiled for the use of the fair sex* (London: R. Bentley, 1690).
11. Joseph Addison's essay on ransacking the globe for female adornments (*Spectator 69*) is another post-Evelyn example.

12. A "croche" is not a religious object but rather a jeweled ornament in the shape of a hook from which a woman could hang a watch, but the similarity in sound between "croche" and "cross" seems to have caught Pope's attention.
13. Tita Chico, *Designing Women: The Dressing Room in Eighteenth-Century English Literature and Culture* (Lewisburg, PA: Bucknell University Press, 2005), p. 81.
14. *The Works of John Dryden*, ed. Edward N. Hooker, Hugh T. Swedenborg, Vinton Dearing, and Alan Roper, Vol. 4 of 20 (Berkeley: University of California Press, 1956–1989), pp. 36–37.
15. Jane Collier, *An Essay on the Art of Ingeniously Tormenting*, ed. Katharine A. Craik (Oxford University Press, 2006). Jonathan Swift, *Directions to Servants* (Dublin, 1745).
16. *The Works of John Dryden*, 4:415.
17. G. Richards, *An Essay on the characteristic differences between ancient and modern poetry, and the several causes from which they result* (Oxford, 1789), p. 9.
18. Giles Jacob, "An Introductory Essay, on the rise, Progress, Beauty, &c. of all Sorts of Poetry" in *The Poetical Register: or, the Lives and Characters of all the English Poets. With an Account of their Writing*, Vol. 2 (London: A. Bettersworth, 1723), p. xviii.
19. *A Satyr against common-wealths* (Printed for John Hindmarsh ... and Francis Hicks, 1684), "Preface to the Reader."
20. Domna Stanton, "Autogynography: Is the Subject Different?" in *Women, Autobiography, Theory: A Reader*, ed. Sidonie Smith and Julia Watson (Madison: University of Wisconsin Press, 1998), pp. 118–19.
21. Anonymous, *A Satyr Against Common-wealths* (London, 1684), preface.
22. Jonathan Swift, *Meditation Upon a Broom-Stick* (London: 1710), p. 7.
23. Hammond, *Pope Among the Satirists*, p. 5.
24. Claudia Johnson, *Equivocal Beings: Politics, Gender, and Sentimentality in the 1790s: Wollstonecraft, Radcliffe, Burney, Austen* (University of Chicago Press, 1995), p. 12, 2.
25. Johnson, *Equivocal Beings*, p. 2.
26. James Gillray, *The New Morality* in *The Anti-Jacobin*, Vol. 1 (August 1, 1798).
27. Johnson, *Equivocal Beings*, p. 31.
28. Johnson, *Equivocal Beings*, p. 15.
29. Johnson, *Equivocal Beings*, p. 5.
30. Johnson, *Equivocal Beings*, p. 8.

10

NICOLA PARSONS

Early fiction

In 1730, Henry Fielding's play *The Author's Farce* brought the literary marketplace on stage in the Little Theatre in Haymarket. The final act of this play, performed at least thirty-two times in its first season, was a showstopper. It depicted the rehearsal of a new play, penned by the impecunious poet Harry Luckless in a desperate attempt to turn a profit from his writing. Drawing on the conceit of Alexander Pope's just-published poem *The Dunciad*, Luckless's play represents characters embodying dramatic writing, prose fiction, and poetry (as well as popular entertainments such as opera, pantomime, and oratory) as they vie for the favor of the Goddess Nonsense. The literary genres and forms of popular entertainment brought together in this staged rehearsal are almost exclusively represented by male characters, their shared gender foregrounded by the collection of masculine honorifics with which they are addressed. In this diverse group of genres and forms, only prose fiction is represented by a woman – Mrs. Novel – a character modeled on Eliza Haywood (1693?–1756), arguably the most popular and prolific producer of fiction in the early eighteenth century.

Fielding's dramatized literary marketplace both suggests a strong link between femininity and fiction in the early eighteenth century and demonstrates that women were recognized as prominent producers of prose fiction in this period. In fact, women not only outnumbered men as authors of prose fiction but, in sharp distinction to their male contemporaries, were more likely to use the term "novel" to refer to their writing. Further, in entreating the Goddess's favor, Mrs. Novel refers to her collected corpus of writing as "romances."[1] The conjunction of this generic marker with her emblematic character name suggests the lack of distinction between romance and novel, particularly in fiction by women, in the early eighteenth century. This chapter takes as its subject the prominence of women as fiction writers in early eighteenth-century Britain. It examines the constitutive connections between romance and the developing genre of the novel in both the eighteenth century and subsequent critical accounts of the field.

I aim to demonstrate both how women's participation in the early market of prose fiction has been understood and to elucidate what may be excluded or misrepresented by these dominant models.

Critical traditions

The rise of the novel looms large in critical accounts of early eighteenth-century fiction, with much discussion centering on identifying the key features of the genre and accounting for its origins. At its inception, academic study of the eighteenth-century novel aligned the genre with realism and referential detail and established the form as a wholly masculine endeavor. In his seminal *The Rise of the Novel* (1957), Ian Watt identifies "formal realism" – that is, the set of narrative techniques enabling fictional stories to approximate everyday life – as the novel's defining feature and establishes Daniel Defoe, along with Samuel Richardson and Fielding, as realism's principal practitioners. This critical model not only effectively eclipses Haywood's eighteenth-century reputation as Mrs. Novel but also, in drawing a direct line of influence from Defoe to Richardson, entirely elides the fiction writers at work in the early decades of the eighteenth century, many of them women. In positing an absolute break between the novel and the romance, Watt translated a problem of definition into one of distinction and suggested the genre was independent of its predecessors. Although subsequent scholarship has departed from the idea of a definitive break, providing alternate models of relation and influence, romance is still positioned as a mode that is anterior or historically prior to the novel proper; in contrast, Michael McKeon, in *Origins of the English Novel* (1987), argues that the novel results from a dialectic between romance and history.

In seeking to challenge these models, feminist discussions of critically and institutionally excluded women writers identified the vast number of women writing in the early eighteenth century. For example, in her pointedly titled *The Rise of the Woman Novelist* (1986), Jane Spencer identifies Haywood and her near-contemporaries Aphra Behn (1640?–89) and Delarivier Manley (c. 1670–1724) as members of an alternative tradition of women's writing. By focusing on these three writers and identifying a shared interest in the representation of romantic or sexual passion as the most noteworthy aspects of their published fiction, contemporary criticism reiterates an eighteenth-century practice. In a commendatory poem prefacing Haywood's *Secret Histories, Novels and Poems* (1725), James Sterling lauds Haywood's feeling representations of desire. He names her "the Great Arbitress of Passion" and claims that she joins "Pathetick Behn" and "Manley's greater Name" to close "the fair Triumvirate of Wit."[2] That Behn, Manley, and Haywood were influential writers whose passionate fictions constituted a visible tradition was crucial to the important work of recovering women writers. If the trope of the "fair triumvirate" allowed Sterling to suggest that the achievements and reputation of Behn, Manley, and Haywood were such that they collectively rivaled the original triumvirate of wit of William Shakespeare, Ben Jonson, and John Fletcher described by John Denham,[3] it also enabled feminist critics to establish a productive counterpoint to the masculine trio of novelists – Defoe, Richardson, and Fielding – institutionalized by Watt. The persistence of romance in texts authored by women, and not just the numbers in which women wrote, became an important way of highlighting the blind spots in existing explanatory models and a means of arguing for the vital role of women novelists in the development of the genre.

Scholarship of the last decade has highlighted the semantic ambiguity surrounding "romance" and "novel" in the early eighteenth century, drawing attention to the fact that the terms were often used interchangeably to describe long fictional narratives and suggesting the impossibility of distinguishing absolutely between the two forms. However, elucidating the persistence of romance – as structure, content, and perhaps even strategy – has enabled critics to make important claims for early fiction by women and assert the centrality of these texts to the development of the novel. In what follows, I focus first on the claims that can be made for women writers by concentrating on the representation of seduction in their fictional texts, before going on to suggest some limitations of this model.

Reconfiguring romance

In writing fiction that adopted the structure and preoccupations of romance, Behn, Manley, Haywood, and their female contemporaries were influenced by French authors of the late seventeenth century. In this period, writers including Madeleine de Scudéry (1607–1701) reconfigured romance by reworking the preoccupations of earlier examples to produce heroic or sentimental narratives. In the process, romance became associated increasingly with a "feminine and feminized urban aristocratic culture."[4] The influence of French precursors such as Scudéry on English authors is well known. The preface to *The Secret History of Queen Zarah* (1705), a libelous account of Sarah Churchill, the Duchess of Marlborough (1660–1744) once thought to be written by Manley, offers a literal translation of a French essay to account for the literary tastes of specifically English authors and their readers.[5] Similarly, booksellers forged associations with repeated strategic decisions to pair narratives by English authors with recent translations of French texts. The complex connections between English and French fiction to which this material history attests is significant, as Ros Ballaster has demonstrated, not just for the textual models they provide but also for the fact that these narratives constitute a feminocentric tradition.

The specifically English reconfiguration of romance is most commonly termed "amatory fiction," a category Ballaster defines as a body of fiction authored by women "explicitly erotic in its concentration on the representation of sentimental love."[6] Amatory fictions share recognizable narrative preoccupations and tropes: typically, a young, naïve woman is seduced by an older, and often duplicitous, man who is able to awaken and exploit her unconscious desires; that desire is furthered through illicit correspondence, which acts as both a substitute for and an invitation to sexual congress; and considerable narrative attention is devoted to the pleasurable transport of passionate feeling. In these fictions, the plot motif of seduction serves a double function: it is a means of engaging the imaginative sympathies of readers and a way of figuring broader ethical, epistemological, and political issues. Readers were encouraged to find a political frame for sexual pleasure that supplemented, rather than superseded, the fictional narrative. For this reason, Catherine Gallagher describes the early eighteenth century as "an extraordinary moment in the history of English women's writing" because politics and femininity became imbricated in a way that produced "a third term, 'fiction.'"[7]

Manley's *Secret Memoirs and Manners of several Persons of Quality, of both Sexes. From the New Atalantis, an Island in the Mediterranean* (1709), more commonly known as the *New Atalantis*, is the best-known example of amatory fiction that was written *à clef* and featured obvious partisan political allegories. The representation of illicit desire and sexual irregularities in this text are associated with specific and recognizable Whigs. Published in two successive volumes in 1709 and suppressed shortly afterward, the *New Atalantis* earned Manley a brief stint in prison on charges of seditious libel and a belated honorarium of fifty pounds from Robert Harley in recognition of her service to the Tory party. Although it is often presented in contemporary critical accounts as if it contained incendiary and immediate political scandal, the narrative of the *New Atalantis* is explicitly positioned as historical. The narrative unfolds in 1702, immediately after the death of William III and Anne's accession to the English throne, and it retails gossip and scandal that is specifically marked as out of date. The pleasure of reading the *New Atalantis* lies not in uncovering new scandal but in discovering how old scandals are amplified in the pages of Manley's fiction. The pleasure, in other words, lies in the interchange between the fictional and the referential levels of the text.

The *New Atalantis* is a collection of anecdotes, loosely held together by its frame narration in which gossip is related by the Lady Intelligence to two allegorical figures, Virtue and Astrea, as they tour the island of Atalantis. As a narrator, Intelligence is compulsively digressive, unable to resist telling her companions everything she knows about everyone they encounter. In the crowded, episodic, narrative that results, several stories are repeatedly singled out for critical attention. These stories – the temptation and betrayal of Charlot by her guardian, the Duke; the affair and frustrated elopement between Diana de Bedamore and Chevalier Thomaso; and Germanicus's seduction of the Duchess de l'Inconstant through the display of his naked and pliable body – are also those Manley highlighted as representative in her fictionalized autobiography, *The Adventures of Rivella* (1714). In praising the *New Atalantis*, one character rhapsodizes that these three interpolated tales "are such Representatives of Nature, that must warm the coldest Reader; it raises high Ideas of the Dignity of Human Kind, and informs us that we have in our Composition, wherewith to taste sublime and transporting Joys."[8] These stories not only represent the systematic association of sexual scandal with real-life figures, but they also demonstrate the engaging fictional aspects of the narrative that lie beyond the frisson of scandalous discovery.

The story of the Duke's seduction of his ward Charlot, described by Intelligence as "a landmark" to warn her innocent readers, has become emblematic of Manley's narrative innovation. The Duke, identified by readers as William III's close confidant Hans Willem Bentinck, is represented as a consummate politician: his ostensible admiration of virtue disguises a flexible morality and a preference for expedience rather than ethics. Nowhere are the Duke's failings more apparent than in his treatment of Charlot. Intending that she will become his son's wife, he forbids her fashionable entertainment and limits her conduct to the strictest notions of feminine propriety; then, once he is seduced by her unwitting charms, he sets out to undo the principles he has inculcated so as to render her susceptible to his advances. The Duke's method of awakening desire in his ward is especially telling: he supplies her with literary texts that introduce her to the "raptures of enjoyment" and the "speculative joys of love."[9] This course of reading has the desired effect and he is soon able to make her his mistress. Once conquered, Charlot is besotted with the Duke and has absolute faith in his constancy, refusing to heed wiser counsel that encourages her to be suspicious of the durability of his desire and take immediate steps to secure their union through marriage. Predictably, his "wonderful loyalty" proves but a sham, and he is seduced away from Charlot and into a hasty marriage with another. This story not only contributes to the bleak portrait of the Whigs that accumulates throughout the novel; in defining sexual desire in part as literary experience, it also highlights what Ballaster has argued is Manley's most important innovation: plots of seduction that are also seductive plots. Charlot's tale, together with other instances of women seduced and betrayed by men's deceitful stories, educates the reader into more sophisticated (if not, suspicious) principles of reading by encouraging interpretation that goes beneath the surface.

Haywood's first novel, *Love in Excess* (1719–20), is another important example of how early eighteenth-century female authors reworked romance into the distinctive form of amatory fiction. This novel follows the intrigues of the ambitious Count D'Elmont as he goes from libertine seducer to a sincere lover, redeeming his past indiscretions by his faithful love for the "matchless Melliora."[10] Unlike the allegorical seduction plot Manley develops in the *New Atalantis*, the representation of sexual agency in *Love in Excess* speaks implicitly – not explicitly – to political questions concerning agency and accountability, as Toni Bowers has shown. In this novel, passion is an overwhelming force to which concession and even capitulation are not only unavoidable but, in some circumstances, may be aspects of virtue.[11]

Love is truly an excessive force in Haywood's novel: it not only possesses body and soul, but it also overwhelms language. When D'Elmont catches Melliora in his arms, for example, he is dumbstruck with desire. The narrator comments approvingly on this circumstance, remarking "there is no greater proof of a vast and elegant passion, than the being uncapable of expressing it" (106). To fill the gap created by this inevitable and repeated failure of description, readers must exercise their imagination. At times, the acts of imaginative sympathy required are prompted by the narrator – we are told that Alovysa's sorrow, for example, is "more easily imagined than expressed" – but more often it is aroused by the disordered and broken syntax of the narration (68). The narrative register of these heightened scenes has been described as a "grammar of eroticism" constituted by "the gasping effect of dashes, inverted syntax, and other arrhythmic prosody."[12] In this way, as G. Gabrielle Starr has established, Haywood's fictions are chiastic forms that aim to reach their readers and produce passionate imaginative responses.[13]

Amatory fiction intensifies the iterability of all romance, producing a kind of formula fiction. The sheer volume of Haywood's fictional publications in the 1720s alone suggests her command of the marketplace, but her novella *Fantomina* (1725) demonstrates her exploitation of amatory fiction's patterns more completely. In this novella, an unnamed lady disguises herself as a prostitute to experience the pleasures of close conversation and unrestrained male desire in which she has witnessed others indulge. She quickly attracts Beauplaisir's eye, and not long after she grants him the last favor, he tires of her "rifled charms" just as her own ardor increases. Rather than seeking to revive his waning passion, Fantomina sets out to engage it anew: she assumes a series of disguises (prostitute, maidservant, widow, aristocratic libertine) to seduce her inconstant lover. In this way, the novella repeatedly rehearses the serial seduction tropes of amatory fiction. The mastery of convention this text represents is acknowledged in the narrator's assessment of the story, expressed in the novella's reflexive final sentence: "thus ended an Intreague, which, considering the Time it lasted, was as full of Variety as any, perhaps, that many Ages has produced."[14] In stressing variety as Fantomina's ultimate virtue, these concluding remarks insist that entertaining plots have value and remind us that Haywood was knowing in her exploitation of popular literary trends.

The formulaic nature of amatory fiction has not escaped critical attention, and neither has Haywood's seemingly close association with the serial pleasure of repetitious plots. Bowers's argument provides a way of redeeming the formulaic – what might be read as mere repetition is recast as a way of working through political issues that remained urgent and seemed intractable throughout the period. From this perspective, the recurrence of narrative structures and plot motifs is a symptom of continued experimentation with persistent political questions rather than a sign of an impoverished creativity. Moreover, as Helen Thompson and Jonathan Kramnick have demonstrated respectively, the legible patterning of amatory fiction – in particular, the relation between (and at times, confusion of) the singular experience of love and the serial pleasure of seduction – speaks to broader questions of how individual agency and its relation to the social may be conceived.[15]

The prevalence and popularity of this fictional form are attested to by the ease with which other authors could identify and parody its conventions. For instance, Mary Davys's (1674–1732) *Familiar Letters betwixt a Gentleman and a Lady* (1725) engages the conventions of amatory fiction to tell a very different story. The impropriety that conventionally attends the exchange of letters in amatory fiction is dismissed through association with the opinions of an overly precise older woman and with reference to the practical demands of friendship. Letters here are part of everyday life, interrupted only by events as mundane as a boiling teakettle.[16] The idea that fictional narratives could sustain discussion of political events only if that discussion is coded is similarly reworked. Politics are addressed directly in these letters, and the correspondents, Berina and Artander, vigorously debate the relative merits of the Whig and Tory parties. Berina attempts to dissuade Artander from his Tory principles, claiming that the party has "nothing in view but the subversions of their religions and laws and the utter ruin of their native land" (269); Artander counters, asking her to point to "one text in either Old or New Testament, that tolerates Rebellion, and I'll recede from all my past Opinions, and become as strenuous a Whig as Berina" (274). Davys's *Familiar Letters* both demonstrates the popularity of amatory fiction and indicates that it was not the only kind of fiction written by women in this period.

Refocusing on early fiction

In highlighting the potential limitations of "amatory fiction" for understanding early eighteenth-century women's prose fiction and arguing against its predominance as an explanatory model, Kathryn King posed the following challenge: "[f]ew ask what it means that this 'tradition' consists only of three writers – Behn, Manley, and Haywood – or consider the implications of a critical move that assimilates a broad and complex move to its sexiest moments."[17] In suggesting women writers constituted an autonomous tradition that existed independently of (or perhaps in opposition to) their male contemporaries and by linking these women writers in a model of influence that depends on exploring romance – whether it be the experience of seduction or an exploration of its effects – this model has perhaps outlived its usefulness. The fair triumvirate of wit, now an overly familiar model, limits our understanding of the range and versatility of women's fiction writing; it also encourages us to overlook the important and influential links female writers developed with their male peers.

Perhaps the best example of how focusing on a feminocentric tradition of amatory fiction might distort, rather than clarify, our understanding of women as fiction writers in the early eighteenth century is provided by Haywood. For much of the twentieth century, Haywood was identified solely as a writer of amatory fictions. In his landmark study of popular fiction published before Richardson's *Pamela* (1740), John Richetti's assessment of Haywood's texts is colored by what he takes as her excessive focus on "palpitating passion," particularly the repetitive rhetorical and narrative devices she employs to produce "sexual 'intensity.'"[18] Reading Haywood through her contemporary critics, such as Pope and Richard Savage, a scandalous impropriety was assumed to attend her reputation for representing passion. This assumption is contested not only by the praise Haywood's passionate fictions attracted from her peers but also by the material history of her signature work *Love in Excess*. Recent bibliographic work on Eliza Haywood indicates that far from a disposable and slightly disreputable popular text, this novella was marketed toward a genteel readership.[19]

Advertisements for *Love in Excess* appended to Haywood's later novel *The British Recluse* (1722) stress the quality and production values of the text, suggesting it might have been regarded as leisure reading suited to a polite audience.

We have always known that Haywood wrote prodigiously and experimented with almost all available forms, but the fact that she deliberately marketed her fictions – and her own authorship – in different ways has only just been demonstrated. King has discovered that the title pages of Haywood's perhaps polite amatory fictions display her name as "Mrs. Eliza Haywood," while her secret histories, published in the same period, appeared anonymously. From this evidence, King concludes "her titles were marketed in clustered product lines manipulated by Haywood in conjunction with the bookseller."[20] No doubt regarding Haywood as the producer of scandalous, amatory fiction has brought her to the attention of modern-day readers and critics and helped claim a place for her in the revised story of the novel. Yet, as the foregoing examples indicate, this framework has also flattened her career and diminished the significance of her example.

Elizabeth Rowe

As seduction is de-centered as an explanatory framework, the full picture of women who experimented with fictional writing in the early eighteenth century comes into clearer focus. Elizabeth Singer Rowe (1674–1737) was arguably the most popular female writer in the eighteenth century and, according to Margaret Ezell, one of the two most published.[21] Her poems dominated the pages of *The Athenian Mercury*, one of the most widely read Whig periodicals of the late seventeenth century. An entire issue of the *Mercury* was devoted to Rowe's poems, a fact that distinguished her from the periodical's many other contributors and suggested her popularity with readers. Her importance to the paper was later confirmed by the proprietor's decision to dedicate the fifteenth volume to her as a "testimony of respect." Rowe's epistolary fictions, *Friendship in Death, In Twenty Letters from the Dead to the Living* (1728) and *Letters Moral and Entertaining in Prose and Verse* (1729–32), were similarly successful, going through multiple editions in the eighteenth century and sustaining a vigorous readership well into the nineteenth. As evidence of Rowe's popularity, Paula Backscheider notes that more editions of Rowe's prose fictions were issued over the course of the eighteenth century than novels now considered canonical. Despite Rowe's evident popularity with eighteenth-century readers, until recently her texts have not been the subject of sustained critical interest and still less is her example integrated in theoretical accounts of early eighteenth-century fiction.[22]

Rowe's reputation for pious polemic, cultivated in her published works and confirmed in a biographical sketch originally penned by her friend Henry Grove and then extended by her brother-in-law Theophilus Rowe, has limited assessments of the significance of her work. Her piety appears to have influenced the characterization of her fictional works, along with her poetry, as rhapsodic expressions of overly sincere feelings. In a representative example of prevailing critical judgments, Richetti characterizes Rowe's epistolary fictions as "written in ecstatic and overly inflated prose and full of the most explicit and tedious moralizing."[23] But the devotional element of Rowe's fiction reflects an important aspect of eighteenth-century literary tastes: as J. Paul Hunter has established, the early novel was often explicitly didactic and the "rhetoric associated with didactic aims remains crucial to its tone, pace and affects."[24] Rowe's work, then, represents an aspect of eighteenth-century fiction that is often ignored. Moreover, the particular expression of Rowe's Christian faith, which manifests itself as both a matter of intense feeling and anticipated physical gratification, is connected in important but sometimes overlooked ways with the amatory fiction penned by her contemporaries.

Friendship in Death (1728), Rowe's first fictional work, takes the form of twenty letters written by recently deceased correspondents to their mortal friends. With the exception of two letters that share the same paired correspondents, each letter is a stand-alone narrative. Framed by a preface that stresses their role as "serious entertainment," some letters aim explicitly at reforming their living recipients by impressing on them the eternal rewards of a virtuous life, but all stress that the intimate connections of love and friendship are durable and "not extinguish'd with the Breath of Life."[25] Rowe followed *Friendship in Death* with a second epistolary fiction, *Letters Moral and Entertaining* (1729–32), published in three volumes over as many years. This text follows the pattern established by *Friendship in Death*, with two important variations. The correspondents of these later volumes are more diverse: letters are most often exchanged between living correspondents who address each other with literary pseudonyms. The letters themselves are also more varied: the collection contains epistles that rework Ovid's *Heroides*, letters that translate sections of Tasso's *Jerusalem Delivered*, and imagined correspondence between historical figures (such as between Lady Jane Grey and her husband Lord Guildford Dudley and between Rosamund Clifford, better known to posterity as "Fair Rosamund," and Henry II). Interpolated verse, most often by Rowe but also by her near-contemporaries Abraham Cowley, John Milton, Pope,

Richard Blackmore, Edward Young, James Thomson, and Isaac Watts, forms an important part of the fiction sustained in each letter. The letters are intricately sequenced, with stories unfolding across the three volumes and names of correspondents appearing in letters exchanged between seemingly disconnected correspondents suggesting sustained and complex narrative lines.

The letters in both *Friendship in Death* and *Letters Moral and Entertaining* explicitly employ the tropes of romance, or amatory fiction, something her eighteenth-century readers noted. In remarking on the "copiousness and luxuriousness" of Rowe's fictions, Samuel Johnson commented that she uses "the ornaments of romance in the decoration of religion."[26] Rowe re-stages familiar scenes of seduction in her letters but revises their conventions. In a striking example, Clerimont vows to resist his illicit desire for his ward Leonora and dies as a result of the effort and pain of his virtuous restraint. Likewise, Rowe inverts a number of the conventional tropes of amatory fiction. In amatory fiction, male libertines happen with alarming frequency on innocent women reading material that renders them susceptible to seduction in amenable outdoor settings that are redolent with the fragrance of jasmine and tuberoses. In Rowe's fictions, this trope is reworked so a scene that would normally enable seduction instead facilitates instruction. For instance, in *Letters Moral and Entertaining*, when Laura happens upon Philocles, a young man of unsurpassed beauty, reading in an arbor perfumed by "Jessamine, Woodbine, and Roses," he is not reading a literary preparative to real-life seduction but *A Discourse on the Government of the Passions* and *A Treatise of the Immortality of the Soul* (vol. 3, pp. 112–13). These generic titles employ phrases commonly incorporated in the titles of published sermons and are likely meant to conjure types of texts rather than particular works. Further, Philocles is neither struck by Laura's charms, as she anticipates, nor does he attempt to take advantage of their seclusion. Instead, Laura's vanity is humbled when he "treats [her] with as much indifference and respect, as if I had been his Great Grandmother" (3.113). Episodes such as this suggest an expanded range of stories and preoccupations for female writers.

Moreover, the conventions of amatory fiction – the purling streams, luxurious bowers, and fragrant flowers – associated with scenes of sexual seduction in amatory fiction are the features of heaven in Rowe's fictions. In *Friendship in Death*, the recently deceased Delia reveals to her correspondent that the glories of heaven encompass romantic love, describing her reunion with a man for whom she bore a "tender and innocent passion" that has now "kindled" and taken "eternal possession" of her soul. As Delia describes it, the "divine enjoyment" of falling in love eclipses all earthly experiences in its "sanctity and grandeur." For Delia, the rapture of heaven is that of consummation; she writes, "hope and languishing expectation are no more, and all desire is lost in full and compleat fruition" (24). In this way, Rowe establishes a connection between the sexual gratification and the realization of spiritual desire: both are appetitive desires and both are experienced sensually. Sharon Achinstein identifies "holy ardour and carnal eroticism" as the "double register" of Rowe's spirituality and suggests her fictions reclaim romance to frame narratives of Christian devotion by employing its structure of deferral that projects yet postpones a desired end.[27]

Rather than expressions of strict or sincere sentiment, Rowe's fictions engage and experiment with trends in popular fiction. She eliminates the cynical and amoral pursuit of pleasure that typifies amatory fiction but preserves its eroticism, using it to serve a vision of Christian love. To modern readers, the concentration on passionate love in Rowe's works and her reputation for piety can seem incongruent, but this was not necessarily the case for her original readers. A fictional correspondent in *Letters, Moral and Entertaining* draws attention to the shared dependence on love, broadly understood, of religious and sexual desire, remarking that "in whatever Character I act, whether the Saint or the Libertine; Love is the animating Motive, the leading Principle" (Vol. 2, p. 88). Rowe's example is helpful in complicating dichotomies relating to early eighteenth-century fiction authored by women.

Jane Barker

The dominance of amatory fiction in critical accounts of early eighteenth-century fiction has meant that consideration of women's formal innovation has been limited. Yet, formal experimentation is central to the prose fictions of many women writers of the period, including those by Manley and Rowe already considered. Its importance is perhaps most apparent in Jane Barker's (1652–1732) three interconnected novels, *Love Intrigues; Or the Amours of Bosvil and Galesia* (1713), *A Patchwork Screen for the Ladies* (1723), and *A Lining of the Patchwork Screen* (1726). Barker was a poet before she was a novelist, writing and exchanging verse with a small network of male writers she appears to have met through her brother, then studying medicine at Cambridge. When she began writing prose fiction two decades later, Barker revisited her poetic oeuvre and incorporated her earlier verse in her novels. These interpolated poems are fundamental to the progress of her novelistic narratives, often supplying crucial details of the protagonist's story that are then retold in the prose narrative. *Love Intrigues*, Barker's first novel, provides the best example of the vital connection between poetic and novelistic form in her works. This novel was initially published prematurely and the advent of a second edition, published six years later in 1719, allowed Barker to make clear that it had initially appeared without her approval. It also provided an opportunity for Barker to silently revise aspects of the narrative to make it fit for a large and anonymous readership she now anticipated. Significantly, the narrative balance between poetry and prose is substantially revised as new poems are added and existing poems expanded.

The publication history of *Love Intrigues* provides one important indication of the importance of manuscript poetry to Barker's published novels, but the structure of the novel that follows, *A Patchwork Screen for the Ladies*, brings Barker's innovative aesthetic practice into clearer focus. This novel focuses on Galesia's experiences following her disappointed courtship with her cousin Bosvil (the subject of *Love Intrigues*), but it begins with a frame narrative that enables this story to unfold. This frame narrative foregrounds formal experimentation, emphasizing its importance to the narrative that follows. Here, Galesia is invited into the country estate of an unnamed lady after the stagecoach in which she is traveling north overturns, delaying her journey. Seeking both to repay her benefactor's hospitality and to enter into sociable exchange, Galesia agrees to collaborate on a fireside screen created by many generations of women that will complete the estate's lavish furniture. Galesia's unconventional circumstances – she is both unmarried and a poet – mean her traveling trunk is filled not with the "bits of one thing or other" for which the lady initially hopes, but with poetic manuscripts.[28] These unusual contents provide material necessary to complete the screen while Galesia's account of the circumstances surrounding the composition of each piece effectively narrates her life story. Consequently, the narrative that follows moves between interpolated material in different modes and genres: from Galesia's account of the medical advice she was able to provide her friends and acquaintances and the remedies she prescribed to an occasional poem, "On the Apothecaries filling my Recipes amongst the Doctors," written by Galesia to memorialize her medical skill (cf. 116–19).

In her final novel, Barker extends her practice. The narrative situation here is slightly different: no longer the beneficiary of an unnamed lady's hospitality, Galesia, now in her own home, extends her own hospitality to a stream of visitors. This time, instead of telling her own story, a narrative task dependent on her poetic rendering of her own experience, Galesia listens to the stories of others. Although these stories do not rely on poetic iteration, they do reprise other forms. As has long been recognized, the stories incorporated in this novel retell stories authored by female novelists who were near-contemporaries of Barker: "The Story of Tangerine, Gentleman Gypsy," narrated by an unnamed lady to company assembled at Lady Allgood's drawing room, and the "Story out of the Book," narrated by Philinda, retell two of Behn's novellas, respectively *The Wandering Beauty* and *The History of the Nun*.[29] These retellings testify to both Barker's commitment to aesthetic experimentation and her engagement with a female-authored tradition.

Aesthetic patchwork is central to Barker's novels, which in many ways represent an anomalous case in the early eighteenth century. The construction of Manley's scandal fiction – particularly the *New Atalantis* – in which story follows story might be viewed from a similar perspective. The fragmentary nature of the *New Atalantis* increases as the narrative progresses, culminating in the introduction of twenty-two new characters in the final pages whose stories stand only in paratactic relation to one another, occasioned, at the level of the narration, by the fact they are all gathered together in the Divan (or, Westminster Hall). Formal capaciousness also characterizes Haywood's novels of the 1720s. All these novels begin with a poetic epigraph, a practice that is conventional in the period. What is not conventional, however, is that, in the 1720s, Haywood's novels were regularly advertised by their title and their poetic epigraph. For instance, the list of "novels &c, writ by Mrs. Haywood" that prefaced the published text of *Lasselia: Or the Self-Abandon'd. A Novel* (1723) listed four of Haywood's most recent publications. Under the title, the four-line poetic epigraph that appears on the title page of each novel is reprinted and attributed to its original author. Familiar lines from well-known poems, these epigraphs appeared in thematic dictionaries of poetic quotations such as E. Bysshe's *The Art of English Poetry* (London, 1718). This intriguing practice adds further weight to King's conclusions about Haywood's carefully crafted and various authorial identities. It also indicates that poetry was an important part of the way Haywood framed and marketed her prose fiction.

Early eighteenth-century novels authored by women do, in fact, epitomize Nancy Armstrong and Lennard Tennenhouse's well-known definition of the novel as a "perfect creole."[30] It is helpful here to return briefly to Fielding's characterization of the novel in *The Author's Farce*. Mrs. Novel does not occupy the stage alone but instead is surrounded by embodiments of popular forms of entertainment – theatrical and written. She interacts with characters who represent competing ways of entertaining their audiences and, consequently, distinct discursive modes – farcical, tragic, pantomimic, operatic – and, toward the end of the sketch, revives her marriage with Signior Opera. Her capacity to enter into easy alliances with other discursive forms is burlesqued. Her death, her passport to Nonsense's court, comes about while laboring to birth an illegitimate child, the result of an affair outside the bounds of marriage with Signoir Opera. Although this representation is designed for patently satiric ends, it also highlights a significant aspect of early eighteenth-century novels authored by women: their capaciousness and capacity for formal experimentation.

NOTES

1. Henry Fielding, *The Author's Farce* (London, 1730), p. 42.
2. James Sterling, "To Mrs. Eliza Haywood, on her Writings," in Eliza Haywood, *Secret Histories, Novels and Poems* (London, 1725), Vol. 1, sig. a2r.
3. In his commendatory poem, "On Mr John Fletcher's Workes," published as part of the prefatory material to *Comedies and Tragedies written by Francis Beaumont and John Fletcher* (London: 1647), sig. a2v, Denham wrote, "When Johnson [sic], Shakespear[e], and thy self did sit / And sway'd in the triumvirate of wit."
4. Barbara Fuchs, *Romance* (New York: Routledge, 2004), p. 101.
5. The attribution of *The Secret History of Queen Zarah* to Delarivier Manley was first challenged by J. A. Downie in "What if Delarivier Manley did *not* write *The Secret History of Queen Zarah?*" *The Library* 5 (2004), 247–64, and, subsequently, by Rachel Carnell in *A Political Biography of Delarivier Manley* (London: Pickering and Chatto, 2008).
6. Rosalind Ballaster, *Seductive Forms: Women's Amatory Fiction from 1684 to 1740* (Oxford: Clarendon Press, 1992), p. 29.
7. Catherine Gallagher, *Nobody's Story: The Vanishing Acts of Women Writers in the Marketplace, 1670–1820* (Berkeley: University of California Press, 1995), pp. 90–91.
8. Delarivier Manley, *The Adventures of Rivella*, ed. Katherine Zelinsky (Peterborough, ON: Broadview, 1999), p. 44.
9. Delarivier Manley, *The New Atalantis*, ed. Rosalind Ballaster (Harmondsworth: Penguin, 1992), p. 37.
10. Eliza Haywood, *Love in Excess: or, the Fatal Enquiry*, ed. David Oakleaf (Peterborough, ON: Broadview, 1996), p. 89.
11. Toni Bowers, *Force or Fraud: British Seduction Stories and the Problem of Resistance, 1660–1760* (Oxford University Press, 2011) pp. 223–39.
12. Kathleen Lubey, "Eliza Haywood's Amatory Aesthetic," *Eighteenth-Century Studies* 39.3 (2006), 316.
13. G. Gabrielle Starr, *Lyric Generations: Poetry and the Novel in the Long Eighteenth Century* (Baltimore, MD: The Johns Hopkins University Press, 2004), p. 64.
14. Eliza Haywood, *Fantomina: or, Love in a Maze*, 1724, in *Fantomina and Other Works*, ed. Alexander Pettit, Margaret C. Croskery, and Anna C. Patchias (Peterborough, ON: Broadview, 2004), p. 71.
15. Helen Thomson, 'Plotting Materialism: W. Charleton's *The Ephesian Matron*, E. Haywood's *Fantomina*, and Feminine Consistency', *Eighteenth-Century Studies* 35.2 (2002), pp. 195–214; Jonathan Kramnick, *Actions and Objects from Hobbes to Richardson* (Stanford, CA: Stanford University Press, 2010).

16. Mary Davys, *Familiar Letters betwixt a Gentleman and a Lady* in *The Works of Mrs. Davys*, Vol. 2 (London: 1725), p. 283.
17. Kathryn R. King, "Female Agency and Feminocentric Romance," *The Eighteenth Century*, 41.1 (2000), 56.
18. John J. Richetti, *Popular Fiction before Richardson: Narrative Patterns, 1700–1739* (Oxford: Clarendon Press, 1969), pp. 179, 201.
19. Al Coppola, "The Secret History of Eliza Haywood's *Works*: The Early Novel and the Book Trade," *1650–1850: Ideas, Aesthetics and Inquiries in the Early Modern Era*, 19 (2012), 133–61.
20. Kathryn R. King, *A Political Biography of Eliza Haywood* (London: Pickering and Chatto, 2012), p. 33.
21. Margaret J. M. Ezell, *Writing Women's Literary History* (Baltimore: The Johns Hopkins University Press, 1995), p. 105.
22. Paula R. Backscheider, *Elizabeth Singer Rowe and the Development of the English Novel* (Baltimore: The Johns Hopkins University Press, 2013).
23. Richetti, *Popular Fiction before Richardson*, p. 245.
24. J. Paul Hunter, *Before Novels: The Cultural Contexts of Eighteenth-Century English Fiction* (New York: Norton, 1990), pp. 54–56.
25. Elizabeth Rowe, *Friendship in Death; in Twenty Letters from the Dead to the Living* (London, 1727), pp. 7, 9.
26. Johnson described Rowe's fiction in this way in a review of Elizabeth Harrison's *Miscellanies on Moral and Religious Subjects, in Prose and Verse* (1756), published in *The Literary Magazine* 1 (September 5, 1756–October 15, 1756), p. 282.
27. Sharon Achinstein, "Romance of the Spirit: Female Sexuality and Religious Desire in Early Modern England," *ELH*, 69.2 (2002), 414, 415, 435.
28. Jane Barker, *A Patchwork Screen for the Ladies*, in *The Galesia Trilogy and Selected Manuscript Poems of Jane Barker*, ed. Carol S. Wilson (Oxford University Press, 1997), p. 74.
29. Jacqueline Pearson, "The History of *The History of the Nun*," in *Rereading Aphra Behn: History, Theory and Criticism*, ed. Heidi Hutner (Charlottesville: University Press of Virginia, 1993), p. 235.
30. Nancy Armstrong and Lennard Tennenhouse, *The Imaginary Puritan: Literature, Intellectual Labour, and the Origins of Personal Life* (Berkeley: University of California Press, 1992), p. 198.

11

KATHERINE BINHAMMER

Later fiction

The primary form women's fiction takes in the later eighteenth century is the sentimental or domestic novel. Women also wrote didactic novels, moral tales, and children's stories, but it is the sentimental novel that dominates. Its conventions were so firmly in place by the end of the century that Mary Alcock (1741?–98) could satirize them in her poem "A receipt for writing a novel" (1799), recommending such "ingredients" as a "fainting fit," a "frantic fever," a "masquerade," and an "[overset] carriage."[1] Her directions for a perfectly baked conclusion were followed with some improvisation in Frances Burney's *Evelina* (1778), *Indiana Danby* (1765), and *Miss Melmouth* (1771): "Suppose your hero knows no mother – / Suppose he proves the heroine's brother – ... Clear the mistake, and introduce / Some tatt'ling nurse to cut the noose ... And ere your reader can recover, / They're married – and your history's over."[2] As Katherine Sobba Green noted in *The Courtship Novel*, novels written by women in this period principally narrate "the time between a young woman's coming out and her marriage."[3] The major obstacles faced by the heroine in this sexual *bildungsroman* are social and economic as she most often enters the story compromised by a downwardly mobile status. Orphaned and left economically dependent on the first page or arriving alone in London after a father dies having squandered the family fortune, the poor but genteelly born heroine begins the story vulnerable and confronts a status barrier to marriage with the aristocratic hero. After Samuel Richardson's *Pamela* (1740) with its tale of upward mobility through marriage, the reader learns to recognize the heroine's inner worth and virtue as guaranteeing that the problem of inequality will be resolved, perhaps through the arrival of an unexpected West Indian inheritance or the discovery of a secret aristocratic genealogy.

Because of the repetition of the "virtue in distress" motif, many second-wave feminist critics read this body of fiction as disappointingly conservative and as attesting to a "great divide" between earlier risqué amatory fiction and the moral modesty of mid-century. Jane Spencer's germinal 1986 work,

The Rise of the Woman Novelist, discusses writers such as Sarah Fielding (1710–68) and Frances Burney (1752–1840) under the rubric "terms of acceptance," and Janet Todd writes that mid-century women's novels such as those by Frances Sheridan (1724–66) and Frances Brooke (1724–89) "collud[ed] with the new ideology of femininity."[4] The emphasis on sexual chastity and heteronormative marriage certainly frames these plots as conforming to an ideal of domestic femininity, but the large body of critical work amassed since the feminist recovery movement of the late twentieth century has revealed a more complicated vision of the sentimental novel, including an impressive diversity within its supposed restrictive conventionality. Recent work by Betty Schellenberg, Susan Carlile, and Jennie Batchelor listed in the "Guide to Further Reading," for example, has refuted the "great divide" thesis, showing mid-century women writers as savvy professionals negotiating a changing print culture and as producing highly experimental and thematically complex texts. Eliza Haywood's *The History of Miss Betsy Thoughtless* (1751), a sentimental novel narrating the moral reformation of a witty coquette, used to be read as evidence that Haywood was forced for propriety to reject her previous erotic fiction, but critics now foreground the similarities between her early and later works, especially in their representation of marriage. The number of post-1740 novels with heroines who remain imprisoned in castles and convents (*Ophelia, Lady Barton, Henrietta, Cornelia*) or who use disguise and cross-dressing to gain mobility (*Munster Village, Harriot Stuart, Cornelia, Sally Sable*) attests to the continuity between amatory and sentimental fiction.

With this understanding of complexity and multiplicity marking the terrain of later fiction, we can turn our interpretative gaze away from the frame of a restrictive domestic ideology toward the intricate pictures of women that they paint. The frame does matter, but it is not determining. In this way, the courtship plot functions in women's novels as Judith Butler formulates gender operating in women's lives: simply because the courtship plot is *the* plot women must write, "it is not for that reason automatic or mechanical. On the contrary, it is a practice of improvisation within a scene of constraint."[5] Once we look for the improvised moments, a different shape of the sentimental novel emerges. Far from a single plot line following feminine self-sacrifice and acquiescence, we notice an array of intelligent, physically aggressive, and witty heroines confronting the major social questions of their day. "Virtue in distress," in fact, legitimates decisive and forceful action as heroines are authorized to use unfeminine means to preserve their feminine virtue. The threat of incest from her uncle-guardian justifies the heroine's solo travels to France in Sarah Scott's (1720–95) *The History of Cornelia* (1750). While the quixotic Arabella only imagines her virtue is in danger in Charlotte Lennox's (1730/31–1804) *The Female Quixote* (1752), this danger gives her permission to gallop across fields and leave her father's house unattended. Richardson's über-self-sacrificing heroine Clarissa provides an important intertext for women novelists, but while Clarissa responds to sexual assault by threatening to take her own life with a penknife, heroines in novels by women often turn that penknife on their male attackers. Emily in *The Old Maid* (1771) stabs her assaulter with a pair of scissors, and in *All's Right at Last* (1774), Fanny pulls out her rapist's sword and thrusts it into his body.[6] Charlotte Lennox's *Harriot Stuart* (1762) provides a comic twist on the penknife scene when the pathetic hero Belmein threatens to use the penknife on himself if Harriot does not give in to his demands. Harriot refuses and manages to escape her imprisonment by Belmein in the wilds of America, finding her way through the forest to arrive home with her virtue intact.

When read collectively, later women's novels also demonstrate that the supposed straight line to marriage in fact runs sideways or continues past the conventional ending. The most striking divergence from the recipe's directions "[marry] and your history's over" is how many novels by women continue beyond this ending and narrate the challenges of marriage. For example, Haywood's *The History of Miss Betsy Thoughtless* (1751), Fielding's *The Adventures of David Simple* (1744) and *The History of the Countess of Dellwyn* (1759), Sheridan's *Memoirs of Miss Sidney Bidulph* (1761), Scott's *The History of Sir George Ellison* (1766), Griffith's *The Delicate Distress* (1769) and *The History of Lady Barton* (1771), and Georgiana, Duchess of Devonshire's *Emma; Or, The Unfortunate Attachment* (1773) all illustrate this pattern. Multiple heroines marry out of familial duty, giving their "hand without their heart," only to find themselves loving another man (Sidney Bidulph, Betsy Thoughtless, Emma, Lady Barton). As the title of *All's Right at Last* promises, sometimes the convenient death of a first husband allows for a happy second marriage, but sometimes the heroine, for example, Lady Barton, must die for daring to feel. Whether the ending is tragic or comic, such plots query the gendered ethics of the new world of companionate bourgeois marriage and the social mobility promised by an increasingly commercial culture. The sentimental novel only makes sense in a culture that is negotiating changing marriage practices, one in which bourgeois love is increasingly valued over heredity lines. Women use the genre to probe questions such as: Can one marry for love without familial consent, especially if one's parents are tyrants? Is love without money enough for happiness? What is the difference between loving outside marital bounds and inside if that love is true? Is mercenary marriage not a form of "legal prostitution"?

Women writers return surprising answers to these questions, ones that anticipate modern feminist sentiments and critique the disenfranchisement of the female sex. The man of feeling, Ed Rivers, in Frances Brooke's epistolary novel *The History of Emily Montague* (1769) goes further than simply rejecting arranged and mercenary marriages by criticizing the arbitrary power husbands have over their wives: "I have always wished the word OBEY expunged from the marriage ceremony ... Equality is the soul of friendship: marriage, to give delight, must join two minds, not devote a slave to the will of an imperious lord."[7] The right of women to choose their marriage partner based on their own feelings is universally endorsed and women's novels repeatedly portray the conditions wrongly restricting this right. The barriers to freedom of choice are most often represented as economic and familial. How can a woman freely choose a husband when her economic survival depends on marriage? Does the duty to one's parents outweigh the claims of one's own heart? Though many heroines proclaim they would prefer to remain single rather than marrying a man they do not love, a single life required an economic independence genteel women rarely achieved. This material fact animates the multiple women's tales in Sarah Scott's *Millenium Hall* (1762). With nowhere else to turn, this group of virtuous women finds refuge in the Hall against the world's inhumanity to "toad-eaters," the derisive term for economically dependent unmarried women. Mrs. Morgan founded the female community after being forced into a mercenary marriage because she had no viable alternatives to marriage. Mr. Morgan, her alcoholic tyrannical husband, fortunately dies, leaving her Millenium Hall, and she is able to build a utopia for similarly disenfranchised women, including her chosen life partner Louisa Mancel.

Even with the variety of renditions of the courtship plot chronicled so far in this chapter, we do a disservice to this body of fiction to attribute its critical importance to its plots. Their historical significance does not lie so much in *what* stories are told but in *how* those stories are narrated. If women's fiction in the first half of the century contributes dynamic and complex plotting to the history of the novel, women's novels in the second half introduce original experimentations with narrative voice. "Who is speaking?" replaces "what happens next?" as the central concern of fiction by women. The turn away from plot and external action toward character and psychological interiority is not isolated to fiction by women as it is rooted in the larger cultural shift to sentimentalism. But the turn has particularly gendered effects that uniquely position women writers to experiment with the female voice. Samuel Richardson's comparison of Sarah Fielding with her brother Henry metaphorically captures this sexual difference; in a letter to Sarah, praising

David Simple (1744) for its "knowledge of the human heart," he writes: "His was but as the knowledge of the outside of a clock-work machine, while your's [sic] was that of all the finer springs and movements of the inside."[8] The perceived proximity between the woman writer and the newly privileged subject of fiction – the human heart – explains why "by a Lady," the pseudonymous attribution of a large percentage of novels in this period, was as likely to be used by a male as a female writer. James Raven's research reveals that 11 percent of all novels between 1770 and 1790 were published as "By a Lady" or a near variant.[9] Sentimentalism places social emphasis on affective relations and charitable giving and for this reason has been referred to as a "feminization" of culture. The historical event that Virginia Woolf famously described in *A Room of One's Own* as of "greater importance than the Crusades or the War of the Roses" – middle-class women entering the marketplace of fiction – was caused by the radical new authority ascribed by the sentimental revolution to the thoughts and feelings of women.

The "rise of feminine authority," to use Nancy Armstrong's phrase, however, is not precisely coextensive with the rise of the woman novelist.[10] James Raven and Antonia Forster's definitive bibliographic research has revealed that male novelists continued to dominate fiction writing until the 1780s, well after Sarah Fielding published the first novelistic portrait of a "man of feeling" in *David Simple*. Raven notes that "[o]nly 14 per cent of all new novel titles published between 1750 and 1760 can be identified as by women writers" and that "[n]ovels by identified male writers outnumber those by women writers by more than two to one in the 1770s." By the 1780s, "the balance shifts, with slightly more novels by women than by men identified for the 1780s and 1790s." The most remarkable statistical profile that Raven and Forster's bibliography reveals, however, is not the sex of known writers but the fact that the overwhelming majority of novels were published anonymously and remain without attribution: "Over 80 per cent of all novel titles published in the 1770s and 1780s were published anonymously."[11] My own calculation has determined that of the 126 anonymously published novels that name characters in their titles in the 1770s, 55 percent name women, 15 percent name both men and women, with the remaining 30 percent referring to men. In other words, before women dominate the field of fiction writing in the last decades of the century, women's lives prevail as the novel's central concern. The answer to "who speaks?" is clearly "woman."

When the focus of our literary analysis of women's later fiction shifts from what stories are told to how they are told, we notice two interrelated phenomena. First, the critical tendency to collapse the "heroine's text" (to use Nancy K. Miller's signature phrase) with the first-person epistolary narrative mode made famous by Richardson should be resisted.[12] Of the novels surveyed for this chapter, the largest single category of narrative form is third-person omniscient. A close second is the multivocal epistolary novel (which most often includes letters written by both male and female characters), with the univocal epistolary or memoir form in which the "I" is female accounting for only 14 percent. Of the forty-five surveyed novels, eighteen are third person; sixteen are multivocal epistolary; six are first person (univocal epistolary or memoir); and five are "other," which includes, for example, the dramatic dialogue of Sarah Fielding and Jane Collier's (1754) *The Cry*. This data does not mean that women writers avoid narrating the female voice; what it points toward is the complex and varied ways they went about doing so.

The second – and, I argue, related – phenomenon that emerges when we highlight narrative form is the deep metafictional nature of women's novels. Women writers are not only concerned with telling female stories, but their novels foreground which stories are authorized as "true" and the discursive conditions under which that truth is heard. In their preface to *The Cry*, Sarah Fielding and Jane Collier (1715–55) note that the dangers that confront their heroine are not the results of dark forests and kidnappings but of "the perverse interpretations made of her words."[13] Their experimental novel narrates both Portia's history and the hypocritical world's willful misreading of that history; the split between the two constitutes the plot at the meta-level as the battle for female truth. What are the conditions under which the crowd would recognize Portia's truth? Whose story counts and why?

The split between narrator and female "I" that structures third-person narration may explain the popularity of this form since the distance allows women writers to ironically depict the social constraints on women's voice. The most accomplished text in this mode is Charlotte Lennox's *The Female Quixote*, a novel about a heroine, Arabella, who believes the world functions like a romance in which she is the heroine. The quixotic conceit allows Lennox to question the conventions of women's life stories that operate in the "real" world within the fiction, a *mise-en-abyme* she exploits to great feminist effect. Frances Brooke also used the third-person satiric form in *The Excursion* (1777), a comic novel of manners whose humor stems from the divide between its socially aware narrator and its naïve and innocent heroine. The orphaned Maria inherits two hundred pounds and decides to travel alone to London where she meets Lord Melvile and believes it is love at first sight. While Maria's ignorance empowers her to imagine herself the object of a lord's legitimate affection, the reader is fully aware that his designs are not virtuous. When he offers her a "settlement," their competing versions of truth come to a crisis: "As her idea of the word settlement differed very essentially from his lordship's, she looked on their marriage as concluded."[14] The dramatic irony with which the reader follows Maria's actions as she assumes herself worthy of marrying Lord Melvile documents the cruelness of a world in which a woman's value is determined not by her inner virtue but by the size of her dowry. Maria's misreading of social codes, like Arabella's, works to satirize, not herself, but the injustice of the social rules. She is unquestioningly virtuous and intelligent, but her "sincere, simple, unaffected" character translates into her lack of awareness of the divide between who she is and who she is perceived to be, a split that introduces the social hypocrisies that are the novel's satiric target: "As to calumny, such was her knowledge of the world, that she thought herself secure from its attacks, only by resolving not to merit them."[15] The lesson Maria needs to learn is a cynical one: the world writes the truth of woman in a way that does not correspond to her own.

Third-person satiric fictions often include an array of self-referential nods to novel reading and writing, inside jokes that position the reader as a female wit, well read enough that when Lennox's Arabella concludes her circumstances are unique and there is no precedent in which a heroine "voluntarily left her father's house," the reader recognizes that she is incorrect.[16] In *The Excursion*, the humor involves Maria's overconfidence in her value as a writer. She heads to London with a suitcase full of manuscripts, grossly overestimating her novel to be worth two hundred pounds (an unknown writer selling a novel to a circulating library was more likely to receive a lowly five guineas). A tag search in *The Orlando Project* on "earnings" reveals a large discrepancy in remuneration for fiction. The standard price for a first novel sold to a circulating library publisher such as the Noble brothers was five guineas (see entries for Jean Marishall, A. Woodfin, Phebe Gibbes). Better connected writers received more: Millar paid Sarah Fielding sixty guineas for *The Countess of Dellwyn*, and Sarah Scott received one hundred pounds for *Sir George Ellison*. Frances Brooke, having already published periodical writing and plays, received an impressive one hundred guineas for her first novel, *The History of Julia Mandeville*, but only thirty pounds for *Emily Montague*. The unknown Frances Burney received twenty pounds for *Evelina* but then two hundred and fifty pounds for *Cecilia*. Novels were far less lucrative than plays or history; for example, Catharine Macaulay was paid nine hundred pounds for *The History of England*.

The jokes at Maria's expense assume the implied reader and narrator share a high level of literary knowledge, about both print culture and the conventions of the novel. For instance, when Lord Melvile's father tries to contract Maria to be his son's kept mistress, Maria decides her lover is not aware of the offer because duplicitous "avaricious fathers" are common, "[s]he had read of them in an hundred novels, and at least half a dozen true histories" (115). The pleasure of the text for the reader comes from recognizing the ironic deployment of these conventions; after all, Maria has previously missed countless signs of Lord Melvile's libertine intentions. Thus, the predictability of the "virtue in distress" plot is the launching ground for the reader's hermeneutic mastery. The reader immediately identifies the kind old woman to be the evil bawd though the heroine does not, producing a pleasurable satisfaction akin to correctly guessing the murderer in a mystery novel on page ten. For instance, in the opening pages of Lennox's novel *Henrietta*, the eponymous heroine, alone and without friends, accepts a recommendation to board at a milliner's shop that the reader knows enough to instantly suspect.

From *Betsy Thoughtless* to Lennox's *Henrietta* (1758) to Fielding's *The History of the Countess of Dellwyn* (1759), women writers employ the satiric third-person form to ironically focus attention on the way conventions of fiction mimic discourses of femininity in that both rely on the repetition of codes to produce a truth that does not correspond to women's self-knowledge. While the irony is used for comic effect, the ultimate insight such sophisticated narrative play leads to is often dark and sobering. Arabella must be "cured" and cannot remain in her fantasy world where her desire and will rule. In *Betsy Thoughtless*, Betsy's spirited character repeatedly places her in situations where sexual violence is threatened, and, though she manages to survive these episodes unscathed, Haywood reminds us that "innocence is no defence against scandal," a lesson Betsy learns the hard way when she is forced to marry the abusive misogynist Mr. Munden to save her reputation (though not her virtue).[17] The lack of correspondence between women's internal truths and the external forces surrounding her provides the plot of the metafictional stories these novels tell.

If third-person narration exploits the distance between narrator and heroine to satirize the codes of femininity, then the multivocal epistolary mode uses the repetition of an event told from multiple first-person points of view to produce a similar critique of the constraints placed on the female voice. For instance, the tragic story of a controlling and jealous husband in the Duchess of Devonshire's (1757–1806) *Emma; Or, The Unfortunate Attachment* (1773) is made doubly so as the reader watches it unfold with dramatic irony. The novel opens with Emma's narration of her young and passionate but unconsummated love for Augustus in letters to a friend; thus, when her future husband William Walpole describes her at their first meeting as "an absolute novice in the ways of the world," the reader recognizes his mistake.[18] He has decided that his wife must be absolutely pure and unsullied and convinces himself that Emma is this woman ("it is not enough for me that she seems angelic; I must be sure of her being more so than any female I have yet met with" [58]). When he later discovers his errors and abandons her, the novel registers the injustice of judging women by so narrow a definition of sexual purity. Emma is innocent, having relinquished her impossible early love for Augustus as the reader knows from reading her self-sacrificing letters.

The narrative mode that emerges as the most forceful weapon in the battle for female truth is ultimately not a particular form of voice but of shifting narrative levels. Embedded tales – stories within stories – are ubiquitous in women's novels whether those novels are written in third-person, first-person, or epistolary form. A woman's story, this fiction ultimately suggests, necessitates the telling of other women's stories. Why and to what effect? As narrative theorists such as Tzvetan Todorov and Mieke Bal have shown, embedded tales are constitutively metafictional insofar as they provide "the narrative of a narrative."[19] By representing scenes of storytelling within a scene of storytelling, they highlight the narrative act itself. When the narrative level shifts to Arabella listening to "The History of Miss Groves," Lennox provides a meta-commentary on how women's stories are used and abused and what it might mean that Miss Groves's maid hopes to gain financially by gossiping about her lady's infidelities while Arabella believes she is hearing a heroic tale akin to Cleopatra's.[20] Stories within stories prompt us to query a fiction's context since the narrative's situation often determines its meaning. To whom is the story told, why, and to what effect? Susan Lanser, in her formative work on feminist narratology, argues that the most relevant characteristic of women's narration, one missed in traditional narratology, is the use of "private" narratees, that is, that the person to whom the story is told is almost always a character in the novel and not a "public" narratee or someone external to the text.[21] While not necessarily the case in terms of the main level of the plot (as noted earlier, third-person "heterodiegetic" narrators are common[22]), her observation is correct in relation to embedded stories within women's fiction. An internal scene of storytelling in which the listener or reader of the inset tale is a character in the novel is so pervasive that one could argue it is the defining feature of women's later fiction. Fielding's *David Simple* provides an early model of a novel that is centrally concerned with storytelling as David incites countless characters, including the novel's two heroines, Cynthia and Camilla, to tell their stories of distress as part of his quest "to seek out one capable of being a real Friend."[23] Whereas Lanser interprets the omnipresence of private narratees as indicative of the restrictions placed on women's public speech, I read these scenes of storytelling as intentional metafictions employed by women writers to mirror the discursive and material conditions authorizing women's voices.

Reading acts of narrative in women's fiction for what they tell us about the material conditions governing the authority and truth of female stories reveals that the single most important determinant is a woman's place within the marriage market. Narrative exchange turns out to be, for women, fundamentally an exchange of sex and money. The sexual exploitation that economic dependency submits women to, especially genteel women, frames many of the embedded tales as women tell their tales of distress. Gerard Genette identifies three main functions that embedded tales serve and women employ all three to critique the marriage market: (1) an "explanatory" function whereby the embedded story explains something in the main diegesis such as a character's past; (2) a "thematic" function in which the story is unrelated to the diegesis but has a thematic link (e.g., Leonora's tale in Henry Fielding's *Joseph Andrews*, probably written by sister Sarah); and (3) an actional function whereby the narrating act is the event as it merges with the present of the diegesis (the classic example is *One Thousand and One Nights* in which telling a story to remain alive constitutes the plot).[24] This last type describes the narrative structure of *The Histories of Some of the Penitents in the Magdalen-House* (1760), published anonymously, often attributed to Sarah Fielding and possibly by Sarah Scott, and written to demonstrate the need for the charity founded to assist penitent prostitutes.[25] The novel consists of inset narratives by four Magdalens whose stories perform the penitential act proving they are properly contrite and thus appropriate objects of charity. The women take very different paths to arrive at the hospital's door, but their plots end in the same place: having to engage in sexual commerce to survive before entering the charity. The cumulative effect of their narratives maps the dangers facing genteel single women without economic independence. The servant Emily fell for the promises of love and marriage made by her employer's son, and, left penniless and ruined, she tries multiple ways of making a living before being reduced to selling her body to feed her child. Another woman is forced into a mercenary marriage to an abusive old man, and, after he imprisons her and she escapes, she runs away with her first love who dies, leaving her with no means of support since needlework does not bring in enough money to feed their children and she turns to prostitution. The actional embedded tales collectively demonstrate the need for women's legal employment without which even virtuous women will be forced into selling sex.

Elizabeth Griffith's (1727–93) novels overflow with thematically linked inset narratives, and the overall result of the shifts in narrative level is to create bonds of female solidarity. In her first novel, *The Delicate Distress* (1769), the main plot of a husband's infidelity is related by the heroine Emily in letters to her sister Fanny; Fanny, in turn, writes to Emily about her own marriage. Their letters raise ethical questions concerning a wife's responsibilities to her husband (e.g., is it alright for Fanny to inoculate her children for small pox without telling her husband?) and within them are many narrative acts in which other women tell their stories to Fanny or Emily who then tells the other, a doubling of private narratees. The inset stories narrate failed attempts at marriage or failed marriages and thus create counterpoints to the ethical concerns of the diegesis. Emily reproduces the "Memoir of Lady Harriet Hanbury" in which Harriet relates how she became engaged to a man whose family refused to consent to the marriage because she was poor and her fiancé abandons her for a woman with more money. Fanny later narrates the story of Lady Somerville, whom she meets when her coach breaks down and she seeks shelter in a neighboring cottage (Griffith here follows Alcock's recipe to include a carriage accident). In the time it takes to fix the carriage, Lady Somerville tells her story of marrying for love, breaking her parent's ban against her interfaith marriage, and being left poor and alone with her children after her disinherited husband dies. In this case, the shift in narrative levels is not marked by a separate manuscript as Harriet's is or even by the insertion of quotation marks; Fanny simply writes "[w]ithout more ceremony, she began: I am a native of Italy."[26] The shift effects a merging of "she" into "I" as it links Fanny's and Lady Somerville's points of view through the collapse of grammatical subjects. In Griffith's *The History of Lady Barton* (1771) as well, the multiplying stories not only give rise to a collective "I" of sentimental identification, uniting women under a shared right to a free heart, but also scenes of storytelling produce *acts* of feminist solidarity. A woman's story turns out to be worth the help of another woman. In exchange for entertaining Fanny while the carriage is being fixed, Lady Somerville receives Fanny's assistance and Emily and her husband take Harriet in, providing her with a refuge in exchange for her tale.

One of the more interesting uses of the technique of embedded storytelling is found in Frances Sheridan's *Memoirs of Miss Sidney Bidulph* (1761). In this novel, it is significantly the *absence* of an explanatory inset tale that would contain Miss Burchell's true history that causes the tragic events in Sidney's life. Sidney dutifully accepts her mother's request that she reject marriage to Orlando Faulkland, the man she loves, because her mother is convinced he has previously seduced Miss Burchell, a fact the mother thinks she has confirmed after she meets Miss Burchell and hears her story. Instead of marrying for love, Sidney gives her hand without her heart to her mother's choice, Mr. Arnold, and ends up in a disastrous marriage that includes her husband's infidelity, abusive jealousy, and promiscuous spending. The untold story of "Miss Burchell's History" haunts the narrative. We ultimately find out that Miss Burchell was less than innocent in the affair with Faulkland, and Sidney was incorrect in breaking her engagement with him. The untold embedded story *acts* in the narrative to criticize Sidney for too easily believing other's – in particular, her mother's – interpretation of the tale and not hearing and judging stories for herself. The story that the story within the story tells concerns how women have a moral duty to interpret the world for themselves and not to trust traditional authorities' assertion of truth.

If women's fiction in the later half of the century is defined by the way it deploys private narratees in inset narratives for metafictional commentary on the economics of marriage, what do we make of the fact that the most accomplished novel by a woman at the end of this period – Frances Burney's *Cecilia* (1782) – does not shift narrative levels to first-person scenes of storytelling? The absence of embedded first-person tales in Burney's novel provides a bookend to this discussion of narrative voice because it is the variance that clarifies the rule.

First-person empathetic scenes of storytelling are missing precisely because Burney takes an opposite approach to representing the economics of marriage. *Cecilia* turns the story of the downwardly mobile heroine inside out and for this reason, the narration is framed by the desire to listen and not to tell female stories, a desire Burney shows can never be fulfilled for a single woman. The novel announces its plot to be about sexual economics in its subtitle – "Memoirs of an Heiress" – and proceeds to recount the misfortunes that befall Cecilia because of the inheritance her uncle has given her on condition that her future husband must take her surname (a plot device earlier deployed in *All's Right at Last*). Unlike most sentimental novels that begin with a poor and dependent but genteel heroine, this one opens with an independent woman of fortune whose "scheme of happiness" is to give her money away to precisely those women in distress.[27] As the mirror to sentimental novels that plot the heroine's economic and romantic gains, Burney's novel proceeds through the emotional and romantic losses caused by Cecilia's independent fortune. Cecilia's money should give her agency to freely chart her path through life since she is not, like Evelina, a "toad-eater," but the demands of sexual propriety impose increasing restrictions on Cecilia. Her money does not buy her freedom from sexual commodification since it turns her into a much sought-after object on the marriage market, literally sold by one of her guardians, the fiscally profligate Mr. Harrel, in payment of a gambling debt. The novel's bleak and deeply conservative ending of a woman's dispossession seems to suggest that living independently according to the rules of sexual propriety is an impossibility. Cecilia ultimately relinquishes her fortune to marry Mortimer Devile and to take his name, implying that a woman must lose everything, including not only her money but her self (Cecilia ends up losing her mind along with her name), to accumulate a husband.

In a novel that begins with a rich heiress seeking to give her money away and ends with her financial debt forgiven through marriage, it is significant that embedded first-person tales are largely absent. Such storytelling in earlier fiction results in financial and sentimental gain for the teller – Fanny Williams, the "fair cottager" in *Emily Montague*, writes Emily her tale of woe and the letter results in an annuity that saves her from destitution and provides her with new friends – but Cecilia is not allowed a life of independence and benevolence; thus, her charity is at best ineffective and at worst counterproductive as she gives in to Harrel's coercive demands for money. Cecilia even mistakes the poor widow Mrs. Hill's solicitation as an exchange of a tragic story for her charity, when Hill is simply requesting payment for work her dead husband performed. When the novel does shift narrative levels to provide a story within a story, for instance, the history of the Belfield family, it does so without the attending shift to a first-person narrator. The reader learns the family's story through reported speech when Henrietta tells it to Cecilia ("Her father, who had been dead only two years, was a linen-draper"[212]).

Burney's use of the narrative technique of reported speech, also known as free indirect discourse, marks an important development in women's narrative experimentations. While Jane Austen has often been credited with developing this quintessentially modern form in which the third-person narrator seamlessly shifts into the point of view of a character, Burney had previously pioneered the style in *Cecilia* (a novel that certainly influenced Austen, providing her with the title of *Pride and Prejudice*). Free indirect discourse, as critics have noted, paradoxically combines the opposing tendencies of distance and proximity between narrator and character. On the one hand, free indirect discourse is used to produce an ironic distance between the narrator and the character whose point of view is being narrated (the most common example is the opening sentence of *Pride and Prejudice*: "It is a truth universally acknowledged ... "). On the other hand, the use of free indirect discourse can effect greater empathy as the positions of narrator and character merge, for instance, when the reader is taken into Cecilia's internal thoughts. Interestingly, these two narrative effects – ironic distance and sympathetic identification – are the main narrative techniques I charted earlier in relation to women's third-person satires and shifts of narrative levels. The fact that Burney merges them into one and the same narrative act suggests women's fiction has achieved a high level of narrative sophistication. It also complicates the earlier metafictional effect that aligned telling stories with economic independence as, like the women of *Millenium Hall* or *Delicate Distress*, scenes of storytelling provide women with relief from the distress of the marriage market. *Cecilia* is less optimistic about the utopic potential of storytelling, and its heroine is never able to translate her benevolent desires into a progressive narrative. Burney's experimental voice, a voice that combines distance with proximity and satire with empathy, matches the conflicting claims on her heroine of resistance and submission, agency and passivity, gendered social demands that the novel ambivalently portrays. In other words, it encapsulates both the "scene of constraint" that defines domestic femininity for women in this period and the innovative "improvisations" women writers performed within the scene. The future of women's fiction post 1780s will be to polarize those conflicting demands into either the radical first-person feminist novels of the 1790s or the conservative anti-Jacobin satires of the turn of the nineteenth century. For the period from the 1740s to the 1780s, women combined the normative and the transgressive in their experiments with narrative voice and their fiction ultimately attests to their successful battle in making their voices heard.

NOTES

1. Mary Alcock, "A receipt for writing a novel," in *Eighteenth-Century Women Poets*, ed. Roger H. Lonsdale (Oxford University Press, 1989), pp. 466–68.
2. Alcock, p. 468. Frances Burney, *Evelina, Or, the History of a Young Lady's Entrance into the World*, ed. Edward A. Bloom and Lillian D. Bloom (Oxford University Press, 1998); 'By a Lady,' *The History of Miss Indiana Danby* (London: 1765); Sophia Briscoe, *Miss Melmoth; Or, The New Clarissa* (London: 1771). The sex of the author of *Indiana Danby* has not been identified; I have included it and a few other anonymous novels reviewers assumed were by women to recognize that the widespread use of "anon" included many women writers who will never be identified.
3. Katherine S. Green, *The Courtship Novel 1740–1820: A Feminized Genre* (Lexington: University Press of Kentucky, 1991), p. 2.
4. Jane Spencer, *The Rise of the Woman Novelist: From Aphra Behn to Jane Austen* (Oxford: Basil Blackwell, 1986); Janet Todd, *The Sign of Angellica: Women, Writing and Fiction, 1660–1800* (London: Virago Press, 1989), p. 160. Susan Staves's important literary history maintains the conservative interpretation, calling the sentimental novel "a claustrophobic discursive space." *A Literary History of Women's Writing in Britain, 1660–1789* (Cambridge University Press, 2006), p. 289.

5. Judith Butler, *Undoing Gender* (New York: Routledge, 2004), p. 1.
6. Ann Masterman Skinn, *The Old Maid; Or, The History of Miss Ravensworth* (London: 1771), Vol. 1, p. 86; *All's Right at Last: Or, The History of Miss West* (London: 1774), Vol. 1, p. 93.
7. Frances Brooke, *The History of Emily Montague*, ed. Mary J. Edwards (Ottawa: Carleton University Press, 1985), p. 205.
8. *Selected Letters of Samuel Richardson*, ed. John Carroll (Oxford: Clarendon Press, 1964), p. 330.
9. James Raven, "Historical Introduction: The Novel Comes of Age," in *The English Novel 1770–1829: A Bibliographical Survey of Prose Fiction Published in the British Isles*, ed. James Raven and Antonia Forster (Oxford University Press, 2000), p. 42.
10. Nancy Armstrong, "The Rise of Feminine Authority in the Novel," *Novel*, 15.2 (Winter 1982), 127–45. Armstrong later developed her argument into her important *Desire and Domestic Fiction: A Political History of the Novel* (Oxford University Press, 1987).
11. Raven, "Historical Introduction," pp. 48, 41.
12. Nancy K. Miller, *The Heroine's Text: Readings in the French and English Novel, 1722–1782* (New York: Columbia University Press, 1980).
13. Sarah Fielding and Jane Collier, *The Cry: a New Dramatic Fable* (London: 1754), Vol. 1, p. 13.
14. Frances Brooke, *The Excursion*, ed. Paula R. Backscheider and Hope D. Cotton (Lexington: University Press of Kentucky, 1997), p. 91.
15. Brooke, *The Excursion*, pp. 7, 11.
16. Charlotte Lennox, *The Female Quixote; or The Adventures of Arabella*, ed. Margaret Dalzeil (Oxford University Press, 1998), p. 35.
17. Eliza Haywood, *The History of Miss Betsy Thoughtless*, ed. Christine Blouch (Peterborough, ON: Broadview Press, 1998), p. 84.
18. Georgiana, Duchess of Devonshire, *Emma; Or, The Unfortunate Attachment*, ed. Jonathan D. Gross (Albany: State University of New York Press, 2004), p. 57.
19. Tzvetan Todorov, *The Poetics of Prose*, trans. Richard Howard (Ithaca: Cornell University Press, 1977), p. 72. See also Mieke Bal, *Narratology: Introduction to the Theory of Narrative* (University of Toronto Press, 2009), pp. 134–48.
20. Lennox, *The Female Quixote*, p. 77.
21. Susan Lanser, "Toward a Feminist Narratology," *Style* 20.3 (Fall 1986), 341–63.
22. "Heterodiegetic" is Gerard Genette's term for a narrator who is not also a character in the story.
23. Sarah Fielding, *The Adventures of David Simple and Volume the Last*, ed. Peter Sabor (Lexington: University Press of Kentucky, 1998), p. 21.
24. Gerard Genette, *Narrative Discourse: An Essay in Method* (Ithaca: Cornell University Press, 1980), pp. 232–33.
25. *Histories of Some of the Penitents in the Magdalen House, As Supposed to be Related by Themselves*, ed. Jennie Batchelor and Megan Hiatt (London: Pickering & Chatto, 2007). See Batchelor and Hiatt's "Introduction" for

>   the most comprehensive discussion of the attribution, which is still at issue, pp. xx–xxiii.
> 26. Elizabeth Griffith, *The Delicate Distress*, ed. Cynthia B. Ricciardi and Susan Staves (Lexington: University Press of Kentucky, 1997), p. 102.
> 27. Frances Burney, *Cecilia, Or, The Memoirs of an Heiress*, ed. Peter Sabor and Margaret Doody (Oxford University Press, 1999), p. 55.

12

HARRIET GUEST

Travel writing

In the late summer of 1774, two women set out to travel from London to Wales. Hester Lynch Thrale (later Piozzi) (1741–1821), accompanied by her husband, the brewer Henry Thrale, and Samuel Johnson, traveled across the breadth of North Wales to the Llyn peninsula, visiting her recently inherited property at Bach y Graig en route. Mary Darby Robinson (1756/58–1800) and her husband ventured into Wales only as far as Tregunter, at the foot of the Black Mountains, near the small market town of Talgarth in the county of Brecknock or Brecon (now Powys). Hester Thrale had been born and raised in rural Wales, and Robinson spent her early childhood in Bristol, on the Severn estuary, before moving to London. Of the two, it was Mary's husband, Thomas Robinson, who had stronger Welsh connections as the natural son of Thomas Harris, who lived with his daughter and housekeeper at Tregunter. Thrale kept a journal of her journey, in keeping with her habit of recording a commentary on the events of her life; Robinson's account is retrospective, revised or written probably shortly before her death at the turn of the century. But both write vividly about their experience of travel from perspectives that are distinctively gendered, and both bring to Wales the preconceptions and preoccupations of the metropolis. Their accounts illuminate what it meant for women to travel within the mainland, and they also have a more far-reaching significance, despite their short and somewhat fragmentary nature. Both Thrale and Robinson used their travel writings, based on these journeys as well as on others, to shape and advance their identities as authors in a period in which the cultural and literary authority of women was markedly increasing.

There is no obvious evidence that Thrale ever intended to publish her Welsh journal, though Johnson was that summer preparing his *Journey to the Western Islands of Scotland* (1775) for publication the following year, and both travelers might well have had at least occasional thoughts about the possibility of producing corresponding accounts of Wales. Robinson's *Memoirs* (in which her journeys to Wales were narrated) were more obviously prepared for publication, though she may have had no intention of their being published before her death. But whether or not the travel accounts of Robinson and Thrale were written for publication or at least circulation in manuscript, they provided these authors with occasions to write themselves into new scenes. Mary Wollstonecraft (1759–97) commented in her *Vindication of the Rights of Woman* (1792) on the difference between male and female attitudes to travel:

> A man, when he undertakes a journey, has, in general, the end in view; a woman thinks more of the accidental occurrences, the strange things that may possibly occur on the road; the impression that she may make on her fellow-travellers; and, above all, she is anxiously intent on the care of the finery that she carries with her, which is more than ever a part of herself, when going to figure on a new scene; when, to use an apt French turn of expression, she is going to produce a sensation.[1]

Wollstonecraft's female traveler is interested in the sights and experiences that the road has to offer, but she is also aware that her journey culminates in a performance; her dramatic appearance on a new scene. She handles her finery with care to exercise control over the sensation she produces. For Robinson and Thrale, the figure they would each make as a writer in the public arena was shaped out of their reflections on the accidental occurrences of the journey, and they used their journals to rehearse their public appearances. Both women, not surprisingly, took a keen interest in their own reputations, but they were also concerned with the status of women writers more generally. Thrale told her nephew that she valued her status as an author, observing, with some pride, that "I would not lose my own little Sprig of Laurel, or exchange it for Queen Proserpine's Golden Bough," though she acknowledged that her literary learning "had made many People averse to me," and was not likely to help women "find or form a permanent Felicity." She remained pessimistic about the possibilities for progressive change and advised her nephew not to encourage his daughters' interest in literature.[2]

Thrale's emphasis on the value of domesticity for women, however, should not be mistaken for a rejection of public life. It involves what Jon Mee has recently identified as "manipulation of domestic conversation and the language of affect" within the *salon* of the learned and professional elite that she and her husband gathered around them at their country house in Streatham, and that enabled her to emerge in the 1780s as a literary and cultural authority who could rival Bluestockings such as Elizabeth Montagu (1718–1800).[3] The combination of personal feeling and social observation in Thrale's tour journal molds a literary form that, like her social practices, is more conversable and more hospitable to women and their concerns than were the tour writings of Johnson or her contemporary Welsh tourist, the antiquarian and natural historian Thomas Pennant. Robinson, in contrast, wrote extensively about the need to carve out space for women in the literary market place and engaged much more positively with the possibilities of a newly commercialized press. She argued that as a result of education, women would become "citizens of the world" and "Prejudice will be palsied," and she used her own scandalous notoriety, and its incongruous relation to her growing literary reputation, to produce a memoir of her journey to Wales that reinforces feminine cultural authority.[4]

Wollstonecraft concluded her comparison of modes of traveling with a dismissive comment on the preoccupations she attributed to women, asking, "Can dignity of mind exist with such trivial cares?" (61). She represents the travel habits of men and women as indicative of their different attitudes toward professionalism and social responsibility, and strongly favors a masculine teleological and linear sense of purpose, disowning the awareness of circumstance and the demands of sociability, as well as the self-conscious sense of anticipation, that dissipate feminine purposiveness. But it is clear from their travel accounts that neither Robinson nor Thrale thought that personal appearance was a trivial issue – indeed, both connected it strongly with their sense of "dignity of mind." They use clothing as a means to assess the women they meet, and Robinson, in particular, sees her own finery as a marker of the cultural gulf separating her from the women she encounters.

Robinson first visited her husband's relations in Wales late in 1773, having been married that April. She was not much more than fifteen years old at the time of her marriage, but she had already impressed David Garrick, the most prominent actor and theater manager of the day, with her potential as an actress. After enjoying an extravagant life in the fashionable world, interrupted by a stay in debtors' prison with her husband, she embarked on a career as an actress in 1776. She was briefly successful on the stage, and – more enduringly – as a leader of fashion, and almost as a part of that role, she became the lover of several of the most powerful men of the period, successfully extracting a pension from the Prince of Wales after a short but well-publicized affair in 1780. Her first collection of poetry appeared in 1775, and when her mobility was seriously affected by illness in the winter of 1783, she was able to turn to writing to develop a second career. From an early stage, she recognized the central role of the press in the modern metropolis, and she became adept in manipulating her own publicity to the advantage of both her first and her second careers. The account in her *Memoirs* of her two visits to Tregunter in the winter of 1773 and the late summer of 1774 presents the recollections of a young girl suddenly made aware of the vast contrast between rural life in Wales and the attractions of the fashionable metropolis; but those recollections are complicated and filtered by the retrospective opinions of the older woman who conceives of herself primarily as a poet, novelist, and polemicist, closely involved in liberal political debate.

It seems probable that Robinson had kept notes or a journal, perhaps in preparation for writing her memoirs, from an early stage in her life. The narrative of her trips to Wales in 1773 and 1774 is vivid, and rich in detail. The first journey to Tregunter illustrates one of the most striking characteristics of her *Memoirs*: the ability to document with complete confidence exactly what she was wearing on particular occasions. She recalled what she wore as well as the admiration it elicited, and she was also punctilious about the contrastingly archaic appearance of her husband's sister, who, "though not more than twenty years of age, was Gothic in her appearance and stiff in her deportment." The sister's clothes were unfashionable, her countenance excessively ruddy and "peculiarly formed for the expression of sarcastic vulgarity." When she rode out in the old-fashioned tall bonnet commonly worn by Welsh women, Robinson reflected contentedly that in her own more modish dress, she at least "looked like something human." Robinson habitually inspected clothing with a keen and knowledgeable interest, and the detailed sketch of her sister-in-law's appearance confirmed the antiquated rusticity of her husband's relations. Immediately on her return to London, she and her husband entered fashionable society, where the impeccably modern good taste with which she presented her own youth and beauty ensured that "all eyes were fixed upon me"; a recollection in which she could almost allow herself to admit to an irresponsible pleasure because she was then "scarcely emerged beyond the boundaries of Childhood, in[to] the broad hemisphere of fashionable folly."[5]

On this first visit to Tregunter, Harris, the old squire, treated her, she thought, as though he would have "liked me for his wife," and though she found his clothing and manners quaint, she aimed stronger criticism at the women of the house. She condemned them for possessing "vulgar illiberal natures" because they dismissed her accomplishments, telling her that "a good housewife had no occasion for harpsichords and books; they belonged to women who brought wherewithal to support them." Robinson establishes herself, even at this young age, as able to appreciate the value of cultural capital, and to see that in the modern world the claim to it overrides the distinctions of class and wealth that the women allude to in reminding her that she is neither a "woman of fortune" nor a duchess. When she and her husband returned to Tregunter in 1774, however, they were fleeing their creditors, and the squire responded with hostility to their designs on his purse. Robinson's account focuses on his animosity toward herself, her husband almost fading from the picture, and she emphasizes her father-in-law's boorish antagonism to the signs of her cultural refinement. In a paragraph added on the reverse of a page of the manuscript, she wrote:

> The mansion of Tregunter presented but few sources of amusement for the female mind. Mr Harris had acquired a considerable fortune in trade, and however the art of accumulating wealth had been successfully practised, the finer pursuits of mental powers had been totally neglected. Books were unknown at Tregunter, excepting a few magazines or periodical publications, which at different periods Miss Robinson borrowed from her juvinile [sic] neighbours.

When she attempted to console herself with music, "which had been one of my early delights," she recalled that Harris greeted her efforts with insults reminiscent of the preceding visit, telling her that she had better "think of getting my bread; women of no fortune had no right to follow the pursuits of fine Ladies, Tom had better married a good tradesman's daughter than the child of a ruined merchant who was not capable of earning a living." Here Robinson manages to extract self-respect from her father's failures in trade, implying that her own poverty is the mark of sensibility, whereas Harris's wealth has stultified his mind and denied him the ability to appreciate the accomplishments of the modern woman. Harris and his family at Tregunter, she suggests, have denied themselves access to the cultural enlightenment of which she, as an educated young woman of sensibility with the world before her, is a prime example.[6]

Thomas Harris leased some of his land at Trefecca (or Trevecca), a few hundred yards across the valley from Tregunter, to his younger brother, the dissenting preacher Hywel (or Howell) Harris, who had established a small religious community there, which by 1773 had developed into a larger college for members of the Countess of Huntingdon's "connexion," or sect. The site at Trefecca had been extended from the original sixteenth-century farmhouse with the addition of a set of buildings and workshops, and the Countess, who took over the lease from Hywel before his death in 1773, had further improved it. On her first visit, Robinson had implied that the establishment at Trefecca was further evidence of the cultural impoverishment of Wales. She mentioned that her sister-in-law was a member of the sect and added that although Mr. Harris was not, he worshiped there every Sunday: "His zeal was indefatigable and he would frequently fine the rustics (for he was a justice of the peace, and had been Sherif [sic] for the County) when he heard them swear, though every third sentence he uttered was attended by an oath that made his hearers shudder." The charges of zeal and hypocrisy here were a common feature of attacks on dissenting religion, which suggested that it was narrow-minded and fanatical and so, like the women of Harris's household, vulgar and illiberal. Calvinistic dissent of the kind promoted by the Huntingdon connection could be seen as implicitly antiquated and enthusiastic, lacking the polite urbanity of metropolitan modernity. In this context, the squire's religion seems an affront to Robinson's sensibilities both because he is hypocritical and because he is not.[7]

But by the following year, Robinson's attitude to the establishment at Trefecca has changed. She contrasts the coarse rustic sociability of Tregunter, where the squire embarrasses her in front of his bucolic friends, with the peace she finds when, because she is about to give birth, she takes up residence:

> I there avoided the low taunts of uncultivated natures, the insolent vulgarity of pride, and the overbearing triumphs of a family, whose loftiest branch was as inferior to my stock as the small weed is beneath the tallest tree that overshades it. I had formed a union with a family who had neither sentiment nor sensibility[.] I was doomed to bear the society of ignorance and pride; I was treated as though I had been the most abject of beings, even at a time when my conscious Spirit soared as far above their powers to wound it, as the mountain towered over the white battlements of my then Solitary habitation. ("Memoirs," 230)

The Countess of Huntingdon liked her followers to be able to disseminate their uncompromising creed within elegant surroundings, and her chapel at Bath, for example, combined ornamental architectural touches with severe demands on its polite attendees. Trefecca had been redeveloped as a substantial building in the fashionable neo-Gothic style, and its gleaming mock fortifications and arched windows seem to have helped prompt Robinson's reveries; but she may also have had to work hard to abstract herself from her surroundings. In 1773, at least twenty-four students were in residence at the college, and in the summer of 1774, around the time when Robinson moved in, many of the students were experimenting with enthusiastic prayer, consisting of "loud talking, as well as of loud singing," and leaping or jumping until they were "obliged to fall down on the floor."[8] On her first visit, Robinson might have seen this as an example of archaic enthusiasm, but what she is keen to emphasize on this visit is the power of her educated sensibility to turn the humiliation heaped on her by her Welsh relations into a kind of sublime elevation.

This emphasis on her interior strength seems to make it necessary to efface the presence of her husband from this episode, for this was the triumph of

Robinson's cultural resources, and not of marital solidarity. Harris, the gothic villain, told her bluntly that her husband would die in jail, and she would have to tie her child to her back and work for it, but she remains confident that her familiarity with literary culture, as both consumer and producer, will secure her access to an enlightened modernity that is civilized and humane and will be appalled by his barbarity. Her portrait of him drew on the traditional image of the Welsh as a primitive people lacking politeness or refinement. This metropolitan perception of them as archaic, as culturally and financially impoverished, is the staple diet of novels and popular prints portraying Welsh curates and squires such as Isaac Cruikshank's *Welch Politeness* (1798) and *A Welsh Feast on St David's Day* (1790) or Robert Dighton's *The Welch Curate* (c. 1770–1780). In Robinson's "Memoirs," it was also an important part of the retrospective process of establishing her claims to distinction as a metropolitan intellectual who, like Wollstonecraft, did not disavow her provincial origins but used them to mark how far she had come and how great was the distance between her enriched sensibility and modern refinement and the impolite wastes of Brecon, where to her eyes polish or progress seemed impossible.

Robinson's reflections on the dress and manners of her husband's family might best be understood not as the trivial concerns Wollstonecraft dismisses as childish folly but as a use of the conventions of travel writing to lend documentary credibility to the personal memoir. Attention to the manners or customs of people encountered in strange lands was a characteristic feature of the genre in the period, which was expected to include accurate accounts of dress, combining ethnographic observation with the accumulation of information potentially useful to trade. James Boswell (1740–95), for example, listed as one of chief deficiencies of Thomas Pennant's *A Tour in Scotland* (1771) that he "shews no philosophical investigation of character and manners," implying that he shows no interest in the quotidian and characteristic details that should flesh out his account.[9] Hester Thrale's narrative draws on the close relation between natural philosophical inquiry – in which Pennant's work excelled – and the observation of manners and customs in her startling comparison of the limestone cave at Poole's Hole in Derbyshire with Miss Hill, the daughter of Sir Rowland Hill of Hawkstone Park near Shrewsbury. She acknowledged that the most remarkable feature of the cave was its size, which she had not fully explored, though she saw enough to find it "gloomy and lofty," and adds the following:

> The petrefactions, too, hanging down in odd figures, seemed ornaments perfectly suited to the solemnity of the place, where imaginative people might dress up a thousand ideas of horror, but cool examination could, I think, find

little except disgust. In the *Lady* too ... there is an odd mixture of sublimity and meanness. Her conversation is elegant, her dress uncommonly vulgar, her manner lofty if not ostentatious, and her whole appearance below that of a common house-maid. She is, however, by far the most conversible Female I have seen since I left home, her character, I hear, is respectable, and her address is as polite as can be wished.

She concluded that she "could wish to see her very often."[10] Thrale's comparison parodies the objective empiricism or disinterested antiquarianism of work such as Pennant's by treating Miss Hill as though she were an odd natural phenomenon; disowning kinship with her by emphasizing the absence of metropolitan style in her dress and manner rather as Robinson had dehumanized her sister-in-law. But Thrale almost immediately contradicts her own satirical sketch by claiming Hill as a conversable, equal, or sympathetic companion, shifting abruptly from aesthetic disapprobation of the appearance of cave and woman to the more sentimental register of desire and regret.

Hester Thrale produced her uncomfortably comic juxtaposition of cavern and Hill on July 28, 1774, the day she entered Wales, and her comments may be colored by her attitude to the transition, which was very different from that of Robinson, the child bride. The younger woman was acutely aware of the need to maintain a sense of her own dignity, and on both her visits to Tregunter, she kept her husband's relations at arm's length, ensuring that the nature of her association with them confirmed and did not detract from her status as a member of polite metropolitan society. But for Thrale, Wales was not an alien land. For her, the journey was at least in part a sentimental tour of the scenes of her childhood, and a pilgrimage of mourning for her mother, who had died in June 1773. She recorded a poignant sense of loss that profoundly destabilized her confidence in her own social status, noting that her uncle, Sir Thomas Salusbury, "has long ago cast me off, & Mr. Thrale & Mr. Johnson are the mere Acquisitions of Chance; which chance, or change of Behaviour, or Intervention of new Objects or twenty Things besides Death can rob me of. One solid Good I had & that is gone – my Mother!"[11] The awkward juxtapositions and uneasy humor of the travel journal can be understood as characteristics of its private and occasional status, but they are also the marks of Thrale's sense of her own contingency and impermanence following her mother's death. James Clifford commented that "For the first time she was completely adrift from all the old ties."[12] Her journey to Wales renewed her connections with her past and with her family, but her journal also indicates a reassessment of the relationships that defined her, and a fresh assertion of her sense of herself as an intellectual, a figure of consequence in the social world of the learned and professional that she cultivated in Streatham.

In the first few weeks of the tour, Thrale repeatedly lamented the lack of her mother's companionship and used her sense of that loss also to mark how excluded or alienated she felt by the friendship of Johnson and her husband – or her master, as she more usually named him. In a typical entry quite early in the tour, she observed sadly that "'tis so melancholy a thing to have nobody one can speak to about one's clothes, or one's child, or one's health, or what comes uppermost. Nobody but *Gentlemen*, before whom one must suppress everything except the mere formalities of conversation and by whom everything is to be commended or censured." A month later, she again regretted "the loss of my Mother" as a companion with whom she could discuss her children's minor ailments and reflected that "My present Companions have too much philosophy for me. One cannot disburthen one's mind to people who are watchful to cavil, or acute to contradict before the sentence is finished." It is curious that the topics she longed to discuss with her mother were precisely contingent – the accidental and quotidian trivia of domestic life that she felt unable to discuss with her male companions because their concerns seemed to her exclusively philosophical and critical. They wanted to weigh and assess serious and solid matters, while she wanted to chat about whatever "comes uppermost." But her mother's death deprived her of a "solid Good" and left her isolated in a world of chance, as though in her absence Thrale's sense of the relation between her domestic concerns and her social and literary ambitions became uncertain or unworkable.[13]

This insecurity about the status of domestic concerns is frequently apparent in Thrale's assessment of the women she meets on her travels. When they stayed with the family of Thrale's cousin, Robert Cotton, at Lleweni Hall near Denbigh, she envied the domestic virtues of her cousin's wife:

> I expected letters from home and had none ... I have not Mrs. Cotton's even sweetness of temper, so I am come into my room to cry. She loves her children as well as I do, but she would not have cried from fretful impatience like me. Why does every body on some occasion or other perpetually do better than I can?

She was careful to point out that Mrs. Cotton was not one of the many Welsh women whose lack of education she deplored. She was

> a most amiable being, charitable, compassionate, modest, and gentle to a degree, almost unequalled by any woman whose want of fortune, person, or understanding did not set her apparently below her husband. She is however,

proportionately equal to him in both knowledge and riches, but so pliant, so tender, so attentive to his health, his children, and his expenses, that I sincerely think of all the people I ever yet knew – he is the *happiest* in a Wife.

Thrale suggested that she expected to find the self-denying and feminine virtues she first listed here only in women who were inferior in rank to their husbands – perhaps in the unequal marriages that she suggested clergymen entered into early in their careers and regretted as they achieved promotion. She implied that domestic women usually developed these virtues because they lacked refinement or education. But Mrs. Cotton made Thrale feel inferior because her "even sweetness" of temper was not compensated for by any obvious deficiency. There is some sign of what reconciled her to what she briefly saw as her own shortcoming in her comment that Mrs. Cotton's education and wealth were "proportionately equal" to her husband's, an assessment that hints that what was proportionate or fitting for the Cottons might not have been adequate to the ambitions of Hester Thrale, the metropolitan hostess and learned lady. Johnson built on this suggestion that Mrs. Cotton's temper was a proportionate good in his reflection that her sweetness was like that of a honeycomb, and merely "in her nature"; it was involuntary and unearned, and though Thrale wrote that he undervalued Mrs. Cotton, the fact that she recorded the opinion suggests that she also found it consoling.

Thrale wished to be able to discuss her maternal concerns, and she clearly admired Mrs. Cotton's domestic virtues, in contrast to those of, for example, Lady Catherine Wynn of Glynllifon, whom she castigated as both ignorant and a poor housewife, who gave them a "vile dinner ... on such linen as shocked one; no plate, no china to be seen."[14] In general she thought that among those she perceived as of "genuine Welch folks," the "women were vastly below the men in proportion," which meant that the women's behavior was even less elegant or polite, and their English vocabulary still "more contracted" than that of the men (106). But her longing for her mother was not about any simple need for reconfirmation of her domestic and maternal role. It was as much about her sense of being excluded from the conversation of her male companions as about the absence of a domestic collaborator.

The farthest point of their trip was Thrale's birthplace at Bodfel Hall, on the Llyn peninsula. She wrote that "Everything here is to me as a monument" to her mother, commemorating "her virtue and her sufferings, and every rough road I feel reminds me of the pain with which she passed these mountains, which I am now crossing for pleasure." Thrale was intensely moved by the recollection of her mother's sufferings, which she felt deeply, and which reinforced her sense of closeness to her; but the place also reminds her of how distant her own life is from her mother's, as she takes pleasure in a journey that had given her pain. On the preceding evening, she writes that the landscape of the Llyn is a pressing reminder of how far she is from England:

> The mountains on your right hand fatigue the eye with looking upward, and the sea, stretched out before you, tire it equally with looking upon total vacuity. Woods, however, of Mr. Griffith's planting shelter the left side, and the garden relieves your imagination from the terrors which such a prospect as this naturally forces on the mind. This is indeed a retreat from the World which seems wholly excluded, and in effect it is so, by mountains and by seas.

Sentiment and nostalgia are undoubtedly important ingredients of the trip for Thrale, and the visit to Bodfel helps her reflect on her mother's life with sympathy, but her account of the prospect from Griffith's house signals a determination to resist any temptation to discover the roots of her own identity there. The view had a negative sublimity of the kind that threatened to annihilate the perceiving subject by forcing on her the qualities of its own "total vacuity." At Poole's Hole, earlier in her travels, she had rejected the horrors of the sublime as flights of fancy cultivated by overactive imaginations and dismissed them as distasteful, but here she found terrors were forced on her mind, and the experience transformed her relationship to her own past.[15]

Once Thrale had visited Bodfel Hall, she went on to the parish church where she was baptised, which she found "truly wretched"; on the same day, she visited the neighboring town of Pwllheli, which she thought was a "piteous place" now, although improved since her childhood, when it had been so primitive and benighted that "all the country flocked thither to see a Sign." Subsequently, they drove to see some churches where Thrale has inherited the right to apportion clerical livings, and she affirmed, "They shock me with their poverty and misery. I never imagined to myself anything half so bad. I do not know what to do for them, they are worse than one can easily conceive." The pilgrimage to her birthplace enabled Thrale to pay sentimental homage to her mother's virtues, but it also established with absolute clarity that this was not her home. She concluded her account of the view from Griffith's house with the comment, "The distance one is at from all relief if an accident should happen fills one with apprehension, and when I have surveyed the place of my nativity, I shall be glad to return to a land fuller of inhabitants." She rejected wholeheartedly the notion that this might be a desirable "retreat from the World," or that it might offer the kind of romantic solitude in which Mary Robinson had delighted while she enjoyed the elegant architecture of Trefecca. The solitude of the Llyn peninsula was for Thrale freighted with her mother's suffering, and she escaped from it with pleasure, taking from it a renewed sympathy with her male companions, whose kindness during this painful visit she accepted with gratitude.[16]

The contrast between Robinson and Thrale in their responses to solitude as a characteristic of the Welsh sublime had more to do with the relative comfort of Trefecca over the isolation and poverty of the Llyn, and with the ways in which the two women forged their identities as writers, than it did with any retrospective revision on Robinson's part. Her taste for solitude is not necessarily more characteristic of the late century than of 1774. Wollstonecraft, in her *Letters from Sweden, Norway and Denmark* (1796), for example, counterbalanced her appreciation of sublime wilderness with a more practical admiration for well-cultivated fields and was confident that towns were essential to the modern way of life. Robinson presented her pleasure in the solitude she imagined at Trefecca as an alternative to the coarse bucolic society available at Tregunter, and as only a brief and enforced respite from the more sophisticated pleasures of the metropolis. For Thrale, the remoter parts of Wales in particular may have offered temptations she felt she needed to resist. Only a couple of days after her stay near Bodfel, she passed near the "barren magnitude" of Snowdon and was able to comment on the scene with complacence: "Goats frisking on the hills and a cataract playing at a small distance so finished the scene, that nothing, I think, could be wished for." Perhaps this enthusiastic response was colored by her relief at escaping from her birthplace, and from the confirmation of identity it might have seemed to offer.

The final stages of Thrale's "Journal" are a good deal more cheerful than the first. She seemed to feel less excluded from the company of the men, and although it became apparent to her that she was pregnant again, and suffering as a result, she also showed a renewed confidence in her identity as a writer and critic. This confidence was demonstrated most clearly during their trip to Hagley Park, in Worcestershire, the country seat of the Lyttelons. When the ladies press Thrale to play cards, she wins "three shillings, which they paid for the pleasure of enjoying my inferiority in the only science wherein I could be found inferior to them." Thrale regards card playing as a "cruel vexation," an activity that she, like the women of the Bluestocking circle, regarded as the height of fashionable and anti-intellectual foolishness. She confirmed her contempt for aristocratic frivolity and ostentation, and her preference for more private and domestic space, when she argued that the garden created by the poet William Shenstone at The Leasowes, where the cascades were "so lovely, so unartificial to appearance," was what she would choose for herself, while the more formal landscape gardens of "Keddlestone or Hagley should be reserved for the gardener to show on a

Sunday to travelling fools and starers."[17] At The Leasowes, she felt able to sit by the boathouse and compose a short poem – an activity she showed no sign of engaging in during her tour of Wales.

Thrale was, of course, proud of her Welsh heritage and keen to develop the land and house at Bach y Graig, a mission she was later able to accomplish with her second husband, Gabriel Piozzi. If during her tour of 1774, she found her re-encounter with Wales difficult, the landscape and the people often rebarbative and alienating, and the company she traveled with unsympathetic, these feelings were indicative of her struggle to accept the awareness of contingency thrust on her by her mother's death. In the first half of her tour journal, her tone or choice of manner was uncertain, and she seemed to find it difficult to position herself, and to determine the kind of account she was writing. After the visit to Bodfel, she became more confident in her ability to move fluently between the domestic and maternal concerns she associated with her mother on the one hand and the learned and literary substance of the men's conversation on the other. She accepted that the world of chance and discontinuity that she had found in the metropolis, and where she could thrive in sociable circles of her own making, was preferable to the solid sense of belonging and of rootedness she had sought in Wales.

When Wollstonecraft wrote of the differences between male and female travelers in 1792, it seemed to her obvious that the masculine method of travel, keeping "the end in view," was preferable. The male traveler fulfils his intention without hesitation or question; he exposes himself to no new experiences and entertains no moments of reflection, no hindrance from doubt or uncertainty; as if in accordance with Wollstonecraft's distinction, travel accounts written by men frequently seem to need to erase or deny the presence of the observing subject and to claim an objectivity and purposiveness on which the truth of their observations is made to depend. Wollstonecraft's female traveler, in contrast, finds that the journey confirms the contingent and discontinuous nature of her subjectivity – its dependence on "accidental occurrences" and extraneous ornament. If she is perceptive, and eager to take note of the "strange things" and people she encounters, these observations disclose her own fluctuating identity, for the female traveler makes no claims to detachment and is changed by her experiences. Thrale and Robinson both position the subjects of their accounts, like Wollstonecraft's traveler, in full view like a figure on the stage at the center of the narrative. As Wollstonecraft herself clearly recognized by the time she published her own tour journal of Scandinavia in 1796, for women travel writers the development of the subject through "the accidental occurrences, the strange things that may possibly occur on the road" produced a narrative enriched with a new kind of value.[18]

NOTES

1. Mary Wollstonecraft, *A Vindication of the Rights of Woman*, ed. Carol H. Poston (New York: W. W. Norton & Co, 1988), p. 61.
2. Harvard Piozziana, 3:126, cited in William McCarthy, *Hester Thrale Piozzi: Portrait of a Literary Woman* (Chapel Hill: University of North Carolina Press, 1985), p. 62.
3. Jon Mee, *Conversable Worlds: Literature, Contention, and Community, 1762–1830* (Oxford University Press, 2011), p. 112.
4. Mary Robinson, *A Letter to the Women of England and The Natural Daughter*, ed. Sharon M. Setzer (Peterborough, ON: Broadview Press, 2003), p. 82.
5. "Memoirs of Mrs. Mary Robinson," in *The Works of Mary Robinson*, Vol. 7 of 8, ed. Hester Davenport, gen. ed. William D. Brewer (London: Pickering and Chatto, 2010), pp. 216, 217. I have chosen to use the text of the manuscript draft of the "Memoirs" because the printed version, in [Mary Robinson and Mary Elizabeth Robinson], *Memoirs of the Late Mrs. Robinson, written by herself. With some posthumous pieces* (London: R. Phillips, 1801), 4 vols., may in some details be additionally edited or filtered by Robinson's daughter, Mary Elizabeth, to reflect the views of a later generation.
6. "Memoirs," pp. 217, 229.
7. On the lease and building work at Trefecca, see Edwin Welch, *Spiritual Pilgrim: A Reassessment of the Life of the Countess of Huntingdon* (Cardiff: University of Wales Press, 1995), pp. 114–15. Robinson, "Memoirs," p. 216.
8. John Evans, *A Sketch of the denominations of the Christian World* (1811), cited in Welsh, p. 179, and see p. 177.
9. James Boswell, *Life of Johnson*, ed. R. W. Chapman, intro. Pat Rogers (Oxford University Press, 1980), p. 933.
10. Hester Thrale, "Journal of a Tour in Wales with Dr. Johnson," in *Dr Johnson & Mrs Thrale's Tour in North Wales, 1774*, ed. Adrian Bristow (Wrexham, Clwyd: Bridge Books, 1995), p. 100, July 28.
11. Quoted from the Children's Book, Thrale's unpublished journal in James L. Clifford, *Hester Lynch Piozzi (Mrs Thrale)* (Oxford: Clarendon Press, 1941), p. 104.
12. Clifford, *Piozzi*, p. 104.
13. Thrale, "Journal," p. 95, July 16, and p. 109, August 14.
14. Thrale, "Journal," p. 107, August 9 and 8; on clergymen's marriages, see p. 103, July 31; Johnson's comment, p. 109, August 12; Glynllifon, p. 113, August 21.
15. Thrale, "Journal," p. 114, August 23; pp. 113–14, August 22.
16. Thrale, "Journal," pp. 115–16, August 23; p. 116, August 24; p. 114, August 22.
17. Thrale, "Journal," p. 122, September 16; p. 123, September 19.
18. Wollstonecraft, *Vindication*, p. 61.

13

RUTH PERRY

Ballads

> It was a woman ... who made the ballads and the folksongs, crooning them to her children, beguiling her spinning with them, or the length of the winter's night.
>
> Virginia Woolf, *A Room of One's Own*

In his anonymous article in *The Nation* on "Ballad Books," published in 1868, Francis J. Child, the great nineteenth-century codifier of popular ballads, pleaded with his audience to hunt down whatever ballads might yet remain unnoted in the world. "Where are the Mrs. Farquhars, the Mrs. Browns, the Mrs. Arnots, the Miss Rutherfords?" he asked, naming the most significant tradition bearers of the previous century. "[I]t cannot be that the diffusion of useful knowledge, the intrusion of the railroads, and the general progress of society, have quite driven all the old songs out of country-women's heads – for it will be noted that it is mainly through women everywhere –

> 'The spinsters and the knitters in the sun,
> And the free maids that weave their thread with bones' –

that ballads have been preserved."[1] Child was quoting Shakespeare's *Twelfth Night*; even in Shakespeare's time, the "old sad songs," the "antique" songs were understood to be carried by women with time to sing – spinsters and free maids. In this chapter, I describe the cultural context for one of the women balladeers invoked by Child in this passage, Anna Gordon (1747–1810) or "Mrs. Brown," and to account for her prominence in the recovery and transmission of ballad texts in the eighteenth century.

First, it may be in order to spell out what Child meant by "popular ballads" and to establish the connection between women and balladry. Child meant those ballads that had been carried in the oral tradition during some period of their existence, ballads that had actually been sung by people and that had therefore lived longer in human memory than the brief lifespan of the topical broadsides sold by the thousands since the dawn of printing. To be sure, many ballads circulated in and out of print during the course of several hundred years; some popular ballads may have been kept alive by print. But Child wanted to specify ballads that had had an oral life as well as a print life.

Child again calls attention to the centrality of women as ballad preservers in his plea in *Notes and Queries* of 1873, for all "*unprinted* manuscripts of ballads in existence." There he asked his readers to try to recall and to send him any ballads they may have learned as children.

> Something also must still be left in the memory of men, or better, of *women* who have been the chief preservers of ballad-poetry. May I entreat the aid of gentlewomen in Scotland, or elsewhere, who remember ballads that they have heard repeated by their grandmothers or nurses?[2]

The association between women and ballads on which Child was drawing was established long before his engagement with collecting. With few exceptions, most historical references to ballad singing in the early modern period mention women as the singers. In 1653, Dorothy Osborne (1627–95) tells Sir William Temple that she has received from her brother a ballad "much older than my Lord of Lorne" – although we do not know what it is because it has not been preserved. And then she writes,

> [T]he heat of the day is spent in reading or working and about sixe or seven a Clock, I walke out into a Common that lyes hard by the house where a great many young wenches keep Sheep and Cow's and sitt in the shade singing of Ballads; I goe to them and compare theire voyces and Beauty's to some Ancient Shepherdesses that I have read of and finde a vast difference there, but trust mee I think these are as innocent as those could bee. I talke to them, and finde they want nothing to make them the happiest People in the world, but the knoledge that they are soe.[3]

Izaak Walton, in chapter 4 of his *Compleat Angler* (1653), printed the same year as Dorothy Osborne's letter, refers to "a handsome milk-maid, that ... sung like a nightingale" whose mother offers him a drink of milk and a syllabub of "new Verjuice" while her daughter sings him "one of her best Ballads, 'Come Shepheard: deck your beards,' or, 'As at noon Dulcina rested; or, 'Philida flouts me;' or, 'Chevy Chase' or 'Johnny Armstrong' or 'Troy Town.'"

A little later in the century, among people of a higher class, Samuel Pepys preserves in his diary the occasion on which he went "to my Lord Bruncker's, and there find ... my dear Mrs. Knipp, with whom I sang, and in perfect pleasure I was to hear her sing, and especially her little Scotch song of 'Barbary Allen.'"[4] Whether or not Mrs. Knipp's version of "Barbara Allen" *was* Scottish, folk songs were often called "Scotch" or "Northern" in the late seventeenth and eighteenth centuries, whatever their provenance – a state of affairs that reflected the craze for Scottish folk music in the rest of Europe.[5]

Women were also at the lowest end of the business – ballad hawkers and ballad street singers – for as Paula McDowell has shown, the oldest and poorest women were to be found on London streets selling broadsides in the late seventeenth and early eighteenth centuries. It was very ill-paid work, and perhaps indigent old women were the only people desperate enough to distribute political broadsides because it was a risky business to be caught doing it. Several of these female ballad singers ended up in jail for distributing treasonous material. Song could be extremely effective politically, as that ardent student of popular culture of his day, Daniel Defoe, declared, writing under the pseudonym of Jeffrey Sing-Song, in "The Balladsmaker's Plea" (1722). There, he refers to the "Universal Benefit" of that "important" song "The King shall enjoy his own again" at the time of the Restoration of Charles II and cites "Lillibulero" (sometimes spelled "Lillbulero"), the satiric song from the time of the Glorious Revolution said to have sung James II out of three kingdoms. Closer to his own time, Defoe reports that

> the Riots in Scotland were usher'd in with a Song, call'd AWA *Whigs*, AWA. The mobs of Dr. *Sacheverell*'s Time had *Down with the Round Heads*, an old Ballad revived. The Hurries of the late Reign had the reviv'd Ballad of Chevy Chase; nay, even the Solicitations for the late *Callico Bill* were introduced with the Ballad of a *Callico Madam*.[6]

The connection between women and the oral tradition of balladry was especially strong in Scotland. For that reason, scholars and antiquarians interested in collecting such cultural artifacts often appealed to their female relatives – their mothers and their aunts – as well as their female servants, for oral versions of old songs and ballads. As Willa Muir argues, the interest in Scottish ballads spread outward from Allan Ramsay's bookshop in Edinburgh, reinforced in 1765 by what is now known as Percy's *Reliques*, or the *Reliques of Ancient English Poetry*, a collection of ballads and popular songs gathered by Thomas Percy. Ballads "were then widely collected and taken down, mostly from the singing of old women who had learned them as girls from the singing of other old women," Muir summarizes. Muir also suggests that the devaluation of ballads in the seventeenth century stems precisely from their being relegated to "women and bairns" (children) and asserts that "women have always tended to conserve a tradition of song and story, as they conserve the ramifications of kinship networks."[7] Indeed, by the time intellectuals were interested in ballads, the fact that a ballad had been collected from an old woman was often enough to authenticate it.

Henry MacKenzie reports that in his youth, "the ladies of Edinburgh used to sing those airs without any accompaniment ... at tea and after supper, their position at table not being interrupted as now by rising to the pianoforte."[8] Accomplished Englishwomen, of course, also sang to entertain their friends and guests, but they might sing art songs or Italian songs or any other song. Scottish women were likely to have learned Scottish songs. In March 1749, an old friend of Archibald Campbell named Charles Stewart wrote of his coming visit to Inveraray Castle, anticipating that he would pass his time agreeably "learning Wisdom from Miss [Betty] Fletcher, Economy from her mother & in hearing Miss Mally sing the Highland Lady by way of desert [sic]."[9] When Samuel Johnson and James Boswell toured Scotland in 1773, they were well entertained in many places by Scottish women singing them folk songs. Scottish women were expected to know their songs and to sing them in company as a respectable diversion.

Anna Gordon was one of the first of such tradition bearers to whom intellectuals and collectors turned in their efforts to find versions of the old ballads. She was the daughter of Thomas Gordon, a professor of Humanity (Greek and Latin classics) at King's College in Aberdeen, Scotland, and Lilias Forbes of Disblair, his wife. Anna Gordon had learned her old ballads as a girl, and her repertoire excited her father's longtime friend, William Tytler, Lord Woodhouselee, who asked Gordon to get them written down for him. Tytler had written *A Dissertation on the Scottish Musick* (1779) to establish the antiquity of Scottish folk songs, and he cared deeply about the history of this music.[10] Much later, Thomas Gordon explained to Tytler's son, Alexander Fraser-Tytler, how his daughter came to learn her old songs and how she came to record them for his father shortly before 1783:

> An Aunt of my children, Mrs. Farquherson [sic] now dead, who was married to the proprietor of a small estate near the sources of the Dee, in the division of Aberdeenshire called Braemar, a sequestered, romantic pastoral country, if you ever went to your estate by the way of the castle of that name, you are not such a stranger to it as need a description. This good woman, I say, spent her days, from the time of her marriage, among the flocks & herds at Allanaquoich her husbands seat, which, even in the country of Braemar is considered as remarkable for the above circumstances. She had a tenacious memory, which retained all the songs she heard the nurses & old women sing in that neighborhood. In the latter part of her life she lived in Aberdeen; & being maternally fond of my children when young, she had them much about her, & was much with us. Her songs & tales of chivalry & love were a high entertainment to their young imagination. My youngest daughter Mrs Brown, at Falkland, is blessed with a memory as good as her aunts, & has almost the whole store of her songs lodged in it. In conversation I mentioned them to your Father [i.e., William Tytler], at

whose request my Grandson Mr Scott, wrote down a parcel of them as his aunt sung them. Being then but a meer novice in musick, he added in his copy such musical notes as he supposed, notwithstanding their correctness, might give your father some imperfect notion of the airs; or rather lilts, to which they were sung. Both the words & strains were perfectly new to me, as they were to your father, & proceeded upon a system of manners, & in a stile of composition, both words & music, very peculiar & of which we could recollect nothing similar ... Mrs. Farquherson, I am sure, invented nor added nothing herself.[11]

Thomas Gordon here credits his sister-in-law with having taught his daughter these ballads, although Anna Gordon herself asserted that she learned them "all when a child, by hearing them sung by [Mrs. Farquharson], by my own mother, and an old maid-servant that had been long in the family."[12] Since Anna Gordon was born in 1747 and learned these songs before she was twelve, and her mother and aunt presumably learned their ballads in *their* youth, her repertoire of ballads must date back to at least the early eighteenth century and probably much earlier.

Moreover, these were not ballads sung everyday on the streets of Aberdeen but were a collection from the wider bounds of Northeast Scotland, probably from a specifically women's singing tradition. "Both the words & strains were perfectly new to me, as they were to your father," Thomas Gordon had written of the ballad manuscript he sent to William Tytler, "& proceeded upon a system of manners, & in a stile of composition, both words & music, very peculiar, & of which we could recollect nothing similar."[13] Thus, although Gordon and Tytler were both musically literate, Anna Gordon's ballad repertoire was apparently unknown to those two well-educated men.

In the years that followed, Anna Gordon – by then Mrs. Brown – was importuned a number of times more for copies of her ballads, including by William Tytler's son, her childhood friend Alexander Fraser-Tytler. Manuscript copies of her ballads were shared by the major ballad connoisseurs of the day – Joseph Ritson, Robert Jamieson, Matthew "Monk" Lewis, Walter Scott, Robert Anderson, and Thomas Percy – who thought her ballads superior to others they had heard or read. They gossiped among themselves about whether or not she had "improved" her texts, as so many collectors did in the eighteenth century. She denied that she had changed them and claimed that she sang them or wrote them down just as she remembered them. As Robert Anderson wrote to Thomas Percy, "her character places her above suspicion of literary imposture, but it is wonderful how she should happen to be the depository of so many curious and valuable ballads."[14]

However, ballad singers never sing the same thing exactly the same way twice. They might smooth out the edges of a phrase, rearrange a word here or there, drop out what is clumsy and choose instead a vivid detail – perhaps from another ballad – all in the process of singing it and without consciously tampering with what they have learned. Chances are that the ballads that passed through Anna Gordon's consciousness were honed by her literary mind – refined, purified, their effects heightened – but not intentionally. The result was a magnificent repertoire, selected brilliantly and rendered fully, each ballad a satisfying whole. Francis J. Child prized her ballads above others in his collection and wrote, "There are no ballads superior to those sung by Mrs. Brown of Falkland in the last century."[15] This, then, was Anna Gordon Brown's contribution to literary history.

Anna Gordon's ballads

A closer look at Gordon's early history helps one better understand the wellsprings of her unique repertoire – her mother's musical family, the stories with which she grew up, and the ballads that were part of her father's family's lore. Aberdeenshire, where Anna Gordon was born and raised, was steeped in balladry. Local traditions of stories and songs abounded in that part of Scotland and were sung and told locally by tinkers, servants, laborers, and artisans as well as by gentlewomen. The names of the characters who peopled these ballads were familiar names in the northeast. Many people could share details about the ballad stories that were not in the sung versions; the countryside was rife with ballad references – where the main characters who peopled them were born or died or lived. And many families passed on stories of their own that corroborated the truth of the events in the ballads. For example, Gordons appear in more than twenty ballads, and their relationship to Anna Gordon's family could be directly traced in some cases.

Thus for Anna Gordon, the world of ballads was continuous with her everyday world. The stories they told were true stories, and most of them had happened in places that she had seen or heard about. She heard them sung and talked about by her mother, by a maidservant in the Gordon household at Humanity Manse, and by her maternal aunt Anne Forbes Farquharson, who frequently came down from her husband's estate, Allanaquoich, to stay with Anna's family. When visiting Farquharson in the summer, Anna Gordon and her sisters also heard local laborers singing ballads and songs in old Scots. Anne Farquharson herself had learned some of their ballads as well, which she taught to her eager young niece.

Anna Gordon wrote to Alexander Fraser-Tytler in 1800 about some Aberdeenshire ballads she had just found in a "by corner" of her memory, ballads that were not ancient but perhaps only a century old or so.[16]

She questions their "poetical merits" but goes on to state that the "family incidents upon which they are founded" and "the local allusions which they contain may perhaps render them curious and not uninteresting." The five ballads she then offered to send him were

>   1st the Baron of Braickly [sic]   2d the Lass of Philorth
>   3d the tryal of the Laird of Gycht
>   4th the death of the Countess of Aboyne
>   5th the Carrieng off of the Heiress of Kinady[17]

In her letter to Fraser-Tytler, she assured him that "all these I can recollect pretty exactly. I never saw any of them either in print or Manuscript but have them entirely from hearing them sung when a child." Aboyne and Philorth are still recognizable places in the northeast, and the names that occur in these ballads – Brackley, Lord Saltoun, Frasers, Auchenachie, and above all Gordon – continue to this day. The area is like a patchwork of ballad references.

When she sent Jamieson "The Baron of Braickly" some months later, she told him that she had seen the place where the incidents recorded in that ballad actually happened: "I have been at Braickly & seen the ruins of the Barrons Castle little of which now remain they show'd me the gate he rode out at about one half of which was then extant & a hollow way between two little knolls where the Farquharsons fell upon him."[18] She then narrated the historical events as she had heard them described that had given rise to the ballad, assuring him that it was a "true story," and that she had been told it really happened, probably at the end of the seventeenth century:

> John Gordon of Braickly or as he was alwise call'd the Baron of Braickly w[as a fin]e man universally esteem'd he was of the Family of Aboyne Farquharson of Inveray had a personal ill will to him, & came with a train of Armed followers & drove off his Cattle the Baron went out to remonstrate with him & was instante surrounded & cut to pieces not many yards from his own gate. Inveray fled & was outlaw'd but was allow'd afterwards to return.[19]

This account, which must have been what local people repeated to one another about the facts of the case, differs markedly from the ballad itself. That John Gordon was a "fine man, universally esteemed" is not apparent in the ballad; neither is the fact that he came from the Aboyne Gordons. Nor does the ballad include the name "Farquharson," but Inveray is enough for locals to know to whom the ballad referred. The teasing and treacherous behavior of Gordon's wife Peggy in the ballad, which gives the ballad story its flavor, seems not to be part of the version as passed on in the family.

Other examples of the vivid, living reality of the ballads of the northeast in the eighteenth century exist. "The Lass of Patie's Mill," still sung today, apparently originated with a woman named Anderson who lived in Keith-Hall in Fintray. The Statistical Account for that parish, commissioned by Sir John Sinclair and published in 1791, observes that "a great grandson of hers, aged 89, and a number of her descendents, reside in this district, and in the parishes of Kinnellar and Dyce." Not far from Disblair, where Anna Gordon's mother and aunt were raised, lived a family that believed itself to be descended from the "lass of Patie's mill" – a family that prized and spoke about the connection.

Another famous ballad story involved the grandfather of the man who married Anna Gordon's sister, Elizabeth Gordon. In 1699, the Reverend John Scott was robbed at Saint Ruffer's Fair of £40 by some "Egyptians" or gypsies, probably while he was attending King's College in Aberdeen. Four of these "Egyptians" were tried and hanged at Banff, one of whom was apparently James McPherson, whose immortality is assured by the song "McPherson's Farewell." A very well-known standard to this day sung to the tune "McPherson's Rant,"[20] it comes from the point of view of the condemned man who tells the story of his capture as he stands below the gallows right before he is hung. The protagonist of the song is also a musician, and he asks that his hands be untied so that he can break his fiddle rather than letting it fall into another's hands and be played by someone else. McPherson was a notorious thief, and his captors were so eager to get rid of him that they set the clock early to foil the reprieve that was coming over the bridge of Banff, or so the song recounts.

Ballad lore was pervasive in this part of the world at this time as indicated by notes that Anna Gordon's father, Thomas, took on the ballads of "Edom o' Gordon" (Child #178) and "The House of Frendraught" (Child #196). Both ballads involve Gordons and the notes were among Thomas Gordon's papers on the family genealogy. Annotating the incidents in "Edom o' Gordon" under the heading of "Sir Adam Gordon of Auchindown," Thomas Gordon, scholar that he was, included a page and a half of notes from historians of Scotland Spottswood and Crawford in English and Buchanan in Latin.[21] Most interesting of all, he also wrote down what Thomas Percy had to say about the ballad in his *Reliques*. The significance of his daughter's "little hoard of solitary entertainment" to a larger intellectual community apparently whetted Gordon's own curiosity about them, although these notes on the historical accuracy of certain ballads suggest his interest lay more in their accuracy as Gordon family history rather than their wider cultural value.

However, a sentence near the bottom of the first page contains information that does not come from any historian's tome, but could only come from current local knowledge. As such, it testifies further to the way these ballads were woven into the living landscape of Aberdeenshire. "[I]n the neighborhood of Towie," Gordon wrote, "they show a grave which they call Lady Campbell's grave, supposing that her ashes & those of her children &c. were there deposited,"[22] referring to the tragic denouement of "Edom o' Gordon" in which Captain Ker (Carre), acting as a proxie for Adam Gordon of Auchindoun (Edom o' Gordon), burns down his enemy's castle with his lady (Margaret Forbes, née Campbell) and her children in it. Thus, once his daughter's repertoire of old songs attracted the notice of other scholars, even Anna Gordon's father was beginning to notice how ballads were part of the texture of life in the northeast, and he interested himself in the locally known details. He appears to have caught the enthusiasm for old ballads that was spreading among intellectuals in the later eighteenth century.

Anna Gordon's everyday ballad world

The family stories told in Anna Gordon's household were hardly less marvelous than the stories carried in ballads, and knowing them contributes to one's sense of the richly imagined world in which she grew up. Our source for these family stories is a daughter of her older sister Elizabeth, said to have heard them from her mother – as Anna Gordon herself must have – further proof that the reliques of kinship were carried matrilineally in this society. These family stories resemble ballads in their spare recounting of astonishing incidents. We learn what happened, but not much about the motivation of the actors or the emotional consequences. No judgment is passed on the life-changing, catastrophic events relayed. Like ballads, the flat tone of the narratives memorably contains the charged and powerful content of these stories. These family stories illustrate the texture of the imaginative life in Gordon's family and give the flavor of Anna Gordon's everyday ballad world.

Of Anna Gordon's paternal great grandfather, Patrick Gordon, the first in a long line of King's College professors, the family told the following story:

> There resided on the border of the Hielands of Scotland a certain Laird of the House of Gordon. His family consisted of his wife, a son, and daughter. His son was educated at King's College, Old Aberdeen, and while there displayed a peculiar talent for acquiring different languages. He was master of thirteen

different languages when he graduated, and he returned home the joy and pride of his parents, who invited his friends to visit him to form shooting parties. His sister was handsome and much admired by the youths of the neighborhood. One morning she entered the room where her brother and his friends were making ready for the chase, and expressed great alarm at seeing them loading their pieces in doors. Her brother laughingly said he intended to punish her for her cruelty to her admirers. She cried out "Do not shoot Laddie! do not shoot!" but he not heeding her the gun accidentally went off and she fell. The shock was so great to her brother than he instantly left his Parents, and all search for him proved vain; in this disconsolate situation they remained for two years.[23]

It is said that the horrified young man joined the army on the Continent, where "his conduct was such as to render him a favorite with men and officers." One night, while standing guard, he overheard a dispute among some officers about the pronunciation of a Greek word. It was observed that young Gordon paid close attention to the argument and he was asked for his opinion. His answer displayed such learning that the men present wanted to know "who and what he was. He related his misfortune which greatly excited their sympathies." When his story reached the commander, he sent for young Gordon and

> recommended him to return to his mourning Parents, remarking it was a sufficient misfortune to lose one child, and the evil was doubled in the loss of both. He accordingly returned and was soon after elected Professor of Ancient and Modern languages, in the College of Old Aberdeen. He married and had a family. His eldest son succeeded him in the Professorship, and was the father of my Grandfather Gordon, who, in a like manner, was elected to fill his father's place.

On her mother's side, Anna Gordon also had some remarkable forebears. Her mother's father, William Forbes, was a composer and a musician; when he died, he left a great deal of music and many valuable instruments. His musical compositions – of which a number survive – made use of Scottish folk melodies and songs, setting them in baroque forms, such as the sonata or concerto, but retaining their Scottish titles. Neither Anna Gordon's mother Lilias nor her aunt Anne who learned some of their ballads as girls ever referred to their father or their English mother as the source of their ballads – but they did mention a maidservant. Nonetheless, it was obviously a musical household, and one that valued Scottish song. Yet Forbes's personal story itself is subject for a ballad. As the story was told by Anna Gordon's niece, William Forbes

> possessed a handsome estate, and married, very early in life, a lady remarkable for her beauty. He became giddy and extravagant, neglected his affairs; and his

wife, finding she could not reclaim him, separated from him, after which they did not see each other for 20 years. They then accidentally met at the house of a mutual friend. He did not recognize his wife, but was charmed with her beauty, and after she had left her friend's house Mr. Forbes spoke in raptures of her and lamented his hard fate that he was not at liberty to offer himself. The lady of the house smiling, asked him if he had no recollection of seeing that lady before. He replied 'None.' She then informed him that lady was his *wedded wife*. He then implored her to bring about a reconciliation and she promised to do her best, on condition he could convince her he was a changed man. After the preliminaries were settled they were reunited, and [Lilias Forbes], the first wife of Professor Thomas Gordon, was born after their second union. Their eldest daughter was married to Professor Thomas Gordon's older brother ... there [were] twenty-five years between the two sisters.[24]

That Anna Gordon's grandfather did not recognize his own wife and that her own mother was the child of their reconciliation is the stuff of ballads. No wonder, as the literary biographer Robert Anderson remarked to Thomas Percy, Anna Gordon was "fond of ballad poetry, writes verses, and reads everything in the marvelous way."[25] Her everyday world was suffused with romantic adventures. Even in her own generation, love played dramatic tricks in her family. Her older sister Elizabeth met the man she married, John Scott, an American, when he fled to Aberdeen to avoid the consequences of a duel in his native Virginia. He had "called out" a Mr. Baylis, whose "scurrilous" insults of himself and his father were insupportable. But then on the field of battle, Baylis picked a second fight with Scott's brother-in-law Bullitt, who had come along to try to prevent bloodshed. Baylis and Bullitt exchanged pistol fire, and Baylis fell. Bullitt was tried and acquitted, but Scott was forced to leave the country both because he provoked the duel in the first place and because he was then pursued by Baylis's friends for revenge. He and his younger brother Gustavus left Virginia and came to Aberdeen, where they entered King's College to finish their education. There John Scott met and secretly married Elizabeth Gordon, Anna Gordon's older sister, without her father's knowledge, although Thomas Gordon soon forgave the impetuous couple. Whether or not Anna Gordon was in on the secret of her sister's clandestine marriage to John Scott, she must have known the story of the misfiring duel told by this handsome stranger from Virginia. Reality blended into romance in her family, blurring the line between real life and fiction. Ordinary people did extraordinary things. The dramatic events of ballads were like the things that happened in everyday life; it was all on one continuum.

Anna Gordon – Mrs. Brown – was a significant link in the chain of oral transmission of a valuable repertoire of Scottish ballads. She retained them in her memory, having learned them as a child; she did not compose them or even consciously alter them. Scholars and antiquarians who remarked on their quantity – more than three dozen – and excellence understood just how rare and precious this hoard of ancient ballad poetry was. They wondered at her remembering so many complete ballads and even intimated that but for her sterling reputation, they would have suspected her of adding verses or improving the ones she knew. She was a rare source: an educated woman with a developed sense of poetry and a taste for this genre. Her family was musical and, on her mother's side, held a particular interest in Scottish tunes. Her female relatives shared her interest in ballads. Her own talents and her social context together encouraged her enthusiasm for ballad lore.

However, Anna Brown may indeed have written one song text, and it would be a mistake to omit this composition from an assessment of her contribution to the history of Scottish ballads. A set of words to "**Auld Lang Syne**" was found in a large folio album of literary extracts belonging to Mrs. Turner of Turnerhall, Aberdeenshire, circa 1796 that may well have been written by Anna Brown.[26] Moreover, there were precedents for writing new verses to this old song, which appears both in James Watson's *Choice Collection of Comic and Serious Scots Poems* (1711) and in Allan Ramsay's *Poems* (1721) long before Burns's example in the *Scots Musical Museum* (Vol. V, 1796). Anna Brown must have written these verses when her husband was minister at Falkland, sometime between 1789 and 1802; indeed, she may well have seen Burns's verses in the *Scots Musical Museum*, published that same year, and been inspired to write a woman's riposte to his classic depiction of lifelong male comradeship. His version is a celebration of male friendship, with a few details of shared boyhood pleasures, and hers is a celebration of female friendship.

Auld Lang Syne

I
Should auld acquaintance be forgot,
Or friendship ere grow cauld?
Should we not tighter draw the knot;
Aye, as we're growing auld?
How comes it then, my worthy friend,
Wha used to be sae kin'
We dinna for each other speer [ask],
As we did lang syne?

II
Tho' many a day be past and gane
Sin we did ither see;
Yet gin the heart be still the same,
It matters not a flee.
Gin ye hae not forgot the art
To sound your harp divine,
Ye'll find still I can bear my part
And sing as lang syne.

III
I think upon the mony days
When I, in youthfu' pride,
Wi' you aft rambled o'er the braes
On bonny Bogie side.
The birdies frae the Arn tree,
Wha mixt their notes wi' mine,
Were not mair blyth, nor fu' o' glee
Than we were lang syne.

IV
I think upo' the bonny springs [tunes],
Ye used to me to play;
And how we used to dance and sing,
The live-lang summer day.
Nae fairies on the haunted green,
Where moonbeams twinkling shine
Mair blythly frisked around their Queen
Than we did lang syne.

V
What tho' I be some aulder grown,
And ablins [perhaps] not so gay;
What tho' my locks o' hazel brown
Be now well mixed wi' grey;
I'm sure my heart's nae caulder grown,
But as my years decline,
Still friendship's flame mair kindly glows
Than it did lang syne.

VI
Tho' ye live on the banks of Don,
And I besouth the Tay,
Well might ye ride to Falklan's Town
Some bonny simmer's day.

> And in that place where Scotland's Kings
> Aft birl'd baith Beer and Wine,
> Let's meet, an' laugh, an'dance, an' sing,
> And crack [gossip, chat] of lang syne.

These verses demonstrate Anna Gordon's abiding sense of her own identity as a singer. She remembers how both she and Mrs. Turner sang out loud as they walked along the banks of the river, their voices mixing with birdsong of summer. And now she is encouraging her old friend to visit her in Falkland Palace where she now resides so that they can renew the pleasures of their early friendship, laughing and singing as they did lang syne. Old friends mean even more now than they did then, she writes, the "flame mair kindly glows." But now as then, the expression of that friendship, and the pleasure of each other's company, lies in being able to make music together.

Anna Gordon could have written her poem in any stanza form, using any rhythm and rhyme scheme; no one commissioned it – it was an occasional poem intended only for her friend's eyes, yet the verses display an accomplished command of idiom and a nimble sense of the interplay of words and melody. Her choice to convey her sentiments in the form of a song – to use a traditional Scottish song as the armature to build on – is telling. She obviously felt comfortable working in that medium, her musical "mother tongue." Moreover, her reference to Scotland's kings drinking beer and wine is both literal and also a ballad reference, for the famous "Sir Patrick Spence" begins with the king drinking wine. She writes in educated Scots rather than English, with a sprinkling of Scots words in their northeast forms. The diction is simple but cultivated, not colloquial but dignified, with elevated touches as in the ballad. She has also coined an interesting neologism – "brisked" – demonstrating both a literary sensibility and a willingness to invent rather than simply to repeat formulas.

Thus, in her choice of a song form, her ballad allusion, and her representation of her friendship as an essentially musical connection, Anna Gordon Brown reveals her preoccupation with songs and ballads in this, the only poem of hers that we have. It is a fitting memento for the woman who remembered and thus preserved for posterity three dozen of the finest old Scottish ballads. Her literary legacy for the Anglophone world has proved an enduring gift to those who love the stories and songs that people have managed to save.

NOTES

1. Francis J. Child, "Ballad Books," *The Nation*, September 3, 1868, p. 193.
2. "Old Ballads. Prof. Child's Appeal," *Notes and Queries*, Series 4, Vol. 11 (January 4, 1873), p. 12.

3. Letter 24, Thursday–Saturday, June 2–4, 1653. *The Letters of Dorothy Osborne to William Temple*, ed. G. C. Moore Smith (Oxford: Clarendon Press, 1947), pp. 51–52.
4. January 2, 1666.
5. Roger Fiske, *Scotland in Music A European Enthusiasm* (Cambridge University Press, 1983) documents the craze for Scottish songs in eighteenth-century Europe.
6. Reprinted in the Appendix of Natascha Wurzbach, *The Rise of the English Street Ballad, 1550–1650* (Cambridge University Press, 1981), pp. 283–84.
7. Willa Muir, *Living With Ballads* (Oxford University Press, 1965), p. 196.
8. *The Anecdotes and Egotisms of Henry Mackenzie 1745–1831*, ed. H. W. Thompson (Oxford and London: Oxford University Press and Humphrey Milford, 1927), p. 79.
9. From NLS MS 16668 f. 123, as quoted in Katharine Glover, *Elite Women and Polite Society in Eighteenth-Century Scotland* (Woodbridge, Suffolk: The Boydell Press, 2011), p. 82.
10. Published as an Appendix to Hugo Arnot's *The History of Edinburgh* (Edinburgh: W. Creech, 1779), pp. 624–42.
11. National Library of Scotland (NLS), Acc. 3640. Letter dated January 19, 1793.
12. John B. Nichols, *Illustrations of the Literary History of the Eighteenth Century consisting of authentic memoirs and original letters of eminent persons*, 8 Vols. (London: Nichols, Son and Bentley, 1817–1858), Vol. 7 (1848), p. 178. Letter from Anna Brown to Alexander Fraser-Tytler, April 21, 1800.
13. Letter from Thomas Gordon to Alexander Fraser-Tytler, January 19, 1793. NLS Acc 3639 and also William Tytler Brown manuscript Harvard University.
14. *The Correspondence of Thomas Percy & Robert Anderson*, ed. W. E. K. Anderson, Vol. 9 of *The Percy Letters*, gen. ed. Cleanth Brooks and Alexander F. Falconer (New Haven and London: Yale University Press, 1988), p. 43.
15. Francis J. Child, Advertisement prefacing Vol. I of *The English and Scottish Popular Ballads*, 10 vols. (Boston: Houghton, Mifflin, 1882–1898).
16. NLS Acc. 3639 ff. 278. Letter dated December 23, 1800.
17. *The Ballad Repertoire of Anna Gordon, Mrs. Brown of Falkland*, ed. Sigrid Rieuwerts, Scottish Text Society Fifth series, No. 8 (Woodbridge, Suffolk: The Boydell Press, 2011), p. 50. According to Sigrid Rieuwerts, these five ballads can be identified as Child #203, "The Baron of Brackley"; Child #239, "Lord Saltoun and Auchanachie"; Child #209, "Geordie"; Child #235, "The Earl of Aboyne"; and Child #234, "Charlie MacPherson" (*Ballad Repertoire*, p. 51)
18. Child #203.
19. Edinburgh University Library MS Laing III 473. Letter dated Falkland, June 18, 1801.
20. Rev. Horace E. Hayden, *Virginia Genealogies A Genealogy of the Glassell Family of Scotland and Virginia, also the families of Ball, Brown, Bryan, Conway, etc.* (Baltimore: Genealogical Publishing Company, 1966), p. 588.
21. John Spottiswood, *The History of the Church and State of Scotland* (London: R. Royston, 1655).
22. Aberdeen University Library, MS 988, (7) Sir Adam Gordon, Spaulding 104.
23. Hayden, *Virginia Genealogies*, p. 615.

24. Hayden, *Virginia Genealogies*, p. 616.
25. Anderson, *Correspondence of Thomas Percy and Robert Anderson*, p. 43.
26. The information about these verses, and the conjecture that Anna Gordon Brown wrote them, appeared in the *Aberdeen Journal* on July 16, 1921 in an article titled "Auld Lang Syne: The Authorship of the Old Aberdeenshire Version," signed by "W," who was most probably the scholar William Walker.

14

MARY WATERS

Periodical writing

In eighteenth-century Britain, literary culture became professionalized and literacy spread to a mass reading audience partly through the development of periodicals. This new genre appeared in the last decade of the seventeenth century, when legal restrictions on publication began to relax. In particular, the 1695 lapse of the Licensing Act ended prepublication censorship and relaxed limitations on the number of printers. These numbers then expanded rapidly, competition became more vigorous, and the political contentiousness of the early eighteenth century found a venue for expression in periodicals. As literacy spread, especially among women and those with limited financial means, periodicals brought affordable reading matter to many whose income placed books out of reach. Women were not just consumers of this new expansion in print culture, but producers as well, with their cultural influence growing in consequence. As Paula McDowell affirms, "Women at all levels of the press helped to shape literary tastes, cultural habits, structures of feeling, and public opinion."[1] McDowell refers to the broad range of participatory avenues that Grub Street afforded women, but limiting the view to periodicals does not alter the truth of her observation. As periodicals developed over the eighteenth century, those by and for women made political and public concerns accessible to a non-elite audience. They offered readers education, entertainment, and a sense of community. They provided a venue for testing one's literary gifts. They contributed to the development of literary commentary pitched to nonspecialist readers. And as the century progressed, periodicals allowed women access to the professionalism of print culture, eventually affording sustained career opportunities that supported increasing numbers of professional woman writers.

Periodicals by and for women originated from general interest predecessors, especially John Dunton's *Athenian Mercury* (1691–97). Conducted by the members of a largely fictional "Athenian Society," the *Athenian Mercury* included letters from correspondents, most of whom were probably fictional as well. The appearance of reader participation was more important than whether real readers actually wrote in. After Dunton's model, correspondence became a usual feature in early periodicals. In the case of the *Athenian Mercury*, these letters soon included inquiries purportedly from women readers on topics such as conduct, love, sex, and marriage, at times treated informatively and explicitly enough to constitute sex education. The feature drew enough interest to prompt a monthly issue devoted to women's concerns, followed in February 1693 with the launch of the *Ladies' Mercury*, the first periodical addressed to women. Although it lasted only four weeks, the *Ladies' Mercury* demonstrated that women, especially the non-elite women of the *Athenian Mercury*'s original audience, might constitute a readership with definable, characteristic concerns. As with the *Athenian Mercury*, the *Ladies' Mercury* included correspondence, much of it probably authored by Dunton and his male associates, but Dunton claimed a number of female associates as well. Among these were Mary Astell (1666–1731), who soon after attained celebrity with her feminist tract *A Serious Proposal to the Ladies* (1694) and bookseller Abigail Baldwin (1658–1713), who later published the *Female Tatler* (1709–10).

Although a pioneer in recognizing the appeal of periodical features by and for women, Dunton was soon followed by other publishers as "ladies" periodicals began to spring up. Some of these new publications, such as *Records of Love, or Weekly Amusements for the Fair Sex* (1710), which specialized in sentimental poetry and fiction, upheld a narrowly traditional view of feminine style and subject matter. Indeed, Kathryn Shevelow delineates a world where periodicals' editorial policies and representational practices "served as an emerging ideology" that progressively enclosed women in the home and coerced them toward a femininity that was apolitical, non-scholarly, and moral, with interests bounded by topics such as "love, marriage, women's education, and conduct."[2] While some new publications fit this outline, others offer women a surprising assortment of topics and features.

Although the subtitle of the *Ladies' Diary: or, Woman's Almanack* (1704–1841), a long-running annual, declared its purpose as "the Use and Diversion of the Fair Sex," along with the dates, chronologies, and medicinal advice more usual in an almanac, its diverting features set light fare such as stories and riddles alongside complex mathematical puzzles and discussions on scientific and natural history topics. Whether a general interest publication with features addressed to women, an enterprise authored or edited by an actual woman or a fictitious female persona, a periodical claiming to be designed for women, or some combination of the three, diverse subject matter and the frequent incorporation of masculine voices lead Iona Italia to observe,

> [I]t is almost impossible to identify a separate tradition of periodical writing by or for women. While the titles of many papers – *Ladies' magazines, museums, companions* and others – suggest that they were aimed at a female readership, there is evidence to suggest that male readers constituted a sizable proportion of the audience of these periodicals.[3]

Dunton's model of spinning off a women's publication from an established general interest one was not soon repeated. Instead, whether ostensibly or actually conducted by women or simply directed toward a female audience, for the next several decades most women's periodicals followed the successful essay periodical format of Richard Steele and Joseph Addison's *Tatler* (1709–11) and its successor, Addison's *Spectator* (1711–15). The *Tatler* and the *Spectator* brought new topics, including public affairs and literary commentary, to a diverse audience that explicitly included women.

In the *Tatler*, Richard Steele gave Dunton's practice of incorporating fictional correspondence a new twist by fabricating the fully elaborated personae, "Isaac Bickerstaff, Esquire" and Bickerstaff's staff of reporters. Under this imaginary editor and his staff, the *Tatler* reported news and gossip from the London coffeehouses while commenting on social foibles from a middle-class perspective. Coffeehouse reporting by nature assumed male journalists, and the *Tatler* could be harsh toward women, but Steele nevertheless occasionally added a female perspective in the fictional persona of "Jenny Distaff," the half-sister of Isaac Bickerstaff. Although the artifact of a male writer, Jenny Distaff advances the ploy of female correspondents pioneered by Dunton an additional step by presenting entire *Tatler* issues as the product of a feminine voice. While some of her concerns fall within the purview of conventional femininity, this persona delves into her half-brother's mail to present a feminine perspective on surprising content such as news of foreign and military affairs.

Before its first year was out, the *Tatler* had spawned several imitators indicating their connection to Steele's paper through their titles, the editorial personae, or in some cases both. Some presented themselves as female alternatives to the paper that inspired them. *The Whisperer* (1709), for example, a witty thrice weekly, was launched as the mouthpiece of Mrs. Jenny Distaff, now a stoutly independent persona who claimed to have set up on her own after refusing to marry the man her half-brother selected. Like the *Tatler*, *The Whisperer* reported news and gossip from a corrective perspective, but just as its title and editorial persona promise a more feminine voice, in this case the paper's scuttlebutt came from household domestics and the social circles associated with women. The author of *The Whisperer* is unknown, and Steele himself cannot be ruled out. Steele certainly used female as well as male editorial personae and directed periodicals to women. Besides his masculine-leaning sequels to the *Tatler* such as the *Guardian* (1713) and the *Englishman* (1713–14), he used male editorial personae to direct the *Lover* by Marmaduke Myrtle, Gen. (1714), *Town Talk, in a Letter to a Lady in the Country* (1715–16), and *Chit-Chat, in a Letter to a Lady in the Country* by Humphrey Phylroye (1716) to a female readership, and in 1719 he produced the *Spinster* under the pseudonym Rachel Woolpack. But whether *The Whisperer*'s author was male or female in actuality, all these *Tatler* sequels demonstrate a continued sense that women could constitute a significant audience interested in concerns other than those traditionally defined as feminine, and that interest in traditionally feminine concerns, including when discussed from the perspective of a female voice, could attract readership from among men as well as women. In the next few decades, publications appeared that brought feminine voices to bear on the most public and controversial topics.

Among the *Tatler*'s imitators, the *Female Tatler*, a thrice weekly, extended the *Tatler*'s milder social corrective and gossip model into a scandal report and political diatribe under the pseudonym "Mrs Crackenthorpe, a Lady that knows Everything." It appeared in two rival versions, the first beginning on July 8, 1709, printed by B[enjamin] Bragge. Five weeks later, this paper was moved to printer Abigail Baldwin but, as Fidelis Morgan observes, Bragge "had obviously enjoyed success with the paper for, despite the loss of his authoress, he continued to print a spurious paper, still ostensibly by 'Mrs Crackenthorpe' but infinitely inferior in style and content."[4] Several people, male and female, have been suggested as the *Female Tatler*'s author, with attorney and playwright Thomas Baker as the most likely candidate and playwright, novelist, and Tory political satirist Delarivier Manley (c. 1670–1724) as another possibility.[5] Whether or not behind the *Female Tatler*, Manley reappeared as a periodical editor in 1711 when she succeeded Jonathan Swift at the virulently Tory *Examiner*, remaining in that position from mid-June through the end of July. Meanwhile, whether the author behind Mrs. Crackenthorpe was male or female, the femininity of the editorial persona was important to the paper's claims for authenticity. Each *Female Tatler* denounced the other as the spurious product of a male author. Either way, the tirades of Mrs. Crackenthorpe demonstrate that a feminine perspective on political and other public issues might be distinctive yet neither reserved nor conciliatory.

Fictional personae remained the most common means of presenting an ostensibly female perspective through the end of the century, but Elizabeth Powell is one woman who made provocative forays into the public sphere under her own name. Powell headed her family publishing business after her Jacobite husband fled prosecution for treasonous publications and then died while in hiding. In his absence, Elizabeth Powell founded several anti-government papers. She was imprisoned briefly after publishing the first and only issue of an intended weekly, the *Orphan*. Following her release, she founded the *Charitable Mercury* and *Female Intelligence*, a weekly launched in 1716 that featured a diatribe against the hardships she suffered as an opponent of established interests. Arrested a second time, she allowed this paper to lapse as well. One might think two arrests would make her more reticent, but in 1718 she founded the *Orphan Reviv'd; or, Powell's Weekly Journal*, another anti-government paper, which she conducted sometimes from hiding and even briefly from prison until April 1720. Powell's first two papers had provoked her arrest for their subversive content; conversely, she used the *Orphan Reviv'd* as a venue to build sympathy for her case after her arrest for printing the seditious pamphlet *Vox Populi, Vox Dei*.[6] Although family political opinions were strong enough for both Elizabeth and her husband to risk arrest or worse, publishing was as much a professional enterprise as a venue for expression. It provided the family livelihood, so much so that another newspaper attributed Elizabeth Powell's early release after her first arrest to "Commiseration to the extream Poverty of her and her numerous Family."[7]

In assessing women's political journalism, Alison Adburgham notes that periodicals could provide access to the public sphere for aristocratic women whose concern for politics arose from their social connections with statesmen and foreign dignitaries. But Elizabeth Powell and Delarivier Manley exemplify cases whereby non-elite women professionals in the literary and publishing trades might include confrontational periodicals as part of their literary production. Lady Mary Wortley Montagu (1689–1762) better fits Adburgham's profile, for her political journalism had no connection to a professional literary career. Montagu's first known publication was her sole contribution to Addison's *Spectator*, an unsolicited letter in the guise of Mrs. President of a club of widows.[8] The essay shows the feminist bent that was later to inform her assessments of political affairs in her shortlived weekly the *Nonsense of Common-Sense* (1737–38). That paper's principles were Whig, generally but not invariably pro-government and supportive of Prime Minster Robert Walpole. Montagu conducted it in direct reply to *Common Sense*, a successful opposition paper. In contrast to the vituperative gossiping of the *Female Tatler*'s Tory Mrs. Crackenthorpe, Montagu implicitly addresses women in the voice of a male persona who eschewed "lewdness and obscenity, gossip and personal defamation."[9] Montagu claimed indifference toward professionalism, disavowing interest in monetary rewards both to her printer, who was concerned about receipts, and to family members, who were concerned that professional writing would compromise her social standing. Instead, she claimed corrective morality and public support of Walpole as her main concerns.

As these examples show, both real women and fictitious feminine personae might speak on public concerns, sometimes in unreservedly provocative ways. By mid-century, three intertwining trends become evident. For one, periodicals by and for women routinely combine traditionally feminine topics such as conduct and domestic advice and light literature with interest in public issues, including government and foreign affairs, often presented from a female perspective or framed in ways that show how public issues bear on women's concerns. At the same time, commentary on literature and the arts takes on increasing importance. And finally, as British literary culture shifted toward professionalism, periodicals offered some women access to that trend. James Basker points out that in generating a vast amount of literary employment, periodicals "contributed as much as any other single cause to the rapid transition from patronage to professional writing."[10] Lady Montagu's example notwithstanding, women's professional involvement in publishing and literary culture often included operating or contributing to periodicals.

One of the most industrious women writers in the eighteenth century was also one of its most inexhaustible producers of periodicals. An actress, playwright, poet, conduct book author, journalist, translator, even at times a publisher, as well as a prolific novelist, Eliza Haywood (1693?–1756) was one of the most professional literary women of her day. Her fame rests most heavily on her many novels, but one of her periodicals, the *Female Spectator*, a monthly running from April 1744 to May 1746, holds the station of first periodical written exclusively by and for women. The *Female Spectator* had several predecessors, including not only Joseph Addison's *Spectator*, from which it takes both name and format, but Haywood's own earlier periodicals as well. In the *Tea Table*, a semi-weekly running from February to June 1724, Haywood inaugurated the conversations between several personae that marked most of her subsequent journalism, reporting the discussions of a fictional gathering of women who canvassed topics that included literature and public events. Soon after, Haywood's *Parrot* (1728), a short-lived, weekly, reform-minded meditation on social vices, featured the editorial persona of Mrs. Penelope Prattle. But as with Addison's original, none of Haywood's earlier offerings especially addressed a female audience.

The *Female Spectator*, on the other hand, presented itself as conducted by a club of four women, the Female Spectator herself and three others: Mira, Euphrosine, and the Widow of Quality. In fact, as had been the case for many periodical editors as far back as John Dunton, Haywood probably authored the entire content of most issues even after the paper launched a section supposedly transmitting reader correspondence. Topics such as sexual morality and the temptations of fashionable life were illustrated with ostensibly factual anecdotes, and the central Female Spectator persona is presented as one who, having strayed at times from the path of ideal virtue, can speak to questions of female morality because of her experience. In the cross-play of multiple contributing personae, however, Haywood dramatizes contending viewpoints and, as Kathryn Shevelow argues, she "illustrates the fallibility of a single moral authority" and "offers an illustration of the subjectivity of moral pronouncement."[11] Meanwhile, like several of its predecessors, the *Female Spectator* demonstrates the range of topics deemed to interest women. Along with moral and social questions, the essays incorporate literary and drama criticism, travel narrative, and commentary on history, public affairs, and even philosophical and scientific topics. The *Female Spectator* was so successful that Haywood continued it much longer than she originally intended, and a reprint collection went through more than half a dozen editions in the next few decades.

Soon after its end, Haywood followed the *Female Spectator* with a new version of the *Parrot* (1746), a weekly that ran for nine weeks. As Catherine Ingrassia has noted, Haywood's prior periodicals had addressed political issues on some level but, published in the immediate aftermath of the Jacobite Rebellion with its subtitle promising "a Compendium of the Times," this new version of the *Parrot* "addressed the political and topical concerns of a post-rebellion audience and depended on the political context for interest and marketability."[12] Haywood was still conducting a periodical shortly before the end of her life, the biweekly *Young Lady* (1756), featuring Euphrosine, the youngest of her personae in the *Female Spectator*. While emphasizing questions of courtship and social conduct, a later number containing an essay that contrasts satire with *ad hominem* literary criticism may signal an intention of incorporating more arts commentary.[13] Haywood's was a long and productive literary career, and having once experimented with conducting a periodical, she not only returned to the form with regularity but advanced it significantly over more than three decades.

The *Female Spectator* had several successors by other women writers, one of which was Frances Brooke's *The Old Maid, by Mary Singleton, Spinster* (1755–56). Brooke (1724–89) is best known as a novelist, but her periodical, with its dramatization of a witty central voice and interactions between that voice, secondary characters, and correspondents male and female, fictional or real, helped her hone her craft for her drama and fiction. Brooke took Samuel Johnson's *Rambler* as her most direct model, but she followed

Haywood in featuring literary and theatrical criticism and commentary on public affairs interwoven with conduct advice and censure of folly. She offers a tongue-in-cheek nod to views that publishing might be improper for women in Mary Singleton's claim that "an Englishwoman has a natural right to expose herself as much as she pleases,"[14] but she upends gender stereotypes in a letter from a correspondent comparing a coffeehouse crowd gathering to criticize the paper to "witches round a conjuring cauldron, every one throwing in his invidious ingredient."[15] Brooke shows no reticence even when canvassing the political world of antiquity, weighing prior commentary on Shakespeare and classical texts or treating Milton in a context that explicitly recalls Addison's landmark *Spectator* essays. She reflects on literary professionalism in an essay on the neglect of the arts when she derides the "embroidered beau" who regards with disdain "*a fellow that writes for bread*," when, she says, "almost all mankind are pursuing the same end, though not all of them by means so laudable."[16] Meanwhile, by placing national prominence in the context of public fostering of the arts, this essay is one of several that links literary criticism to a concern for public affairs.

Charlotte Lennox's *The Lady's Museum* (1760–61) followed a similar vein with reader correspondence (real or not), poetry, narratives exposing folly, history, biography, natural history, geography, conduct and education advice, and literary commentary, all choreographed by a central persona, provocatively dubbed "The Trifler." Assisted for a time by playwright, novelist, and periodical essayist Hugh Kelly, Lennox (1730/31–1804) offered variety enough to prompt one correspondent to suspect "that you artfully mean to cajole your fair readers into sense and seriousness, and that you only bait your periodical labours with a Trifler merely to captivate our attention, while you mean nothing less than our acquaintance with all useful and polite literature."[17] A versatile literary professional like Brooke and Haywood, Lennox took the women's essay periodical format a step further when she serialized her novel *The History of Harriot and Sophia* (1760–61). Although this work met with a cool reception, Lennox capitalized on her prior literary fame in advertising her paper as "by the author of *The Female Quixote*." Lennox includes comments distancing herself from motives of financial gain, but in fact her personal circumstances, including repeated appeals to the Royal Literary Fund, suggest that she undertook most of her writing, including *The Lady's Museum*, with potential profit in sharp focus.

As these instances of periodicals operated by and for women suggest that subgenre was coming into its own, a separate trend emerged as well. Before the century's close, the essay periodical format gave way to the magazine, modeled on Edward Cave's long-running *Gentleman's Magazine*, founded in 1731. Among Cave's many imitators were four *Lady's Magazines*. The first, the *Lady's Magazine, or Monthly Intelligencer*, was announced in 1733, but since no copies survive, Adburgham conjectures that it may have been prevented, perhaps by Cave himself. The second met with more success. A weekly running from October 1738 into 1739, it advertises its content in its full title, *The Lady's Magazine, or Compleat Library, containing a very curious collection of histories, travels novels, poems, songs, letters, &c.* Two decades after this magazine's demise, a fictitious female persona, "The Hon. Mrs Stanhope," graced the masthead of *The Lady's Magazine, or Polite Companion for the Fair Sex* (1759–63), edited from 1760 by Oliver Goldsmith. Finally, *The Lady's Magazine, or Entertaining Companion for the Fair Sex* (1770–1832), a popular monthly operated for many years by George Robinson, featured not only fashion, recipes, and household medicine but essays on history, geography, travel, science, and the theater as well as foreign and domestic news.

Variations on the title "Lady's Magazine" appeared during the intervening years. The *Ladies' Magazine, or the Universal Entertainer*, a fortnightly running from 1749 to 1753, featured an editorial persona named Jasper Goodwill of Oxford, Esq., who promised readers "Subjects in the Circle of Wit, Gallantry, Love, History, Trade, Science and News," and social commentary intended to amuse not only women but "young Masters" as well.[18] Its success, however, probably depended more on its serialized fiction and sensational accounts of notorious criminals. Another, *The Royal Female Magazine* (1760), was conducted by Charles Honeycombe, a pseudonym for the poet Robert Lloyd. Similarly, "Matilda Wentworth & others," ostensible editors of *The Court Miscellany, or Ladies' New Magazine* (1765–69), was a pseudonym for Hugh Kelly, the actual editor, who had earlier collaborated with Lennox. And in the *New Lady's Magazine, or Polite & Entertaining Companion for the Fair Sex* (1786–95), Rev. Charles Stanhope serialized epistolary novels and offered fancywork patterns, poetry, book reviews, travel narratives, and reports on domestic and foreign affairs.[19] Most of these productions show that "women's" magazines might reach out to male readers while aspiring to improve women's minds in a wide range of intellectual fields. Authored and/or edited by men, however, what they do not demonstrate is an expansion of professional literary opportunities for women. While a few women managed to leverage remuneration for the stories, poems, essays, translations, and other work they provided to these publications, as Adburgham observes, "women's magazines contrived to get most of their contributions for nothing." [20] As the example of Montagu's *Spectator* paper shows, women contributed creative work such as poetry, stories, and entertaining essays to periodicals almost from the first, but often in the form of unsolicited and unremunerated correspondence.

Nevertheless, women writers were not excluded from the trend toward professionalization in Britain at the end of the eighteenth century. The establishment in 1790 of the Royal Literary Fund, from which Lennox hoped to benefit, is one marker of increasing professionalization in literary work. A second, earlier marker is the inauguration of critical reviews. By making affordable reading matter available to a broad audience that included large numbers of women, periodicals did much to extend literacy and create demand not only for literature, but for guidance on what and how to read. While women comprised a considerable part of this new audience for criticism, many of the educated elite believed that women lacked the analytical abilities needed to produce it. Others, however, believed that women's innate sensibility conferred a natural taste that afforded them a special capacity for literary commentary. The mid-century essay periodicals operated by women included commentary on literature, a practice that followed the masculine models set by Addison and Johnson. Meanwhile, general interest periodicals, including giants such as the *Gentleman's Magazine*, incorporated ever more frequent literary commentary by women. But with the advent of the literary review, a new benchmark arrived. As literary culture evolved from reliance on patronage to professionalism, one way women took part in this trend was through authoring literary criticism, including for literary reviews.

The first periodical devoted exclusively to literary criticism, the *Monthly Review*, was founded in 1749 by bookseller Ralph Griffiths, who published and edited it for half a century before passing it on to his son during the early nineteenth century. Griffiths's wife Isabella, a better business manager than her husband, seems to have had a hand in the *Monthly Review*'s operations nearly from the first. Moreover, skepticism from competing editors and critics did not restrain her from contributing critical articles to this giant in the history of British periodicals, and she collaborated on many others, with the consent of the article's main author or otherwise. The tradition of anonymity can make reviewer identification difficult. Editors and proprietors often believed that anonymity facilitated objectivity. Reviewer embarrassment over writing for money sometimes played a part as well. In the case of women reviewers, anonymity might shield both reviewer and proprietor from imputations that the publication was compromised because it employed women. The *Critical Review*'s numerous swipes at Isabella Griffiths's work at the *Monthly Review* show how the question of female competence offered a ready target. Accordingly, where reviewers were identified at all, it was usually by pseudonym or initials. The *Monthly Review* conformed publicly to the practice of anonymous reviewing, and even private records fail to identify all article authorship. Nevertheless, Betty Rizzo attributes to Isabella Griffiths a series of reviews published between 1757 and 1763 and signed "N."[21] With such a beginning, it should be no surprise that by the end of the century, the major review periodicals were providing some women with opportunities to exercise their critical and intellectual skills in a professional capacity.

The case of Elizabeth Moody (1737–1814) offers one example of how, by the later decades of the eighteenth century, contributing to a periodical could facilitate a woman's transition into professional and public literary culture. Born into a well-to-do suburban London family, Moody, née Elizabeth Greenly, made a name among the local literary luminaries by privately circulating her poetry. She enjoyed an unusually long career as a local celebrity and single woman of fashion until 1777, when at age forty she married the young Dissenting clergyman Christopher Lake Moody. An industrious literary professional, Reverend Moody was a prolific contributor to the *Monthly Review* and a shareholder in the *St. James's Chronicle*, a thrice-weekly newspaper launched in 1761 in which Ralph Griffiths was involved as well. Under the protection of this family connection, Elizabeth Moody soon began contributing poetry, reviews, and letters on literary and social subjects to the *St. James's Chronicle*, becoming one of the paper's marketable attractions under the pseudonym "The Muse of Surbiton." The couple probably assumed editing responsibilities as well, particularly for the paper's poetry section.[22] By 1789, Elizabeth's literary commentary had become professional reviewing for the nation's leading literary review when she joined her husband reviewing for the *Monthly Review*. Between the years 1789 and 1808, she authored some thirty reviews, mostly on novels or poetry; during a gap in her reviewing between 1791 and 1800, she published her only poetry volume, *Poetic Trifles* (1798). With facility in Italian acquired from her fashionable education, she particularly found a niche reviewing *belles lettres* publications in that language. Over the decades of her involvement with literary periodicals, she grew from a local amateur into a professional bringing distinctive skills to the literary marketplace.

At the time of her tenure at the *Monthly Review*, Elizabeth Moody was the only known regular woman contributor. But shortly after her contributions ceased, those of a far more famous woman writer, Anna Letitia Barbauld (1743–1825), began. In Barbauld's case, however, instead of periodical contributions leading to literary professionalism, the reverse seems to have been the case – it was probably Barbauld's standing as a literary figure, including her reputation as a professional literary critic, that led to her joining the *Monthly Review* staff. Barbauld, née Aikin, had established her reputation by publishing her volume *Poems* in 1773 and *Miscellaneous Pieces in Prose*, a collection of essays and short tales coauthored with her brother John Aikin and published the same year. Shortly after this debut, she married a Dissenting clergyman, and the couple opened a school for boys. Barbauld was well loved for the educational, children's, and devotional literature she produced over the next decade and a half, but by the mid-1790s, after turning out a series of political poems and pamphlets, she for the first time came before the public as a literary critic with a critical introduction to a 1794 edition of Mark Akenside's *The Pleasures of Imagination*. Over the next few years, Barbauld not only published several other major critical essays but also contributed reviews to the *Monthly Magazine*, the *Analytical Review*, the *Annual Review*, the *Athenæum*, the *Gentleman's Magazine*, and probably other periodicals as well. Finally, in 1809, Barbauld began authoring what eventually totaled several hundred short reviews for the *Monthly Review*. With her established reputation in a wide variety of literary forms including criticism, Barbauld was enlisted by what was still the most prestigious among eighteenth-century literary periodicals to assess publications from across the full spectrum of her expertise.

If reviewing emerged as the culmination of Barbauld's professional writing, Mary Wollstonecraft (1759–97) developed into a formidable literary professional in a relatively brief but memorable career that was set in motion in 1788 by her work at the *Analytic Review*, a monthly edited by London dissenting bookseller Joseph Johnson. Wollstonecraft scholars know well the story of her involvement with this radical-leaning publication. Arriving in London in 1787 after a series of unsuccessful forays into the world of traditionally feminine, semi-genteel occupations, Wollstonecraft brought her just-completed novel *Mary; A Fiction* (1788) to Johnson, who had recently published her conduct book, *Thoughts on the Education of Daughters* (1787). Johnson not only accepted the novel but assured Wollstonecraft that he could supply her plentifully with work, urging her to acquire skills such as facility with major continental languages to broaden her professional range.

Beginning as a translator and reader, Wollstonecraft soon took on the roles of reviewer and editorial assistant. She became one of Johnson's most important reviewers on topics ranging far wider than those traditionally thought to be the purview of women. By the end of her career, the *Analytical Review* had featured Wollstonecraft's articles on fiction, travel, sermons, poetry, drama, collections of letters, essays, educational materials, conduct literature, natural philosophy, social reform, biography, the performing arts, aesthetics, music history, and even boxing. Although most active between 1789 and her departure for Paris in 1792, Wollstonecraft resumed work for Johnson in 1796 after returning permanently to England. By the time of her death in 1797, her reviews numbered in the hundreds.

Her financial mainstay, the *Analytical Review* led Wollstonecraft into other areas of literary professionalism as well. Although she began as a conduct book author, over the next few years she not only expanded her range to include an original work of history, her own correspondence edited for public consumption, an unfinished but significant novel, and the abundance of literary reviews, but under Johnson's aegis she authored the political works for which she is best known, *A Vindication of the Rights of Men* (1790) and *A Vindication of the Rights of Woman* (1792). Through her reviews, Wollstonecraft developed intellectual credibility as well as the capacity to address a broad, often demanding audience.

As a staff writer for Johnson, Wollstonecraft recognized she had attained a level of literary professionalism new for women, one that made her "the first of a new genus."[23] What is more, in her position with Johnson she offered professional mentoring to another woman writer, Mary Hays (1759–1843). Besides contributing fiction, poetry, and essays on literary and philosophical topics to the *Universal Magazine* and the *Monthly Magazine*, Hays had published a pamphlet in defense of dissenter worship and reviewed literature for the *Critical Review*. Hays admired Wollstonecraft and solicited her interest with Johnson. Over the next few years, Wollstonecraft provided Hays with some canny publication advice as well as opportunities for literary work, including reviewing for the *Analytical Review*, and she offered Hays practical suggestions for improving her literary criticism. In her roles as staff writer, editorial assistant, and mentor, Wollstonecraft stands as an example of a new level of professionalism among literary women, the foundation of which was her work for a literary periodical.

As the eighteenth century drew to a close, women contributed to periodicals in increasing numbers. Not all desired to make these contributions part of a professional literary career. Poet Anna Seward (1742–1809), for example, contributed not only poetry but criticism to periodicals such as the *Gentleman's Magazine* and the *Critical Review*. Seward edited her own literary commentary for posterity, but in presenting it she clung to the gentility associated with amateurism.[24] Although Johnson solicited her help in founding the *Analytical Review*, she only sent her comments on his plan, declining the role of regular contributor. On the other hand, Clara Reeve (1729–1807), Seward's sparring partner for a series of critical debates in the *Gentleman's Magazine*, leverages her periodical contributions into a professional literary standing that becomes evident in her dealings with (or declining to deal with) the *Lady's Magazine*. As Jeanine Casler details, Reeve conducted ultimately unsuccessful but nevertheless highly professional negotiations for remuneration from the *Lady's Magazine*. And Mary Robinson (1756/58?–1800), whose professional life began with acting, supplemented her publication of numerous novels, political tracts, and volumes of poetry with prolific contributions to the *Evening Mail*, *Town and Country*, the *Whitehall Evening Post*, the *Monthly Magazine*, the *World*, the *Oracle*, the *Morning Post*, the *Gentleman's Magazine*, and other periodicals, becoming the editor of the *Morning Post* poetry section in December 1799. The careers of many other women writers show it to a varying degree, but overall the drift was toward increasing professionalism, with periodical work an important element in that trend.

Through the nineteenth century and beyond, periodicals supplied the backbone to the careers of many women writers, and ever more frequently editing and literary criticism were part of these careers. Harriet Martineau (1802–76), for example, began her career with literary criticism for periodicals, especially the *Monthly Repository*. Letitia Landon (1802–38) struggled through headaches brought on by overwork to author not only poetry but literary essays for the *Literary Gazette*, the *New Monthly Magazine*, and other periodicals, and she held editorial responsibilities at the *Literary Gazette* as well. Sydney Owenson (1783–1859) supplemented the income earned by her husband, himself a professional critic, with a variety of publications that included fiction and political essays as well as a substantial body of criticism authored for periodicals such as the *New Monthly Magazine* and the *Athenaeum*. The far less well-known Mary Margaret Busk's (1779–1863) voluminous commentary on French, Spanish, Portuguese, Italian, German, Scandinavian, and even Armenian literature was featured in *Blackwood's Edinburgh Magazine* and the *Foreign Quarterly Review*. As the century progressed, the careers of these and many other nineteenth-century women writers followed from the vital and diverse impact on the development of periodicals and professional literary culture of their eighteenth-century women forebears.

NOTES

1. Paula McDowell, "Women and the Business of Print," in *Women and Literature in Britain 1700–1800*, ed. Vivien Jones (Cambridge University Press, 2000), pp. 135–54, 135.
2. Kathryn Shevelow, *Women and Print Culture: The Construction of Femininity in the Early Periodical* (London and New York: Routledge, 1989), pp. 1, 36.
3. Iona Italia, *The Rise of Literary Journalism in the Eighteenth Century: Anxious Employment* (London and New York: Routledge, 2005), p. 4.

4. Fidelis Morgan, "Introduction" to *The Female Tatler*, ed. Fidelis Morgan (London: J. M. Dent; Rutland, VT: Charles E. Tuttle, 1992), p. vi.
5. Morgan summarizes some of the contemporary evidence for attributing authorship of the original *Female Tatler* to Delarivier Manley, but attribution remains a vexed question. Italia offers an updated and more detailed summary of evidence that incorporates discussions unavailable when Morgan published her essay. Present consensus favors crediting lawyer Thomas Baker (1656–1740) with the Mrs. Crackenthorpe papers of the legitimate (Bragge/Baldwin) *Female Tatler*, and Bernard Mandeville (1670–1733) with others, possibly including playwright Susanna Centlivre (1669?–1723), for those beginning November 1709, when "Mrs. Crackenthorpe" was retired and the paper had been handed over to "a society of ladies," who continued it with a softened tone through March 1710. Most recently, Rachel Carnell, *A Political Biography of Delarivier Manley* (London: Pickering and Chatto, 2008) finds evidence for Manley's authorship unconvincing and leans toward Baker.
6. McDowell, "Women and the Business of Print," p. 148.
7. *Weekly Journal*, March 31, 1716, quoted in McDowell, p. 147.
8. *Spectator* No. 573 (Wednesday, July 28, 1714).
9. Alison Adburgham, *Women in Print: Writing Women and Women's Magazines from the Restoration to the Accession of Victoria* (London: George Allen and Unwin Ltd., 1972), p. 86.
10. James Basker, "Criticism and the Rise of Periodical Literature," in *The Eighteenth Century*, Vol. 4 of *The Cambridge History of Literary Criticism*, ed. H. Barry Nisbet and Claude Rawson (Cambridge University Press, 1997), pp. 316–32, 325.
11. Shevelow, *Women and Print Culture*, p. 171.
12. Catherine Ingrassia, *Authorship, Commerce, and Gender in Early Eighteenth-Century England: A Culture of Paper Credit* (Cambridge University Press, 1998), p. 122.
13. *Young Lady*, VI (Tuesday, February 10, 1756).
14. *The Old Maid* no. 1 (Saturday, November 15, 1755).
15. *The Old Maid* no. 18 (Saturday, March 13, 1756).
16. *The Old Maid* no. 3 (Saturday, November 29, 1755).
17. Charlotte Lennox, *The Lady's Museum* No. IX in *The Lady's Museum, By the Author of The Female Quixote*, Vol. 2 (London: Printed for J. Newbery in St. Paul's Church-Yard, and J. Coote in Pater Noster Row, 1760–1761), p. 641.
18. *Ladies' Magazine, or the Universal Entertainer* (Saturday, November 18, 1749).
19. "Rev. Charles Stanhope" does not appear in the Church of England Clergy database theclergydatabase.org.uk or in the *DNB*.
20. Adburgham, *Women in Print*, p. 217.
21. Betty Rizzo, "Isabella Griffiths," *A Dictionary of British and American Women Writers, 1660–1800*, ed. Janet Todd (Totowa, NJ: Rowman and Allanheld, 1985), p. 143. Antonia Forster, however, departs from this opinion, suggesting that although Griffiths supported women writers, he said explicitly that his wife had not written a word in the journal. Antonia Forster, "Griffiths, Ralph (1720?–1803)," *Oxford Dictionary of National Biography* (Oxford University Press, 2004), www.oxforddnb.com.

22. Jan Wellington, "Elizabeth Moody," *Encyclopedia of British Women Writers*, rev. ed., ed. June Schlueter (New Brunswick, NJ: Rutgers University Press, 1999), pp. 461–62.
23. Mary Wollstonecraft to Everina Wollstonecraft, London, November 7 [1787], *Collected Letters of Mary Wollstonecraft*, ed. Ralph M. Wardle (Ithaca, NY: Cornell University Press, 1979), pp. 163–65.
24. Anna Seward, *Letters of Anna Seward 1784–1807*, 6 vols. (Edinburgh: A. Constable, 1811).

GUIDE TO FURTHER READING

This list represents a selection of secondary materials related to the scholarship of women's writing in England during the Restoration and eighteenth century. Titles are generally not duplicated among the lists although many pertain to multiple chapters; a title appears in connection with the genre or topic to which it is most relevant.

Introduction and general background

Ballaster, Ros, ed. *The History of British Women's Writing, 1690–1750*, Vol. 4. Basingstoke and New York: Palgrave, 2010.

Brown, Susan, Patricia Clements, and Isobel Grundy, ed. *Orlando: Women's Writing in the British Isles from the Beginnings to the Present.* Cambridge University Press Online, 2006; orlando.cambridge.org.

Ezell, Margaret J. M. *Social Authorship and the Advent of Print.* Baltimore and London: The Johns Hopkins University Press, 1999.

Writing Women's Literary History. Baltimore: The Johns Hopkins University Press, 1996.

Jones, Vivien, ed. *Women and Literature in Britain 1700–1800.* Cambridge University Press, 2000.

Labbe, Jacqueline, ed. *The History of British Women's Writing: 1750–1830*, Vol. 5. Basingstoke and New York: Palgrave, 2010.

McDowell, Paula. *The Women of Grub Street: Gender, Press, and Politics in the London Literary Marketplace 1678–1730.* Oxford: Clarendon Press, 1998.

Raven, James. *British Fiction, 1750–1770: A Chronological Checklist of Prose Fiction Printed in Britain and Ireland.* London and Toronto: Associated University Press, 1987.

The Business of Books: Booksellers and the English Book Trade 1450–1850. New Haven: Yale University Press, 2007.

Siskin, Clifford. *The Work of Writing: Literature and Social Change in Britain 1700–1830.* Baltimore and London: The Johns Hopkins University Press, 1998.

Stanton, Judith P. "Statistical Profile of Women Writing in English from 1660 to 1800." In *Eighteenth-Century Women and the Arts*. Ed. Frederick M. Keener and Susan E. Lorsch. New York: Greenwood Press, 1988: 247–54.
Staves, Susan. *A Literary History of Women's Writing in Britain, 1660–1789*. Cambridge University Press, 2006.
Todd, Janet M. *The Sign of Angelica: Women, Writing and Fiction, 1660–1800*. New York: Columbia University Press, 1989.
Turner, Cheryl. *Living by the Pen: Women Writers in the Eighteenth Century*. London: Routledge, 1992.
Watt, Ian. *The Rise of the Novel: Studies in Defoe, Richardson, and Fielding*. Berkeley and London: University of California Press, Chatto and Windus, 1957.

Women as readers and writers

Allan, David. *Commonplace Books and Reading in Georgian England*. Cambridge University Press, 2010.
  Making British Culture: English Readers and the Scottish Enlightenment, 1740–1830. New York: Routledge, 2008.
  A Nation of Readers: The Lending Library in Georgian England. London: British Library, 2008.
Colclough, Stephen. *Consuming Texts: Readers and Reading Communities, 1695–1870*. Basingstoke: Palgrave, 2007.
Darnton, Robert. "What Is the History of Books?" *Daedalus* 111.3 (1982): 65–83.
Fergus, Jan. *Provincial Readers in Eighteenth-Century England*. Oxford University Press, 2007.
Flint, Kate. *The Woman Reader, 1837–1914*. Oxford: Clarendon Press, 1993.
Glover, Katharine. *Elite Women and Polite Society in Eighteenth-Century Scotland*. Woodbridge, UK: The Boydell Press, 2011.
Kaufman, Paul. *Libraries and Their Users: Collected Papers in Library History*. London: Library Association, 1969.
Pearson, Jacqueline. *Women's Reading in Britain, 1750–1835: A Dangerous Recreation*. Cambridge University Press, 1999.
Raven, James, Helen Small, and Naomi Tadmor, ed. *The Practice and Representation of Reading in England*. Cambridge University Press, 1996.
St. Clair, William. *The Reading Nation in the Romantic Period*. Cambridge University Press, 2004.
Towsey, Mark. "'Observe her Heedfully': Elizabeth Rose on Women Writers." *Women's Writing* 18.1 (2011): 15–33.
  Reading the Scottish Enlightenment: Books and Their Readers in Provincial Scotland, 1750–1820. Leiden: Brill, 2010.
Vickery, Amanda. *The Gentleman's Daughter: Women's Lives in Georgian England*. New Haven: Yale University Press, 1998.
Whyman, Susan E. *The Pen and the People: English Letter Writers, 1660–1800*. Oxford University Press, 2009.

The professional female writer

Batchelor, Jennie. *Women's Work: Labour, Gender, Authorship, 1750–1830.* Manchester University Press, 2010.
Carlile, Susan, ed. *Masters of the Marketplace: British Women Novelists of the 1750s.* Bethlehem, PA: Lehigh University Press, 2001.
Griffin, Dustin. *Literary Patronage in England, 1650–1800.* Cambridge University Press, 1996.
Hammond, Brean S. *Professional Imaginative Writing in England, 1670–1740: 'Hackney for Bread.'* Oxford: Clarendon Press, 1997.
King, Kathryn R., "Elizabeth Singer Rowe's Tactical Use of Print and Manuscript." In *Women's Writing and the Circulation of Ideas: Manuscript Publication in England, 1550–1800.* Ed. George L. Justice and Nathan Tinker. Cambridge University Press, 2002: 158–81.
A Political Biography of Eliza Haywood. London: Pickering and Chatto, 2012.
McCarthy William. *Anna Letitia Barbauld: Voice of Enlightenment.* Baltimore: The Johns Hopkins University Press, 2008.
Myers, Sylvia Harcstark. *The Bluestocking Circle: Women, Friendship, and the Life of the Mind in Eighteenth-Century England.* Oxford: Clarendon Press, 1990.
Rose, Mark. *Authors and Owners: The Invention of Copyright.* Cambridge, MA: Harvard University Press, 1993.
Schellenberg, Betty A. *The Professionalization of Women Writers in Eighteenth-Century Britain.* Cambridge University Press, 2005.
Schürer, Norbert, ed. *Charlotte Lennox: Correspondence and Miscellaneous Documents.* Lewisberg, PA: Bucknell University Press, 2012.
Spencer, Jane. *Aphra Behn's Afterlife.* Oxford University Press, 2001.
Todd, Janet. *The Secret Life of Aphra Behn.* New Brunswick, NJ: Rutgers University Press, 1996.
Woodmansee, Martha. *The Author, Art, and the Market: Rereading the History of Aesthetics.* New York: Columbia University Press, 1996.
Zionkowski, Linda. *Men's Work: Gender, Class, and the Professionalization of Poetry, 1660–1774.* New York: Palgrave, 2001.

Place and publication

Borsay, Peter. *The English Urban Renaissance: Culture and Society in the Provincial Town, 1660–1770.* Oxford University Press, 1989.
Charnell-White, Catherine, ed. *Beirdd Ceridwen: Blodeugerdd Barddas o Ganu Menywod hyd tua 1800.* Llandybïe: Cyhoeddiadau Barddas, 2005.
Coolahan, Marie-Louise. *Women, Writing, and Language in Early Modern Ireland.* Oxford University Press, 2010.
Ellis, Joyce M. *The Georgian Town, 1680–1840.* Basingstoke and New York: Palgrave, 2001.
Ezell, Margaret J. M. *The Patriarch's Wife: Literary Evidence and the History of the Family.* Chapel Hill: The University of North Carolina Press, 1987.
Gavin, Michael. "Critics and Criticism in the Poetry of Anne Finch." *ELH* 78.3 (2011): 633–55.

Gifford, Douglas and Dorothy McMillan, ed. *A History of Scottish Women's Writing*. Edinburgh University Press, 1997.
Gray, Catherine. "Katherine Philips in Ireland." *English Literary Renaissance* 39.3 (2009): 557–85.
  Women Writers and Public Debate in Seventeenth-Century Britain. Basingstoke: Palgrave Macmillan, 2007.
Hackel, Heidi Brayman and Catherine E. Kelly, ed. *Reading Women: Literacy, Authorship, and Culture in the Atlantic World, 1500–1800*. Philadelphia: University of Pennsylvania Press, 2008.
Kerrigan, Catherine. *An Anthology of Scottish Women Poets*. Edinburgh University Press, 1991.
Lonsdale, Roger, ed. *Eighteenth-Century Women Poets: An Anthology*. Oxford University Press, 1989.
Overton, Bill. "The Poems of Jean Adam, 1704–65." *Women's Writing* 10.3 (2003): 425–51.
Prescott, Sarah. "The Cambrian Muse: Welsh Identity and Hanoverian Loyalty in the Poems of Jane Brereton (1685–1740)." *Eighteenth-Century Studies* 38.4 (2005): 587–603.
  Eighteenth-Century Writing from Wales: Bards and Britons. Cardiff: University of Wales Press, 2008.
  Women, Authorship, and Literary Culture, 1690–1740. Basingstoke and New York: Palgrave Macmillan, 2003.
Schneider, Gary M. *The Culture of Epistolarity: Vernacular Letters and Letter Writing in Early Modern England, 1500–1700*. Newark: University of Delaware Press, 2005.
Shuttleton, David. "Mary Chandler's *Description of Bath* (1733): The poetic topographies of an Augustan tradeswoman." *Women's Writing* 7.3 (2000): 447–67.
Sweet, Rosemary. *The Writing of Urban Histories in Eighteenth-Century England*. Oxford: Clarendon Press, 1997.

Women and popular culture

Asleson, Robyn, ed. *Notorious Muse: The Actress in British Art and Culture, 1776–1812*. New Haven: Yale University Press, 2003.
Backscheider, Paula. "The Paradigms of Popular Culture." In *The Eighteenth-Century Novel: Essays in Honor of John Richetti*. Vol. 6–7 (2009): 19–59.
Engel, Laura. *Fashioning Celebrity: Eighteenth-Century British Actresses and Strategies for Image Making*. Athens: Ohio State University Press, 2011.
Luckhurst, Mary and Jane Moody, ed. *Theatre and Celebrity in Britain, 1660–2000*. New York: Palgrave Macmillan, 2005.
Nussbaum, Felicity. *Rival Queens: Actresses, Performance, and the Eighteenth-Century British Theater*. Philadelphia: University of Pennsylvania Press, 2010.
Potter, Tiffany, ed. *Women, Popular Culture, and the Eighteenth Century*. University of Toronto Press, 2012.
Russell, Gillian. *Women, Sociability and Theatre in Georgian London*. Cambridge University Press, 2007.

Genre crossings

Anderson, Emily Hodgson. *Eighteenth-Century Authorship and the Play of Fiction: Novels and the Theatre, Haywood to Austen.* New York and London: Routledge, 2009.

Aravamudan, Srinvas. "In the Wake of the Novel: The Oriental Tale as National Allegory." *Novel* 33 (1999): 5–31.

Armstrong, Nancy. *Desire and Domestic Fiction: A Political History of the Novel.* Oxford University Press, 1987.

Bahktin, Mikhail M. "Epic and Novel." In *The Dialogic Imagination.* Ed. M. Holquist. Trans. Caryl Emerson and Michael Holquist. Austin: University of Texas Press, 1981.

Ballaster, Ros. "A Gender of Opposition: Eliza Haywood's Scandal Fiction." In *The Passionate Fictions of Eliza Haywood: Essays on Her Life and Work.* Ed. Kirsten T. Saxton and Rebecca P. Bocchicchio. Lexington: University Press of Kentucky, 2000: 143–67.

Batchelor, Jennie. "'[T]o strike a little out of a road already so much beaten': Gender, Genre, and the Mid-Century Novel." In *The History of British Women's Writing, 1750–1830.* Ed. Jacqueline M. Labbe. Houndsmills, Basingstoke, Hampshire: Palgrave Macmillan, 2010: 84–101.

Brant, Claire. "Varieties of Women's Writing." In *Women and Literature in Britain 1700–1800.* Ed. Vivien Jones. Cambridge University Press, 2000: 285–305.

Carlile, Susan. "*Henrietta* on Page and Stage." In *Masters of the Marketplace: British Women Novelists of the 1750s.* Ed. Susan Carlile. Bethlehem, PA: Lehigh University Press, 2011: 128–41.

Cohen, Roger. "Genre Theory, Literary History, and Historical Change." In *Theoretical Issues in Literary History.* Ed. David Perkins. Cambridge, MA, and London: Harvard University Press, 1991: 85–113.

Colie, Rosalie Littell. *The Resources of Kind: Genre-Theory in the Renaissance.* Berkeley: University of California Press, 1973.

Gardiner, Judith Kegan. "First English Novel: Aphra Behn's *Love Letters*, the Canon, and Women's Tastes." *Tulsa Studies in Women's Literature* 8 (1989): 201–22.

Greer, Germaine, ed. *Kissing the Rod: An Anthology of Seventeenth-Century Women's Verse.* New York: Farrar Straus Giroux, 1988.

Ingrassia, Catherine. "'The Stage Not Answering My Expectations': The Case of Eliza Haywood." In *Teaching British Women Playwrights of the Restoration and Eighteenth Century.* Ed. Bonnie Nelson and Catherine Burroughs. New York: Modern Language Association of America, 2010: 213–22.

King, Kathryn R. *Jane Barker, Exile: A Literary Career 1675–1725.* Oxford: Clarendon Press, 2000.

A Political Biography of Eliza Haywood. London: Pickering & Chatto, 2012.

Lacroix, Constance. "Wicked Traders, Deserving Peddlers, and Virtuous Smugglers: The Counter-Economy of Jane Barker's Jacobite Novel." *Eighteenth-Century Fiction* 23 (Winter 2010–11): 269–94.

Merritt, Juliette. *Beyond Spectacle: Eliza Haywood's Female Spectators.* University of Toronto Press, 2004.

Radway, Janice. *Reading the Romance: Women, Patriarchy, and Popular Literature.* 1984, rpt. Chapel Hill: University of North Carolina Press, 1991.

Schofield, Mary Anne and Cecilia Macheski, ed. *Curtain Calls: British and American Women and the Theater, 1660–1820*. Athens: Ohio University Press, 1991.

Spencer, Jane. *The Rise of the Woman Novelist: From Aphra Behn to Jane Austen*. Oxford: Basil Blackwell, 1986.

Starr, G. Gabrielle. *Lyric Generations: Poetry and the Novel in the Long Eighteenth Century*. Baltimore and London: The Johns Hopkins University Press, 2004.

Swenson, Rivka. "Representing Modernity in Jane Barker's Galesia Trilogy: Jacobite Allegory and the Patch-Work Aesthetic." *Studies in Eighteenth-Century Culture* 34 (2005): 55–80.

Zimbardo, Rose. "Aphra Behn: A Dramatist in Search of the Novel." In *Curtain Calls: British and American Women and the Theatre, 1660–1820*. Ed. Mary Anne Schofield and Cecilia Macheksi. Athens: Ohio University Press, 1991: 371–82.

Poetry

Armstrong, Isobel and Virginia Blain, ed. *Women's Poetry in the Enlightenment: The Making of a Canon, 1730–1820*. Basingstoke: Macmillan and New York: St. Martin's Press, 1999.

Backscheider, Paula R. *Eighteenth-Century Women Poets and Their Readers; Inventing Agency, Inventing Genre*. Baltimore: The John Hopkins University Press, 2005.

Backscheider, Paula R. and Ingrassia, Catherine E., ed. *British Women Poets of the Long Eighteenth Century: An Anthology*. Baltimore: The Johns Hopkins University Press, 2009.

Barash, Carol. *English Women's Poetry, 1649–1714: Politics, Community, and Linguistic Authority*. Oxford: Clarendon Press, 1986.

Ferguson, Moira. *Eighteenth-Century Women Poets: Nation, Class and Gender*. Albany: State University of New York Press, 1995.

Greene, Richard. *Mary Leapor: A Study in Eighteenth-Century Women's Poetry*. Oxford: Clarendon Press, 1993.

Grundy, Isobel. *Lady Mary Wortley Montagu: Comet of the Enlightenment*. Oxford University Press, 1996.

Hinnant, Charles H. *The Poetry of Anne Finch: An Essay in Interpretation*. Newark: University of Delaware Press, 1999.

Juhas, Kirsten. *"I'le to My Self, and to My Muse Be True": Strategies of Self-Authorization in Eighteenth-Century Women Poetry*. Frankfurt am Main and Oxford: Lang, 2008.

Kairoff, Claudia Thomas. *Anna Seward and the End of the Eighteenth Century*. Baltimore: The John Hopkins University Press, 2011.

"Eighteenth-Century Women Poets and Their Readers." In *The Cambridge Companion to Eighteenth-Century Poetry*. Ed. John Sitter. Cambridge University Press, 2001: 157–76.

Labbe, Jacqueline M., *Charlotte Smith: Romanticism, Poetry, and the Culture of Gender*. Manchester University Press and New York: Palgrave, 2003.

Landry, Donna. *The Muses of Resistance: Labouring-Class Women's Poetry in Britain, 1739–1796*. Cambridge University Press, 1994.

Lavoie, Chantel M. *Collecting Women: Poetry and Lives, 1700–1780*. Lewisburg, PA: Bucknell University Press, 2009.
Lonsdale, Roger, ed. *Eighteenth-Century Women Poets: An Oxford Anthology*. Oxford University Press, 1989.
McGovern, Barbara and Charles H. Hinnant, ed. *The Anne Finch Wellesley Manuscript Poems: A Critical Edition*. Athens, GA, and London: University of Georgia Press, 1998.
Prescott, Sarah and David E. Shuttleton, ed. *Women and Poetry 1660–1750*. Basingstoke and New York: Macmillan, 2003.

Drama

Anderson, Misty Gale. *Female Playwrights and Eighteenth-Century Comedy: Negotiating Marriage on the London Stage*. Basingstoke: Palgrave 2002.
Cotton, Nancy. *Women Playwrights in England, c. 1363 to 1750*. Lewisburg, PA: Bucknell University Press, 1980.
Donkin, Ellen. *Getting into the Act: Women Playwrights in London, 1776–1829*. London: Routledge, 1995.
Freeman, Lisa. *Character and Identity on the Eighteenth-Century English Stage*. Philadelphia: University of Pennsylvania Press, 2002.
Hook, Lucyle, ed. *The Female Wits*. Augustan Reprint Society, No. 124. William Andrews Clark Memorial Library. Los Angeles: University of California, 1967.
Howe, Elizabeth. *The First English Actresses: Women and Drama 1660–1700*. Cambridge University Press, 1992.
Hughes, Derek, gen. ed. *Eighteenth-Century Women Playwrights*. 6 Vols. London: Pickering and Chatto, 2001.
Kelley, Anne. *Catharine Trotter: An Early Modern Writer in the Vanguard of Feminism*. Aldershot, Hampshire: Ashgate Publishing, 2002.
Mann, David, Susan G. Mann, and Camille Garnier. *Women Playwrights in England, Ireland, and Scotland, 1660–1823*. Bloomington: Indiana University Press, 1996.
Nelson, Bonnie and Catherine Burroughs, ed. *Teaching British Women Playwrights of the Restoration and Eighteenth Century*. New York: Modern Language Association, 2010.
Quinsey, Katherine M., ed. *Broken Boundaries: Women and Feminism in Restoration Drama*. Lexington: University Press of Kentucky, 1996.
Rosenthal, Laura. *Playwrights and Plagiarists in Early Modern England: Gender, Authorship, Literary Property*. Ithaca: Cornell University Press, 1996.
Russell, Gillian. *Women, Sociability, and the Theatre in Georgian London*. Cambridge University Press, 2007.

History

Bannet, Eve Taylor. "'Secret History': Or, Talebearing inside and outside the Secretory." In *The Uses of History in Early Modern England*. Ed. Paulina Kewes. San Marino, CA: Henry Huntington Library, 2006: 367–88.

Brewer, David. "'Haywood,' Secret History, and the Politics of Attribution." In *The Passionate Fictions of Eliza Haywood: Essays on Her Life and Works.* Ed. Kirsten T. Saxton and Rebecca Bocchicchio. Lexington: University Press of Kentucky, 2000: 217–39.

Brownley, Martine W. *Clarendon and the Rhetoric of Historical Form.* Philadelphia: University of Pennsylvania Press, 1985.

Bullard, Rebecca. *The Politics of Disclosure, 1674–1725: Secret History Narratives.* London: Pickering and Chatto, 2009.

Burke, Peter. "Publicizing the Rise of the Private: The Rise of 'Secret History.'" In *Changing Perceptions of the Public Sphere.* Ed. Christian J. Emden and David Midgley. Oxford: Berghan Books, 2012: 57–74.

Carnell, Rachel. *Partisan Politics, Narrative Realism, and the Rise of the British Novel.* New York and Basingstoke: Palgrave Macmillan, 2006.

Cohen, Roger. "History and Genre." *New Literary History* 17.2 (1986): 203–18.

Gallagher, Noelle. *Historical Literatures: Writing about the Past in England, 1660–1740.* University of Manchester Press, 2012.

Grundy, Isobel. "Women's History? Writing by English Nuns." In *Women, Writing, History: 1640–1740.* Ed. Isobel Grundy and Susan Wiseman. Athens: University of Georgia Press, 1992: 126–38.

Kasmer, Lisa. *British Women Writing History, 1760–1830.* Lanham, NJ: Fairleigh Dickinson University Press, 2012.

Kucich, Greg. "Romanticism and Feminist Historiography." *Wordsworth Circle* 24.3 (1993): 133–40.

Lewis, Jayne E. *Mary Queen of Scots: Romance and Nation.* London and New York: Routledge, 1998.

Looser, Devoney. *British Women Writers and the Writing of History, 1670–1820.* Baltimore: The Johns Hopkins University Press, 2005.

Mack, Ruth. *Literary Historicity: Literature and Historical Experience in Eighteenth-Century Britain.* Stanford University Press, 2009.

Phillips, Mark Salber. *Society and Sentiment: Genres of Historical Writing in Britain, 1740–1820.* Princeton University Press, 2000.

Spongberg, Mary. *Writing Women's History since the Renaissance.* Basingstoke: Palgrave, 2002.

Satire

Chico, Tita. *Designing Women: The Dressing Room in Eighteenth-Century English Literature and Culture.* Lewisburg, PA: Bucknell University Press, 2005.

Fabricant, Carole. "The Shared Worlds of Manley and Swift." In *Pope, Swift, and Women Writers.* Ed. Donald C. Mell. Newark and London: University of Delaware Press, 1996: 154–78.

Gill, James E., ed. *Cutting Edges: Postmodern Critical Essays on Eighteenth-Century Satire.* Knoxville: University of Tennessee Press, 1995.

Kairoff, Claudia Thomas. "Gendering Satire: Behn to Burney." In *A Companion to Satire: Ancient and Modern.* Ed. Ruben Quintero. Malden, MA: Blackwell, 2006: 276–92.

Knight, Charles A. *The Literature of Satire.* Cambridge University Press, 2004.

Mason, Nicholas. "Austen's *Emma* and the Gendering of Enlightenment Satire." *Persuasions: Journal of the Jane Austen Society of North America* 25 (2003): 213–19.
Nussbaum, F. *The Brink of All We Hate: English Satires on Women 1660–1750*. Lexington: University Press of Kentucky, 1984.
Rabb, Melinda A. *Satire and Secrecy in English Literature 1650–1750*. New York and London: Palgrave, 2007.
Sabor, Peter. "Jane Austen: Satirical Historian." In *Swift's Travels: Eighteenth-Century British Satire and Its Legacy*. Ed. Nicholas Hudson and Aaron Santasso. Cambridge University Press, 2008: 217–32.
Young, Elizabeth V. "De-Gendering Genre: Aphra Behn and the Tradition of English Verse Satire." *Philological Quarterly* 81 (2002): 185–205.

Early fiction

Ballaster, Ros. *Seductive Forms: Women's Amatory Fiction from 1684 to 1740*. Oxford: Clarendon Press, 1992.
Bowers, Toni. *Force or Fraud: British Seduction Stories and the Problem of Resistance, 1660–1760*. Oxford University Press, 2011.
Gallagher, Catherine. *Nobody's Story: The Vanishing Acts of Women Writers in the Marketplace, 1670–1820*. Berkeley: University of California Press, 1995.
Hunter, J. Paul. *Before Novels: The Cultural Contexts of Eighteenth-Century English Fiction*. New York: Norton, 1990.
McKeon, Michael. *The Origins of the English Novel, 1660 to 1740*. Baltimore: The Johns Hopkins University Press, 1987.
  The Secret History of Domesticity: Public, Private and the Division of Knowledge. Baltimore: The Johns Hopkins University Press, 2005.
Richetti, John J. *Popular Fiction Before Richardson: Narrative Patterns, 1700–1739*. Oxford: Clarendon Press, 1969.
Spencer, Jane. *The Rise of the Woman Novelist: From Aphra Behn to Jane Austen*. Oxford: Basil Blackwell, 1986.
Warner, William B. *Licensing Entertainment: The Elevation of Novel Reading in Britain, 1684–1750*. Berkeley: University of California Press, 1998.

Later fiction

Backsheider, Paula R., ed. *Revising Women: Eighteenth-Century Women's Fiction and Social Engagement*. Baltimore: The Johns Hopkins University Press, 2000.
Castle, Terry. *Masquerade and Civilization: The Carnivalesque in Eighteenth-Century English Culture and Fiction*. Stanford University Press, 1986.
Langbauer, Laurie. *Women and Romance: The Consolations of Gender in the English Novel*. Ithaca, NY: Cornell University Press, 1990.
Perry, Ruth. *Novel Relations: The Transformation of Kinship in English Literature and Culture, 1748–1818*. Cambridge University Press, 2004.

Poovey, Mary. *The Proper Lady and the Woman Writer: Ideology as Style in the Works of Mary Wollstonecraft, Mary Shelley, and Jane Austen*. University of Chicago Press, 1984.
Schofield, Mary Anne and Cecilia Macheski, ed. *Fetter'd or Free: British Women Novelists, 1670–1815*. Athens: Ohio University Press, 1986.
Spacks, Patricia Meyer. *Desire and Truth: Functions of Plot in Eighteenth-Century English Novels*. University of Chicago Press, 1990.
Spender, Dale. *Mothers of the Novel: 100 Good Women Writers Before Jane Austen*. London: Pandora, 1986.
Thompson, Helen. *Ingenuous Subjection: Compliance and Power in the Eighteenth-Century Domestic Novel*. Philadelphia: University of Pennsylvania Press, 2005.
Tompkins, J. M. S. *The Popular Novel in England, 1770–1800*. Lincoln: University of Nebraska Press, 1961 [1932].

Travel writing

Bass, Robert D. *The Green Dragoon: The Lives of Banastre Tarleton and Mary Robinson*. 1957, Orangeburg, SC: Sandlapper Publishing Co., 1973.
Bohls, Elizabeth A. *Women Travel Writers and the Language of Aesthetics, 1716–1818*. Cambridge University Press, 1995.
Bohls, Elizabeth A. and Ian Duncan, ed. *Travel Writing 1700–1830: An Anthology*. Oxford University Press, 2005.
Bristow, Adrian, ed. *Dr Johnson & Mrs Thrale's Tour in North Wales, 1774*. Wrexham, Clwyd: Bridge Books, 1995.
Byrne, Paula. *Perdita: The Life of Mary Robinson*. London: Harper Perennial, 2004.
Clifford, James L. *Hester Lynch Piozzi (Mrs Thrale)*. Oxford: Clarendon Press, 1941.
Craciun, Adriana. *British Women Writers and the French Revolution: Citizens of the World*. London: Palgrave, 2005.
De Bolla, Peter. *The Discourse of the Sublime Readings in History, Aesthetics, and the Subject*. Oxford: Blackwell Press, 1989.
Dougal, Theresa A. "'Strange Farrago of Public, Private Follies.' Piozzi, Diary, and the Travel Narrative," *The Age of Johnson: A Scholarly Annual* 10 (1999): 195–218.
Eger, Elizabeth, ed. *Bluestockings Displayed: Portraiture, Performance and Patronage, 1730–1830*. Cambridge University Press, 2013.
  Bluestockings: Women of Reason from Enlightenment to Romanticism. New York: Palgrave Macmillan, 2010.
  and Lucy Peltz, ed. *Brilliant Women: 18th-Century Bluestockings*. New Haven: Yale University Press, 2008.
Foster, Shirley and Sara Mills, ed. *An Anthology of Women's Travel Writing*. Manchester University Press, 2002.
Guest, Harriet. *Small Change: Women, Learning, Patriotism, 1750–1810*. University of Chicago Press, 2000.
Janowitz, Anne. *Women Romantic Poets: Anna Barbauld and Mary Robinson*. Tavistock: Northcote House, 2004.
Klancher, Jon. "Discriminations, or Romantic Cosmopolitanisms in London." In *Romantic Metropolis: The Urban Scene of British Culture, 1780–1840*. Ed. James Chandler and Kevin Gilmartin. Cambridge University Press, 2005.

Major, Emma. *Madam Britannia: Women, Church, and Nation 1712–1812*. Oxford University Press, 2011.
McAllister, Marie E. "Gender, Myth, and Recompense: Hester Thrale's Journal of a Tour to Wales." *The Age of Johnson: A Scholarly Annual* 6 (1993): 265–82.
McCarthy, William. *Hester Thrale Piozzi: Portrait of a Literary Woman*. Chapel Hill: University of North Carolina Press, 1985.
Mee, Jon. *Conversable Worlds: Literature, Contention, and Community, 1762–1830*. Oxford University Press, 2011.
Mills, Sara. *Discourses of Difference: An Analysis of Women's Travel Books and Colonialism*. London and New York: Routledge, 1991.
Pascoe, Judith. *Romantic Theatricality: Gender, Poetry, and Spectatorship*. Ithaca, NY: Cornell University Press, 1997.
Pratt, Mary Louise, *Imperial Eyes: Travel Writing and Transculturation*. New York: Routledge, 1992.
Turner, Katherine. *British Travel Writers in Europe 1750–1800*. Aldershot, Hampshire: Ashgate, 2001.
Welch, Edwin. *Spiritual Pilgrim: A Reassessment of the Life of the Countess of Huntingdon*. Cardiff: University of Wales Press, 1995.

Ballads

The Ballad Repertoire of Anna Gordon, Mrs. Brown of Falkland. Ed. Sigrid Rieuwerts. Scottish Text Society Fifth series, No. 8. Woodbridge, Suffolk: The Boydell Press, 2011.
Bronson, Bertrand H. "Mrs. Brown and the Ballad," originally published in *California Folklore Quarterly* 4.2 (1945) and reprinted in *The Ballad As Song*. Berkeley: University of California Press, 1969: 64–78.
Brown, Mary Ellen. "Old Singing Women and the Canons of Scottish Balladry and Song." In *A History of Scottish Women's Writing*. Ed. Douglas Gifford and Dorothy McMillan. Edinburgh University Press, 1997: 44–57.
Cowan, Edward J., ed. *The Ballad in Scottish History*. East Linton: Tuckwell Press, 2000.
Dugaw, Dianne. *Warrior Women and Popular Balladry, 1650–1850*. Cambridge University Press, 1989.
Fumerton, Patricia and Anita Guerrini. *Ballads and Broadsides in Britain, 1500–1800*. Farnham, Surrey, England and Burlington, VT: Ashgate, 2010.
English Broadside Ballad Archive. ebba.english.ucsb.edu.
McCue, Kirsteen. "Women and Song 1750–1850." In *A History of Scottish Women's Writing*. Ed. Douglas Gifford and Dorothy McMillan. Edinburgh University Press, 1997: 58–70.
McLane, Maureen N. *Balladeering, Minstrelsy, and the Making of British Romantic Poetry*. Cambridge University Press, 2008.
Perry, Ruth. "The Famous Ballads of Anna Gordon, Mrs. Brown." In *Cultural History of Women in the Age of Enlightenment*. Ed. E. Pollak. London and New York: Bloomsbury, 2013: 187–208.
"'The Finest Ballads': Women's Oral Traditions in Eighteenth-Century Scotland." *Eighteenth-Century Life* 32.2 (2008): 81–98.

Pettitt, Thomas. "Mrs. Brown's 'Lass of Roch Royal' and the Golden Age of Balladry." *Jahrbuch für Volksleidforschung.* 29. Jahrg. (1984): 13–31.

Periodical writing

Adburgham, Alison. *Women in Print: Writing Women and Women's Magazines from the Restoration to the Accession of Victoria.* London: George Allen and Unwin Ltd., 1972.
Ballaster, Rosalind, Margaret Beetham, Elizabeth Frazer, and Sandra Hebron. *Women's Worlds: Ideology, Femininity and the Woman's Magazine.* Basingstoke: Macmillan, 1992.
Ellis, Markmann. "Coffee-women, *The Spectator* and the Public Sphere in the Early Eighteenth Century." In *Women Writing and the Public Sphere: 1700–1830.* Ed. Elizabeth Eger, Charlotte Grant, Clíona Ó Gallchoir, and Penny Warburton. Cambridge University Press, 2001: 27–52.
Italia, Iona. *The Rise of Literary Journalism in the Eighteenth Century: Anxious Employment.* London: Routledge, 2005.
Maurer, Shawn Lisa. *Proposing Men: Dialectics of Gender and Class in the Eighteenth-Century English Periodical.* Stanford University Press, 1998.
Powell, Manushag N. *Performing Authorship in Eighteenth-Century English Periodicals.* Lewisburg, PA: Bucknell University Press, 2012.
Shevelow, Kathryn. *Women and Print Culture: The Construction of Femininity in the Early Periodical.* London: Routledge, 1989.
White, Cynthia. *Women's Magazines, 1693–1968.* London: Michael Joseph.

INDEX

Adam, Jean (1704–65), xii, xvi, xix, 58, 60, 66–7, 69
Adburgham, Alison, 230, 234, 240n9, 20, 253
Addison, Joseph (1672–1719), xii, 21–2, 76, 158, 162n11, 228, 230–1, 233, 235
advice literature, 40, 45; periodical and, 227; women and, 23, 31, 231–3
Aikin, John (1747–1822), 237
Akenside, Mark (1721–70), 30, 237
Algarotti, Francesco (1712–64), xvii, 46, 47
Allan, David, 27, 35n4, 243
Alliston, April, 146n28
Altick, Richard, 25, 35n13
amatory fiction, 10, 13, 40, 87, 91, 93, 136, 149; devotional literature and, 173, 174–5, 180; novel and, 167, 169–75
Analytical Review, The, 237–8
Anderson, Robert (1749–1830), 214, 220, 224n14, 225n25
Annual Register, 26
anonymous and pseudonymous publication, 3, 15, 105, 121, 172, 176, 184, 189
archipelago; archipelagic approach, 11, 17, 55–6, 67
Armstrong, Nancy, 87, 95, 177, 179n30, 184, 194n10; *Desire and Domestic Fiction* 87, 100n18
Arnold, Matthew (1822–88), 103
Astell, Mary (1666–1731), xi, xiii, xvi, 32, 36n38, 106–7, 227; *A Serious Proposal to the Ladies* (1694), 31; *Reflections on Marriage* (1700), 107
Athenæum, The, 237, 239
Athenian Mercury, The, 60, 108, 172, 226–7
Aubin, Penelope (1679?–1738), xii, xv, 91
Austen, Jane (1775–1817), ix, 147–8, 158, 162, 192

Authorship: professional, 37–53; women and, 32, 38, 57–62, 66, 90, 148, 160, 172, 226–7, 230–1, 236, 240n5

Backscheider, Paula, 9, 10, 11, 12, 13, 14n4, 18n26, 59, 68n7, 84n14, 85n20, 95, 99n6, 100n17, 166n4, 172, 179n22, 194n14
Baillie, Joanna (1762–1851), xix, 51, 118–19, 121, 126, 132–3
Baker, Thomas (b.1680/81), 229, 240n5
Bakhtin, M. M., 91; novelization and, 91–2
Baldwin, Abigail (1658–1713), xiv, 227, 229, 240n5
ballads, 13, 25, 104, 210–25; oral transmission of, 67, 210–15; women as preservers and transmitters of, 210–25; women as singers of, 212–13; individual ballads: "Auld Lang Syne," 221–3; "Barbara Allen," 211; " Baron of Braickly," 216; "Chevy Chase," 211, 212; "Edom o' Gordon," 217–8; "House of Frendraught," 217; "Johnny Armstrong," 211; "Lass of Patie's Mill," 217; "Lillibulero," 212; "McPherson's Rant," 217
Ballard, George (1705/6–55), xviii, 2, 103
Ballaster, Ros, 9, 87, 125, 134n14, 141, 146n16, 167, 169, 178n6, 178n9
Banks, John (1652/3–1706), 72, 136
Barbauld, Anna Letitia (née Aikin) (1743–1825), xvii, xix, xx, 11, 29, 36n25; periodicals and, 236–7; poet as, 112, 113; professional author, as 40, 42, 47, 49–51, 52, 53, 54n19
Barbauld, Rochemount (1749–1808), 50
Barber, Mary (c.1685–1755), xii, xvi, 5, 18n13, 63, 105, 110, 116
Barker, Jane (1652–1732), xiii, xiv, xv, xvi, 8, 9, 144; novel and, 175–7; "patchwork narratives" of, 86, 89, 90, 92, 95–9, 100n21; poetry and, 60–1, 116, 175–78; political

INDEX

allegiances of, 60–1, 97–8; provincial poet, as, 60–1, 64, 69n10
Barry, Elizabeth (1656x8-1713), xiv, 72–3, 75, 76–7, 84n5, 84n17, 122–4
Basker, James, 231, 240n10
Batchelor, Jennie, 52, 99n5, 181, 194n25
Beattie, James, 47
Behn, Aphra (1640?–89), xiii, 12, 99; fiction and, 165, 166, 171, 177, 179n29; hybridization and, 90–3; playwright, as, 72–6, 77, 80–1, 82, 83, 84n8, 86, 87, 100n9, 119, 121–2, 127–8, 133n5, 132, 134n12; political affiliations of, 3, 121–2, 127–8, 132; professional author, as, 1, 3, 4–5, 37, 38, 40, 42, 43–4, 52, 53; satire and, 147, 149, 154, 161, 162n3; individual works: *Abdelazer* (1676), xii, 73, 75, 124; *Oroonoko* (1688), xiii, 5, 43, 90; *The Rover* (1671), 127–8
Betterton, Mary Saunderson (c.1637–1712), 74–5
Betterton, Thomas (1635–1710), 73–4, 75, 76, 77, 84n17, 122, 123, 125
Bickerstaff, Isaac, 228
Birch, Thomas (1705–66), 45
Blackwood, Adam, 141, 146n16
Blackwood's Edinburgh Magazine, 239
Blamire, Susanna (1747–94), xvii, 59
Bluestockings, The, 31, 33, 47, 112, 132, 197
(de) Boisguilbert, Pierre le Pesant (1646–1714), 135–9, 141, 145n3
book clubs, 26–7, 31
booksellers (publishers), 4, 7, 24–5, 34, 38, 39, 40, 44, 46–9, 62, 70, 93, 104–5, 108, 166, 172, 227, 235
Borsay, Peter, 62, 68n14
Boswell, James (1740–95), xvii, 34n1, 46, 53n12, 113, 129, 202, 209n9, 213
Bowers, Toni, 169, 170, 178n11
Boyle, Richard (1694–1753), 57, 73
Bracegirdle, Anne (1671–1748), xii, 73, 75, 76, 122–5
Bragge, B[enjamin], 229, 240n5
Brant, Clare, 88, 89, 99n2
Brereton, Jane (1685–1740), xii, xvii, 64–5, 105
Brewer, John, 36n23
broadsides, 210, 212
Brooke, Frances (1724–89), xv, xvii, xviii, xix, xx, 12, 36, 51, 52, 72, 76–9, 81, 84n13, 125–6, 134n15, 181, 183, 185–6, 194n7, 232–3; individual works: *The Excursion*, (1777) xix, 78, 79, 84n14, 126, 185, 186,

194n14; *The History of Emily Montague* (1769), xix, 77, 183, 186, 192, 194n7; *The History of Lady Julia Mandeville* (1763), xix, 77, 186; *Old Maid, by Mary Singleton, Spinster* (1755–6), xviii, 76, 77, 232, 240n14; *The Siege of Sinope* (1781), 76, 125, 182, 194n6, 232, 240
Bullard, Rebecca, 135, 136, 145n5
Burke, Edmund (1729/30–97), 160–1
Burney, Charles (1726–1814), 40
Burney, Frances (1752–1840), xviii, xx, 1, 5, 29, 30, 40, 47–9, 51–2, 53, 54n18, 119, 131–2, 134n21, 161, 180–1, 186, 191, 192–3; individual works: *Cecilia* (1782), xx, 29, 52, 186, 191–3, 195n27; *Evelina* (1778), xx, 51, 180, 186, 191, 193n2; *The Witlings* (1779), xx, 132, 134n22
Burns, Robert (1759–96), xviii, 26, 106, 113, 221
Burr, Esther Edwards (1732–58), 28, 31
Burroughs, Catherine, 88, 100n15
Busk, Mary Margaret (1779–1863), 239
"Butler, Sarah," xv, 64, 69n17
Byron, George Lord (1788–1824), 118

Camden, William (1551–1623), 136
Cappe, Catharine (1744–1821), 23, 35n9
Carnell, Rachel, 178n5, 240n5
Carter, Elizabeth (1717–1806), xv, xvii, xviii, 1, 5, 8, 31, 33; poet, as, 104, 109; professional author, as, 40, 41–3, 46–7, 48, 49, 51, 54n13
Carter, Susannah, 25
Cave, Edward (1691–1754), xiii, xvi, 46, 65, 104, 233–4
Cavendish, Margaret, the Duchess of Newcastle (1623?–73), xii, 41, 97
Celticism; Celtic, 55, 57, 63–6
Centlivre, Susanna (1669?–1723), xii, xiv, xv, 3, 4, 5, 17n10, 18n12, 44, 121, 125, 128–9, 134n18, 240n5
Chandler, Mary (1687–1745), xii, xvi, 6, 62, 67n13, 105, 111
Chapone, Hester (1727–1801), xv, xix, 33, 47
Charitable Mercury and Female Intelligence, The, 230
Charke, Charlotte (1713–60), xiv, 119
Charles II (1630–85), xi, xii, 40, 43, 73, 124, 159, 212
Chetwood, William (d.1766), 94
Child, Francis James (1825–96), 210–11, 215, 217, 223n1, 225n15
children, 30, 152, 154, 156

255

INDEX

children's literature, 38, 50, 106, 180, 237
Chit Chat, in a Letter to a Lady in the Country, 229
Chudleigh, Lady Mary (1656–1710), xiii, xiv, 29, 57–8, 68n3, 107
circulating libraries, 23, 27, 35n14, 186
Cohen, Ralph, 98, 100n24, 135, 136, 143, 145n4
Coleridge, Samuel (1772–1834), xix, 51, 115, 117n20
Colie, Rosamund, 96, 100n20
Collier, Jane (1715–55), xiv, xviii, 89, 149, 154–7, 163n15, 185; individual works: *An Essay on the Art of Ingeniously Tormenting* (1753), 153–7; *The Cry* (1754), 185, 194n13
Collier, Mary (1688?–1762), xiii, xvii, 5, 6, 18n15, 60, 106
Colman, George the Elder (1732–94), xviii, 2, 3, 42, 103
Colonial governance, 81–2
Commodification, 71–2, 78, 129, 191–2
Common Sense, 230
contemporary readerships, 40–1
Coppola, Al, 10, 18n27, 179n19
copyrights, 39, 43, 45–6
coteries, 8, 46–7, 56–7, 60–1, 97, 105, 107
Court Miscellany, or Ladies' New Magazine, The, 234
courtship novel, 42, 180
Cowley, Hannah (1743–1809), xvii, xx, 52, 121, 130–1; *The Belle's Stratagem* (1780), 131, 134n20
Cowper, William (1731–1800), 29
Crackenthorpe, Mrs., 229–30, 240n5
Critical Review, 76, 84n12, 235, 238
Curll, Edmund (d.1747), xvi, 64, 105

Darnton, Robert, 32, 36n41
Darwall, Mary Whateley (1738–1825), xvii, xix, 59–60
Darwin, Erasmus (1731–1802), 113
Davidoff, Leonore, 29, 36n26
Davies, Margaret/Dafydd, Marged (c.1700–85?), xiii, 65
Davys, Mary (1674–1732), xii, xv, xvi, 1, 8, 12, 62–3, 86, 92, 93, 95–7, 99, 171; individual texts: *Familiar Letters betwixt a Gentleman and a Lady* (1725), 171, 179n16; *Northern Heiress; or the Humours of York, The*, xv, 62, 95; *Reform'd Coquet* (1724), xv, 63, 96
Deal, 41, 46–7

dedicatees, 43
Defoe, Daniel (1660?–1731), xi, xv, xvi, 75, 87, 165, 166, 212
didactic fiction, 33, 96, 173, 180
Dissenters, 23, 50, 108, 111, 238
Distaff, Jenny, 228
Dixon, Sarah (1671/72–1765), xii, xix, 59
Dodsley, Robert (1704–64), xiii, 46
Donne, John (1572–1631), 92, 93
drama: ideological vehicle, as, 80–8; popular culture and, 73–6, 78–80; women and, 38, 63, 73–83, 87–9, 91–4, 118–34
Drury Lane Theatre, 84n13, 94, 119, 125
Dryden, John (1631–1700), xi, xiii, 33, 43, 73, 75–6, 104, 148, 153, 158, 163n14
Duck, Stephen (1705?–56), xvi, 106; *Thresher's Labour, The* (1730), xvi, 60, 106
Duncombe, John (1729–86), xviii, 3–4, 17n3, 42, 47, 54n14, 103
Dunton, John (1659–1732), 60, 108, 226–8, 231

economics, 22, 80, 156; literary marketplace, of, 6–7, 37–54; marriage, of, 191
Edgeworth, Maria (1768–1849), xix, 51
editing, 38, 236, 239
educational writing, 41, 42, 50
Egerton, Sarah (née Fyge) (1670–1723), xii, xiii, 106
Elizabeth I, Queen of England (1533–1603), 141, 146n26
Ellis, Joyce M., 62, 66, 68n14, 69n19
employment, women's, 2, 6, 7, 189, 231
Englishman, The, 229
epilogues, 3, 5, 72–3, 75, 76, 79–80, 83, 84n18, 123, 124–7, 129–31
epistolary networks, 56–8, 59
Etherege, George (1636–91/2), 74, 75
Evans, Evan, 66
Evelyn, Mary (c.1665–85), xi, 149–50, 153–4, 162n10; *Mundus Muliebris* (1690), xii, 149–50, 151–3
Evening Mail, The, 239
Examiner, The, 229
Exilius; or, The Banish'd Roman, 90
Ezell, Margaret, 56, 57, 68n3, 88, 172, 179n21

family, 5, 13, 42, 46, 50, 52, 57, 58, 61, 105, 110, 157; ballads and, 214, 215–21; marriage and, 180, 190, 192; publishing and, 229–30, 231, 236; reading and,

22, 24, 30; travel and, 200, 201–2, 203, 204
Farquhar, George (1676/7–1707), 130
Farquharson, Mrs., 210, 214, 216
Female Spectator, The, see Eliza Haywood
Female Tatler, The, xiv, 227, 229–30, 240n4
feminocentric fiction, 167, 171, 179n17
Fergus, Jan, 23, 24, 25, 27, 35n11
Fielding, Henry (1707–54), xiv, xvii, 26, 45, 52, 87, 90, 165, 166, 183; individual works: *The Author's Farce* (1730), xvi, 54n7, 164, 177, 178n1; *Joseph Andrews* (1742), xvii, 189
Fielding, Sarah (1710–68), xiv, 89, 181, 183, 189; individual works: *The Cry* (1754), xviii, 185, 194n13; *David Simple* (1744), xvii, 182, 183–4, 188, 194n23; *The History of the Countess of Dellwyn* (1759), xviii, 186–7
Finch, Anne (Countess of Winchilsea) (1661–1720), xi, 1, 3, 4, 8, 15, 17n4, 41, 60, 72, 89, 93, 103, 105, 113; biography, 107–8; political affiliations of, 57–9, 107–8; provincial writer, as 57–9; individual works: "Ardelia to Melancholy," 107; "Ardelia's Answer to Ephelia," 108; *Miscellany Poems* (1713), xiv, 115; "Nocturnal Reverie," 103; "Petition for an Absolute Retreat," 107–8, 116n6; "The Spleen" xiii, 113, 115
Flint, Kate, 33, 36n43
Forbes, William, 219–20
Fordyce, James (1720–96), 23, 24, 35n7
Foreign Quarterly Review, The, 239
Forster, Antonia, 184, 194n9, 240n21
Fraser Tytler, Alexander (1747–1813), 213–16, 224n12
Freebairn, James, 137–42, 145n10
French Revolution, the, xx, 42, 50, 161

Gallagher, Catherine, 9, 167, 178n7
Gallagher, Noelle, 136, 145n6
Garrick, David (1717–79), xv, 52, 76, 84n14, 125, 126, 130, 198
Garth, Samuel (1660/61–1719), 104
Gavin, Michael, 57, 58, 68n2
Gay, John (1685–1732), xii, 25, 57, 90, 110, 148
gender, 1, 5, 8–9, 12–13, 22, 44, 51, 55, 70–83, 86–92, 98, 105, 108, 124, 135, 137, 144–5, 147–8, 159–62, 164–5, 181–4, 193, 196, 233
genius, 3, 39–40, 110, 144

genre, 12–13, 16, 27, 38, 42–3, 135, 137, 147, 202; choices of, 1–2, 52, 55, 76–7, 83, 106, 119, 127; development of, 70–1, 114; mixing of, 86–100, 115–16, 135–6, 166–78, 143–5
Gentleman's Magazine, The, xvi, 15, 40, 46, 48, 60, 65, 104, 113, 116n3, 233–4, 235, 237, 238, 239
geography, 2, 11, 55–68, 233–4
George III (1738–1820), xix, 41, 159
ghosting, 79–80, 83
Gibbon, Edward (1737–94), 21, 26, 34n1, 144
Gildon, Charles (c.1665–1724), 64
Glover, Katharine, 35n20, 36n28, 224n9
Godwin, William (1756–1836), 71, 83
Goldsmith, Oliver (1728?–74), xvi, 114, 162, 234
Goodwill, Jasper, 234
Gordon, Anna (also Mrs. Brown) (1747–1810), xvii, 13, 213–23; ballad collector, as, 215–18; family of, 218–20; individual ballads: "Auld Lang Syne" 221–3, "Baron of Braichly" 216, 224n17
Gordon, Thomas (1714–97), 213–14, 217, 220; "Edom o' Gordon," annotations to 217–18; "House of Frendraught" and, 217
Gray, Thomas (1716–71), xiv, 66, 104, 114
Greer, Germaine, 87, 246
Grierson, Constantia (1704/5–32), xiv, 5, 104, 116
Griffin, Dustin, 162n6, 244
Griffith, Elizabeth (1727–93), xv, xix, 28, 42, 182, 190, 195n26
Griffiths, Isabella, 235–6, 240n21
Griffiths, Ralph (1720?–1803), 235–6, 240n21
Grundy, Isobel, 53n6, 105, 242, 247, 249
Guardian, The, 229
Guest, Harriet, 13–14, 53n5, 251
Guy, John, 146n17

Hall, Catherine, 29, 36n26
Hall, Joseph (1574–1656), 158
Hall, Stuart, 80, 84n3
Hamilton, Elizabeth (1756?–1816), xviii, 23, 35n10
Hammond, Brean, 38, 53n4, 159, 162n4, 244
Hands, Elizabeth (1746–1815), xvii, 25, 59
Harris, Thomas, 77, 126
Hatton, Julia Ann (1764–1838), xix, 65
Hawkesworth, John (1720–73), 52
Hays, Mary (1759–1843), xviii, 6, 238

INDEX

Haywood, Eliza (1693?–1756), xiii, 1, 4, 11, 12, 13, 15, 40, 75, 86, 87, 90–2, 149, 164–6, 170–2, 231; bibliographic work on, 9–10; political affiliations of, 92–3, 169–70; professional author, as, 7–8, 9–10, 44–6, 48, 52; individual works: *The Arragonian Queen* (1724), xv, 28; *Anti-Pamela* (1741), xvii, 6, 92; *British Recluse* (1722), xv, 95, 172; *City Jilt* (1726), xv, 95; *Eovaai* (1736), xvi, 91, 92; *Fantomina* (1725), 92, 95, 169–70, 178n14; *Fatal Secret* (1725), 90, 99n8; *Female Spectator, The* (1744–46), xvii, 99n12, 231–3, 247; *Frederick duke of Brunswick-Lunenburgh* (1729), xvi, 96; *History of Miss Betsy Thoughtless* (1751), xviii, 45, 92–4, 181–2, 187, 194n17; *Lasselia* (1723), xv, 177; *Love in Excess* (1719–20), xv, 44–5, 53n7, 75, 86, 92–6, 99n14, 169, 171–2, 178n10; *Mary, Queen of Scots* (1725), xv, 135–45; *Parrot, The* (1728), 231; *Parrot, The* (1746), xvii, 232; *The Perplex'd Dutchess* (1727), xv, 28; *Secret Histories, Novels and Poems* (1725), xv, 140, 146n14, 165, 178n2; *Tea Table, The* (1724), xv, 231; *Young Lady, The* (1756), 232, 240n13
Highmore, Susanna (1689/90–1750), xiii, 47
historical discourse, 135–6, 141, 144–5
history: genre, as, 135–7, 143–4; secret history and, 135–40; women and, 135–45
Holt, Jane (*fl.* c. 1682–1717), xiii, xv, 58, 63; *Antiochus the Great: Or, The Fatal Relapse* (1701), xiii, 63
Home, Henry, 59
homosocial desire, 139, 141
Honeycombe, Charles, 234
Hume, David (1711–76), xiv, 22, 26, 32, 144
Hume, Robert, 119, 133n2
Hunter, J. Paul, 38, 135, 173, 170n24, 250

ideological vehicle, drama as, 80–8
imperialism, 80–83
Inchbald, Elizabeth (1753–1821), xviii, xx, 12; playwright, as, 71–3, 77, 80–3, 85n9, 128–9, 134n17; individual works: *A Simple Story* (1791) xx, 81, 85n21; *Every One Has His Faults* (1793), 83; *Nature and Art* (1796), xx, 83, 85n22; *Such Things Are* (1788), xx, 82; *Wives as They Were, and Maids as They Are* (1797), xx, 81–2
Ingram, Anne, Viscountess Irwin (née Howard) (c.1696–1764), xiii; "Epistle to Mr. Pope," xvi, 109

Ingrassia, Catherine, 59, 68n7, 100n15, 116n4, 232, 240n12
interpolated verse, 174–5
Ireland; Irish, 11, 55, 56, 58, 62, 63–5, 67
Italia, Iona, 227–8, 239n3, 240n5, 253

James II (1633–1701), xii, 40, 107, 212
Jamieson, Robert (1772–1844), 214, 216
Jebb, Samuel (1693/4–1772), 136, 141, 146n16; *The History of the Life and Reign of Mary Queen of Scots* (1725), 136
Johnson, Claudia, 161, 163nn24, 25, 27–30
Johnson, Joseph (1738–1809), 237
Johnson, Samuel (1709–84), xiv, xviii, xix, 21, 26, 40, 49, 52, 65, 104, 174, 196, 213, 232; Charlotte Lennox and, 48–9
Jones, Mary (1707–78), xiv, xviii, 59, 105; influenced by Pope, 109; patronized by Frances Seymour, 111–12; individual works: "Epistle to Lady Bower" 109, 111; *Miscellanies in Prose and Verse* (1750), xviii, 111
Jones, Vivien, 99n2, 239n1, 242, 246

Kasmer, Lisa, 249
Kelly, Hugh (1739–77), 162, 233–4
Killigrew, Anne (1660–85), xi, 107
Killigrew, Thomas (1612–83), 73, 127
King, Kathryn R., 9–10, 12, 17, 44, 60, 68n10, 171, 179n17
King's Theatre, 77, 125
Kirkall, Elisha (1681/2–1742), 94
Kucich, Greg, 249

Labanoff, Alexandre, 146n24
Lacroix, Constance, 98, 100n22, 246
Ladies Defence, The, xiii, 57, 107
Ladies' Diary: or, Woman's Almanack, The, 227
Ladies' Magazine, or the Universal Entertainer, The, 234, 240n18
Ladies' Mercury, The, 227
Lady's Magazine, or Compleat Library, The, 21, 25, 32, 234, 239
Lady's Magazine, or Entertaining Companion for the Fair Sex, The, 234
Lady's Magazine, or Monthly Intelligencer, The, 234
Lady's Magazine, or Polite Companion for the Fair Sex, The, 234
Lady's Museum, The, xix, 48, 233, 240n17
Landon, Letitia (1802–38), 239

INDEX

Larpent, Anna (1758–1832), xviii, 28, 30, 35n23
Leapor, Mary (1722–46), xv, xvii, 5, 25, 42, 46, 59, 110, 147; individual works: "Crumble Hall," 106; "An Essay on Woman," 89; *Poems on Several Occasions* (1748), xvii, xviii, 110
Lee, Sophia (1750–1824), xvii, 143–5; *The Recess: Or, a Tale of Other Times* (1783), xx, 143–5, 146n28
Lennox, Charlotte (1730/31–1804), 9, 11, 28; periodicals and, 233–5, 240n17; professional author, as, 40, 42, 47–9, 51–2, 86, 90, 93, 125–6; Royal Literary Fund, and, 49, 233, 235; individual works: "The Art of Coquetry," 48; *The Female Quixote* (1752), xviii, 33, 48, 49, 90, 96, 182, 185, 186, 188, 194n16, 233; *The History of Harriot and Sophia* (1760–61), xix, 233; *Harriot Stuart* (1762), xix, 182; *Henrietta* (1758), xviii, 187; *Lady's Museum* (1760–61), xix, 233–5, 240n17; *Poems on Several Occasions* (1747), xvii, 48; *Shakespeare Illustrated* (1753–4), xviii, 48
letter-writing, 25, 41–2, 51, 58, 88, 105–6, 110, 113, 170–1, 173, 185, 188, 190, 204, 216, 226–7, 233, 243, 245; women and, 31–3
Lewis, Jayne Elizabeth, 144, 146n29, 249
Lewis, Matthew Gregory "Monk" (1775–1818), 214
libraries: book clubs as, 26–27; circulating, 23, 27, 186; communities of readers and, 31, 34; family, 24–5, 58–9; lending, 26; subscription, 26–7; women's access to, 5, 24–7, 35n15, 58–9, 63, 66
literacy, 5, 21–2, 33, 37–8, 212, 226, 235, 245
Literary Gazette, The, 239
literature, 38, 46, 50, 55, 83, 88, 90, 104, 106–7, 148–9, 197, 231, 232–3, 235
Little, Janet (1759–1813), xviii, 106
Lloyd, Robert (1733–64), 234
Locke, John (1632–1704), xiv, 25, 57
London, xi, 3, 8, 11, 27, 55, 58, 62, 73, 107–8, 119–20, 196, 228; literary marketplace in, 41–4, 46–9, 57, 59–60, 64–5, 67, 237
Longleat, 58
Lonsdale, Roger, 63, 64, 87, 100n23, 104, 116n1, 193n1, 245
Looser, Devoney, 9, 36n27, 135, 145n1, 249

Macaulay, Catherine (1731–91), xvi, 144, 187; *The History of England* (1763), xix, 144, 146n30, 187
Macheski, Cecilia, 88, 247, 251
Mack, Ruth, 9, 249
MacKenzie, Henry (1745–1831), 32, 36n42, 114, 162, 213, 224n8
Maese, Sarah (1744–1811), 23
Manley, Delarivier (c.1670–1724), xii, 3, 4, 44, 87, 91, 93, 123–5, 149, 165–6, 171, 175; political allegiances of, 121, 167–8, 229–30, 240n5; individual works: *The Adventures of Rivella* (1714), xiv, 168, 178n8; *Almyna* (1707), xiv, 124; *The Lost Lover* (1696), 121, 134n8; *The New Atalantis* (1709), xiv, 167–9, 177, 178n9; *The Royal Mischief* (1696), xiii, 123, 124, 134n11; *The Secret History of Queen Zarah* (1705), xiv, 178n5
manuscript culture, 22, 33, 38, 41, 55–6, 58, 68n5, 104–5, 176, 197, 214, 244; *see also*, scribal culture
marriage, 6, 30, 41, 50, 57, 60, 64, 76, 80, 82, 95–7, 106–7, 122, 124, 129–30, 131, 133n6, 168, 180–3, 186, 189–93, 198, 205, 209n4, 227
Martineau, Harriet (1802–76), 239
Massey, Doreen, 56–57, 68n1
Masters, Mary (fl. 1733–55), 59
McCarthy, William, 36n25, 50, 51, 54n19, 209n2, 244, 252
McDowell, Paula, 9, 88, 212, 226, 239n1, 240n6, 242
McKeon, Michael, 165, 250
McMurran, Mary Helen, 145n2
Melville, James, 146n18
Millar, Andrew, 46, 48, 186
Mills, Rebecca, 58, 68n4
Milton, John (1608–74), xii, 66, 92, 104, 114, 158, 173, 233
Monck, Mary (Molesworth) (1677?–1715), xii, 58, 63, 68n5; *Marinda: Poems and Translations on Several Occasions* (1716), xiv, 58
Montagu, Elizabeth (1718–1800), xv, xix, 31, 33, 41, 47, 51–2, 54n13, 112, 132, 197
Montagu, Lady Mary Wortley (1689–1762), xiii, xvi, 6, 18n16, 24, 32–3, 41, 104, 230–1, 234, 247; individual works: "The Reasons that induced Dr. Swift," xvi, 89; *Six Town Eclogues* (1746), 104–5; "Verses Addressed to the Imitator of the First Satire of the Second Book of Horace," 109
Monthly Magazine, The, 237–9
Monthly Repository, The, 239
Monthly Review, The, 26, 235–7

259

INDEX

Moody, Elizabeth (1737–1814), xvi, 236, 241n22
More, Hannah (1745–1833), xvii, 32–3, 42, 51, 52, 106, 112–13, 119; as playwright, 126–7; as poet, 106, 112–13, 115–16; Yearsley, Ann and, 33; individual works: "The Bas Blue; Or, Conversation," xx, 112; *Percy* (1778), xx, 126, 134n16; *Sacred Dramas* (1782), xx, 116; "Sensibility," 113, 115–16; "Slavery; a Poem," xx, 112
Morgan, Fidelis, 229, 240n4
Morning Post, The, 70, 239
Muir, Willhelmina Johnston (Willa), 212, 224
Mure, Elizabeth (1700–90), xiii, 21, 34n2
Murphy, Arthur, 52, 79
Myddleton, Mary, 65

Napoleonic wars, 50
narrative level, 188–93
narrative voice, 183, 191–3
nation; national, 3, 4, 13, 22, 37, 41–3, 47, 50, 55–6, 63–8, 82, 113, 125–6, 131–2, 212, 233
Neale, J. E., 146n26
Nelson, Bonnie, 88, 100n15, 246, 248
New Lady's Magazine, or Polite & Entertaining Companion for the Fair Sex, The, 234
New Monthly Magazine, The, 239
Nonsense of Common-Sense, The, 230
novel: amatory fiction and, 13, 40, 87, 91, 93, 149, 167–72, 174, 180; critical tradition of, 165–6; development of, 91–2, 166–72; experimentation and, 175–8; marketing of, 10–11, 172; poetry and, 175–6; romance and, 168–9, 172–4; sentimental, 180–195
novelization, 91–2

Oldfield, Anne (1683–1730), xii, xvi, 72, 93
opera, 43, 77, 79, 82, 112, 130, 164, 178
Oracle, The, 239
Orphan Reviv'd; or, Powell's Weekly Journal, The, 230
Orphan, The (periodical), 230
Orr, Leah, 54n9
Otway, Thomas (1652–85), 72–4, 84n6, 119
Overton, Bill, 67, 69n20, 245
Ovid, 97, 173
Owenson, Sydney Morgan (1783–1859), 239

patronage, 33, 38–9, 43, 48–9, 61, 65, 106, 231, 235, 244, 251
Pearson, Jacqueline, 21–2, 28, 32, 34, 34n3, 35n15, 36n34, 179n29, 243

Penny, Anne Hughes (1729–80/84), xvi, xix, xx, 65–6
Pepys, Samuel (1633–1703), 211
Percy, Thomas (1729–1811), 214, 220, 224n14, 225n25; *Reliques of Ancient English Poetry* (1765) xix, 212, 217
periodical essays, 38, 40, 186, 226–39
periodical press, 30, 41, 46–8, 59–60, 70, 76–7, 104, 226–41, 239n2, 240n10; *see also* names of individual periodicals
Philips, Katherine (1632–64), xi, 3, 56, 58, 60, 64–5, 73, 89, 93, 114
Phillips, Mark Salber, 249
Pilkington, Laetitia (1709–50), xiv, xvii, 1, 3, 4, 17n5, 28
Pix, Mary (c.1666–1709), xi, xiv, 44, 121
playwriting, 44, 95, 120, 131; *see also*, drama
poetry, 2, 3, 5, 12–13, 15, 22, 26, 29, 33, 38, 40, 41–4, 47, 50, 53, 91–2, 97, 103–116, 175–6, 178, 198, 221, 223; biblical and devotional models for 107–8; patronage of, 106–7; periodicals and, 234–5, 236–9; provincial writers and, 57–60, 62–6; sentimentalism and, 112–15; slavery and, 112–13; subscription sale of, 6–7, 105, 109–11
Pope, Alexander (1688–1744), xiii, xiv, xvii, 21, 25–6, 39, 40, 45–6, 57, 72, 90, 104, 105, 162n4, 163n12, 171, 173; model for women poets, 89, 109; individual works: *Dunciad* (1728, 1742), xvi, 45, 53n7, 105, 110, 132, 148, 149, 150, 158, 164; *Eloisa to Abelard* (1717), xv, 114; *Epistle to Dr. Arbuthnot* (1735), xvi, 109, 159, 161; *Epistle to a Lady* (1735), xvi, 109, 119; *Iliad* (1715–20) xiv, 29; *Poems on Several Occasions* (1717), 108, 110; *The Rape of the Lock* (1714), xiv, 152; *Three Hours After Marriage*, 105
popular culture, 11–12, 13, 70–5, 78–9, 80, 81, 82–3, 84n3, 212
Powell, Elizabeth, 229–30
Prattle, Penelope, 231
Prescott, Sarah, 11, 13, 17, 68nn4,9, 108, 116n7, 245, 248
print culture, 2–3, 6, 8, 9, 11, 14, 15, 21–2, 25, 55, 57–8, 70, 181, 186, 226
Procopius, 146n15
professional authorship, 3, 6–8, 37–54, 90–1, 93, 181, 226, 230–1, 233–9, 244
prologues, 3, 72–3, 75, 83
provinciality; provincial, 21, 30, 35n11, 36n28, 55–69, 120, 202, 243

INDEX

Rambler, The, 232–3
Ramsay, Allan (1684–1758), 30, 212, 221
Raven, James, 25, 35n14, 36n34, 42, 46, 53n11, 184, 194nn9,11, 242–3
reading, 2, 4, 5–6, 7, 11, 90, 104, 132, 147, 149, 162, 168–9, 172, 174, 185–6, 211; women and, 21–36
Reeve, Clara (1729–1807), xvi, 238–9
republic of letters, 33, 38, 46–7, 76
Restoration, the, xi, 2, 16, 38, 72; female dramatists and, 119–20, 127, 132, 133n5; satire in, 151, 158, 159; women writers in, 41–2, 43–4, 88–9, 91, 93, 94, 96
reviews, 5, 30, 234–5, 236, 237–8
Reynolds, Sir Joshua (1723–92), 30, 52
Riccoboni, Marie Jeanne, 77, 84n14
Richardson, Samuel (1689–1761), xiii, 18n24, 32, 36n24, 45–8, 50, 51, 52, 62, 87, 91, 110, 114, 162, 165, 166, 179n18, 183, 185, 194n8, 243, 250; individual works: *Clarissa* (1747/48), xvii, 24, 28, 29, 30, 32, 161, 182; *Pamela* (1740), xvii, 6, 28, 31, 104, 116n2, 171, 180; *Sir Charles Grandison* (1753), xviii, 28
Richetti, John, 10, 18n25, 133n2, 171, 173, 179n18, 245, 250
Ritson, Joseph (1752–1803), 214
Robertson, William (1740–1803), 26, 30, 32, 144
Robinson, George (1736–1801), 234
Robinson, Mary (1756/58?–1800), xviii, xx, 14, 70–1, 196–203, 206–8, 239, 251; individual works: *Memoirs* (1801), 196–7, 199–202, 209nn5,7; *The Natural Daughter* (1799), 6, 18n18, 70–1, 84n2, 209n4
romance, 23, 32, 45–6, 64, 86, 87, 90–1, 95, 97, 99n1, 109, 136, 141, 146n29, 220; French romance, 90, 96, 185; novel and, 164–7, 169–70, 171, 174–5, 178n4, 179n17
Roscoe, William (1753–1831), 51
Rose, Elizabeth (1747–1813), 24, 25, 29, 31, 32, 36n35, 36n42
Rowe, Elizabeth Singer (1674–1737), xi, 3; fiction and, 172–5, 179n22; "Philomela," as, 60, 108; "The Pindarick Lady," as, 60, 108; poet, as, 108–9, 111–12, 116, 89; political allegiances of, 108–9; professional author, as, 41, 46–7; provincial writer, as, 57, 58, 59–60, 68n8; individual works: *Friendship in Death* (1728), xvi, 91, 108, 172, 173–5, 179n25; *Letters Moral and Entertaining* (1729–32), xvi, 173–4, 175;

"On the Death of Mr. THOMAS Rowe," 108; *Poems on Several Occasions* (1697), xiii, 108; *The History of Joseph* (1736), xvi, 91, 108
Royal Female Magazine, 60, 234
Royal Literary Fund, 49, 233, 235

Sansom, Martha Fowke (1689–1736), xiii, 45
Savage, Richard (1696/97–1743), xiii, 45, 93, 99n14, 171
satire, 12, 71, 92, 103, 109, 147–63, 119, 232, 249–50; female-authored, 147–8, 149–55; gendering of, 158–60; literary history and, 148–9; manliness and, 158–60, 161–2; poetry and, 103; women and, 104, 107, 119, 132, 193
scandal, 37, 40, 43, 45, 121, 147, 167, 187, 229; fiction and, 44–5, 86, 140, 168–9, 172, 177, 246; personal, 4, 132, 160, 168, 171, 198; professional, 11, 45
Schneider, Gary, 57, 245
Schofield, Mary Anne, 88, 99n9, 247, 251
Scotland; Scottish, 48, 55, 58, 106, 137, 142, 143, 196, 202, 223, 224n5, 243, 248, 252; ballad and, 13, 66–7, 211, 212–9; readers in, 21, 24, 28–9, 35nn15,16,20, 36nn28, 29; women writers and, 11, 55, 63, 66–8
Scott, Sarah (1720–95), xv, xviii, 89, 181, 182, 186, 189; *Millenium Hall* (1762), xix, 183
Scott, Sir Walter (1771–1832), xix, 51, 113, 214
Scottish folk music, 211–3, 219, 223
Scottish Gaelic, 64, 67
scribal culture, 46–7; see also, manuscript culture
Secker, Thomas (1693–1768), 47
secret history, 135–8, 140–5
seduction, 91, 95, 166–7, 168–70, 171–5
Select Scotish songs, ancient and modern (1810), 66
sentimentalism, 113, 161–2, 183–4
Seward, Anna (1742–1809), xvii, 5, 8, 9; friendship with Honora Sneyd, 114; James Boswell and, 113; periodicals and, 238; poet, as, 112, 113–14; "queer" readings of, 114; Samuel Johnson and, 113; "Swan of Lichfield" as, 59, 113; individual works: "Elegy for Captain Cook," 113; "Llangollen Vale," 114; *Louisa, A Poetical Novel* (1784), xx, 114, 117
sex object, 77–9
Seymour, Frances, (Thynee), Countess of Hertford (1699–1754), xiii, xvi, 3, 111–12

261

Shadwell, Thomas (1640–92), xiii, 43
Shakespeare, William (1554–1616), 25, 30, 37, 48, 93, 104, 125, 166, 210, 233
She-tragedy, 72, 77, 79
Shellenberg, Betty A., 11, 181, 244
Sheridan, Frances (1724–66), xv, xix, 129–30, 181, 182, 190–1
Sheridan, Richard Brinsley (1751–1816), 23, 35n8, 52
Shevelow, Kathryn, 227, 232, 239n2, 241n11, 253
Shiels, Robert (d. 1753), 103
Shuttleton, David, 12–3, 17, 62, 68n4, 13, 116n7, 245, 248
Siddons, Sarah (1755–1831), xviii, 78, 119
Siskin, Clifford, 1, 17n2, 242
Smith, Charlotte Turner (1749–1806), xvii, 25, 52, 114–5; individual works: *Elegiac Sonnets* (1784), xx, 115; *The Emigrants* (1793), 115; *Beachy Head* (1807), 115
Smock Alley Theatre, Dublin, 94
sociability, 31–2, 62, 198, 201, 245
Society of Friendship, 56
Some Specimens of the Poetry of the Antient Welsh Bards, 66
Spectator, The, 112, 158–9, 162n11, 228, 230–1, 233–4, 240n8
Spedding, Patrick, 10, 45, 54n8
Spence, Sir Patrick, 223
Spencer, Jane, 9, 44, 87, 100n19, 165, 180, 193n4, 244, 247, 250
Spinster, The, 229
St. Germain, 60–61, 97
St. James's Chronicle, The, 236
Stage Licensing Act (1737), xvii, 44, 125
Staines, John, 136, 145n8
Stanhope, Charles (1753–1816), 234, 240
Stanhope, Mrs., 234
Starr, Gabrielle, 91–3, 99n11, 13, 169, 178n13, 247
status ambiguity, 79–80
Statute of Anne (1709), xiv, 39
Staves, Susan, 61–63, 64; *A Literary History of Women's Writing in Britain*, 88, 193n4
Steele, Sir Richard (1672–1729), 57, 76, 228
subscription libraries, 26–7; *see also* libraries
subscription, publication by, 6–7, 11, 33, 38–9, 46–7, 52, 56, 59, 63–4, 65, 105, 109–10, 111
Sweet, Rosemary, 60
Swenson, Rivka, 13, 98, 100n22
Swift, Jonathan (1667–1745), xii, xvii, 21, 25, 63, 90–1, 104–5, 110, 148, 151, 158, 160, 161, 229; influence on women poets, 63–4; individual works: "A Beautiful Young Nymph Going to Bed" (1734), xvi, 150–1, 161; *Directions to Servants* (1745), 154–7; *Gulliver's Travels* (1726), xv, 91; "The Lady's Dressing Room" (1732), xvi, 89, 150–2; *Modest Proposal* (1729), xvi, 152, 157; *Tale of a Tub* (1704), 160–1

Tadmor, Naomi, 30, 35n14, 35n34
Talbot, Catherine (1721–70), xv, 31, 33, 47
Taliesin, 66
Tatler, The, 228–9
Thomas, Elizabeth (1675–1731), xii, xvi, 4, 6, 17n7, 18n17, 58, 98, 105, 107
Thomson, James (1700–48), xiii, 29, 104, 111, 174
Thornton, Bonnell (1725–68), xviii, 2–3, 103
Thrale, Hester (later Piozzi) (1741–1821), xvii, 14, 24, 49, 51, 118–19, 131–2, 133, 133n1, 196–8, 202–8, 209n2
Todd, Janet, 53n1, 84n8, 87, 133n5, 134n12, 181, 193n4, 240n21
Tonson, Jacob (1655/6–1736), 63
Town and Country, 239
Town Talk, in a Letter to a Lady in the Country, 229
transatlantic feminism, 67
translation, 2, 3, 5, 12, 38, 40, 43, 45–8, 52, 63, 71, 76–7, 79, 90, 93, 104, 125, 135, 138, 142, 145, 166, 234
Trifler, The, 233
Trotter, Catharine (later Cockburn) (1674?–1749), xii, xiii, 3, 44, 121–3
Tytler, William (1711–92), 213

Universal Magazine, The, 238
Universal Spectator, The, 159

Vesey, Elizabeth (1715–91), xiv, 24, 31, 112
Vickery, Amanda, 21, 30, 34n3, 35n14, 36n29

Wales, 11, 14; poets from, 55, 56, 58, 63–6, 67, 114; travels to, 196–208
Walton, Isaac (1651–1719), 211
Warner, William B., 23, 35n12, 45, 149, 162n9, 250
Warrington Academy, 49
Watt, Ian P., 10, 18n25, 59, 87, 165, 166
Watts, Isaac (1674–1748), 59, 109, 111, 174
Wells, Mary (Becky) Davies (1762–1829), xix, 73, 84n7

Whisperer, The, 228–9
Whitehall Evening Post, The, 239
Williams, Anna (1706–83), xiv, 33
Williams, Raymond, 135
Wilmot, John, Earl of Rochester (1647–80), 124, 154
Wollstonecraft, Mary (1759–97), xviii, xx, 22, 51, 107, 162, 197–8, 202, 207, 208, 237–8
women: ballads and, 210–35; educational opportunities for, 5–6, 22–3, 30, 33–4, 38, 47–9, 90, 104, 204–5; employment for, 6–7, 189, 231; libraries and, 5, 24–7, 35n15, 58–9, 63, 66; literacy and, 5, 21–2, 33, 37, 226; periodicals and, 226–41; popular culture and, 70–85; reading and, 21–36; satire and, 147–163
women writers: canon and, 16, 42, 43, 46, 87–8, 103–4, 115, critical tradition of, 1–2, 11–12, 52, 87–8, 103–4, 164–6, 180–1; cultural resistance to, 2–6; manuscript culture and, 22, 33, 38, 41, 55–6, 58, 104–6, 176, 197; patronage and, 33, 38–9, 43, 48–9, 61, 106, 231; poets, as, 103–17; subscription publishing and, 6–7, 11, 33, 38–9, 46–7, 52, 56, 59, 63–4, 65, 105, 109–10; recovery project of, 1–2, 8–10, 14–16, 21–2, 87–90, 103, 149, 181. *See also* novel; playwriting; poetry; and individual authors
Woolf, Virginia (1882–1941), 1, 17n1, 37, 38, 42, 53n2, 103, 184, 210
Woolpack, Rachel, 229
Wordsworth, William (1770–1850), xix, 103, 115
World, The, 239
Wroth, Mary (1587?–1651/53), 162n2

Yates, Mary Ann (1728–87), xv, 72, 76–80, 84n18, 125–6
Yearsley, Ann (1753–1806), xviii, xx, 6, 33, 60, 106, 112
Young Lady, The, 232

Cambridge Companions to ...

AUTHORS

Edward Albee edited by Stephen J. Bottoms

Margaret Atwood edited by Coral Ann Howells

W. H. Auden edited by Stan Smith

Jane Austen edited by Edward Copeland and Juliet McMaster (second edition)

Beckett edited by John Pilling

Bede edited by Scott DeGregorio

Aphra Behn edited by Derek Hughes and Janet Todd

Walter Benjamin edited by David S. Ferris

William Blake edited by Morris Eaves

Jorge Luis Borges edited by Edwin Williamson

Brecht edited by Peter Thomson and Glendyr Sacks (second edition)

The Brontës edited by Heather Glen

Bunyan edited by Anne Dunan-Page

Frances Burney edited by Peter Sabor

Byron edited by Drummond Bone

Albert Camus edited by Edward J. Hughes

Willa Cather edited by Marilee Lindemann

Cervantes edited by Anthony J. Cascardi

Chaucer edited by Piero Boitani and Jill Mann (second edition)

Chekhov edited by Vera Gottlieb and Paul Allain

Kate Chopin edited by Janet Beer

Caryl Churchill edited by Elaine Aston and Elin Diamond

Cicero edited by Catherine Steel

Coleridge edited by Lucy Newlyn

Wilkie Collins edited by Jenny Bourne Taylor

Joseph Conrad edited by J. H. Stape

H. D. edited by Nephie J. Christodoulides and Polina Mackay

Dante edited by Rachel Jacoff (second edition)

Daniel Defoe edited by John Richetti

Don DeLillo edited by John N. Duvall

Charles Dickens edited by John O. Jordan

Emily Dickinson edited by Wendy Martin

John Donne edited by Achsah Guibbory

Dostoevskii edited by W. J. Leatherbarrow

Theodore Dreiser edited by Leonard Cassuto and Claire Virginia Eby

John Dryden edited by Steven N. Zwicker

W. E. B. Du Bois edited by Shamoon Zamir

George Eliot edited by George Levine

T. S. Eliot edited by A. David Moody

Ralph Ellison edited by Ross Posnock

Ralph Waldo Emerson edited by Joel Porte and Saundra Morris

William Faulkner edited by Philip M. Weinstein

Henry Fielding edited by Claude Rawson

F. Scott Fitzgerald edited by Ruth Prigozy

Flaubert edited by Timothy Unwin

E. M. Forster edited by David Bradshaw

Benjamin Franklin edited by Carla Mulford

Brian Friel edited by Anthony Roche

Robert Frost edited by Robert Faggen

Gabriel García Márquez edited by Philip Swanson

Elizabeth Gaskell edited by Jill L. Matus

Goethe edited by Lesley Sharpe

Günter Grass edited by Stuart Taberner

Thomas Hardy edited by Dale Kramer

David Hare edited by Richard Boon

Nathaniel Hawthorne edited by Richard Millington

Seamus Heaney edited by Bernard O'Donoghue

Ernest Hemingway edited by Scott Donaldson

Homer edited by Robert Fowler

Horace edited by Stephen Harrison

Ted Hughes edited by Terry Gifford

Ibsen edited by James McFarlane

Henry James edited by Jonathan Freedman

Samuel Johnson edited by Greg Clingham

Ben Jonson edited by Richard Harp and Stanley Stewart

James Joyce edited by Derek Attridge (second edition)

Kafka edited by Julian Preece

Keats edited by Susan J. Wolfson

Rudyard Kipling edited by Howard J. Booth

Lacan edited by Jean-Michel Rabaté

D. H. Lawrence edited by Anne Fernihough

Primo Levi edited by Robert Gordon

Lucretius edited by Stuart Gillespie and Philip Hardie
Machiavelli edited by John M. Najemy
David Mamet edited by Christopher Bigsby
Thomas Mann edited by Ritchie Robertson
Christopher Marlowe edited by Patrick Cheney
Andrew Marvell edited by Derek Hirst and Steven N. Zwicker
Herman Melville edited by Robert S. Levine
Arthur Miller edited by Christopher Bigsby (second edition)
Milton edited by Dennis Danielson (second edition)
Molière edited by David Bradby and Andrew Calder
Toni Morrison edited by Justine Tally
Nabokov edited by Julian W. Connolly
Eugene O'Neill edited by Michael Manheim
George Orwell edited by John Rodden
Ovid edited by Philip Hardie
Harold Pinter edited by Peter Raby (second edition)
Sylvia Plath edited by Jo Gill
Edgar Allan Poe edited by Kevin J. Hayes
Alexander Pope edited by Pat Rogers
Ezra Pound edited by Ira B. Nadel
Proust edited by Richard Bales
Pushkin edited by Andrew Kahn
Rabelais edited by John O'Brien
Rilke edited by Karen Leeder and Robert Vilain
Philip Roth edited by Timothy Parrish
Salman Rushdie edited by Abdulrazak Gurnah
Shakespeare edited by Margareta de Grazia and Stanley Wells (second edition)
Shakespearean Comedy edited by Alexander Leggatt
Shakespeare and Contemporary Dramatists edited by Ton Hoenselaars
Shakespeare and Popular Culture edited by Robert Shaughnessy
Shakespearean Tragedy edited by Claire McEachern (second edition)
Shakespeare on Film edited by Russell Jackson (second edition)
Shakespeare on Stage edited by Stanley Wells and Sarah Stanton

Shakespeare's History Plays edited by Michael Hattaway
Shakespeare's Last Plays edited by Catherine M. S. Alexander
Shakespeare's Poetry edited by Patrick Cheney
George Bernard Shaw edited by Christopher Innes
Shelley edited by Timothy Morton
Mary Shelley edited by Esther Schor
Sam Shepard edited by Matthew C. Roudané
Spenser edited by Andrew Hadfield
Laurence Sterne edited by Thomas Keymer
Wallace Stevens edited by John N. Serio
Tom Stoppard edited by Katherine E. Kelly
Harriet Beecher Stowe edited by Cindy Weinstein
August Strindberg edited by Michael Robinson
Jonathan Swift edited by Christopher Fox
J. M. Synge edited by P. J. Mathews
Tacitus edited by A. J. Woodman
Henry David Thoreau edited by Joel Myerson
Tolstoy edited by Donna Tussing Orwin
Anthony Trollope edited by Carolyn Dever and Lisa Niles
Mark Twain edited by Forrest G. Robinson
John Updike edited by Stacey Olster
Mario Vargas Llosa edited by Efrain Kristal and John King
Virgil edited by Charles Martindale
Voltaire edited by Nicholas Cronk
Edith Wharton edited by Millicent Bell
Walt Whitman edited by Ezra Greenspan
Oscar Wilde edited by Peter Raby
Tennessee Williams edited by Matthew C. Roudané
August Wilson edited by Christopher Bigsby
Mary Wollstonecraft edited by Claudia L. Johnson
Virginia Woolf edited by Susan Sellers (second edition)
Wordsworth edited by Stephen Gill
W. B. Yeats edited by Marjorie Howes and John Kelly
Zola edited by Brian Nelson

TOPICS

The Actress edited by Maggie B. Gale and John Stokes

The African American Novel edited by Maryemma Graham

The African American Slave Narrative edited by Audrey A. Fisch

African American Theatre by Harvey Young

Allegory edited by Rita Copeland and Peter Struck

American Crime Fiction edited by Catherine Ross Nickerson

American Modernism edited by Walter Kalaidjian

American Poetry Since 1945 edited by Jennifer Ashton

American Realism and Naturalism edited by Donald Pizer

American Travel Writing edited by Alfred Bendixen and Judith Hamera

American Women Playwrights edited by Brenda Murphy

Ancient Rhetoric edited by Erik Gunderson

Arthurian Legend edited by Elizabeth Archibald and Ad Putter

Australian Literature edited by Elizabeth Webby

British Literature of the French Revolution edited by Pamela Clemit

British Romanticism edited by Stuart Curran (second edition)

British Romantic Poetry edited by James Chandler and Maureen N. McLane

British Theatre, 1730–1830, edited by Jane Moody and Daniel O'Quinn

Canadian Literature edited by Eva-Marie Kröller

Children's Literature edited by M. O. Grenby and Andrea Immel

The Classic Russian Novel edited by Malcolm V. Jones and Robin Feuer Miller

Contemporary Irish Poetry edited by Matthew Campbell

Creative Writing edited by David Morley and Philip Neilsen

Crime Fiction edited by Martin Priestman

Early Modern Women's Writing edited by Laura Lunger Knoppers

The Eighteenth-Century Novel edited by John Richetti

Eighteenth-Century Poetry edited by John Sitter

English Literature, 1500–1600 edited by Arthur F. Kinney

English Literature, 1650–1740 edited by Steven N. Zwicker

English Literature, 1740–1830 edited by Thomas Keymer and Jon Mee

English Literature, 1830–1914 edited by Joanne Shattock

English Novelists edited by Adrian Poole

English Poetry, Donne to Marvell edited by Thomas N. Corns

English Poets edited by Claude Rawson

English Renaissance Drama, second edition edited by A. R. Braunmuller and Michael Hattaway

English Renaissance Tragedy edited by Emma Smith and Garrett A. Sullivan Jr.

English Restoration Theatre edited by Deborah C. Payne Fisk

The Epic edited by Catherine Bates

European Modernism edited by Pericles Lewis

European Novelists edited by Michael Bell

Fairy Tales edited by Maria Tatar

Fantasy Literature edited by Edward James and Farah Mendlesohn

Feminist Literary Theory edited by Ellen Rooney

Fiction in the Romantic Period edited by Richard Maxwell and Katie Trumpener

The Fin de Siècle edited by Gail Marshall

The French Enlightenment edited by Daniel Brewer

The French Novel: from 1800 to the Present edited by Timothy Unwin

Gay and Lesbian Writing edited by Hugh Stevens

German Romanticism edited by Nicholas Saul

Gothic Fiction edited by Jerrold E. Hogle

The Greek and Roman Novel edited by Tim Whitmarsh

Greek and Roman Theatre edited by Marianne McDonald and J. Michael Walton

Greek Comedy edited by Martin Revermann

Greek Lyric edited by Felix Budelmann

Greek Mythology edited by Roger D. Woodard

Greek Tragedy edited by P. E. Easterling

The Harlem Renaissance edited by George Hutchinson

The History of the Book edited by Leslie Howsam

The Irish Novel edited by John Wilson Foster

The Italian Novel edited by Peter Bondanella and Andrea Ciccarelli

The Italian Renaissance edited by Michael Wyatt

Jewish American Literature edited by Hana Wirth-Nesher and Michael P. Kramer

The Latin American Novel edited by Efraín Kristal

The Literature of the First World War edited by Vincent Sherry

The Literature of London edited by Lawrence Manley

The Literature of Los Angeles edited by Kevin R. McNamara

The Literature of New York edited by Cyrus Patell and Bryan Waterman

The Literature of Paris edited by Anna-Louise Milne

The Literature of World War II edited by Marina MacKay

Literature on Screen edited by Deborah Cartmell and Imelda Whelehan

Medieval English Culture edited by Andrew Galloway

Medieval English Literature edited by Larry Scanlon

Medieval English Mysticism edited by Samuel Fanous and Vincent Gillespie

Medieval English Theatre edited by Richard Beadle and Alan J. Fletcher (second edition)

Medieval French Literature edited by Simon Gaunt and Sarah Kay

Medieval Romance edited by Roberta L. Krueger

Medieval Women's Writing edited by Carolyn Dinshaw and David Wallace

Modern American Culture edited by Christopher Bigsby

Modern British Women Playwrights edited by Elaine Aston and Janelle Reinelt

Modern French Culture edited by Nicholas Hewitt

Modern German Culture edited by Eva Kolinsky and Wilfried van der Will

The Modern German Novel edited by Graham Bartram

The Modern Gothic edited by Jerrold E. Hogle

Modern Irish Culture edited by Joe Cleary and Claire Connolly

Modern Italian Culture edited by Zygmunt G. Baranski and Rebecca J. West

Modern Latin American Culture edited by John King

Modern Russian Culture edited by Nicholas Rzhevsky

Modern Spanish Culture edited by David T. Gies

Modernism edited by Michael Levenson (second edition)

The Modernist Novel edited by Morag Shiach

Modernist Poetry edited by Alex Davis and Lee M. Jenkins

Modernist Women Writers edited by Maren Tova Linett

Narrative edited by David Herman

Native American Literature edited by Joy Porter and Kenneth M. Roemer

Nineteenth-Century American Women's Writing edited by Dale M. Bauer and Philip Gould

Old English Literature edited by Malcolm Godden and Michael Lapidge (second edition)

Performance Studies edited by Tracy C. Davis

Piers Plowman by Andrew Cole and Andrew Galloway

Popular Fiction edited by David Glover and Scott McCracken

Postcolonial Literary Studies edited by Neil Lazarus

Postmodernism edited by Steven Connor

The Pre-Raphaelites edited by Elizabeth Prettejohn

Pride and Prejudice edited by Janet Todd

Renaissance Humanism edited by Jill Kraye

The Roman Historians edited by Andrew Feldherr

Roman Satire edited by Kirk Freudenburg

Science Fiction edited by Edward James and Farah Mendlesohn

Scottish Literature edited by Gerald Carruthers and Liam McIlvanney

Sensation Fiction edited by Andrew Mangham

The Sonnet edited by A. D. Cousins and Peter Howarth

The Spanish Novel: from 1600 to the Present edited by Harriet Turner and Adelaida López de Martínez

Textual Scholarship edited by Neil Fraistat and Julia Flanders

Theatre History by David Wiles and Christine Dymkowski

Travel Writing edited by Peter Hulme and Tim Youngs

Twentieth-Century British and Irish Women's Poetry edited by Jane Dowson

The Twentieth-Century English Novel edited by Robert L. Caserio

Twentieth-Century English Poetry edited by Neil Corcoran

Twentieth-Century Irish Drama edited by Shaun Richards

Twentieth-Century Russian Literature edited by Marina Balina and Evgeny Dobrenko

Utopian Literature edited by Gregory Claeys

Victorian and Edwardian Theatre edited by Kerry Powell

The Victorian Novel edited by Deirdre David (second edition)

Victorian Poetry edited by Joseph Bristow

War Writing edited by Kate McLoughlin

Women's Writing in Britain, 1660–1789 edited by Catherine Ingrassia

Women's Writing in the Romantic Period edited by Devoney Looser

Writing of the English Revolution edited by N. H. Keeble